THE AUTOBIOGRAPHY OF DANIEL PARKER,

FRONTIER UNIVERSALIST

The Autobiography of DANIEL PARKER

Frontier Universalist

Edited and Annotated with an Introduction and Epilogue by

David Torbett

Ohio University Press / Athens, Ohio

Ohio University Press, Athens, Ohio 45701
ohioswallow.com

Printed in the United States of America
Ohio University Press books are printed on acid-free paper ∞ ™

31 30 29 28 27 26 25 24 23 22 21 5 4 3 2 1

Library of Congress Cataloging-in-Publication Data
Names: Parker, Daniel, 1781-1861, author. | Torbett, David, editor.
Title: The autobiography of Daniel Parker, frontier universalist / Daniel Parker ; edited and annotated with an introduction and epilogue by David Torbett.
Description: Athens, Ohio : Ohio University Press, [2020] |
Includes bibliographical references and index.
Identifiers: LCCN 2020029606 (print) | LCCN 2020029607 (ebook) | ISBN 9780821424292 (hardcover) | ISBN 9780821447239 (pdf)
Subjects: LCSH: Parker, Daniel, 1781-1861. | Universalists--United States--Biography. | Abolitionists--United States--Biography.
Classification: LCC BX9969.P36 A3 2020 (print) | LCC BX9969.P36 (ebook) | DDC 289.1/34092--dc23
LC record available at https://lccn.loc.gov/2020029606
LC ebook record available at https://lccn.loc.gov/2020029607

Publication of this edition of
The Autobiography of Daniel Parker, Frontier Universalist
has been made possible by funding
from Marietta College Library.

CONTENTS

ILLUSTRATIONS

Figures

Maps

ACKNOWLEDGMENTS

Transcribing, researching, annotating, editing, submitting, revising, and resubmitting this book for publication has been a years-long journey and the product of the effort of many people.

First and foremost, I am grateful to Dr. James Parker, who brought Daniel Parker's manuscript, along with its handwritten copy, to Marietta College. In so doing, he was acting on behalf of other family members who shared ownership of the manuscript and supported this project: Scot Buchanan Parker, Elizabeth Irene Spencer, Jennifer Lynn Parker, Gailen Lee Tillotson, Thomas Parker Goebel, Julia Ann Goebel, and Ellen Elizabeth Daugherty.

A pleasant unexpected consequence of this project is that it brought together members of an extended family who did not previously know each other. I am grateful to Margaret McDiarmid, who represents another branch of Daniel Parker's family tree, for donating so many family documents and items to the Clermont Academy Collection at Northern Kentucky University. They have been invaluable resources for researching and illustrating this edition. I thank her brother, Walter Colvin, who serendipitously had just recently restored portraits of Daniel and Priscilla Parker painted by John Frankenstein, and who took photographs of them for this book. Though I never met her, I am grateful to their great aunt, Bertha Currier Hardman, the daughter of Fannie Parker Currier, the granddaughter of James K. Parker, and the great granddaughter of Daniel and Priscilla Parker, for making the effort to preserve the memories of her family members and their witness to the history of the Ohio valley region.

I thank Ray Swick, historian of the West Virginia State Park System (before his retirement), who helped bring Parker's manuscript to the attention of Marietta College and has encouraged its publication for many years. I am grateful to Marietta College librarian Douglas Anderson, who helped to conceive and recruit me for the project and supported its completion and publication in countless ways. Linda Showalter, the manager of special collections at MC's Legacy Library, has helped me from the beginning, tracking down documents, finding information, photocopying and scanning, and in many other ways. I am grateful to other current and former Special Collections staff who have provided assistance, including Sally Norton, Georgene Johnson, and director Katy Scullin, as well as to the library staff in general.

I am grateful to Marietta College, its faculty, staff, and administration, for the opportunity to teach students and to engage in this kind of scholarly work. I thank my colleague, Matthew Young, professor of history and expert in geographic information systems, for his excellent maps for this book. Brandon Downing, our early American historian, has suggested avenues of research that have greatly helped my understanding of Parker's context. I am grateful to my department chair, Kathryn McDaniel, for her constant support. I thank our administrative assistant Amy Williams for her work, especially in the last stages of preparing this manuscript for publication.

I thank the faculty, staff, and students of Northern Kentucky University who are part of the Parker Academy Archaeological Project. On my several visits, public history professor Brian Hackett has given an inordinate amount of time and effort to provide hospitality and assistance. On one visit he brought me to several locations in the area that were significant to my research, including the former Parker homestead and the site of Clermont Academy. At the homestead site I was pleased to meet Don and Julie Leukebe, who invited me into what was then their home, the house where Daniel and Priscilla Parker once lived. Brian has continued to answer my questions and provide scanned copies of documents and pictures from the Clermont Academy Collection at NKU, as have undergraduate and graduate students Liza Vance, Chelsea Hauser, and Andrea Shiverdecker, along with former staff member Autumn Shuler and other members of the NKU community. Robert K. Wallace, professor of English, who has been researching a book on antislavery activism in Cincinnati, provided me with relevant information about some of the people we have encountered in our overlapping studies, which I am thankful for, as well as for his general enthusiasm for my project. Greg Roberts, a local historian of New Richmond, whose current home was once the girls' dormitory of Clermont Academy, has been ready with support and helpful answers to my questions.

I am grateful to the volunteer staff at the Gallia County Historical Society for helping me track down information about some of Daniel Parker's friends and associates, as well as to the staff of the Ohio History Connection for maintaining documents related to Daniel Parker and for providing images from Ohio history for this publication.

I am grateful to Ohio University Press for committing to this project. I thank its staff members for their diligence in every phase of the preparation, publication, and promotion of this book, especially Laura André, Tyler Balli, Nancy Basmajian, Zoë Bossiere, Sandra Dixon, Ricky S. Huard, Jeff Kallet, Beth Pratt, Ed Vesneske, Jr., Sally Welch, and Stephanie Williams.

My personal thanks go to my mother, Alice Torbett, and my father, David Jesse Torbett, who have supported me in all my efforts. My father passed away during the years I was preparing this book. Working on Daniel Parker's autobiography impressed on me the importance of remembering the life experience of passing generations and inspired me to record some of my father's stories before he died. I am grateful for the love and support of my family: my son, Thomas, my daughter, Nora, and my wife, Jill, on whom I depend.

Lastly, I am thankful to Daniel Parker himself for writing his autobiography. It was an honor to carry out his intention to share his life story with a broader audience. In his writing, Daniel's historical limitations are clear, but through the century and three quarters since he wrote his narrative, his generous personality still shines through. He wrote this memoir at the request of his family and friends. He shared his beliefs, his struggles, and his joys with the hope that they would be a benefit to others. It is my sincere hope that with this publication, those benefits will be realized.

Figure I.1. Daniel Parker, portrait by John Frankenstein. (Photograph by Walter Colvin)

EDITOR'S INTRODUCTION

Itinerant preacher Daniel Parker expected opposition when he promoted his unorthodox doctrine of universal salvation. It was, according to most Christians, a heresy, after all. At times, however, his self-proclaimed allies frustrated him as much as his opponents.

Knowing Parker's reputation in the Ohio valley as a preacher who denied the doctrine of hell, religious skeptics occasionally sought to enlist him in an early nineteenth-century version of an American culture war. "Men of no religious profession, and sometimes destitute of even moral principle," would invite him to travel a day's journey to speak, offering to "make suitable returns" for his efforts. Parker accepted these invitations in good faith, only to discover to his "mortification" that "they only wanted me to oppose orthodoxy." To make matters worse, Parker was "exceedingly tried" by "drunken fellows" who saluted him as one of their own. "Such persons," Parker speculated, "having always associated religion with the idea of preaching never-ending torment to the wicked, supposed that a minister who did not preach it must be wicked himself."[1]

What these skeptics and "drunken fellows" misunderstood, and what the highly principled, but patient and conciliatory, preacher sought to explain, was that his universalism was not merely a revolt against orthodoxy. It had nothing to do with moral laxity. It had only partly to do with the afterlife. Parker's rejection of the idea of eternal punishment was only one aspect of what he called the "glorious doctrine" of universal "restoration," a comprehensive vision of reconciliation that embraced both time and eternity. His own efforts to improve human society through the promotion of temperance, education, and the abolition of slavery were part and parcel of this vision. Parker saw himself and other social reformers of his time as agents of God, on a divine mission to "overcome evil with good."[2]

Daniel Parker

Daniel Parker was born in Newburyport, Massachusetts, in 1781 to William and Mary Parker, the fifth of their eleven children.[3] In 1788, when Daniel was seven years old, his family moved to what was then the frontier of the young United States, intending to settle on their share of the nearly one-million-acre purchase of the Ohio Company, an association of New Englanders who would establish the "first settlement" (more accurately, the first officially recognized European-American settlement) in the Old Northwest Territory. After crossing the Alleghenies, the Parker family, anxious about Indian wars on the eighteenth-century frontier, delayed the remainder of their westward trek, living a number of years in western Pennsylvania. In 1802 they at last settled on their land in Leading Creek, near the village of Rutland in Meigs County, in what the following year would become the state of Ohio.

Like his father, Daniel Parker made his living primarily as a carpenter and mechanic. From 1809 to 1813 he attempted a career as itinerant salesman of a newly patented washing machine (made to order), traveling by flatboat as far south as New Orleans, gradually returning to Ohio by land, living for extended periods in Tennessee and Kentucky, and encountering several misadventures along the way. In his thirties he was married to a young widow, Priscilla Mulloy Ring. Ultimately the Parkers settled in Clermont County, Ohio, near Cincinnati and New Richmond, in an area that is now part of Monroe Township, on a homestead prosaically named Mount Hygiene. Together they had eight children. Among his other projects, he with his wife and son James founded Clermont Academy, which thrived for over fifty years as a racially integrated, coeducational, private secondary school—the first such institution in Ohio. Parker was also a self-taught vocal and instrumental musician, "considered by backwoods people a tolerable performer on the flute and violin."[4]

However, Daniel Parker's real vocation was as a self-appointed itinerant preacher of his own brand of universal salvation, or, as he preferred to put it, the "final restoration" of "all the human family" from "sin to holiness, and consequently from misery to happiness."[5] Raised a Presbyterian, he experienced a dramatic conversion to the Halcyon Church, an alternative, millenarian religious movement, in 1803. After a tense (and ambivalent) parting of ways with the Halcyonists in 1807, Parker privately continued his own biblical and theological studies, eventually arriving at the conclusion that all human beings would ultimately, after a postmortem purgative period, enjoy a blessed eternal life.

After some initial hesitation, and the diversion of an attempted career as a traveling salesman, Parker eventually embraced the life of an itinerant minister. Continuing to make his material living as a carpenter and by other means, he preached, never asking for compensation (though accepting it when freely given), for any group who would have him, in any hall or home they could offer, throughout the Ohio valley—including, for a time, his own First Restorationist Church in Cincinnati. In so doing, "he contributed no small amount of influence in spreading the knowledge and acceptance of Universalist views," according to one prominent historian of American Universalism.[6] Parker defended his position in print in his one published book, a theological treatise written in an epistolary style, *Familiar Letters to a Brother: On the Final Restoration of All Mankind.*[7] Parker's other major literary effort was unpublished: this autobiography, handwritten on some 260 pages, "mostly from memory" but with occasional references to old journals, "in the 64th year of his age, 1845."[8]

Parker's Autobiography

The author gives a number of reasons for writing his memoir: to satisfy "the request of his family and friends,"[9] to teach moral lessons, to advocate causes, to record observations of the world around him, and to record his "inward . . . travel" toward salvation and happiness.[10] Whatever his intended purposes, he consistently wrote with the understanding that people would read what he had to say. Parker occasionally interrupted his narrative to address his readers: both his children and "others who may read this memoir," hinting that he hoped he might reach a broader audience.[11]

For generations after the author's death, Daniel Parker's manuscript has been handed down to his descendants, who have read, occasionally copied, and referred to it in correspondence and family histories.[12] Two gifts of Daniel Parker's descendants have made the author's hope of 175 years ago, to reach a general audience, a possibility for the present time. In 2011, Dr. James Parker, a direct descendant of Daniel Parker, with other members of the Parker family, made Daniel Parker's manuscript, along with a handwritten copy from his son Charles Coleman Parker,[13] available to Marietta College as a long-term loan, with the hope that Daniel Parker's story could at last be transcribed, annotated, and published. Serendipitously, in 2015, Northern Kentucky University, located in Highland Heights, Kentucky, initiated its Parker Academy Archaeological Project, an interdisciplinary effort of its history, public history, archeology, and anthropology programs. Students and faculty have been excavating the site of the Parker family's Clermont Academy in nearby Monroe Township, Ohio.[14] In support of this project, another Daniel Parker descendent, Margaret McDiarmid, lent a large collection of manuscripts, printed documents, photographs, and other items related to the academy, including diaries, letters, and memoirs written by Daniel Parker and his family. These documents have provided invaluable context for this introduction and the notes of this edition of Daniel Parker's autobiography.

Parker's Decades of Change

For those it reaches, Parker's memoir offers many rewards, especially as a witness to history. Daniel Parker was a humble and essentially ordinary man, with a local reputation as a preacher and at best a few prominent family connections (his sister Sally was the second wife of Ephraim Cutler, a respected Ohio statesman). Nevertheless, Parker had an uncanny ability to step into the frame of events of national consequence, something like a Forrest Gump of the old frontier, albeit not always a very punctual one, occasionally arriving a year early or a year late. For example, in 1810, Parker, then an itinerant salesman traveling through the old Southwest, acquired two hundred acres of land in the Missouri Territory that would be partially sunk a year later by the New Madrid earthquakes, the most powerful ever to hit the contiguous United States east of the Mississippi. That same year he stayed at Grinder's Stand, a lodging house in Tennessee where the explorer Meriwether Lewis (of Lewis and Clark) had died a year earlier—presumably by suicide, though a persistent minority to this day have alleged murder. Parker vividly remembers meeting his host, Mrs. Priscilla Grinder, who was, according to some conspiracy theorists, a suspect in Lewis's death.[15]

More important than Parker's proximity to this or that (literally) earth-shattering or controversial event, however, is his reflection on the broader trends of his time. Daniel Parker's narrative stretches from the end of the eighteenth century into the 1840s, decades of rapid change and increasing complexity for the old western territories and for the United States as a whole. The era is fittingly represented by scholars as a prism of overlapping and coinciding periods of American history.[16] It was the period of the early republic, during which the identity and sovereignty of the newly independent United States was established by a constitution and tested by domestic and international conflicts: the Whiskey Rebellion of 1794 and the War of 1812, events which color Parker's narrative.[17] The period of the early republic overlapped an era of accelerating westward expansion and migration, in the vanguard of which was the Parker family.[18] Westward expansion coincided with the era of market revolution, in which Daniel Parker, traveling down the Mississippi selling a new invention, was an early participant.[19] The market revolution coincided with the beginning of the age of expanded American democracy, characterized by the populism that Parker satirized in his description of an election day in Kentucky.[20] These same decades have also been construed as an era of religious ferment and diversity,[21] as a period of expansion of and increasing sectional conflict over African American slavery,[22] and as an age of reform during which a "benevolent empire" of voluntary associations sought to morally revitalize American society.[23] Parker was deeply engaged in these facets of his time as well.

In sum, Daniel Parker was, in one way or another, present for every chapter of his transformative era, offering an ordinary person's perspective on historical trends, made extraordinary by his particular temperament and style. Parker was, among other things, a keen observer, both of his own thoughts and feelings and of the world around him. He records the social interactions, the work habits, the speech patterns, the clothing, the medical practices, and other aspects of the daily lives of the people he knew. As a carpenter and mechanic, Parker takes a particular interest in the making of things, describing in detail the construction of a pioneer log cabin and the workings of a hand mill. Similarly, he also describes archeological discoveries, natural landscapes, animals, and plants, painting a picture of an environment that was rapidly changing—from the frontier territories, in which isolated pioneer families hunted for their food, traded with Indians, and traveled by horseback and flatboat, to the central United States, in which a growing population lived in busy cities like Cincinnati and traveled the rivers on modern steamboats and the newly dug canals via a transit system of mule-drawn packet boats. His reflections are a rich source of data for historians following various approaches, including in the areas of political, intellectual, cultural, social, material, environmental, and gender history.

Parker and American Religion

As Parker's memoir is primarily a spiritual autobiography, he pays special attention to the religious beliefs and practices of the people he encounters. During the first decades of the nineteenth century, Old World precedents, evangelical fervor, Enlightenment ideas, and an emerging American individualism converged to make the United States in general, and the frontier in particular, a fertile ground for religious diversity. Daniel Parker documents the religious life of the Ohio valley with characteristically irenic curiosity, revealing a rich and varied landscape that parallels, or even predates, the "burned-over district" of western New York.[24]

In his account of his childhood, Parker alludes to the early and long-lasting influence of John Calvin and the Reformed Protestant tradition on American religious life, stretching back to the Puritans of the seventeenth century.[25] Daniel Parker's parents were unusual among New Englanders in that they belonged to the Presbyterian rather than the Congregationalist stream of American Calvinism, a consequence of the particular ecclesiastical history of their hometown of Newburyport, Massachusetts.[26] Parker remembers them "instructing their children in both the scriptures and catechism," undoubtedly the Westminster Catechism, which provided theological guidance for English-speaking Calvinists of all stripes.[27] He also describes his brother John's anxious reaction against the Calvinist doctrines of limited atonement and double predestination. John's fear that he was not among the elect for whom Christ died, and was therefore predestined for damnation, tempted him to suicide.

Parker describes his encounters with Methodists and Baptists, the popular "evangelical" denominations that were rapidly expanding during the early nineteenth century,[28] a period of religious revival many historians call the Second Great Awakening.[29] Parker, with his unusual ideas, had conflicts with Methodist and Baptist ministers, who viewed the preacher as a rival. Even so, he shared many of their values: their Arminian emphasis on human free will and God's universal love (and consequent rejection of Calvinist predestination),[30] their high regard for the Bible, their emphasis on heartfelt religious experience, their distaste for dancing, drinking, and profanity, and their proclivity for social activism and moral reform.

Parker's quest for truth would lead him to broach the most hostile religious boundaries of his time. Traveling through Washington County, Kentucky, "where Catholics were pretty thickly settled," Parker had a civil theological conversation with a priest and became friendly with several Catholic families. He read the books that they lent him "with care, and found in them much to approve."[31] Considering the long-standing Anglo-American Protestant animosity to the Catholic Church, which would erupt into riotous anti-immigrant nativism in Parker's lifetime, this was remarkable receptivity.[32] Also while in Kentucky, Parker visited a community of Shakers. Their messianic beliefs about their founder, Mother Ann Lee (1736–84), along with their communal living and property arrangements, mandatory universal celibacy, and physically ecstatic worship and dance (from which their name derives), would cause many of their contemporaries to consider them a bizarre cult.[33] Parker, on the other hand, found himself "much pleased" with their singing and dancing rites. Characteristically, however, he objected to the "dogmatic" tone of the sermon, with its "heavy denunciations against their opposers."[34]

Parker also conversed with "skeptics," advocates of the American Enlightenment, the "Age of Reason," who often expressed their views in opposition to traditional Christianity. These included those he labeled as "Deists," who affirmed the existence of God but denied "revelation, prophecies, and miracles." Parker, despite his liberal beliefs about universal salvation, did not consider himself a skeptic or Deist, but argued respectfully with philosophically minded people, knowing that they "would not be put off with dogmatic assertions, but insisted on reasons addressed to the understanding." Parker had a warm friendship with a Scottish immigrant and Kentucky planter named James Kennedy, whom he described as "benevolent, sensible, practical, and the strangest Deist I had ever met with." Kennedy introduced Daniel Parker to his wife Priscilla and was the namesake of his oldest son, James Kennedy Parker.[35]

The American Enlightenment was a facet of a broader phenomenon, especially on the frontier: an emerging individualism, which affected religion as much as it did other facets of American life. Daniel Parker encountered and was himself part of a broad spectrum of self-educated scholars, prophets, and mystics who, separate from formal religious organizations, constructed their own belief systems. He and his brother John held lengthy conversations with an "old man" named Daniel Fink who held the "opinion that washing of feet should be performed as a religious ceremony" and "desired that he might be permitted to wash ours." With characteristic patience, Parker reported, "Although we did not view it as he did, we consented."[36] He was baffled but also intrigued by the musings of Rhoda Fordice (or possibly Fordyce), whose mystical theology included an idiosyncratic explanation of gender and sexuality.[37]

The Halcyon Church

Fordice, like Daniel and John Parker (and perhaps also Daniel Fink), had been a member of the Halcyon Church. Partly in reaction against the Calvinist teachings of their upbringing, both brothers enthusiastically embraced this alternative community as young men, even becoming circuit-riding preachers on its behalf. Indeed, Parker's most valuable contribution to the historical record may be his unique first-hand account of this mysterious group and its visionary leader, Abel Sarjent.[38]

Significant in its time, but almost forgotten today, the Halcyon Church was both a marginalized sect and a representatively American religion with distinctly American elements: an egalitarian ethos, a millennial optimism, and an original interpretation of the Bible (supplemented by personal revelations), all promulgated by a charismatic leader.[39] Abel Sarjent's eclectic theology combined evangelical Christianity, Enlightenment philosophy, revolutionary politics, and even the mysticism of Jewish kabbalah.[40] More remarkable than its influences, however, was the Halcyon Church's anticipation of elements of later religious movements of the nineteenth and even the twentieth centuries. These range from the apocalypticism of William Miller and the Adventist movement to the this-worldly reformism of the Social Gospel,[41] to (most strikingly) another quintessentially "American religion," Joseph Smith's Church of Jesus Christ of Latter-day Saints.[42] Thirty years before the Mormons appeared on the scene, the Halcyon Church followed its own living prophet (of a sort), proclaimed its own "restored" gospel, and expected the emergence of God's new "Zion" on the American continent.[43] Despite these and more uncanny similarities in terminology, there is no clear evidence that Halcyon doctrines directly influenced those of the Latter-day Saints. Nevertheless, the intriguing fact remains that Abel Sarjent's son and namesake became one of the first generation of Mormons.[44]

While many details of Sarjent's life are uncertain, it is clear that he was a strong personality with a sense of mission. Born in 1764, Sarjent was originally from Maryland, where he may have itinerated as a Free-will Baptist preacher.[45] In 1785 he married Sarah Tunis, with whom he would have nine children. In the 1790s Sarjent moved with his family between Maryland, Pennsylvania, New York, and Ohio. During this time he declared himself a Universalist and published his views in four issues of a periodical, the *Free Universal Magazine* (1793–94). He may have briefly served a Universalist congregation in Washington County, Pennsylvania, in 1800. In 1801 he was living in Kenhawa County, Virginia (now Mason County, West Virginia), near Point Pleasant along the Ohio River, and had experienced what he understood to be a divine calling to form a new religious community. The Halcyon Church would be formally organized with fifteen members at Point Pleasant in July of 1802. Sarjent published his ideas in various formats, including pamphlets, supplemental material in *The New Hymn-Book for the Use of the Free Church* (1811), and two short-lived (but long-named) periodicals, the *Aletheian Critic; or Error Exposed, by an Exhibition of Truth* (1804) and the *Halcyon Itinerary and True Millennium Messenger* (1807–8).

For several years Sarjent lived transiently, preaching and baptizing converts and helping the Halcyon movement grow and flourish in southeastern Ohio, northwestern Virginia (present-day West Virginia), Kentucky, and western Pennsylvania. In 1807 the movement peaked with twenty branches, which included "440 regular members, besides 2200 warm friends and open advocates of the doctrines and cause espoused and vindicated in and by this church."[46] Afterward the movement gradually dwindled, divided, and eventually dissolved, with members drifting into other religious communities, including Universalist churches.[47] After attempting to resume his preaching and publishing career in Cincinnati in the 1820s, Abel Sarjent faded into obscurity.[48] He would eventually move to Indiana, where he died in 1839.[49]

The doctrines of the Halcyon Church may be found in Sarjent's own writings, to the extent that they can be discerned through his style, which ranged from sophisticated theological argument to satirical polemic, to cryptic symbolism. His beliefs included, first and foremost, the expectation of a rapidly approaching millennium, in which the reign of Christ would be established on earth in the form of a perfectly just society.[50] Reporting natural, political, and paranormal events as omens of the coming new age,[51] Sarjent alluded to himself as the "messenger," chosen by God to announce the imminent millennium to the world[52] (though he denied any messianic pretensions and even specifically rejected the title of "prophet," saying the term belonged to a past age).[53] Sarjent claimed that the millennial "empire" would first emerge in "Columbia" (a commonly used poetic term for the United States) and then spread throughout the world.[54] The world's people would voluntarily and democratically submit to the principles of Christ's reign in the spirit of "genuine republicanism."[55] The future just society would be one of perfect equality and would mark the end of such evils as African slavery and economic injustice.[56]

Sarjent's depiction of the millennial utopia was strikingly this-worldly. At times it seems he is describing simply gradual, natural, political progress, rather than a supernatural apocalypse.[57] His vision of the future also contained supernatural elements, however, including the general resurrection of the dead, which apparently was to occur after the millennial empire had been established. At this time, Sarjent believed, all who have died would rise again. The righteous would live forever in God's kingdom and the recalcitrantly unrighteous would suffer "the second death" and simply cease to exist.[58]

Implicit in Sarjent's understanding of the final judgment was his conditional concept of immortality. According to this belief, sometimes labeled "Christian mortalism," human beings do not possess souls that are immortal by nature.[59] Rather, human beings receive a contingent immortality as a special gift from God, and such a gift can be lost as well.[60] Sarjent is credited with first bringing the Universalist faith to Ohio—understandably so, as he appropriated the label "Universalist" for himself and a journal he published. However, Sarjent's concept of the afterlife technically stopped short of universal salvation.[61] His "annihilationist" view was closer to that shared by present-day Seventh-day Adventists and Jehovah's Witnesses.[62] Sarjent did not believe that all people would enjoy a blessed eternal life, but he did reject the traditional concept of a fiery hell in which the damned would be tormented forever.

Like other apocalyptic thinkers, Sarjent contrasted future perfection with present corruption.[63] He distrusted all civil governments and his evocative political statements at times had the ring of anarchy,[64] but his most hostile attacks were on established mainline churches, both Catholic and Protestant. Sarjent claimed that institutional Christianity had for centuries been "adulterated from her native purity." Christianity's chief corruption was the adoption of an educated and formally ordained "clergy" who, Sarjent claimed, were by no means true "ministers of the gospel." Sarjent accused the clergy of worldliness, materialism, and the promotion of error—including obscuring the "original sense" of the Bible, which Sarjent believed should be interpreted figuratively rather than literally.[65]

Urim and Thummim

In attacking the legitimacy of the established churches and their clergy, Sarjent laid the groundwork for the necessity of his own alternative Christian community under his leadership. In criticizing biblical literalism, he laid the foundation for his own claims to truth based on his direct revelations from God and his figurative interpretation of the Bible, especially his schema of "Urim and Thummim."

This symbolic interpretation of an Old Testament term (literally, a divining device that was consulted by the chief priest, perhaps two marked stones that were cast as lots) was essential to Halcyon theology.[66] It was the "standard," the key that unlocked the meaning of Scripture, revealing the true nature of God, humanity, Jesus Christ, and salvation. Just like the two stones that the priest Aaron kept in a pouch on his breastplate, the symbolic Urim and Thummim were the human means of access to God.[67]

Daniel Parker devotes several pages of his autobiography to the idea, which continued to "enamour" him long after he had officially parted ways with the Halcyon Church.[68] Parker's autobiography also raises questions about the idea's origin, as he gives credit to Sarjent for explaining only half of the system, the meaning of Urim. Parker claims to have arrived at the meaning of the second half, Thummim, later, independently of Sarjent, an account which is in tension with the usage of the term "Thummim" in older Halcyon publications.

Possible explanations for this discrepancy, along with the specific meaning of the symbolic system, will be further discussed in later chapters and their endnotes. For now, a general explanation must suffice. Urim and Thummim represented respectively a set of seven divine virtues, "love, wisdom, power, holiness, justice, goodness, and truth," and five human faculties for perfecting those virtues, "perception, judgment, affection, will, and memory."[69] Jesus Christ, who was "divinity and humanity in one," was both the exemplar and mediator of these perfected virtues. Faith in Christ was the means by which a believer came under his "influence" and could reach a similar state of perfection.[70]

According to Halcyon literature, the Bible's many references to the numbers seven, five, and twelve (seven plus five) were allusions to the seven principles and five faculties of Urim and Thummim, and these numbers recurred "also in the volume of nature."[71] Daniel Parker enthusiastically elaborated on this pattern: there were not only ten biblical commandments (two times five) but five fingers on each hand; not only seven days in the biblical week but seven colors in the spectrum. These were divinely planted signifiers pointing to the hidden treasure of Urim and Thummim. Anticipating his readers' skepticism toward such numerology, Parker emphasized its experiential practicality: "If these enquiries tend to make us neglect the service of God, we certainly should not pursue them," but as for himself, "I never saw the character of God so attracting, and his service so delightful, as has been the case since these views were made known."[72]

Indeed, by offering an alternative to the commonly accepted penal substitutionary theory of atonement, this apparently esoteric system anticipated similar innovations of prominent liberal Protestant theologians of the nineteenth century. Salvation, in this symbolic system, was a matter of rebellious human beings being reconciled to God through the infusion of virtues, not an angry God being reconciled to humanity by the vicarious suffering of his son.[73]

A Mysterious Death

If Sarjent's own writings were cryptic, writings about him and the Halcyon Church by his contemporaries were mostly condemnatory.[74] Church members are depicted as at best dupes and at worst dangerous.

Sarjent is portrayed as at best a fanatic and at worst dishonest: a wandering charlatan who awed followers with pretended religious ecstasies and staged miracles (bringing fire down from heaven and raising the dead), a deadbeat, and even a thief who did not hedge at stealing fish from a neighbor's line.[75] Such attacks against alternative religious communities and their leaders were not (and are not) uncommon, especially coming from mainstream religious leaders.[76] While Sarjent's moral character was not beyond suspicion,[77] these attacks were at least partly motivated by prejudice against and even jealousy of this strangely successful movement.[78]

Sarjent and the church had supporters as well.[79] Daniel Parker defends the Halcyon Church as a respectable, misunderstood band of believers who suffered verbal (and sometimes physical) abuse for their convictions.[80] He describes Sarjent as a sincere preacher who attracted followers not with ecstatic performances or (real or pretended) miracles, but with the strength of his teaching, which appealed "more to the understanding than to the passions."[81] He defends Sarjent against accusations of imposture and dishonesty and even the rumor of his stealing fish. Parker's essentially complimentary portrait of his mentor is made all the more credible by his recognition of his shortcomings. Characteristically, the irenic Parker recoiled from Sarjent's "great severity of language against his opponents."[82]

Parker also provides insight into what may be the most controversial moment in the history of the Halcyon Church, and probably the most upsetting event of Parker's life: the mysterious death of Amos Parkhurst. In 1807, a small group ("some ten or a dozen . . . pilgrims") within the church, which included John and Daniel Parker as well as Rhoda Fordice, decided to engage in a severe fast, motivated by the apocalyptic belief "that the followers of the Lamb would have to go through great tribulation in order to be prepared for entering the kingdom." Among the "cross-bearing company" who participated in the fast was a young man named Amos Parkhurst, whom Parker reports as having extraordinary spiritual gifts, including, most significantly, his capacity for attaining deep states of trance that lasted for several hours, during which he took on the appearance of death, "his eyes shut, his pulse and breath suspended." Parkhurst would eventually come to, apparently unharmed and even robust, and report the extraordinary visions he received while in his trance. Finally, however, Parkhurst slipped into a trance from which he did not awaken. "How long he had been really dead we could not tell," writes Parker, "for he went into the spell about three days before, and had come to so often we thought it would be wrong to bury him until we had the most irrefutable proof of his death."[83]

The death of Amos Parkhurst brought rumors, accusations, and condemnation down on the "pilgrims" who participated in the fast: "Some said we had killed him; others that we had been trying for three days to raise him from the dead."[84] These rumors of either reckless or intentional homicide, perpetrated by religious fanatics, were reported in various memoirs and local histories, with confused names and details.[85] These reports would be taken at face value and repeated by historians in the twentieth and twenty-first centuries.[86] However, it was not only outsiders of the Halcyon Church who opposed this controversial fast. Sarjent himself did not condone it and even attacked the "pilgrims" as schismatics.[87]

Traumatized by conflict, disappointment, and the death of Parkhurst, Parker quietly withdrew from his association with the Halcyon Church. His departure was not entirely bitter. Parker continued to value his experience with the church as a formative chapter in his spiritual journey. He was cordial with Abel Sarjent when they met years later. Most significantly, Parker retained many of his old mentor's ideas even as he developed his own theology. Taking a hiatus from preaching, Parker traveled for several years with a partner named Alvan Bingham to sell washing machines. Privately, he studied the scriptures and reflected on the question of ultimate human destiny. In April of 1814 he accepted an invitation from a friend to preach one Monday evening to a rapidly assembled audience in Alexandria, Ohio, beginning his career as an itinerating evangelist of universal salvation.

Parker and Universal Salvation

In so doing, Parker joined an American religious movement that had been growing for two generations. Universalism is the theological position that affirms universal salvation: not only that no one will be eternally damned, but that everyone will enjoy the full blessings of eternal life with God. While such beliefs have cropped up in various forms throughout the history of Christianity,[88] the enduring Universalist religious community in North America began in the eighteenth century, pioneered by preachers like the English immigrants John Murray and Elhanan Winchester and maintained in its second generation by intellectual leaders like Hosea Ballou.[89]

In contrast to the more educated and wealthier Unitarians (the other major liberal religious association in the United States), the Universalist movement was populist and democratic. Universalist preachers tended to be like Daniel Parker: working class, self-taught scholars who arrived at their positions from their own examination of the scriptures and took up itinerant preaching to informal congregations.[90] Over time, local congregations united into a General Convention and the informal movement evolved into a new American Protestant denomination, which endured until it merged with the Unitarians to form the Unitarian Universalist Association in 1961.[91] However, even as the movement consolidated, many of its nineteenth-century preachers clung to informality and independence, especially in the West. Parker's contemporary George Rogers, pastor of the First Universalist Society in Cincinnati, complained of "an almost total absence of organization in the West, and a prevalent reluctance, on the part of persons professing our faith, to come into any kind of ecclesiastical order."[92]

Daniel Parker freelanced for over twenty-five years before settling as pastor of his own First Restorationist Church on Race Street in Cincinnati, the first preaching engagement to bring him regular income, according to a later memoir by one of his children.[93] Even afterward, he still seemed to cling to his identity as an itinerant. Despite dedicating his book *Familiar Letters to a Brother* to his congregation in 1844, Parker did not mention them in his 1845 autobiography, but wrote instead, "My ministerial labours since the year 1815 had not been confined to any one place."[94] Neither Parker nor his congregation ever formally united with the Universalist denomination, though Parker maintained "friendly" relations with its members.[95] The congregation eventually disbanded, apparently having had Parker as its only minister.

Universalists identified themselves broadly as Christian. Uniting on the idea of universal salvation, they favored flexibility on particular points of theology, though the General Convention did promulgate a minimal, open-ended statement of faith. The Universalist community was not immune to theological rifts, however.[96] The first generation of American Universalists differed over whether it was necessary to affirm the traditional Christian doctrines of the Trinity and the divinity of Jesus.[97] A major issue of contention among Universalists in Parker's day had to do with the possibility of a limited punishment for sin in the afterlife. Some denied any form of future retribution and maintained that all people would immediately experience complete salvation after death. Others, like Parker, believed that some would have to endure a period of postmortem purgation before being "restored" to unity with God. Members of the latter group took the name "Restorationist" for themselves (a designation that Parker preferred to "Universalist")[98] and referred to their opponents as "Ultra-Universalists."[99] Parker's stance would have separated him from prominent Universalist intellectual leaders in the early nineteenth century. By mid-century, however, the Restorationist position had become the majority opinion of the denomination.[100]

What distinguished Daniel Parker most from his fellow Universalists were the beliefs that he carried over from his formation in the Halcyon Church. Parker went so far as to claim, "with the exception of the one point of final restoration, my sentiments have remained the same as when I was a Halcyonist."[101] For example, even after Parker dropped Abel Sarjent's annihilationist doctrine, he continued to affirm its partner concept of Christian mortalism.[102] Most importantly, Parker continued to affirm the Halcyon schema of Urim and Thummim, of atonement through the infusion of virtues, a belief that he integrated into his Restorationist version of universal salvation.

Alluding to the apostle Paul, Parker described atonement as a process of "overcoming evil with good": overcoming vice with virtue, learning to love God and neighbor, to the point of imitating Christ by loving even one's enemies. This process must continue, for all people, even beyond the boundaries of death, until "the whole human family" is restored to unity with God and each other. Apparently, the process could be painful. While Parker generally avoids specific descriptions of the afterlife, his allusions to a postmortem "just retribution" for sin imply that the wicked will experience a kind of redemptive rather than simply a punitive suffering for their wrongdoing, as they gradually turn from sin and selfishness and embrace unity with God and the human family.[103]

As did the Halcyon Church, Parker linked this-worldly progress toward a just and equal society with millennial expectations of final victory over sin and death. According to Parker, the human race was gradually progressing toward individual and communal regeneration, which would ultimately involve the resurrection of the dead and the establishment of God's eternal kingdom. Parker's eschatology (his religious vision of the future) was a call to active participation, not passive waiting, in anticipation of Christ's millennial reign. Human efforts to create a more virtuous, just, and equal society were organically connected to the final perfection of creation and the restoration of the human family. The "benevolent empire" of religious and moral reform movements of Parker's day "were only so many instrumentalities for accomplishing the great work of *restoration.*" Genuine, as opposed to "nominal Restorationists," must work for "the *practical* redemption of all men from every possible wrong condition."[104]

Parker and Slavery

It follows that Parker's own efforts to right social wrongs, such as his involvement in the temperance movement, were not extracurricular interests but essential expressions of his faith. The "wrong condition" of American society that concerned him the most was African slavery. Parker's opposition to slavery was long-standing and deep-seated, but as was the case for many Americans, his stance evolved over time: from initial silence to private moral disapproval to public activism.

Parker hardly mentions slavery in recounting his life as a child and a young man. Having "had seen little of slavery" before, he witnessed scenes that convinced him of its evils during his commercial travels through the South from 1809 to 1814. In the most extreme instance, Parker and his business partners saw "a savage looking white man" knock a slave off a boat in the port of Natchez, Mississippi. Later they found his body "floating about in a small basin near the boat with his skull broken and much swelled." They buried the man in the sand themselves when no one from the town would help them. Though Parker was yet to engage in any public antislavery activity, his opposition during these years was strong enough to affect his choices concerning his future happiness. When Parker fell deeply in love with the daughter of a slaveholding family in Kentucky, he would not consider proposing marriage until she affirmed "she was willing to live in a free state and give up her slaves."[105] She said she was willing, but chose another suitor.

Parker was most outspoken against slavery during the final episodes recorded in his autobiography, occurring from the 1820s to the early 1840s. Parker and his family had settled near Cincinnati, near the border between the slave state of Kentucky and the free state of Ohio, in the path of the Underground Railroad. His public antislavery action initially took the form of supporting the "colonization enterprise." Parker, like many other White moderate opponents of slavery, believed that the plan, at least as old as American independence, to resettle former slaves in a colony in Africa would encourage slaveholders to manumit their slaves voluntarily and thus gradually "lead to emancipation in this country." For two years in the early 1830s, Parker lectured and raised money on behalf of the "parent society," the American Colonization Society, which had formally organized in 1816 and, with limited help from the United States government, established the African colony of Liberia in 1822 as a homeland for former slaves.[106] While Parker was "simple enough" at first to believe that all supporters of colonization shared his antislavery motivations,[107] he became convinced, through the words of its own literature and actions of its leaders, that the Colonization Society, especially its southern faction, was more interested in ridding the country of the troublesome presence of free Blacks than in actually ending slavery. Parker, like many others, withdrew his support. He did not reject the possibility of former slaves voluntarily establishing their own colonies in Africa, but came to "abominate" the Colonization Society's de facto strategy of making deportation a condition of freedom for Black people in the United States.[108]

Even as Parker struggled with the question of colonization, a more radical movement for emancipation was emerging dramatically on the American public stage. These new, uncompromising "abolitionists" rejected both the colonization scheme and the gradualist policy of the earlier generation of moderate antislavery opponents. In the approving words of Daniel Parker, abolitionists "advocated immediate emancipation, on the soil, as the natural and inalienable right of the slaves; urged the doctrine of human rights contained in our Declaration of Independence and the claims of the gospel upon all mankind, irrespective of color or condition; depicted in glowing language the horrors of slavery with a zeal corresponding to the magnitude and importance of the subject; repudiated worldly expediency, and insisted on the duty of adhering to correct principle, whatever might be the consequences."[109] Abolitionists were most famously represented on the national stage by the White publisher William Lloyd Garrison, whose abolitionist manifesto appeared in the first issue of his newspaper, the *Liberator*, in 1831. Their diverse ranks also included African Americans, like the former slave Frederick Douglass, and women, like the controversially outspoken Sarah and Angelina Grimké. Close to Parker's home in the Ohio valley was the former slaveholder James G. Birney, a zealous convert who advocated the cause in his newspaper, the *Philanthropist*. Also nearby was the Presbyterian minister John Rankin, a conductor on the Underground Railroad whose account of escapees from slavery crossing the Ohio River on cakes of ice was fictionalized by his Cincinnati neighbor Harriet Beecher Stowe in *Uncle Tom's Cabin*.[110]

Parker, who disliked confrontation and controversy, hesitated to join the ranks of the abolitionists even after he broke with the Colonization Society. But by 1837 he "became associated with the abolition movement, having some time before espoused and publicly advocated the cause of temperance." Parker joked that the combination of his "so called heretical opinions on theology" with abolitionism made him "as unpopular as my worst opposer could wish."[111] Even in the North abolitionists were despised as radical anarchists, victimized by riots, tarring and feathering, destruction of printing presses, and even murder. While Daniel Parker's abolitionism was not as famous or dramatic as that of Birney or Rankin (or the publisher Elijah Lovejoy, who died defending his third printing press from destruction in neighboring Indiana),[112] it was consequential enough to make his friends fear for his safety during anti-abolitionist riots in Cincinnati. He delivered antislavery lectures for the Clermont County Antislavery Society and other audiences. He subscribed to and acted as an agent for the *Philanthropist.* As he traveled by steamboat to his various speaking and preaching engagements, he engaged slaveholders and proslavery arguments, defending abolitionism in general and John Rankin in particular. At preaching engagements south of the Ohio River, where a publicized antislavery lecture would be all but impossible, he limited himself to speaking on temperance or universal salvation, but his reputation as an abolitionist preceded him. He was subject to verbal abuse and threatened with violence, but reported having "got off without having my throat cut." He added, "slaveholders respect antislavery men who will fearlessly stand up for their principles much more than cringing dough-faces."[113]

Parker and Race

Undergirding the American conflict over slavery was a more complicated problem, one that pervaded not only slavery but virtually all institutions of American society in the nineteenth century: the problem of race and racism. Parker, a man of his time, made ambiguous references to race. For example, on one hand he decried the unjust treatment of Native Americans in Ohio, saying the Indians he knew were honest and "always fulfilled their promises," in contrast to what "could be said of our government toward them."[114] On the other hand, Parker worried about dying "among savages" on his return journey from New Orleans, and expressed relief at "seeing the first white woman after passing through the Chickasaw nation."[115]

Concerning racial slavery, on one hand Parker attacked it with an instinctive commitment to human equality under God, specifically rejecting race-based proslavery arguments, saying one need only "apply the golden rule" to understand its injustice.[116] Also, once fully disillusioned with the American Colonization Society, he adeptly criticized the racist assumptions ("the prejudice against color") undergirding its implicit strategy of deporting Black people as a solution to the problem of African American slavery.[117] On the other hand, Parker once allowed himself to become entangled with the institution of slavery.

Wishing to be helpful to two men who had shown him hospitality in Kentucky, Parker offered to "take care of the families" while they volunteered their services against the British and their Native American allies in the War of 1812. Parker's task consisted of "superintending the business of a farm worked by slaves." In other words, Parker was an overseer for seven weeks, during which time he complained in his diary about his "set of lazy negroes" who were also "lying and dishonest."[118]

Such outbursts need not be excused, but should be put in context. While punctuation in the manuscript is unclear, the statement was apparently from a journal that Parker kept in 1812 and later quoted in his autobiography. At the time, Parker was overwhelmed by an unpleasant and unfamiliar task, frustrated by a number of financial and personal problems, and still growing in his opposition to slavery.[119] He was not the radical abolitionist he would be when he wrote his autobiography in 1845. Parker may have included this quoted passage from his old journal in his autobiography to illustrate his own antislavery argument, that slavery demoralized both masters and slaves, inculcating a false sense of superiority in the former and discouraging the virtues of industry and honesty in the latter. Being separated from the benefits of their labor, for slaves "the less they did in a given time was to them so much gain."[120] Nevertheless, Parker's resentful language about the slaves' behavior is jarring, especially in contrast to his general emphasis on the injustice of slavery itself. He appears oblivious to the possibility that, rather than being passively demoralized by slavery, his charges were intentionally engaging in "silent sabotage," resisting slavery by the best available means.[121]

Parker was not immune to the prejudices of his time, any more than most other White Americans, including many opponents of slavery such as Abraham Lincoln.[122] Especially in Parker's time and place, the "borderlands" of the antebellum Ohio valley, many White residents north of the river combined opposition to slavery with mild to virulent racism, worrying more about the movement of slave power, slave labor, or simply Black people into their lands than about racial injustice.[123] On a spectrum of his contemporaries, Parker would be much closer to the egalitarian end than to the racist extreme. He certainly differed from his fellow Ohioan William Sawyer, who, while claiming to oppose slavery, said that Blacks were "very little removed from dumb beasts" who "wallowed in the mire like hogs."[124] Most importantly, Parker and his family accepted Black students on an equal standing with Whites at Clermont Academy.

Clermont Academy

Clermont Academy had been in operation six years at the time Daniel Parker wrote his autobiography. His account of the school's origins agrees in essence with other family accounts, including a detailed narrative written in 1884 by his daughter-in-law Sarah Baker Parker, wife of his oldest son, James K. Parker. The project was born out of Daniel and (especially) Priscilla Parker's concern about providing an adequate secondary education for their own children. Dissatisfied with the local "common school" and financially unable to send all their children away to boarding schools, the Parkers decided to send James to college so that he would be "prepared to teach the rest." James would then become principal of a high school to be built on the Parker homestead. Having only slightly more schooling and teaching experience than the "two sessions to South Hanover College, Indiana, and one to Mr. Lang's academy near Cincinnati" that Daniel Parker reported,[125] James Parker became the principal instructor at Clermont Academy, which opened for its first term in 1839 with twenty-six day and boarding students, five of whom bore the name Parker. The class included male and female students, to be taught together in the same classroom, an unusual choice for private schools at that time.[126]

The first class also included their first African American student, Edwin Matthews, who was living with and employed by another abolitionist family in New Richmond. Sarah Baker Parker described his application as a "test of principle" for the abolitionist family.[127] Oberlin College had recently, and controversially, enrolled Black and White and male and female students together at the university level, but there was no known precedent for a racially integrated secondary school in Ohio.[128] A similar policy had sparked a backlash that forced a school to close in Yankee Connecticut.[129] After some discussion, along with the encouragement of a visiting English minister and abolitionist, the Parkers admitted the student. He was one of many African American students at Clermont Academy over the years, a policy that would, as the Parkers correctly predicted, lose them some White students (usually from Kentucky), and gain the "odium" of a few of their White neighbors in Ohio.[130]

The structure of Clermont Academy was such that matching school policy to moral principle depended almost entirely on the Parkers' resolve to do so. It was "a real independent family concern—without charter, trustees, or support from public funds."[131] Independence also allowed for simplicity and flexibility. Admission requirements, curriculum, faculty, tuition, expenses, and even a packing list ("one pair of sheets, one pair of pillowcases," etc.) were all contained on a two-page, occasionally revised, printed circular.[132] Over four years, each divided into three twelve-week terms, students took courses in Latin, history, mathematics, science, religion, and philosophy, but "those who desire to prepare for college will be allowed to deviate from this course as much as may be necessary for that purpose." In keeping with the ethos of the family, all students were to "sustain a good moral character" and "attend the religious exercises of the school and to attend public worship on the Sabbath whenever practicable."[133]

The structure appeared to work well. Despite the loss of some White students over racial integration, enrollments increased from year to year. According to records kept by Sarah Baker Parker, graduates went on to attend colleges (ranging from Marietta College in Ohio to Princeton in New Jersey), join professions (teachers, ministers, physicians, politicians), and send their own children to the school.[134] Annual "exhibitions" in which students demonstrated their compositional and rhetorical skills on such topics as "True and False Philanthropy" and the "Necessity of Liberal Principles" became community-wide events, with music, invocations, and distinguished guests.[135] James Parker, known to students, family, and friends as "Teacher Parker," gained such a reputation that he was invited to become the first professor of the historically Black Wilberforce College. He accepted and filled that position for sixteen months in 1857–58.

He then returned to reopen Clermont Academy, which continued for another thirty years.[136]

James Parker taught most of the classes himself, although, as Daniel Parker explained, the students were "under our care," meaning the care of the whole family. Sarah Baker Parker was an assistant teacher and "Mrs. F. P. Currier" (James Parker's married daughter Fannie) at times was teacher of music and Latin. Daniel Parker's contributions were in helping to conceive, finance, and literally build and maintain the institution with his carpentry skills. He was one of many ministers of different denominations invited to preach and lead occasional "religious exercises," and he generally served as grandfather in residence to students who, along with his family, fondly called him "Father Parker."[137]

Even more engaged in the conception, founding, and day-to-day running of the school was Priscilla, "Mother Parker," whose genius Daniel Parker acknowledged. Daniel gave a speech recounting the history of the academy on the occasion of its twentieth anniversary in 1859. A minister attending the celebration volunteered that the school was "more like the undertaking of a woman than a man." Daniel Parker replied that this was true, "though it took both of their combined energies to see it through."[138]

Priscilla Parker

Daniel Parker rarely missed an opportunity to praise Priscilla, whom he called his "best earthly friend."[139] As we have noted, however, Priscilla was not his first love. Writing decades later, he recalled vividly his feelings ("a kind of agreeable dread") of falling in love for the first time with, and being rejected by, the daughter of a Kentucky planter,[140] making his recollections of his successful romance with Priscilla all the more affecting.

Though almost twelve years younger, Priscilla had gained her own storehouse of experience by the time she was introduced to Daniel Parker by their Deist friend, James Kennedy, in 1816.[141] She, like Parker, was a New Englander, born in the "province" (later the state) of Maine in 1793, the daughter of Revolutionary War veteran Hugh Mulloy and

Priscilla Thompson Mulloy. She too had been in love. She too had been heartbroken, losing her husband, Charles Ring, to a shipwreck after three months of marriage and their child to disease less than two years later. During this time she, like Daniel Parker, had migrated west, joining a company of distant relatives that settled in Clermont County, Ohio. She had earned her living as a school teacher in Ohio and Kentucky.

Parker's highest praise for his wife is as the mother of their children. Remembering fondly his own mother, and in keeping with the nineteenth-century "cult of domesticity," Daniel Parker exalts the vocation of motherhood and exhorts his children to appreciate Priscilla's efforts on their behalf. On the other hand, with notable lack of embarrassment, Daniel credits Priscilla for supporting the family financially through her teaching while he was incapacitated with typhus. He honors her contributions to the founding and running of Clermont Academy. He applauds her reforming activism, upholding her courageous opposition to slavery as an example he tried to emulate. Late one night, the couple was visited by an acquaintance from Kentucky who was hunting runaway slaves in Ohio. Daniel tried diplomatically to persuade the slaveholder that it was in his own best interest to give up the search, but Priscilla spoke directly: "Do go home like a Christian and let the poor things go."[142]

Priscilla's strength of character is such that she merits a biography of her own, and thanks to her son, William Tell Parker, she has one, a forty-three-page manuscript written with love and wry humor shortly after her death in 1874. (There are also two short sketches by her daughter Susanna and grandson Parker Donaldson). "Tell" Parker confirms Daniel Parker's description of Priscilla as a devoted mother and, when necessary, an industrious provider, adding that his father "gladly surrendered nearly all paternal authority into her hands. We always went to her for directions, and permission, and not to him."[143] Tell also confirms that as a social reformer, Priscilla did not shy away from confrontation, whether it was in marching into the taverns of New Richmond to plead the temperance cause or protesting against slavery. Among the Parker family papers is Priscilla's handwritten draft of a petition of 1847 to her local Baptist association, insisting they commit to "drive this disgraceful practice, not only from the churches, but from the face of the earth," and appending her opposition to the "wicked" United States war against Mexico that had "no better foundation than the support of slavery."[144]

Priscilla was and remained, as she stated in the same petition and as her husband and son confirmed in their memoirs, a Baptist. Converted and baptized as a teenager, she recommitted herself to the faith of her youth, joining Ten Mile Baptist Church along with her oldest son, James Parker, during a religious revival of the late 1830s. While her Baptist loyalty was constant, it sometimes mixed with other interests. Tell cannot resist mentioning her dabbling in spiritualism (the nineteenth-century phenomenon of communicating with the dead). However, Priscilla was not a member of Daniel Parker's church in Cincinnati, nor did she fully agree with his particular blend of Halcyon mysticism and Restorationist universalism. Nevertheless, writes Daniel Parker, "We were both willing to exercise mutual charity on the subject of difference in our doctrinal views, and agreed to encourage each other in following the saviour's example."[145] Despite their differences, Priscilla supported her husband's spiritually rewarding (but financially negligible) itinerancy. Even when his travels "threw a great burden" on her, Daniel gratefully recalled, she "was not only willing I should go, but always anxious that my labours might be blessed."[146]

A Human Story

In his relationship with his Priscilla, and in other many ways, Parker showed his human qualities. Whatever else it might be, his autobiography is a human story about an individual who, despite considerable obstacles, sought and ultimately found happiness—in the forms of religious assurance, financial security, a meaningful vocation, and love.

Among his personal traits, his religiosity, his moralism, his occasional short-sightedness, and even his bouts of depression are evident. But so are his humility, his patience, his tolerance, and his openness to different views. Though he stood with the radicals in opposition to slavery, he was generally uncomfortable with any type of belligerence, whether it came in the form of partisan frontier politics, the "war spirit" in 1812, or, worst of all, religious dogmatism. While he appreciated listening to a Presbyterian sermon, watching the circular dance of the Shakers, or engaging in theological conversation with a Catholic priest, he could also criticize each of these groups for their exclusivist tendencies.

Parker's irenic nature distinguished him even from other Universalist preachers. Those culture warriors who "mortified" Parker by hiring him to put on a show of attacking religious orthodoxy had warranted expectations. According to historian Ann Lee Bressler, such a scene was typical in the early nineteenth century: "Supporters as well as detractors of the movement described common folk, often halfhearted churchgoers, gathered around some itinerant Universalist preacher, chortling as he held up 'orthodox theology' to ridicule." Considering these popular displays of "spiritual warfare," it is unsurprising that the consummate showman, P. T. Barnum, was in his early life "a religious controversialist on the side of the Universalists," albeit in print.[147] But such stridency was not Daniel Parker's style.

Parker believed he was divinely called and duty bound to preach those truths that had brought him so much hope and joy. However, he could also soft-pedal his "peculiar sentiments on theology" when he thought it appropriate, such as when he spoke to student assemblies at Clermont Academy. On these occasions, Parker gave general moral admonitions and avoided discussion of universal salvation, "lest their parents might think I took advantage of my position." He added, "Unless particularly requested, I seldom said anything on the subject of Restorationism in my own family."[148]

Parker's reticence might seem like inconsistency, but it was also forbearance, an essential aspect of his belief system. In contrast to his radically anticlerical mentor, Abel Sarjent, who rejected virtually all established religion as "false faith,"[149] Parker developed a theological framework that allowed him to uphold his own position while at the same time respecting and even honoring different views, including those of his Baptist wife and son. In Parker's hopeful narrative, every human being and the universe as a whole was moving gradually but inevitably toward personal and social salvation. Particular beliefs, "doctrinal differences," were not unimportant, but they were not ultimate.

Parker's vision of reconciliation might seem naive, considering that even as he wrote, in the 1840s, the major evangelical denominations in the United States had divided or were dividing into northern and southern factions over slavery. On the eve of his death in 1861, the nation itself was dividing and facing the bloodiest war in its history over the same cause. However, Parker's hope was not simplistic optimism, but part of a comprehensive religious vision, which combined love with justice, personal virtue with social concern, otherworldly hope with this-worldly action, time and eternity.

Nor is his vision irrelevant to the present time. While Daniel Parker's theology is thoroughly grounded in the nineteenth century, he struggled with questions that have arisen in new forms in the twenty-first: about the meaning of life, the possibility of an afterlife, the reality of injustice and oppression, the challenges of increasing religious diversity and potential and actual religious conflict. Present-day readers can take inspiration from the way he cobbled together—from scripture, from mystical contemplation, and from his lived experience—a basis for happiness and the hope of overcoming evil with good.

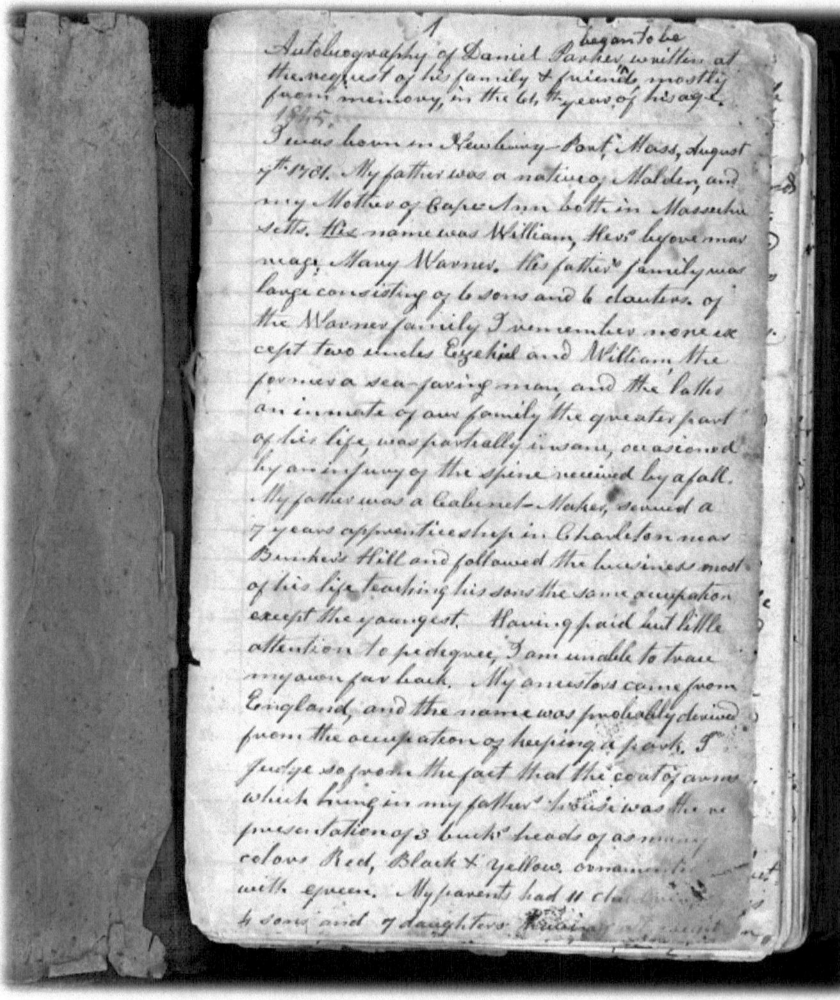

1

Autobiography of Daniel Parker, begun to be written at the request of his family & friends, mostly from memory, in the 61st year of his age. 1845.

I was born in Newbury-Port, Mass, August 7th 1781. My father was a native of Malden, and my Mother of Cape Ann both in Massachusetts. His name was William, Hers before marriage, Mary Warner. His father's family was large consisting of 6 sons and 6 dauters. of the Warner family I remember none except two uncles Ezekiel and William the former a sea-faring man, and the latter an inmate of our family the greater part of his life, was partially insane, occasioned by an injury of the spine received by a fall. My father was a Cabinet-Maker, served a 7 years apprenticeship in Charleston near Bunker's Hill and followed the business most of his life teaching his sons the same occupation except the youngest. Having paid but little attention to pedigree, I am unable to trace my own far back. My ancestors came from England, and the name was probably derived from the occupation of keeping a park. I judge so from the fact that the coat of arms which hung in my father's house was the representation of 3 bucks' heads of as many colors Red, Black & yellow, ornamented with green. My parents had 11 children 4 sons and 7 daughters. [illegible]

Figure N.1. Daniel Parker's manuscript autobiography, open to the first page. (Special Collections, Legacy Library, Marietta College)

NOTE ON TEXT

Beginning in 1845, Daniel Parker wrote his autobiography in sixteen octavo notebooks, which were numbered and bound together into one volume. Decades later, one of Parker's children copied his manuscript by hand. The copyist, who also included a genealogy in the same large notebook, identified Daniel Parker as his or her father, but did not give his or her own name. According to Parker family oral history it was Charles Coleman Parker.[1] The last death recorded in the genealogy was Priscilla Parker's in 1874, indicating the volume was copied around that time.[2]

Both the copy and the original manuscript remained in the possession of one Parker descendant after another until 2011. That year, Dr. James Parker lent them on behalf of the Parker family to Marietta College in Marietta, Ohio, where they have been housed in the Special Collections of the Legacy Library. A typescript of the autobiography, copied from the original manuscript, may be found along with typed copies of other Parker family papers in the archives of the Ohio History Connection (formerly the Ohio Historical Society) in Columbus. These were produced and donated by Daniel Parker's great granddaughter, Bertha Currier Hardman, around 1947. A carbon copy of the typescript, along with many originals and copies of other Parker family papers, were donated by Parker descendent Margaret McDiarmid to the Department of History and Geography of Northern Kentucky University in support of its Parker Academy Archaeological Project.

Considering Daniel Parker's lack of formal education, and considering the fluctuating standards of English spelling, grammar, and punctuation in nineteenth-century America, Parker's manuscript is surprisingly accessible to the modern reader. Nevertheless, it still presents challenges. The author's handwriting, while mostly legible, is at times obscure. He informally makes use of numerals, idiomatic abbreviations, and shorthand symbols. His spelling, while comprehensible (especially when compared to that of many of his peers),[3] is at times irregular and inconsistent. For example, he offers at least three ways of spelling the word "celibacy."[4] Grammatically, Parker had a habit of stringing several clauses in a sentence without conjunctions, of splicing complete sentences together with a comma, and of neglecting to place a subject at the beginning of a clause or even at the beginning of a sentence. Finally, despite his generous personality, Daniel Parker was remarkably stingy with commas and periods, and apparently considered paragraph indentations an extravagance above his station. Hyphens, on the other hand, he was rather free with, putting them in items as small as a "tea-cup" and places as large as "New-York."

In preparing this manuscript for publication, the editor must balance two valid concerns. On the one hand, the published edition should give an accurate presentation of the author's work, preserving the particularity of its style, spelling, and syntax for their historical value. On the other hand, the published edition should be accessible and even enjoyable to a broad audience, which the author himself indicated he hoped to reach. On the basis of either of these two concerns, an editor might veer to one or another extreme. An unedited typescript (or even a photo-facsimile) would be an accurate historical presentation of Parker's manuscript, but not as accessible for present-day readers. At the other extreme, a free adaptation might (possibly) be more interesting to current readers, but of little historical value. This edition has taken a middle path. While striving to preserve Parker's original voice, it has made some accommodations for the sake of clarity.

Two documents have provided editorial guidance. The Family Copy of 1874 is especially helpful in discerning Parker's handwriting.

The copyist has also taken the liberty of adding punctuation and paragraph divisions as well as correcting some of the author's spelling and (less often) his grammar. Much of the copyist's interpretive editing is instructive, though some of these "corrections" are more a matter of preference than clarity. Therefore, this edition follows its lead in some but not all circumstances.[5] In addition, Parker's theological monograph, *Familiar Letters to a Brother: On the Final Restoration of All Mankind*, provides both a precedent and a pattern for preparing his autobiography for publication. While no original manuscript of this published book survives, it is clear, when compared with Parker's unedited handwritten autobiography, that the former work was edited for grammar, spelling, and punctuation in preparation for printing. Perhaps Daniel Parker's wife Priscilla or his son James, who were both teachers, helped him in this capacity. In any case, it is evident in his author's dedication that Daniel Parker approved of the final product. One may assume he would have wished for similar editing for the future publication of his autobiography.

For the sake of authenticity, this edition of Parker's autobiography has refrained from putting words in the author's mouth and resisted the temptation to improve his writing by adding a subjective noun, a conjunction, or a verb that seems to be missing. Parker's grammar has been left essentially intact, even, for example, in the verb-less "sentence" that follows: "Measuring in architecture by twelve inches, seven radical tones in music, seven colours in the rays of light."[6] While the sentence is awkward, its meaning is clear in context. In the few especially problematic sentences that have been revised within the text, revised language is placed in square brackets [like these]. Words within rounded parentheses (like these) are the author's own, not editorial revisions.

For the sake of accessibility and in keeping with *Familiar Letters to a Brother*, Parker's more unusual spelling has been regularized and modernized. A few isolated or inconsistent misspellings, apparent slips of the pen, have been corrected silently, as have some minor inconsistencies in capitalization. Some but not all numerals and abbreviations have been spelled out.

When Parker uses a conventional alternative spelling, and when this same alternative spelling is also used in *Letters*, then it is not altered in his autobiography. Examples include Parker's use of the once-common "shew" (instead of "show") and his frequent use of the British *–our* ending instead of the standard American *–or* ending for such words as "neighbour" (as opposed to "neighbor"). Also, some of Parker's inconsistent alternations between these commonly accepted spellings have been left as they are, along with several other inconsistencies in spelling and style, when imposing uniformity on Parker would involve excessive second-guessing as to his intentions.

An interesting inconsistency, which has been corrected, is the spelling of the last name of the leader of the Halcyon Church. In a few instances near the beginning of his manuscript, Parker refers to "Abel Sargent," a spelling frequently used by his contemporaries and later historians. Throughout the rest of the manuscript, however, Parker refers to "Abel Sarjent," which was the favored spelling of the man himself. Though using two different spellings may have been an appropriate tribute to the mysterious Halcyon "messenger," this edition uses "Sarjent" consistently to avoid confusion.

As almost certainly was the case with *Familiar Letters to a Brother*, formatting and punctuation of Parker's manuscript autobiography have been revised in preparation for printing.[7] Commas, periods, semicolons, and paragraph indentations have been added freely, and some extraneous hyphens and other punctuation have been removed. Punctuating and formatting Parker's manuscript has been an inexact, interpretive effort. When necessary, editorial issues and choices related to the manuscript (discerning handwriting, spelling, punctuation, etc.) are further explained in the endnotes.

Parker quotes, paraphrases, and alludes to the Bible often, but not always with a citation. Biblical chapter-and-verse citations that appear in the text (usually in parentheses) are the author's. Those not given by the author are provided in the notes.

In the introduction, endnotes, and epilogue, I, as editor, capitalize "Black" when the term refers to Black racial identity. This practice is in keeping with the recently revised guidance of *The Chicago Manual of Style*, as well as that of other style guides and media outlets, and is both a matter of clarity and respect.[8] I also capitalize "White" when referring to White racial identity. This is a more controversial choice.

It is made not with the intent of conferring dignity on Whiteness but to indicate clearly that the term does refer to a historically created racial identity, not some "normal" or "neutral" condition.[9] Daniel Parker, on the other hand, does not generally capitalize "white," "black," or "negro" when referring to White or Black ethnicity, and doing so was not a convention of his time. So for the sake of historical clarity, those terms are left in lowercase in his autobiography. Direct quotes within the introduction, notes, and epilogue will retain the capital or lowercase letters of the quoted sources.

The chapter divisions and titles of this volume are not original to the manuscript, but are the editor's. Chapter divisions are based on logical breaks in his narrative and chapter titles are quotes from Parker's text. It is an unplanned coincidence that there are seven chapters, a number of mystical significance in the Halcyon system of Urim and Thummim. Daniel Parker would no doubt be pleased and not at all surprised.

Daniel Parker's Patterns of Irregular Spellings

For the sake of historical linguistic interest, Parker's frequently occurring irregular spellings are listed below. Some others are explained in endnotes. Many of Parker's irregular spellings followed patterns, which are listed below along with selected examples. Parker did not adhere to these patterns with complete consistency. Some words listed as examples below have more than one spelling in the manuscript.

Substituting *i* for *e*: appertinences; attintion; confissed; convirsed; counsil; disigned; disire; dispise; distroyed; gintlemen; imployers; inabled; indeavours; ingrose; inliven; insuing; intangled; inter; intinse; intirely; interprize; intreaty ispecially; ixists; Pinsylvania; sint; spint; tistimony; undirstanding.

Substituting *e* for *i*: derected; destressing; devision; embecile; envestigation; pegeon; rediculous.

Substituting *e* for *a*: deliverence; Gibralter; ignorent; perseverence; repentence; seperated; utterence.

Other vowel substitutions: antitipe (for "antitype"); barbacue; despared; effigee; imperitive; itenerency; persuits; sacrafices; speach; tendancy; testiment; existance; horizen; phisical; susceptable.

Substituting *c* for *k*: scull; sceptical.

Substituting double letters for single letters: acknowleggement; biggot; cabbin; callico; collumns; defference; dilligent; ennamoured; excressences; equallity; forrest; habilliments; holliness; hospitallity; instabillity; loose (for "lose"); oppulence; scurillity; subburbs; reallity; tittle (for "title"); travelling; untill; waggon. Parker also occasionally adds double letters to place names: Collumbia; Flemming (for Fleming County, Kentucky), Cynthianna (for Cynthiana, Kentucky)—though again, these spellings are not always consistent.

Substituting single letters for double letters: agravate; coroding; dispeled; emisaries; eroneous; fulfil; ilgoten ease (for "ill-gotten ease"); insurection; meriment; Mesiah; millenium; narative; occured; paliation; posible; quary; skilful; steped; stoped; terible; unsuported; valey; vilage. This tendency can also be found in a place name: "Harison" County.

Separating compound words: every body (and other compound words beginning with *any–* and *every–*), mean while; slave holders; to day; where ever. This pattern also occurs for place names: Middle Town; Nash Ville; Shelby Ville. Parker is less consistent in this pattern of irregular spelling than in others: he also uses the spellings "slaveholder," "Nashville," etc. Parker also had the countervailing tendency to collide distinct words in place names, such as "Tenmile" (for Ten Mile, Pennsylvania, a spelling he also uses).

Missing silent letters: bath (for "bathe"); diciples; facinating; morgaged; riteous; rout (for "route"); strait (for "straight"—Parker also once substitutes "straights" for "straits").

Added silent letters: fourthe; hopeing; hornes; judgement.

Homophones: As do many writers today, Parker would occasionally and inconsistently confuse homophones, such as using "flower" instead of "flour"; "heal" instead of "heel"; "principle" instead of "principal"; "seller" instead of "cellar"; "their" instead of "there."

Contractions: Parker would often contract the past tense ending *–ed* with an apostrophe (e.g., "strain'd"). In keeping with *Familiar Letters to a Brother*, these contractions have been spelled out (e.g., "strained").

Abbreviations: Most of Parker's abbreviations, such as "Wm." for the name "William," seem to be shorthand informalities, not conventions he would want to be preserved in print. Therefore, most have been spelled out in this edition, though some are historically interesting. For example, before the United States included Oklahoma and Oregon, Ohio could be abbreviated as "O." without confusion. Some of Parker's abbreviations for titles ("Doc." for "Doctor" and "Esqr." for "Esquire") have been retained, as these titles were and are typically abbreviated in print, though with different spellings ("Dr." and "Esq.").

THE AUTOBIOGRAPHY OF DANIEL PARKER,

FRONTIER UNIVERSALIST

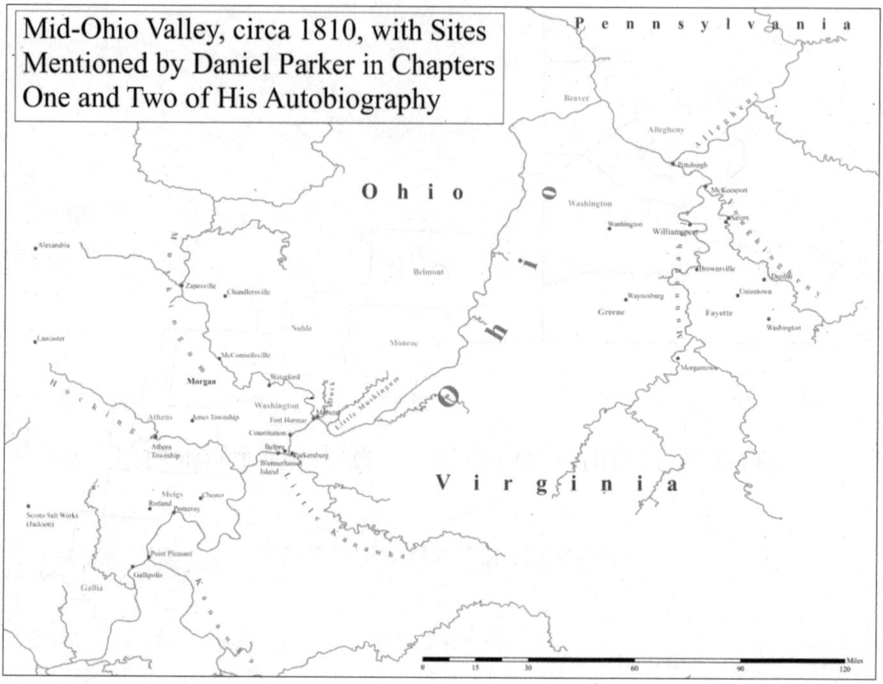

Map 1.1. Map by Matthew Young

CHAPTER 1

"On Our Arrival West of the Mountains"

AUTOBIOGRAPHY OF Daniel Parker, began to be written at the request of his family and friends, mostly from memory in the 64th year of his age, 1845.

I was born in Newburyport,[1] Mass., August 7, 1781. My father was a native of Malden, and my mother of Cape Ann, both in Massachusetts. His name was William;[2] hers, before marriage, Mary Warner.[3] His father's family was large, consisting of six sons and six daughters. Of the Warner family, I remember none except two uncles, Ezekiel and William,[4] the former a seafaring man, and the latter, an inmate of our family the greater part of his life, was partially insane, occasioned by the injury of the spine received by a fall.

My father was a cabinetmaker: served a seven-years apprenticeship in Charlestown[5] near Bunker's Hill, and followed the business most of his life, teaching his sons the same occupation except the youngest. Having paid but little attention to pedigree, I am unable to trace my own far back. My ancestors came from England, and the name was probably derived from the occupation of keeping a park. I judge so from the fact that the coat of arms which hung in my father's house was a presentation of three bucks' heads of as many colors: red, black, and yellow, ornamented with green.

My parents had eleven children, four sons and seven daughters, having all, except the youngest, old fashioned names, in the following order according to age: Betsey Warner,[6] William,[7] Sally,[8] John,[9] Daniel, Polly,[10] Nancy,[11] Suky,[12] Fanny,[13] Ebenezer,[14] Clarrissa[15]—none having middle names but the oldest. All lived to be of mature age and are still alive (1845) except Suky and Clarrissa who have been dead many years. My mother died in 1811 and my father in 1826.

The earliest incident of my life that I can remember was falling down cellar[16] while running through the house in the twilight, crying for my mother, who took me in her arms after being brought up much hurt. Being but seven years old when we left Newburyport, my recollection of the place is but slight. I remember, however, going to school, playing truant once, snow-balling with other little boys, sliding on small sleds down the hillside back of town (head foremost, steering with my toes), going of errands, eating gingerbread, seeing ships launch in the Merrimac River, and going to Mr. Murry's meeting.[17]

I can never forget, while retaining the faculty of memory, the tenderness and assiduity of my dear mother, who kindly restrained my waywardness and taught me little prayers and hymns while putting me to sleep in the trundle-bed. Maternal solicitude is seldom repaid by children.

My mother was of medium size, very comely in person, gentle in disposition, courteous in manners, attentive to the wants of others, beloved by all who knew her. Her skill in vocal music was extraordinary.

My father was of ordinary size, not handsome, though "good-looking"; of plain manners, very industrious and attentive to the wants of his family. He seemed to have a constitutional aversion to seeing human blood, as the following incident will shew. My sister Polly when a small child had her little fingers badly bruised while climbing over a pile of scantling, and bleeding profusely, was brought into his presence. On seeing the blood he rose to leave the room but fainted and fell backward on the floor.

Although my parents were not members of any church, they were religious, attending to both public and family worship, strictly observing the Sabbath and instructing their children in both the scriptures and catechism, being of the Presbyterian persuasion.[18]

In the fall of 1788 we removed from Newburyport in company with several other families to the western part of Pennsylvania. After a very tedious and expensive journey through many hardships, occasioned by bad roads and inclement weather, we arrived on the waters of the Monongahela about twenty miles above Fort Pitt (now Pittsburgh) a few miles northeast from the mouth of the Youghogena[19]—the Ohio

Company having settled in April of the same year at the mouth of the Muskingum.[20] In this company's purchase my father owned a share consisting of 1500 acres of land,[21] which was divided into different sized lots, located in various places, some along the banks of the Muskingum, others on the Ohio, but the larger portion about twelve miles south of the latter stream on the waters of Leading Creek in what is now Meigs County. His intention when leaving New England was to go on to his land the next spring, but before he could make the necessary preparations the Indian War broke out and continued until the treaty of General Wayne at Greenville in 1795.[22]

On our arrival west of the mountains we found the country but little improved, and the people still less, dwelling in rude cabins constructed of round logs, covered with clapboard chinked with triangular hearts split off the clapboard stuff, and daubed with mud. The chimneys were made of what they called "cat and clay" in the following

Figure 1.1. *An American Loghouse*, Georges-Henri-Victor Collot, from *A Journey in North America* (Paris: Arthus Bertrand, 1826), plate 16. This print is based on one of Collot's drawings from his travels in 1796 in the Ohio, Missouri, and Mississippi river valleys. (Edward E. Ayer Collection, Newberry Library)

manner. Mortar mixed with straw was worked into long rolls and laid round alternately with split sticks crossing at the corners and thus preventing the mortar from falling off, the mortar entirely covering the sticks and thus securing them from the fire, the whole resting on a pen of logs projecting from one end of the cabin to form the fireplace. The floors were made from split puncheons hewed on the upper side; the same material formed the door.

Oiled paper served as glass for the window (seldom more than one)[23] while the inside walls were lined round with the woman's dresses hung on wooden pins. A calico dress was a rare sight. They were generally made of linsey[24] and consisted of [a] petticoat and short gown, the latter reaching a little below the waist. A sunbonnet was the common headdress. When the women went to meeting they carried their shoes and stockings in their hands, and put them on before going into church. One might see them in all directions sitting about on logs attending to this adjustment. The men wore linsey hunting shirts, and either buckskin or linsey pantaloons. Fur hats and broadcloth coats were scarce as calico dresses.

It being late in November, snow having fallen, weather wet and cold, my father moneyless, with a family of eight children in a wilderness country, far from friends and without a house, our situation was melancholy enough. The first shelter we found in which to stow the family and goods was a hovel built of round logs, roofed indeed but without chinking, daubing, chimney, or floor. Having no bedsteads, we erected scaffolds with crotches, poles, and clapboards in the corners, hung round quilts and there put the beds. A large fire was built in the centre and bits of clapboards scattered about to keep our feet out of the mud, for when it rained the weather ran across the whole enclosure. We had driven out a flock of sheep belonging to the landlord before taking possession, and in this wretched place we lived one month, during which time my father put a shingle roof on the landlord's house, the first in that section of country, and received in part pay a bagful of sick wheat, which made us all sick before we knew there was such a thing as sick wheat.[25] My mother was blind for three days occasioned by the smoke. She was almost heart-broken when comparing her condition with what it had been, but there was no remedy, for we could not go back if we would.[26]

At the month's end we found a few miles off a hut that had once been inhabited by human beings, but then was occupied by horses. After getting permission and cleaning out the manure, we found it had a floor. It had also chinking, daubing, and a chimney. Here we spent the remainder of the winter, in which time my sister Fanny was born.

It was not long till we heard of two New England families being in the neighborhood. Their names were Sheppard and Porter. Our families soon became intimate, and though strangers before seemed like relations to each other, and soon after settled for a short time near together. This intimacy was, however, soon broken off by their removal to Marietta in the state of Ohio.[27]

For nearly seven years we had no permanent home for any considerable length of time, but moved about, living on rented land which we boys cultivated while our father worked at his trade. Between the two of us we made a comfortable living. During these seven years there was one of great scarcity, so that some families were without bread for many weeks, living on greens and milk—it being most serious in the spring and the fore part of summer, when the winter stock was exhausted. It happened that we had raised a good crop of beans the previous year, so that we did not suffer like many others. I remember of seeing my mother measure off to each child a small piece of Johnny Cake (Indian cornbread baked on a narrow board) and of putting my piece in a box, taking a small portion occasionally that it might last the longer.

My father, hearing that there was corn at Wheeling 100 miles down the river, went thither with some others in a canoe, found some at Mr. Zanes' (afterward proprietor of Zanesville), but he refused to let them have any, because they had money, giving as a reason that he was obliged to supply his poor neighbors who had no money. They returned without a bushel, commending the benevolence of Mr. Zanes to the poor.[28]

Harvest approaching, Mr. John McKee (proprietor of McKeesport at the mouth of the Youghogena),[29] having a field of very early barley, gave out word that if the neighbors would come and reap it they might each have a grist, and pay him when they could. My father went and brought home a bagful, which made the sweetest bread we thought that ever was eaten.

I record these things that my children may be thankful for bread, and instead of wasting what they do not need, give it to the poor. I desire that they may never experience such privation, but should they, it will teach them a lesson of economy which perhaps they may now despise. The sin of Sodom was pride, occasioned by "fullness of bread and abundance of idleness."[30]

Our next residence was on the west bank of the Monongahela opposite McKeesport in what was called "the neck." There we lived the last three of the years before mentioned, during which time the excise law was passed by congress, laying a tax on whiskey. The law was resisted and an insurrection ensued.[31] An army was sent by General Washington, then president, to quell it. We were in the midst of the turmoil. Soldiers passed our house almost every day from one cantonment to another. The house of Presley Neville (excise master and afterward proprietor of Neville in Clermont County, Ohio) was only six miles distant. It was burnt by insurgents, and Mr. Neville escaped with difficulty to Fort Pitt.[32] One Colonel Bradford was a leading man in that business. He made his escape down the Mississippi.[33] Others were caught, taken over the mountains and tried, but were all, I think, pardoned.[34] One distiller said, before the army came, [he] wished he had the heads of all the congressmen in his big still. Some, who were very noisy when there was no danger, soon hid like young partridges at the approach of the army.

At this place my brother Ebenezer was born. Here also the whole family, except Father, was inoculated and had the small pox vaccination, for kine pox was not then known in that country.[35]

My father, becoming tired of living on other men's land and not thinking it prudent to settle on his own in Ohio, which was then a wilderness, there being an uncertainty whether peace with the Indians (although the war was closed) would continue, bought a small place of some twenty acres in the "Forks of the Yough," eight miles up and one mile south of the Youghogena river. On that little place we resided seven years. There my youngest sister was born.

Having a home of our own in a very healthy situation, we began to be quite reconciled to the country, which was much improved, as were also its inhabitants, compared with what they were when we first came to the west. We had excellent neighbors, the greater part professors of

Figure 1.2. In a painting attributed to Frederick Kemmelmeyer (after 1795), *George Washington Reviews the Western Army at Fort Cumberland, Maryland.* The troops depicted would have been part of a massive contingent that President Washington led into western Pennsylvania to quash the Whiskey Rebellion in 1794. Daniel Parker, thirteen years old at the time, witnessed soldiers passing his house every day during the crisis. (Metropolitan Museum of Art)

religion, belonging either to the Presbyterian, Covenanter, or Seceder Church. [They] were plain and honest, open-hearted farmers, mostly of Irish descent.[36] They used some very singular words in conversation, such as:

"Fenent" for "opposite."

"Hanan" for "what did you say?"

"Till" for "to" and "to" for "till": as, "Are you going till the meeting? Well, wait to I get ready."

"Swither" for "quandary": as, "I am in a swither what till do."

"The morrow" for "tomorrow."

"Be to be" for "has to be."

"Childer" for "children."

"Hit" for "it," with many others not remembered.

It was customary when religious people met for worship to kiss each other, doubtless intending to obey the injunction in First Corinthians 16:20, "Greet ye one another with a holy kiss." Baptists and Methodists were scarcely known in that section, and but little theological controversy. One instance of religious disturbance, however, I recollect, occasioned by the preaching of Mr. Black from Fort Pitt, who was a very talented man, a rigid Covenanter and of course strenuously opposed to singing Watts' psalms in worship (calling them counterfeit psalmody). He had drawn away a number of Mr. Henderson's congregation who were Seceders. I recollect a sermon of Mr. Henderson designed to counteract the influence of Mr. Black.-His text was in Solomon's Songs—these words: "Take us the foxes, the little foxes that spoil the vines, for our vines have tender grapes." In alluding to the nature of a fox, he said that the most mischievous of foxes, according to the opinion of the historians, were the *black* foxes, the shrewdness of this remark fixed it in my memory.[37]

With our little farm and cabinet shop we procured a very comfortable living, but could make no surplus. My father being far advanced in years, my elder brother having left home and gone to Marietta, the place too small, and nearly destitute of timber and the soil much worn, Brother John and myself urged our aged parent to sell out and move down to his land while we were yet with him, promising to stay until he should be comfortably settled, to which after much persuasion he reluctantly consented.

We had rented a sawmill and followed building flat boats, which were then called "Kentucky boats," being used principally by emigrants moving to that state then in a course of rapid settlement. We accordingly commenced preparing to build two boats to convey the family goods and stock. The very first day my brother John took sick and was unable to work for one year. The burden falling upon me, and hating to give up, I went to the woods next day and did about two common days' work. I soon found that would not answer, and wrote immediately to my brother William, requesting him to come to my assistance. He did so, and we finished the boats in time to move in the spring of 1802. Previously to leaving, our shop caught fire and was consumed together with all the tools, stuff, and considerable furniture. This was a great misfortune as the trade was our main dependence.

About the same time another severe trial occurred. My brother John had, unknown to the rest of the family, been laboring under great concern of mind on the subject of a future state. Having been brought up to believe the doctrine of partial election and reprobation, supposing himself to be one of those for whom Christ did not die, he was driven almost to despair, but concealed his trouble as much as possible.[38] One day as my mother was walking near the verge of a deep hollow not far from the house, she heard the sound of a human voice coming up from the bottom of the ravine, and approaching the spot she discovered her son on his knees in prayer. They both returned to the house in tears. He then told us that he had been for many months tempted to commit suicide and was praying for strength to resist the temptation when our mother found him, that he had been afraid to handle any implement by which he might commit the dreadful act.

This unexpected and extraordinary development produced a deep impression on all, but especially on me, as we were intimate companions in everything. I then recollected of his refusing some time before to go a short distance for the cows unless I would go with him. I said it was not worthwhile for two to go, as the bell was within hearing. I could go myself if he would not. This was said in a pettish mood. While at the time I thought strange of his refusing, as he was generally more willing to do any such thing than I was. On reminding him of this afterward, he said the reason of his refusing was a fear that he might see a grape vine and be tempted to hang himself. I felt the sting of self-reproach, and in future was very careful not to leave him alone.

In the midst of these discouragements, we embarked for the state of Ohio and arrived without accident at the mouth of Leading Creek the eleventh of April, 1802. The river being very high, we floated our boats up the backwater six miles, found a smaller settlement and met a hospitable reception from the few inhabitants who had gone before us. We had then to cut a road six miles farther, following a section line to find the land.

Leaving most of the family at the settlement (now called Rutland), my elder brother, uncle William Warner, and myself commenced operations on the land. Our first object was to construct a temporary shelter of puncheons to live in till we could build a cabin. In cutting for this purpose a small buckeye, I lodged it against another tree, and while in the act of cutting the latter, it suddenly broke loose above and I only had time to step out of my tracks when it came down exactly where I had stood.[39] Thus my life was preserved from imminent peril.

By the help of kind friends from Rutland, we raised and covered our cabin and, without waiting to finish it, moved the family out. Thus after the lapse of nearly fourteen years from the period of our leaving New England, we found ourselves for the second time located in a new country, less improved than that in Pennsylvania, to which we first emigrated. There were no neighbors except one within six miles distance eastward. On the north, twenty miles off, was Athens. About the same distance on the south was Gallipolis. And on the west twenty-five miles was the Scioto Salt Works (now the town of Jackson).

Almost the whole territory included within these points was one unbroken wilderness. Wild game was abundant. One could scarcely walk a mile without seeing deer or turkeys and occasionally a bear. It was therefore but little trouble to obtain supplies of animal food. We had taken with us a good supply of flour and of course we had no lack of substantial provision for one year at least. Wild pea vine covered the ground with rich food for cattle, so we had plenty of milk. By extremely hard work, often continued after night, we cleared, fenced, and planted in corn and vegetables, about three acres of ground that season. Some was planted in July. This part of Ohio had been a great hunting ground for the Indians, and Leading Creek, it is said, was so named on account of having been the leading route in passing from their northern towns to the mouth of Kenhawa.[40] Deer being still very numerous, they often spent the fall season hunting near and once encamped on my father's land about two miles off.[41] They were very friendly and honest, would bring us venison to exchange for vegetables, and always fulfilled their promises. I wish this could be said of our government toward them.[42]

My brother William, having kindly assisted us in moving and settling, was soon after married and located in Marietta. Brother John's health remained delicate, and being still unable to work, the younger brother but a child, a large portion of care and labor devolved on me. In addition to farming work, I had to make all our coarse shoes for a number of years, there being no shoemaker near us. [We often wore] moccasins in the summer.[43]

After I was of age, my custom was to help my father occasionally in summer and work for myself in winter, my younger brother being unable to manage the place. Although we soon had obtained a plentiful supply of grain, there were no mills nearer than twenty miles, and those horse mills. We had therefore to grind our corn for six years on a hand mill or go that distance. It may not be amiss for those who never saw a hand mill to have it described. The stones were some twenty to twenty-four inches in diameter, about four inches think, some not that. They were furrowed on the face slightly, hung as mill stones usually are, and on the outer edge of the upper one was a small hole into which a gudgeon driven, into [which] a pole was inserted, the upper end of the pole passing through a hole in a board overhead loosely. The runner was turned round by one hand grasping the lower end of the pole while the other supplied the mill with corn.

Our stock of flour brought from Pennsylvania being exhausted, I once took my young brother with two horses and what wheat they could carry, took our own harnesses, went twenty miles to a horse

Figure 1.3. This picture of "women grinding corn in Ireland" from the *Illustrated London News* (1870) depicts a hand mill, also called a quern, fitting Daniel Parker's description.

mill in Virginia, fording the Ohio River on the way at the foot of Eight Mile Island, attended to the grinding, bolted it by hand, and gave one quarter for toll. Short cakes were then a luxury and tasted all the better for being dearly bought. We paid in those days fifty cents per pound for coffee and two dollars for tea and two dollars a bushel for salt (fifty pounds) and had to pack it from the Scioto Salt Works twenty-five miles through the woods.[44] [We made] our own sugar.[45] Our suppers generally consisted of mush and milk or bean broth and we had neither dyspepsia nor doctors. A lawyer would have starved to death if he had depended for a living on his profession. When visitors came, which was seldom, they generally stayed all night. If they had horses, we spancelled them, that is, tied their forelegs about a foot apart, put a bell on, and turned them loose in the woods where the pea vine was up to their eyes. In the morning they would be found probably within one half a mile of the place we left them.

Nobody visited for mere etiquette but all for friendship. No quarreling among neighbors for they lived too far apart. Tattling and scandal were uncommon as luxurious living. Nobody's pigs, fowls, or cattle troubled us but our own, and we made them pay for what they got by furnishing us with meat and milk. When we had no candles; fire light made with pine knots supplied their place. Having no newspapers nor periodicals and but few books, we read what we had the oftener and with greater attention. There being no schools, the children were instructed at home, and no fault to find with the schoolmaster. No one was alarmed about having their money stolen because they had none to lose. The poor did not envy the rich, as nobody had riches. Deprived of many conveniences we relished with greater zest what we had. We seldom heard preaching, but often attended the Sabbath social religious meetings at Rutland. Providence was kind and we were healthy and thankful. The men-folks raised and dressed large quantities of flax, and my sisters spun and wove it into cloth, the surplus of which was exchanged at Gallipolis for store goods after the family wants were supplied.[46]

On one occasion I accompanied my oldest sister thither for the purpose of exchange, and while returning, night came on before we reached our intended stopping place. It being very dark and the path obscure, we were soon entangled among the bushes, and though within hearing of dogs, could not make ourselves be heard by their owners. So wrapping up with our new goods and tying the horses, we sat down by a tree and stayed till morning.

One very extraordinary occurrence took place shortly after our settlement on Leading Creek. My uncle William, though imbecile in mind, was strong and healthy in body, very peaceful and industrious, and could perform common labor that required little judgment. He was one evening at work a short distance from the house, grubbing some bushes, when a deer came bounding by and ran up the front of a ridge, leading westward, in which direction there was no inhabitant for twenty-five miles.

The beauty and agility of the animal attracted his attention so strongly that he followed it some distance for the pleasure of seeing it run. But on attempting to return, the curvature of the ridge deceived him; and taking a different spur from that he went up, traveled directly from home. At dark he came not in, and a tremendous storm of rain, thunder, and lightning in the night prevented our making much search till next morning. We then procured what assistance we could and scoured the county in every direction, making all the noise possible with guns, horns, and hallooing, but to no purpose. Continuing the search one week without success, he was given up for dead.

In twenty-four days from the time of his departure he was found by some hunters near the Scioto Salt Works and taken thence in the most deplorable condition, though still alive. Fortunately for him, a very kind family by the name of Everts took him in, and by the most careful attention restored him sufficiently to be brought home, but in a state of wild distraction. Being, however, gradually recovered, his mind became more sane than before he went away, and continued so several months. During this lucid interval he informed us of what he had suffered—that he lived on roots and berries (it being the month of July); that he killed and ate raw a pole cat or possum (I disremember which); that he sometimes slept in caves, traveling mostly at night for fear of wild beasts finding him while asleep; that in addition to his intense suffering from hunger, he was bitten by a snake on his heel, which was still in a sad condition after his return. He was absent about one month. [He] died at my father's house many years afterward.

Figure 2.1. Daniel Parker worked in Marietta's shipbuilding industry in 1802. The industry was interrupted by the federal Embargo Act of 1807 but was revived in the 1840s, the time of this painting by Charles Sullivan titled *The Ohio River at Marietta.* Locally built ships were sent down the Ohio and Mississippi Rivers to the Gulf of Mexico. (Courtesy of the Ohio History Connection)

CHAPTER 2

"This Cross-Bearing Company"

THE WINTER of 1802 [and] 3, I worked in Marietta (being twenty-one years old the previous summer) part of the time at [the] cabinet business with my brother and one month on a sea vessel then [being built] by Mr. James Whitney,[1] owned by Colonel Lord of that place, called the "*Brig Marietta* of Marietta." The master builder (Mr. Whitney) was a very pious Methodist and superintended with great ability, commanding the respect of all under his control.[2]

The following summer I spent on the farm, Brother John being able to do some light work. His mind had become more calm, though, not satisfied with the doctrinal view he had been taught, he turned his attention closely to studying the scriptures, drew encouragement thence to hope that Christ died for all the human race and that if they were not all saved it would be their own fault.[3] About this time report reached us of a Mr. Abel Sarjent preaching with great success on the Ohio River near the great Kenhawa. Many strange stories were circulated concerning his doctrine and character. Some said he was a good man, others that he was an imposter.[4] My brother, desirous of hearing for himself, attended his ministry, and became convinced soon after that the sentiments he propagated were true, and the reproaches against his character false. The effect upon his mind was most salutary, and he came home rejoicing; was mentally relieved from his former apprehensions and sore temptations of which I have already spoken.

Hitherto I had not been the subject of any very particular religious experience, though often reflecting with horror on the destiny of those who would suffer eternally in a lake of literal fire and brimstone, as I had been taught to believe. Such reflections would arise on looking into the intense flame of a large log heap while burning. I would think of what excruciating torture would result from being cast into its glowing centre and burnt to ashes, then try to compare that with the endless torment of "*living death*,"[5] so frequently made the leading theme of what were called "gospel sermons."[6] But such thoughts made no lasting impression on my mind, much less on my heart. I was, like most young persons, fond of amusement, and frequently called upon by social parties to promote hilarity by rehearsing odd and diverting speeches, committed to memory for such occasions, though not permitted nor having any desire to form vicious associations; never swore an oath nor ever heard my father or any of my brethren do so.[7]

I was excessively fond of music, both vocal and instrumental; acquired some knowledge of the latter, and was considered by backwoods people a tolerable performer on the flute and violin, one or both of which were often used by Brother John (who could play the flute) and myself in concert with the family singing. Being all acquainted in some degree with the pleasing science, we could carry four parts, and were so accustomed to each other's voices that our music obtained quite a reputation in those days.[8]

The remarkable change wrought in my brother's mind by what he had heard from the new preacher excited my curiosity to know something more about it; nor was he backward in giving information. He said the leading themes in the new doctrine were the love of God; his impartial goodness to men; that Christ died for all; that his death was not designed to reconcile God to man, but man to God; that we must be drawn and not driven to be religious; that all might be drawn if they would yield obedience to the gospel; but that those who continued obstinate enemies of Christ to the end of their probation would be utterly destroyed and not eternally miserable.[9]

With the first part of his statement I was delighted, but this last sentiment I thought was a dangerous error, and immediately set about refuting it by an appeal to the Bible. We therefore kept up for many days an earnest controversy. I found he had out-traveled me in the sacred record, and was able by scripture and reason to demolish what had before appeared to me unanswerable proofs of endless misery. This led me to read the Bible with more interest than I had ever felt before, not so much for the benefit of my soul as to find proof of what I supposed a sacred truth in theory. At length I became satisfied that whatever might be the final destiny of the impenitent, the Almighty would not punish without end any portion of the human race. Still I was loath to acknowledge, although convinced. This state of mind, however, did not continue long. The mutual expression of our sentiments tended to strengthen that fraternal union which had always subsisted between us, and which was afterward still closer cemented when we both together drank into the same *spirit.*

Shortly after my theoretical conversion to what was denominated the Halcyon doctrine,[10] I commenced the cabinet business with my very small means on the bank of the Ohio, ten miles above Gallipolis, in what is called Kyger Bottom, in Gallia County, Ohio. A young man by the name of James Weldon, a wheelwright, worked with me in the same shop, both boarding at Mr. John Bing's,[11] who had a large family of sons and daughters. They were from old Virginia—very respectable, kindhearted, industrious farmers. The whole family were of a sociable and lively turn, indulged in what all thought innocent merriment, attending parties of pleasure, and thought it no harm to dance. Though for my part I never had a taste for it, nor yet for fine dress, always keeping a little behind the fashion.

My landlord lived about three miles from Mr. Sarjent, whose residence was nearly opposite in Virginia, where his preaching was producing a great stir. Many were turned from wickedness. Young people began to forsake the ballroom for the meeting house, the service of Satan for that of God. The spirit of persecution arose in proportion to the increase of practical religion. As yet, however, the work had not extended much into Ohio, and although my brother often traveled fifteen miles to attend the meetings, and drank deeply into the spirit of the revival, I remained unaffected except as to the doctrine, which I soon began to defend in argument. But the time was drawing near when something more important than mere doctrine was to sway my mind.

My sister Sally and I were invited to a social party across the Ohio, which we accepted rather more to please others than ourselves. The forepart of the evening was decently spent. There being a large company, and from some cause (not recollected) obliged to stay all night, dancing was introduced by those who practiced it, and some of the young men, to keep up their spirits, took too much strong drink (which in those days was always furnished on such occasions), and the whole company were kept awake till daylight. In the morning we returned to Ohio completely disgusted, resolving in my own mind never to go to another frolic.[12] On our way home we called near the mouth of Leading Creek to hear the Halcyon preacher, and though in a very unfavorable condition through sleepiness and fatigue, my attention was powerfully arrested by the sermon.

Mr. Sarjent was in his prime, strong minded and energetic and searching in his appeals to the understanding and heart. In his address to the youth he pointed out the superior advantages of religion over the frivolous amusements they pursued so carelessly, and impressed upon their minds, with much earnestness and affection, the importance of giving their hearts to the saviour while young. His discourse was directed more to the understanding than to the passions. His language was not that of terror but of love. I not only heard its sound but felt its power. The word of truth penetrated my conscience and the arrows of conviction pierced the inmost recesses of my soul. All my past folly, instead of appearing as innocent amusement, now seemed the natural fruit of a corrupt heart. The purity of God's law when brought to bear upon my best deeds produced only condemnation and swept away the last prop of self-dependence. My heart sunk within me and I viewed myself as loathsome in the sight of God.[13]

This state of mind continued for many weeks and could not be concealed from observation among my associates. They began to fear that the "fanaticism," as they called it, would spread until it would break up all their convivial parties. The old folks feared it, not so much on that account, as on account of what they thought heretical in the doctrine taught. To doubt the truth of the general belief that the wicked would suffer without end was, they supposed, to open the floodgates of every vice.[14] Although at the same time they saw the vicious turning from their evil ways through preaching a different faith.

The intensity of my convictions and consequent distress of mind was so great that I would often forget what I was doing, and have frequently caught myself standing entirely still in the shop, holding in my hand some tool with which I had been working. I appeared to myself utterly unworthy to make an outward profession of religion and feared to do so, lest I should disgrace the cause of Christ. Having lost all relish for vain company and pursuits, and experiencing none of the comforts of religion, I was wretched indeed, often applying to myself the passage of scripture concerning the ass being tied where two ways met.[15] I was neither in the way of folly nor in that of holiness; neither willfully disobedient as I thought, nor yet practically obedient; convinced that the claims of Christ were paramount, and yet afraid to enlist in his service lest I might prove a traitor; tempted with the allurements of this world, yet drawn powerfully to seek the more substantial joys of that which is to come. Knowing that if I openly espoused the Halcyon cause by attaching myself to the church (that was then organized in Virginia), I should not only forfeit the good will of my intimate friends, hurt the feelings of my relations, but also subject myself to persecution.[16]

In the midst of these conflicting thoughts and emotions, I attended a meeting in Virginia at a schoolhouse near Mr. Sarjent's residence. My soul was weighed down and full of trouble. The text from which Mr. Sarjent preached was Isaiah 11:15: "And the Lord shall utterly destroy the tongue of the Egyptian Sea and with his mighty wind shall he shake his hand over the river and shall smite it in the seven streams and make men go over dry shod."

I took my seat on a writing bench (the house being very much crowded), and wondered what the preacher would do with such an odd text. After treating the subject in accordance with history and geography, he went on to spiritualize it, making the river to represent the current of corruption in the human heart; the seven streams to represent the opposites to the seven attributes of God—love, wisdom, power, holiness, justice, goodness, and truth; expatiating with great clearness and cogency on these divine perfections in God; that their influence, received into the affections by faith, would smite their opposites, cast them out, and thus prepare the way for the soul to pass "from darkness to light and from the power of Satan to God."[17]

I had never heard a sermon that took such hold of my mind. The power of truth came home with such force it seemed as if my heart would break, and that if I resisted the Spirit any longer destruction would be my portion. At the height of this severe conflict, I sprang from my seat into the midst of the congregation and publicly confessed the saviour. This was accompanied with an instantaneous release from all my distress. The light of heaven broke in and irradiated my whole soul. Such was the change from deep mental anguish to inexpressible joy that I could scarcely refrain from shouting aloud. Every portion of God's works presented a new aspect. Even inanimate nature seemed vocal with praise. Then indeed was the gospel to me "the power of God unto salvation," and I rejoiced "with joy unspeakable and full of glory";[18] was baptized by pouring in the Ohio River and became a member of the Halcyon Church, as my brother John was already. This event united our hearts still closer, and we were not merely brothers in the flesh but also in the Lord.[19]

Our father's family, although they treated us with kindness, were exceedingly mortified when they heard of our uniting with a society so much despised and persecuted. This was to us a great trial, but we had inward peace. The society increased rapidly notwithstanding the opposition, and many stout hearts were brought to bow, and many who came to mock stayed to pray. The character of our preacher was assailed from various quarters, and we were identified with the reproach or pitied as dupes. We were often threatened with mobs, and on one occasion a company with clubs surrounded the house where we assembled for worship. They did not, however, break in, and some of them were much ashamed of it afterward, becoming warm friends.

Among the converts were two of my landlord's daughters. This enraged their parents so that the old man told me I could not be permitted to speak of the doctrine in his house, though he would always treat me well on condition of my keeping silent on the subject. I told him I could not promise that, and therefore should seek another home. Accordingly my companion (Mr. Weldon) and I built a shop on the opposite bank in Virginia, and boarded with Mr. Thomas Waddle, having but a small family who were very amiable and kind.[20] This was a pleasant, quiet home, and suited the state of my mind, which was for a time calm as the summer's eve. It was also more convenient to the place of worship and nearer the body of the church. This I esteemed a great privilege.

My peace flowed like a river for many weeks, and nothing occurred to mar the tranquility, until an impression came over my mind that the Lord would yet call me to preach the gospel. I tried every way (except giving up religion) to shake it off, but the more I strove against it the stronger would the impression become.[21] When the plea of ignorance would present itself, a text like this would come with force to my mind: "The world by wisdom knew not God"; or to any other plea of inability, such as the following: "My grace is sufficient for thee"; "I will give you a mouth and wisdom, which all your adversaries shall not be able to gainsay nor resist"; "Take no thought beforehand what ye shall say"; with many others of like kind.[22] I was naturally very bashful and dreaded the idea of attempting to speak in public. I often retired, after the day's labor was over, to the woods and prayed, "Lord what wilt thou have me to do?"; "If this impression is from thee, give me some evidence that shall remove all doubt and keep me from presumption." My peace of mind was much disturbed by this exercise, which lasted, as nearly as I can recollect, about a month.

One evening my old landlady, Mrs. Bing,[23] came over the river in company with one of the daughters (who had joined the church with her sister) on a visit to Mr. Waddle's, who had long been an acquaintance of theirs. After supper they were preparing to return, when the wind, which had been blowing some time, increased in violence; so that it became dangerous to cross in the canoe which had brought them over. The old lady had been violent in her opposition, and became very uneasy at the prospect of being compelled to stay all night, and fearing (as she afterward confessed) that the hated subject would be introduced. I saw her embarrassment and offered to take them over if they would venture, but they declined and stayed till morning.

About dusk my mind was agitated to an uncommon degree. I retired to the field and prayed earnestly that God would give me some satisfactory proof if it was his will that I should be called to labour publicly in his service. On returning to the house, the depression began to subside, and it seemed as though I could not hold my tongue—as if the stones would cry out unless I bore testimony to the impartial goodness of God in the presence of that woman.[24] This was a great cross to me, as she had always treated me like her own son until of late. I disliked to hurt her feelings, but duty to God must not be set aside for earthly friendship. I walked the room in great agitation for some time. At length I spoke with warmth on the divine character and the fullness of salvation by Christ, my recent experience, and the happiness enjoyed since I had embraced the Halcyon faith.

In the midst of my discourse the old lady threw herself back on the bed and screamed out in an agony, saying "I have resisted light and there is no mercy for me." At that moment it appeared to me that a cloud was let down upon my head. A heavenly glow beamed through my soul, and something like an electric shock darted through my nervous system, accompanied by a degree of faith such as I have never experienced, neither before nor since. In the full exercise of this faith, I stepped to the bed and, putting my hand on her, spoke very confidently and said that if she would give herself up without reserve to do the Lord's will, she would be immediately relieved. This I said without the shadow of a doubt. It was not, I think, one minute from the uttering of that sentence until she arose in an ecstasy and declared that her soul was in heaven, begging that we would all sing, which we did, I trust, "in the spirit and with the understanding also."[25] I was so struck with this remarkable occurrence, which seemed to be permitted as an answer to my prayers, that I could scarcely doubt thereafter of its being my duty to relinquish worldly pursuits and devote myself to the public service of God.

No one (except those who have had similar experience) can realize the trials I passed through in reference to this subject. Having been brought up in a new country with few facilities for instruction, obliged to labour hard from the time of our first settlement in the west, my education was very limited. All the time I had been to school since seven years of age would not amount probably to more than one year. And what schools we had were of very inferior quality. Scarcely anything was taught except reading, writing, and arithmetic, and these very imperfectly. On this account I felt great embarrassment. My natural inclination was for a domestic life, and nothing was more trying than to be called on to say anything in a public assembly.[26]

What added still more to the difficulty was the formidable opposition with which I should have to contend in advocating a sentiment so unpopular; and I could not conscientiously support the doctrine of endless misery. On this subject I might expect to meet with little countenance from the religious world. I had also a great aversion to controversy, yet knew it would be unavoidable. I liked the good opinion of mankind, and this I knew must be sacrificed.[27] Also, the affectionate remonstrances of my father's family must be met (for all except Brother John were opposed to our views and thought we were deluded).[28] In addition to all this, I had just commenced business for myself; had procured some tools and materials for carrying on my trade. [I] was in the bloom of youth, in which season all the fascinations of life present their most powerful attractions. [I] should be obliged to forego, in a great measure, all these, and undergo many hardships which must necessarily be incurred. All these considerations were weighed over and over, until I became satisfied that it was my duty to forsake all for the cause of Christ.

In the meantime old Mrs. Bing, whose extraordinary experience I have related, united with the Halcyon Church. Her husband, whose temper was naturally violent, became so enraged that he threatened the lives of his wife and two daughters, all of whom were now members of a church which he looked upon as a "synagogue of Satan."[29] They were sometimes driven from home and obliged to seek refuge with their neighbours. He forbid my brother and me from coming to his house, so that we seldom could obtain an interview with the persecuted sisters. On one occasion my brother happened to meet the two daughters in the road, and while conversing together they were discovered by the old gentleman, who came up full of wrath and beat my brother on the head with his cane. John said afterward that it did not hurt much, for he was filled at the time with the spirit of his Master, as his persecutor with that of his. The old man trembled while the young disciples remained composed. Such was the difference between the two spirits.

Those worthy females suffered thus for many months with a degree of patience which nothing but the religion of Christ could inspire. This furious storm gradually abated, and before the old gentleman died he invited us to hold meetings in his house. His wife survived him many years, became very old, continued firm in the faith even unto death. One of the daughters died many years before her mother, strong in hope of blessed immortality,[30] and the other is at this time (1845) still living so far as I know.[31]

In the winter of 1805, having settled up what little temporal business I had, Brother Sarjent and myself set out on a preaching tour up the Ohio. Each too poor to own a horse, we borrowed one apiece of brethren in the church. My own circumstances as to property were very narrow, for after paying my debts I had not enough to buy a comfortable suit of clothes for traveling in a winter so cold as that of 1805. And had I applied to my father for assistance (which I did not like to do, as he was so averse to my going), he could not have helped me much, for though he owned a good deal of wild land, all except the farm was rather a burden than a help, as there was no sale for it, and the taxes had to be paid and money very scarce.

My brother had already officiated some in public speaking and expected to supply in some measure the place of Brother Sarjent, who desired me to accompany him to lead in singing and exhort occasionally. My voice being good, it was no hardship to do the former, but the latter was at first a great trial.

[We] went by way of Athens, and by the time we arrived, a report had reached there that my companion had stolen the horse he rode. This lie we had to combat from that to Pittsburgh.[32] The Methodist preachers were very active in circulating this, with many other stories equally false. Their itinerancy gave them great facilities for circulating these slanders. Some of them probably thought they were "doing God service," as Paul did when he persecuted the ancient church; and I hope they will, like him, be forgiven.[33] Although some of their circuit riders erred in this, yet the Methodists were in general a much more devoted people than they are now. Then they bore a faithful testimony against all sin, slavery not excepted, but now many of them spare this "*Agag* of America," and seek to justify the practice of slaveholding by

Figure 2.2. This print of an engraving by Matthew DuBorg, based on a painting Jacques Gérard Milbert, depicts a *Camp Meeting of the Methodists in North America* (ca. 1819), characteristic of the evangelical revivalism common on the old western frontier. Though Daniel Parker and Abel Sarjent had conflicts with Methodist itinerants, Parker's conversion to Sarjent's Halcyon Church was in many ways a typical evangelical conversion experience. (Library of Congress)

the Bible.[34] Then they were, like all new sects, persecuted by the more popular churches, but now they are "rich and increased in goods and have need of nothing."[35]

In our progress up the river, through storms from without and trials within, the reproachful stories increased. One was that Mr. Sarjent had set a stump on fire in the night with a cigar,. and when the flame arose declared that he saw an angel ascend in it, and from the celestial messenger he had received his commission. This device, they said, had scared my brother and me into the church, and that we, being unsuspecting innocent young men, were objects of pity.[36] Another was that he had stolen fish off the trotline of his neighbour Doctor Bennet. It was true that he had taken fish from his neighbour's line, but it was also true that he had borrowed it the previous evening, and having had good success, he offered the doctor part of the fish next morning, and he refusing to take any, Mr. Sarjent left on the line a number of hooks of his own; but these circumstances were not reported, and thus the truth was turned into a lie.[37]

Notwithstanding all the impediments, our meetings were generally well attended, and many embraced the sentiments when understood, especially in Marietta, where a large society was shortly after established; also at Dilly's Bottom, opposite the flats of Grave Creek, where we met some valuable friends whose minds were prepared by previous experience to receive our views.

Before reaching this place, some distance below at Sunfish Creek, we encountered a very serious difficulty. The water had frozen while the creek was high, and having fallen, the cakes of ice were standing nearly upright along the shore for the distance of a mile up the stream. The hills were exceedingly steep, coming down so near the creek as to leave a very narrow footpath between them and the water. The ground was hard frozen. Up this narrow pass we had to lead our horses to the ford one mile up. On the way, the portmanteau of Mr. Sarjent, being very full and heavy, fell to the frozen surface of the creek. Being the younger and more active, I let myself down the standing ice cakes, holding with one hand to the upper edge, and with the other reaching and drawing it up.

Passing through Pittsburgh, we travelled on without much stopping to Washington County, Pennsylvania, and made a stand on the waters of Ten Mile Creek a few miles south of Washington. Here was soon after established a large branch of the Halcyon Church. A meeting house was built and the society flourished a number of years. Our labours in this place were blessed and attended with great reformations. Many respectable Christians from other denominations united with us, as also many notorious sinners were brought to an acknowledgement of Christ. Among the converts to our faith here was a very pious family of Baptists by the name of Parkhurst.[38] The youngest son, Amos, was baptized by immersion (according to his own faith on that subject) and became afterward a preacher of our order.[39] Of him I shall have occasion to say more hereafter.

I continued to travel as a companion to Mr. Sarjent about one year, during which time we revisited our friends at Dilly's Bottom, Marietta, Leading Creek, and in particular near the Kenhawa, where my brother had laboured and where the report of our success cheered the hearts of the members.

On our return again to Pennsylvania, the calls for Brother Sarjent's preaching were soon greatly increased. His meetings were large and interesting. He was in those days a powerful speaker, full of energy and love. His appeals to the young especially were very searching. His temperament was exceedingly sanguine and, when not under the restraining influence of the gospel, prompted him to great severity of language against his opponents. He had much to try his temper, being assailed from various quarters by the vilest slanders. It required sometimes more patience than he could exercise. When I would say to him that I thought softer words would do better, his reply would be the words of Paul to Titus, "Rebuke them sharply that they may be sound in the faith."[40] His natural disposition was ambitious, and he was unwilling to be second in what was in his estimation a good cause. No one was more willing to suffer for the right. Lukewarmness he could not endure. His attachments and antipathies were of the most ardent character. What he did was done with all his might. I doubt whether he would have flinched from the performance of what he thought to be his duty before a host of armed men. His energy of character has often reminded me of Luther and Bonaparte. He made no provision for retreat.

A delineation of the divine character was his main theme in preaching, and such lucid and forcible descriptions as his I never heard from any other man. He presented the character of God under seven distinct heads in the following order (viz.): first Love, second Wisdom, third Power, fourth Holiness, fifth Justice, sixth Goodness, seventh Truth. These seven attributes he denominated communicable attributes, as contradistinguished from self-existence, self-dependence, omniscience, and immutability. He said that those seven constituted the antitype of the *Urim* in the breastplate of judgment on Aaron's priestly vestment. He insisted that every explanation of the attributes which represented the claims of one as clashing with those of another was false; and that

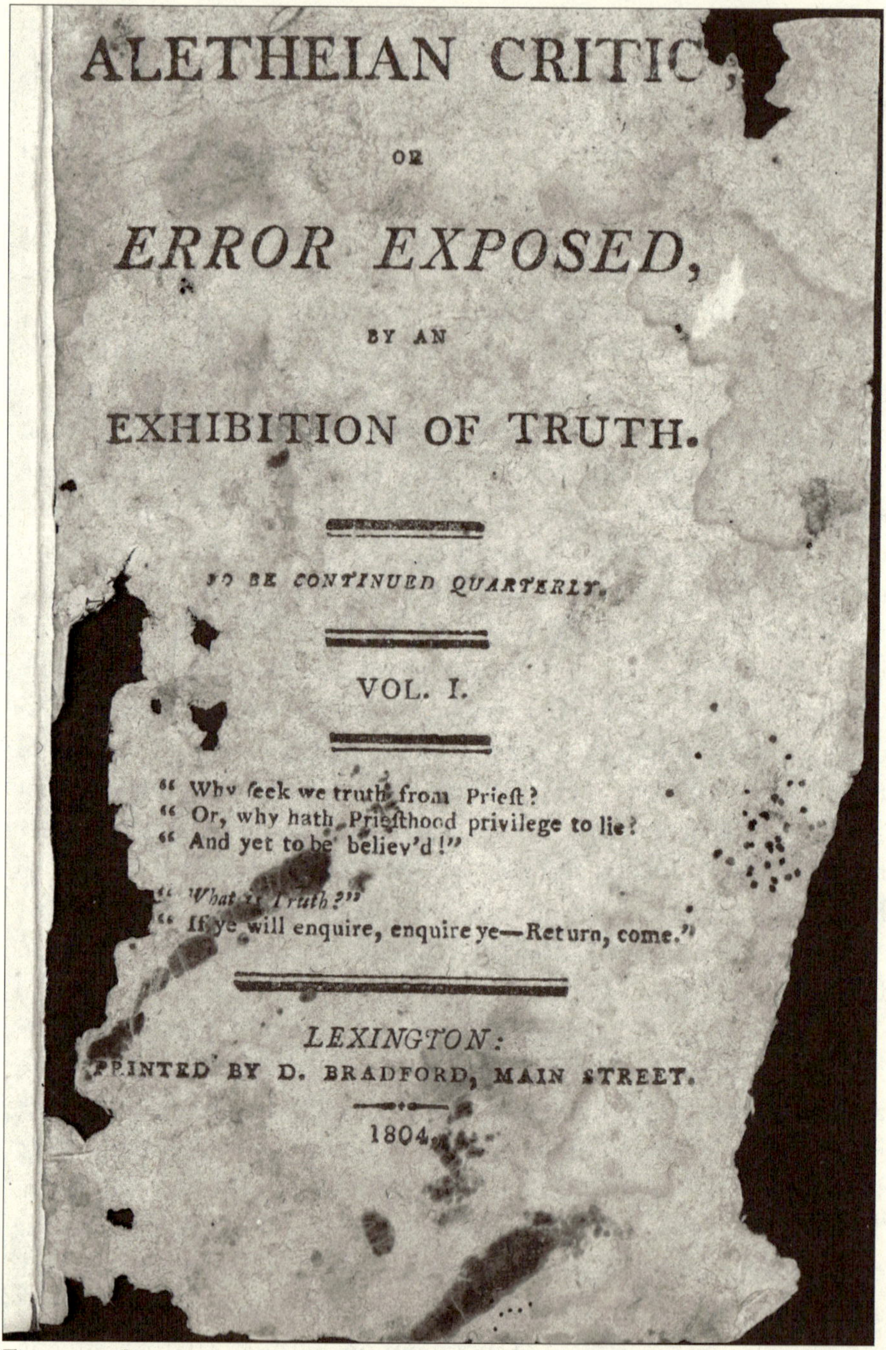

ALETHEIAN CRITIC;

OR

ERROR EXPOSED,

BY AN

EXHIBITION OF TRUTH.

TO BE CONTINUED QUARTERLY.

VOL. I.

" Why seek we truth from Priest?
" Or, why hath Priesthood privilege to lie?
" And yet to be believ'd!"

" *What is Truth?*"
" If ye will enquire, enquire ye—Return, come."

LEXINGTON:
PRINTED BY D. BRADFORD, MAIN STREET.

1804.

Figure 2.3. Cover page of the first (and only) issue of the *Aletheian Critic*, one of the journals of the Halcyon Church, edited by Abel Sarjent. (Special Collections, Legacy Library, Marietta College)

in our investigations of scripture, we should always keep in view this seven-fold criterion, calling it the only infallible *standard* of truth by which to understand the written word of God. That any doctrine which might involve the idea of limit or change in any or all of these perfections in the Creator must be false, and that in seeking after truth we must exercise the reason that God had given us; and in proportion as the soul was brought by a voluntary submission under the influence of the seven attributes it was redeemed.[41]

In expatiating on this glorious subject, he adverted often to the many portions of scripture where the number seven occurs—such as the "seven eyes on the stone laid before Joshua" (Zech 3:9); the plummet in the hand of Zerubbabel with "those *seven*" (Zech 4:10); the *seven* horns and eyes of the Lamb (Rev. 5:6); *seven* spirits of God (Rev. 4:5), etc.—which had reference to the seven attributes of God in Christ, through whom alone salvation flowed to man.[42]

He also called this spiritual *Urim* the key to knowledge: that this key had been concealed from the church, but that the time had come for it to be brought forward and that he was assured providence had called him into the work of publishing it.[43] He was a strong believer in the Millennium, and announced in the most confident manner its near approach, calling it the new dispensation, and predicting the downfall of all unjust government among men, the general diffusion of light and truth, [and] the triumphant and glorious reign of the saviour.[44]

Such a subject, treated by such a man, could not fail to draw attention and excite enquiries in every direction. The persecution began to subside. And although the larger portion of hearers were at first actuated by curiosity, great numbers became sincere enquirers after truth for its own sake.

In proportion to the increase of this spirit was Mr. Sarjent's anxiety to comply with every call, but at length it became impossible. And having sent an appointment to a small village called Salem,[45] a few miles from Brownsville, and meeting with some disappointment not now recollected, he told me that I must go and fill it. I was shocked and began immediately to make excuses, while he insisted that I must make a beginning some time, that I already had some experience in speaking by way of exhortation, and that if I went relying on God he would grant me all necessary aid (for he was a firm believer in the influence of the Spirit, as also was I). After a prayerful consideration, I finally consented and we parted, he to some other appointment and I to the one above mentioned.

The distance was so that I did not reach the place that day. When the next morning came, it seemed to me that I could not go. The idea of filling his appointment was much worse than if it had been made for me. I knew in reason there would be a great crowd and my spirits sunk. I would have given all I was worth to have been excused, but that could not be without running away from duty. In the greatest anxiety of mind and with my heart lifted in prayer that I might be led aright, I opened my pocket Bible, which was my daily companion, and the first passage that struck my eye was the following: Isaiah 54:17. "No weapon that is formed against thee shall prosper, and every tongue that shall rise against thee in judgment thou shalt condemn. This is the heritage of the servants of the Lord, and their righteousness is of me, saith the Lord." I was forcibly struck with these words, and they inspired me with new courage. Several other texts of a similar kind presented themselves to my mind.

On my arrival at the place of meeting, the house was crowded to excess. Even the entry and stairs were so full that I could hardly find room to stand. This was one of the most trying moments of my life. I was all in a tremble. My knees smote together. I began, however, with explaining the disappointment, and then took as a text Rev. 5:6, "And I beheld, and lo, in the midst of the throne and of the four beasts and in the midst of the elders, stood a lamb, as it had been slain, having seven horns and seven eyes, which are the seven spirits of God sent forth into all the earth." I had not spoken many minutes until my embarrassment was all gone, and I preached about two hours. The effect upon the audience astonished me. One young man by the name of Roundtree, after meeting, went through the village from house to house declaring the doctrine of the *Urim*, which had been my leading theme. The people thought he was crazy. He afterward traveled with me for a time in my preaching tours.[46]

After this, having been regularly ordained and receiving a certificate from the church, I established a circuit in which to travel—Brother

Sarjent having left me now to myself. The circuit was performed in five weeks, having five places of meeting, and staying in each neighbourhood one week. The first was on the north fork of Ten Mile, five or six miles east of Washington; the next at Salem, where I preached the first sermon; the next in Morgantown in Virginia on the Monongahela, the next at Waynsburgh, and the other at Williamsport at the mouth of Pigeon Creek, Monongahela. Here I became acquainted with Mr. Alexander McGrew, then a young man just out of his apprenticeship, who settled afterward in Cincinnati, lived there many years, and recently died near that city. This circuit I rode about one year, and had generally very large and attentive assemblies, and there were many evidences that my labours were not in vain.[47]

At Morgantown, my principle home was with a German by the name of Baltzel.[48] On one occasion, just before going to meeting, an old gentleman stepped in who was a noted Deist, by the name of Joseph Reed.[49] [He] lived about four miles off, at the foot of Laurel Hill, [and] had been a great torment to the Christians in that community. [He] was a man of talents and information, [but] had become very intemperate. He asked me if it would be any offense to put a few questions. I said no, I was always willing to answer any question that I could, and if not would say so. He asked me if I believed that day and night were occasioned by the alternate presence and absence of the sun. I said yes. "Well then," said he, "what made the three days before the sun was created, for we are told in Genesis that the sun was created on the fourth day?"

At first I was a good deal puzzled what to say. At length I replied that many parts of the Bible were written according to appearances, such as that God repented of making man; repented again on the repenting of the Ninevites; that the sun and the moon stood still at the command of Joshua; and that our account of the creation had been written in the same way—that during the first three days the earth was probably enveloped with a thick mist sufficiently dense to prevent the sun from being seen, and yet not so thick as to prevent discerning the difference between day and night. That on the fourth day the mist was dispelled so that the sun made its appearance. The history was therefore written according to appearance and not exactly in accordance with the astronomical fact, which was that the sun was, then as now, the centre of the solar system.

This idea was suggested to my mind for the first time on that occasion.[50] Whether this was proper one or not, it had a wondrous effect on the man's mind. He was a few moments silent, and then said it was the best answer he had ever heard, and refrained from any more questions. He then attended meeting, which was large and held in the courthouse. He paid the most strict attention, but said nothing to me after meeting. He went home, returned to Morgantown before night, and then went six miles on my circuit to attend an evening meeting. I discovered an expression of great anxiety in his countenance and felt for him the most intense solicitude. I prayed to the Lord that I might be directed to some suitable passage of scripture that might meet his case, and opening the Bible, my attention was arrested by the first verse of the fourteenth chapter of John: "Let not your heart be troubled. Ye believe in God, believe also in me."

It seemed as though some guardian angel handed it to me. My mind was filled with light and my mouth with arguments. After treating the subject scripturally, showing the impossibility of even knowing God truly unless his full character had been made manifest in Christ—that we could not have access to the Father except through the Son—and quoting such portions of the sacred oracles as teach the doctrine of mediation, without which we could not apprehend abstract deity, I then endeavoured to shew the utter incapacity of man to believe in the existence of abstract life any farther than it was manifested through some medium: asked how we knew there was animal life except by seeing animals move, or vegetable life but by seeing that vegetables grow, or of rational life but by its effects through the reasoning powers, and so on.[51] At the close of my discourse, the man came up to me and said, "You took that text on purpose for me and you beat me as flat as a frying pan. And now, I call this assembly to witness that I have been wandering for five years on the dark mountains of error. I have denied my Lord and master, but now I acknowledge him," while a flood of tears streamed from his eyes. This remarkable instance I could not help construing as another evidence of my call to ministry.

The man insisted that when I came round again I should come and preach at his house, which I did, and there came in contact with one of his neighbours who was worse still than a Deist. He was a pantheist, believing that everything in the universe was a part of God: that he and I were parts of God.[52] I asked him how he reconciled that with the doctrine of unity (for he was a great stickler for the unity of God), observing that God must according to his theory be opposed to himself, inasmuch as he and I, being parts of God, were nevertheless opposing each other in argument. This put him to thinking and he let me alone. Mr. Reed continued faithful while I stayed in that part of the country, but what became of him afterward I know not.

I received no certain compensation for preaching, but depended on what the friends chose to give, and that was scarcely sufficient to keep me in very plain clothes, depending on the church members for the use of a horse. Toward the latter portion of my time in that section, a few generous friends joined together and bought me a very pretty little horse for which, if I recollect rightly, they paid sixty dollars.[53] He was a fine traveler, and I thought the ease I then enjoyed was too pleasant to last long, for I had become so used to suffering hardship that when matters went smoothly I became suspicious.

Being deeply impressed with the belief that the latter days were fast approaching, and that the followers of the Lamb would have to go through great tribulation in order to be prepared for entering the kingdom (especially as first fruits), that a greater cross must be borne, that all ungodliness and worldly lusts must be forsaken, and that to gain the victory over the influences of the world, it would be necessary to fast as well as pray. In accordance with these impressions, some ten or a dozen of us belonging to the Halcyon Church entered gradually into a course of abstinence from every luxury, denying ourselves of everything that would merely gratify taste, repudiating the use of animal food, and living very sparingly on the lightest diet.[54]

This was considered a great extreme by most of the members, among whom was Brother Sarjent, who opposed our course with all his influence and, as we thought sometimes, with a wrong spirit. The result was that a division of the church ensued, some believing we were right and others that we were deluded.[55]

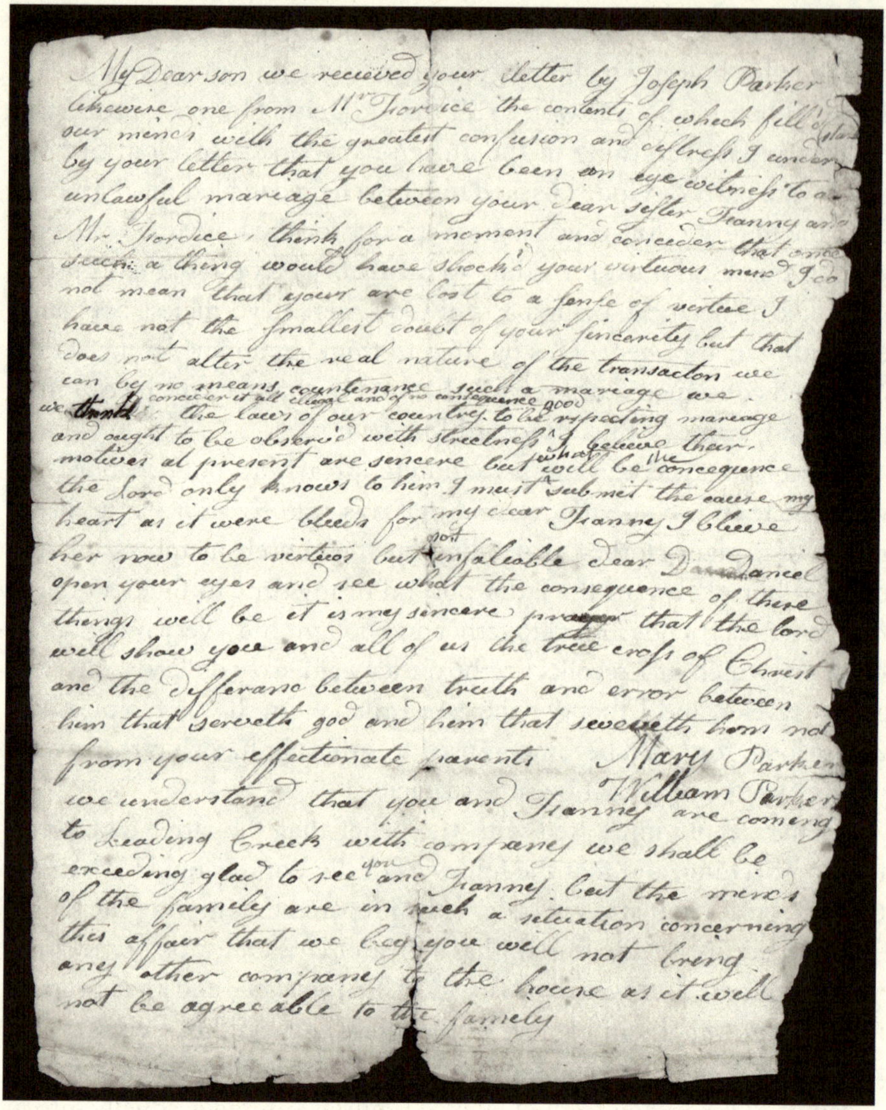

My Dear son we received your letter by Joseph Parker
likewise one from Mr Fordice the contents of which fill'd
our minds with the greatest confusion and distress I understand
by your letter that you have been an eye witness to an
unlawful mariage between your dear sister Fanny and
Mr Fordice, think for a moment and consider that once
such a thing would have shock'd your virtuous mind I do
not mean that your are lost to a sense of virtue I
have not the smallest doubt of your sincerity but that
does not alter the real nature of the transaction we
can by no means countenance such a mariage we
consider it all illegal and of no consequence
we think the laws of our country to be good respecting mariage
and aught to be observ'd with strictness I believe their
motives at present are sincere but what will be the consequence
the Lord only knows to him I must submit the cause my
heart as it were bleeds for my dear Fanny I believe
her now to be virtuous but not infalible dear Daniel
open your eyes and see what the consequence of these
things will be it is my sincere prayer that the lord
will show you and all of us the true cross of Christ
and the differance between truth and error between
him that serveth god and him that serveth him not
from your effectionate parents Mary Parker
William Parker
we understand that you and Fanny are coming
to Leading Creek with company we shall be
exceeding glad to see you and Fanny but the minds
of the family are in such a situation concerning
this affair that we beg you will not bring
any other company to the house as it will
not be agreeable to the family

Figure 2.4. Daniel Parker, not without reason, worried that his newfound faith would strain his relationship with his parents. Mary Parker, who handled her family's correspondence, probably wrote and signed both her and her husband William's name to this letter to their son. She disapproves of the recent marriage of her daughter to a Halcyon Church member, and implicitly of the Halcyon Church as a whole: "you have been an eye witness to an unlawful marriage between your dear sister Fanny and Mr. Fordice. Think for a moment and consider that once such a thing would have shocked your virtuous mind." She prays that the Lord will show Daniel "the difference between truth and error." (Special Collections, Legacy Library, Marietta College)

I of course gave up my circuit, and consequently thought it would be wrong for me to retain the horse the friends had given for the express purpose of my riding that circuit. Accordingly, I took him back and told those friends all the truth, just as it was. They were very sorry and insisted that I should keep him; but I refused and left him, returning on foot to the little company of what might be with propriety termed "pilgrims." We had relinquished the world as far as we could to stay in it. We believed the first resurrection was near and that some even of our little band might never die.[56]

We did not look upon either fasting or prayer as meritorious, or as constituting any claim on God for his grace, but that they only tended to render us more susceptible of the spirit by mortifying the body and thereby diminishing the animal propensities. We dwelt much on those parts of sacred history giving accounts of the ancient saints, their self-denial and humble devotion, and more especially the long fast and sore temptations of the saviour, his injunctions to his disciples to forsake all for his service, even father, mother, wife, children, houses, lands, and whatever might hinder our progress in the divine life. Such were our impressions, and such our practice. The neighbors look on and wonder.[57]

One of this cross-bearing company was Brother Amos Parkhurst,[58] than whom I believe there never was a more humble, self-denying, devoted youth. He was not far from his twentieth year of age, most affectionate in disposition, of simple manners, extremely conscientious, even in the most trifling matter.[59] His whole soul was engaged in seeking salvation and striving for a greater conformity to the saviour. He appeared to be deeply impressed with the belief that some uncommon experience was just before him.

One day as he stood by the fire in his father's house, absorbed in deep meditation, he exclaimed, "I have to go to the bottom of the sepulcher. But brethren," said he, "hold on to the standard." There were several of us present and at a loss how to understand him, for we all thought that if anyone should be permitted to live until the great change, spoken of by Paul in the fifteenth [chapter] of First Corinthians,[60] it would surely be Amos. Not long after this declaration, without any apparent cause, he sunk into a state resembling what is now called "magnetic sleep."[61] He lay on the bed on his back, his eyes shut, his pulse and breath suspended. Not the least sign of life could be detected. I put my hand over his heart to ascertain if it beat, felt of his wrists, the jugular veins, and every part where pulsation might be discerned, but not the smallest motion was there. We then applied light feathers to his mouth and nostrils to detect any impulse of respiration. Then we applied a looking glass to see if any moisture would be left on its surface, but all to no purpose. He was to all appearances a corpse. In this condition he lay, I think, about nine hours; when all of a sudden he rose up without help, turned his feet round off the bed and stood on the floor close by my side. His eyes were little balls of fire and the first words he uttered were, "The Lord God omnipotent reigneth."[62] I sunk to the floor and he assisted me to rise. He then delivered the most searching and wonderful discourse I ever heard from mortal tongue. He said that while in that trance or vision the spiritual world was opened to his view, that he saw the resurrection and the glory of Christ's kingdom, but that he could not find words to express the whole scene. This extraordinary occurrence took place sometime between January and April, 1807 (if I remember rightly, as I write entirely from memory, not having any written document to guide me).

After this strange event, he with several others traveled on foot to Marietta and back,[63] preaching in various places on the way. Having returned again to his father's house, I was there one day when he retired into the field, as we supposed, for devotion (as that was a practice with us all at that time). At length he was seen by us coming over the cornfield, descending toward the house. His step was quick and he appeared to possess great bodily strength, although reduced in flesh, by severe fasting, to a mere skeleton.[64] I was standing by his aged mother when he approached and took her by the hand, speaking some encouraging words, not now remembered, the purport of which was that she must have faith—that he was in possession of strength from on high by the Spirit. The old lady, though astonished at what had already transpired, was quite skeptical as to its being anything more than fanaticism, but she declared afterward that the moment Amos touched her hand she was entirely relieved of a pain in her arm, which had afflicted her many years: that she felt a healing influence dart through her system.

To convince us that he was strong, notwithstanding his emaciated appearance, I saw him lift, carry, and put on the fire, a log of wood that would have required the strength of a common man to carry.[65] These were strange things, and if they can be accounted for upon philosophical principles, I confess my inability to do it. That they did so happen can be proved by many witnesses now living.

Brother Amos passed through several other similar scenes of suspended animation and recovered as he had before. At length on the fourth day of April, 1807, he was found to be actually dead. How long he had been really dead we could not tell, for he went into the spell about three days before, and as he had come to so often we thought it would be wrong to bury him until we had the most irrefutable proof of his death.

No sooner was it known in the surrounding neighbourhood than the most extravagant lies were set on foot. Some said we had killed him; others that we had been trying for three days to raise him from the dead.[66] And on the day of the funeral, the rabble made a jumping stick of his measure,[67] heaping upon us the most scurrilous and abusive epithets. All this, with the mortifying disappointment of our hopes, we had to bear when we were so weak through fasting as rendered us almost unable to walk.

The witnesses of these solemn scenes were of both sexes, of a class too not easily imposed upon by false pretenses, and, excepting myself, were possessed of superior minds—by no means ignorant either of the scriptures or Christian experience. I am entirely unable to account for what has been here related, but know that the facts stated are true.

We remained a short time in the neighborhood of old Mr. Parkhurst, still pursuing an abstemious course of diet, though not such rigorous fasting. My brother John, being one of the company, had gone to such an extreme in abstaining from food that with great difficulty he recovered his former health. It was also a long time before my own was reinstated.

Those who knew the facts in reference to Amos Parkhurst[68] were struck with astonishment and cast no blame on us, but such were the scandalous reports abroad that we were threatened with mobs. Nor was it safe for us to pass by certain places. At one time, a small company of us having to pass through a village where threats had been made, we stayed in the woods nearly all night in cold weather, so that we could go through just before day while the inhabitants were asleep. Those that knew no better called us murderers and charged us with the most licentious conduct, while the truth was we were sacrificing every worldly interest in what we conceived to be the service of God. Nor was there one in the whole company of those who went through the fast but were members of the most respectable families.

After the band was dissolved and the individuals retired to their respective homes, we made occasional visits to each other, for we had suffered so much together that the ties of friendship between us were almost indissoluble. Although our hopes had been blasted in respect of Brother Amos, we yet indulged the belief that the Millennium was near. Our faith in outward organizations, however, was so much weakened that we never reunited formally with the Halcyon Church. It was kept up for several years by Brother Sarjent and some other preachers who came in subsequently. At one time there was quite a number of flourishing societies. There was one in Fleming County, Kentucky, of about 100 members, under the pastoral care for a short time of my brother. Several other branches had 100 and some more.

CHAPTER 3

"It Might Be a Benefit to Travel"

MY TEMPORAL wants required that I should attend to some business for support. I was very destitute of means, but when my strength became sufficient, I commenced once more to work at my trade, pursued the business some time in Marietta, occasionally speaking in public. My brother continued to travel and preach. Having married, his companion accompanied him in the ministry from place to place.[1] My oldest brother bought a farm and settled in Rutland on Leading Creek.[2] He also set up the cabinet business, and with him I worked about one year, being once more located near my father, who by this time was comfortably provided for,[3] his youngest son being able to superintend the farm. While residing with Brother William I studied geography, keeping the book on my work bench, reading and working alternately.

In the mean time, Brother John suggested to me the idea of a deliverance from the second death, which we had held to consist of a final destruction of the soul, as we found no proof in scripture for immortality to man out of Christ, and not seeing how a soul could even exist in the eternal state without immortality. And discovering that it was never predicated of man, in the Bible, as a constituent principle but as one derived, we were driven to the conclusion that the wicked, for want of immortality, must cease to exist as conscious beings.[4]

Although the doctrine of destruction appeared more consistent with the goodness of God than that of endless suffering, inasmuch as putting out of pain incorrigible sinners would be more benevolent

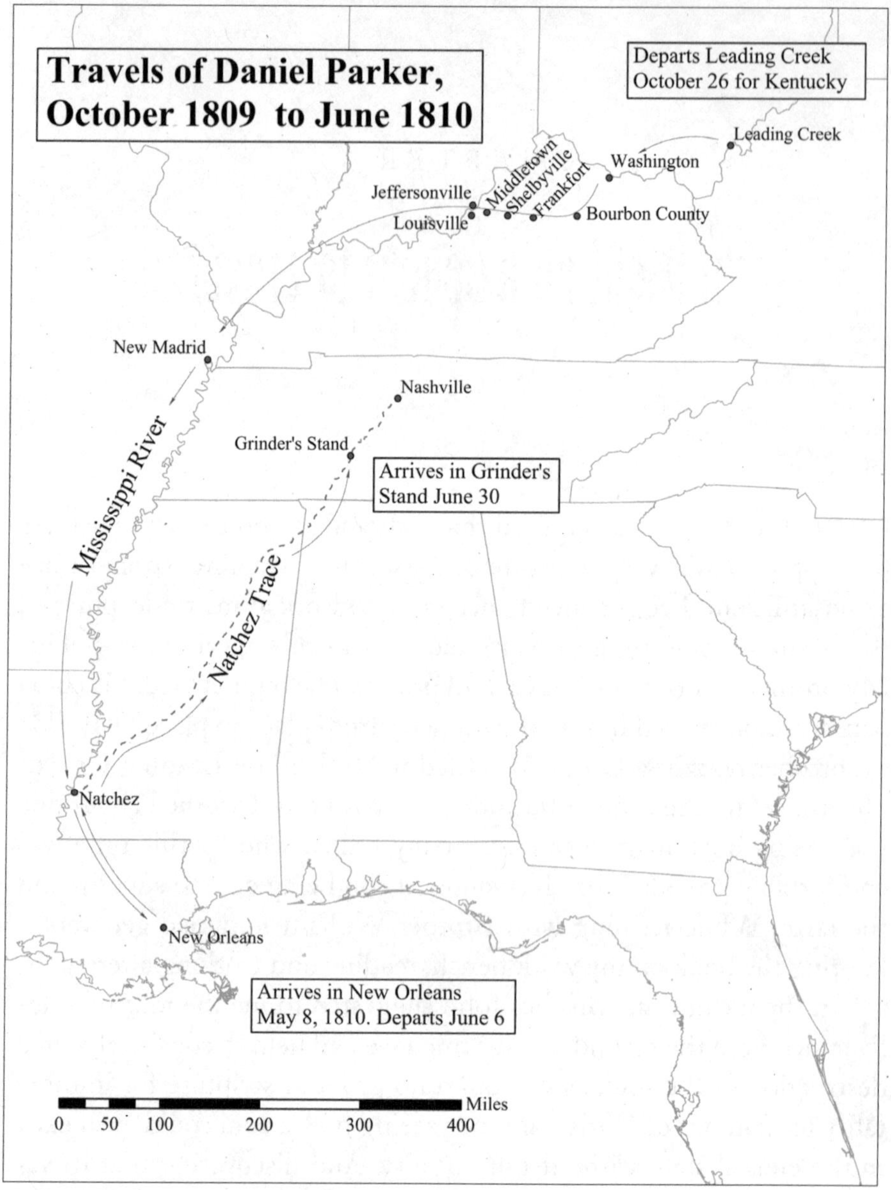

Map 3.1. Map by Matthew Young

than keeping them in it (if reclamation were impossible), yet I had for some time felt a difficulty in reconciling the idea of their being raised from the first death merely for the purpose of consigning them to the second, for our views of God's character forbid the supposition that the almighty would ever be influenced by mere revenge, which the destruction doctrine seemed to involve.

Yet when he first suggested the thought of a final restoration of all mankind, I was astonished and thought surely such a sentiment must be too good to be true, although [I was] not so much shocked as when the doctrine of endless misery was called in question. My mind began to enter a new field of investigation, which I was determined to pursue with prayerful attention. Fearful of adopting so pleasing a sentiment more because it was agreeable than because it was true, and knowing also that we easily believe what we wish may be true, I was exceedingly cautious.[5] Having never seen an author on the subject nor heard a sermon in its defense, my desire was to know whether the scriptures afforded any proof in its favour, resolving like the Bereans to search them thoroughly until satisfied.[6] During this research I did not feel at liberty to preach at all. From what my brother had said, I began to waver, and was once more "tied where two ways met." In this state of mind I called to remembrance the words of our departed brother Amos: "Hold on to the standard" (that has already been explained). I did so, and with that infallible rule constantly in view, became satisfied that no other doctrine could be found to reconcile the record so well as that of the Restoration. At what period my mind became completely settled on this point I cannot now remember, but think it was about a year after the thought was first suggested.[7]

Then came another trial, and that was the expediency of advocating publicly a sentiment so liable to perversion. The caution of the saviour not to "cast pearls before swine" held me back.[8] The conviction of its truth became more and more clear as I compared it with Christian experience, judging from what my own had been: that when the love of God was shed abroad in my heart, it prompted me to desire the salvation of all others. I could not limit that desire to any specific number, and this seemed warranted by the "standard" already alluded to. This difficulty continued much longer than any other, so that several years passed away during which I could not see my way clear to officiate in public—although I had no wish nor intention of giving up religion, resolving still to cultivate it in private, but never to attempt preaching again. This resolution fell in so exactly with my natural feelings that for a time I indulged the thought with a degree of complacency.

In the fall of 1809, a proposition was made to me by Mr. Alvan Bingham of Athens, Ohio,[9] to go with him into Kentucky in company with two other men from New York, who had two patent rights for the whole western country, one for a hemp-breaking and the other for a washing machine.[10] They wanted to hire me as a workman.

My mind had passed through so many straits that I feared the consequences to my nervous system, and thought it might be a benefit to travel, see more of the world, and divert my attention from such incessant mental labour. The wages, I concluded, would keep me in clothes and my employers would bear my travelling expenses. I therefore accepted the proposal, and on the 26th of October, 1809, left Leading Creek and all my relations. In company with Mr. Bingham (the other two having gone forward), [I] went into Kentucky, found Messrs. Jackson and Crocker, the New York men, near Washington, Mason County, at the house of General Henry Lee;[11] where I worked about three weeks on a hemp-breaking machine, and then went to Washington.

Here for the first time on the 20th of November I saw a poor slave mother and an infant child sold at public auction.[12] The following is an extract from my daily journal,[13] which I commenced keeping on leaving home for this tour:

> My attention was called by an officer crying an article for sale. On looking round I discovered it to be a negro woman and child. She sat on a bench at the tavern door, surrounded by a group of men, who were as merry while they bid their several prices as though it had been a cow and calf to be sold. They bid on until she was struck off at 249 dollars. This scene gave rise to a train of deep reflections on the depravity of human nature, and the cruelty of trading in rational beings, who by nature are equal to those that hold them in bondage, for the purpose of supporting themselves in pomp and luxury.

Figure 3.1. No drawing is available of the washing machine Daniel Parker made and sold, invented by Eli Hill and patented in 1809. It may have been similar to this home washing machine and wringer from an 1869 advertisement. (Library of Congress)

HITHERTO I had seen little of slavery, there being but few in those parts of Virginia where I had been. It was quite odd to be waited on in small matters, which I had ever been used to doing myself.

The people about Washington were remarkably hospitable and open-hearted, but I was shocked at the profanity among the young men. The most of them seemed to think it no disparagement, and would scarcely speak ten words without an oath. Having to board at a tavern, I was often annoyed a great part of the night with the vulgar noise of gamblers. I had never before seen so much roughness blended with so much kindness. To me it was a strange mixture. Even genteel females would permit the utterance of oaths in their presence without showing the least sign of disapprobation.[14]

We remained in Washington until the sixth of December, having constructed and put in operation a washing machine; but meeting with little success, we proceeded to Bourbon County and there erected

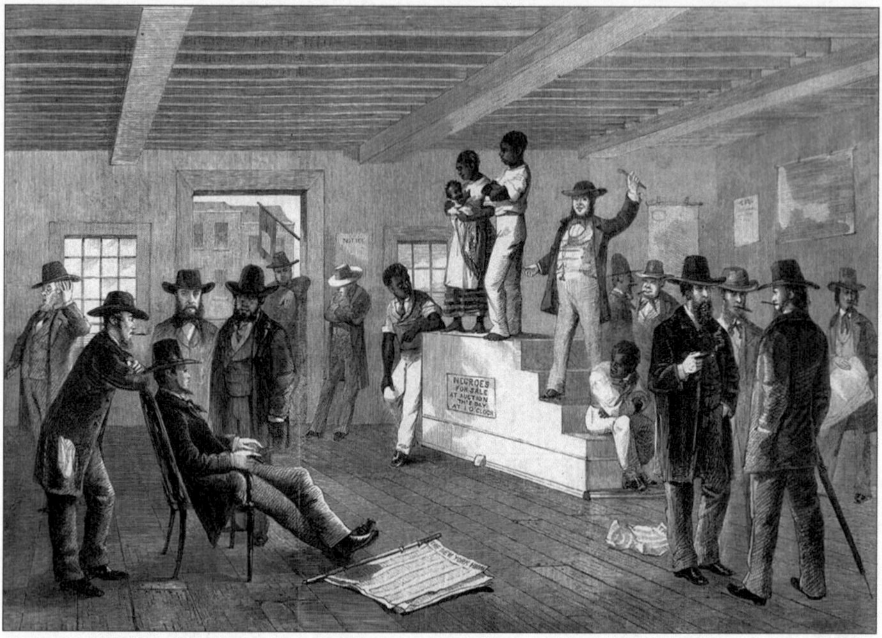

Figure 3.2. *A Slave Auction in Virginia*. (*Illustrated London News*, 1861)

another hemp mill, but it did not answer a good purpose; and the New York men, becoming discouraged, left Mr. Bingham and myself on the fifth of January, 1810. Before returning home, however, they prevailed on us to buy the right of the washing machine for Kentucky, Tennessee, Virginia west of the mountains, and all the territories. I was very reluctant to enter into the business, having no means to pay and disliking both debt and speculation. We were satisfied that the improvement was valuable and if properly made could not fail to answer a good purpose. They offered to credit us and to take the whole in trade, with indulgence as to time. Mr. Bingham was very sanguine and urged me strongly to join him. He was the more so because I was a workman and he could not make an ax-handle as it should be, but was well qualified for trading.

I finally yielded and gave my notes payable at different dates for 700 dollars' worth of such property as we could send to New York, such as horses, watches, etc. I had not at that time ten dollars to spare. I had no sooner entered into the contract than I repented, but it was too late. There was no way of getting out of it, and the only possible chance was to persevere. I therefore set about improving the construction without infringing on the principle embraced in the patent, which had been originally granted to Eli F. Hill.[15] I succeeded in doing so, and the machine being highly approved, we began to feel encouraged.

We made and sold a few in Kentucky, but Mr. Bingham, who was sometimes more sanguine than prudent, thought we could make a fortune by going to New Orleans. Accordingly we passed on west through Frankfort, Shelbyville, Middletown, to Louisville, crossed the Ohio; put up with one Esqr. Lemon in Jeffersonville, who purchased the right for the Mississippi Territory. We also sold the right for Jefferson County, Kentucky. Our horses were exchanged for produce such as would sell on the coast, and having employed a very worthy young man by the name of Denny, a cabinet maker by trade, to assist me in making machines, we procured a flatboat, put in what produce we had, set up a workshop in one end, and on the 23rd of February, 1810, set sail in company with Esqr. Lemon and his brother, who had a boatload of horses.[16]

Figure 3.3. "Sketch of a flat bottom boat, such as are used to descend the Ohio and the Mississippi," Georges-Henri-Victor Collot, from *A Journey in North America* (Paris: Arthus Bertrand, 1826), plate 7. (Edward E. Ayer Collection, Newberry Library)

Mr. Bingham, who was an equal partner with me in the enterprise, did the trading and I the work. In the neighborhood of New Madrid, he traded patent rights for a farm, including a tract of land consisting of 200 acres, situated on the river bank near the little prairie. We then began to think that my friend's anticipations of a fortune were not altogether groundless, but as he got only a little land, it afterward proved to be good for nothing. The Earthquake also sunk a part of it the next year. It was about twenty-five miles below New Madrid.[17] This bargain was concluded on the 19th of March, according to my old diary.

We had provided an ample supply of material for our machines, and what time could be spared from the oars was industriously devoted to the workbench by Mr. Denny and myself, so that we two had but little leisure. We enjoyed, however, some very pleasant seasons by moonlight in good weather. I carried my flute, and Mr. Denny being a pious young man, we often sang hymns together, especially on the Sabbath.

In those days there were unbroken forests for hundreds of miles together. The tall cypress shot up their straight trunks far into the air, surrounded at the bottom with what were called "knees," being excrescences from the roots, varying in height from one to three feet. The Spanish moss hung pendant from their tops, in some places nearly to the ground, forming a kind of mournful drapery. Thousands of acres were thickly covered with rushes, appearing at a distance like a luxuriant wheat field. Unbroken cane breaks, extending many miles, so thick that one could scarcely walk through, elevated their tapering stems from twenty to thirty feet.[18]

Indians of various nations came often in their canoes to trade, especially the Arkansas, Chickasaws, and Choctaws. On one occasion, a Cherokee came into our boat, and perceiving one of another tribe come up the beach, he drew his long knife and began to sharpen it on the whetstone, keeping a sharp and savage eye on the other, whom we supposed he thought to be an enemy. We dreaded the consequences, but when he came up they both shook hands quite friendly.[19] Some had money to pay for what they wanted, while others were importunate beggars.[20] They were delighted with the music of my flute.

After a tedious passage, occasioned by frequently stopping to trade and narrowly escaping boat-wreck, we arrived at Natchez the 15th of April. The forests and fields presented a most lovely aspect. The live

Figure 3.4. Daniel Parker interacted with members of the Choctaw and other Native American groups on his southern journey. George Caitlin painted many Native American portraits in the mid-nineteenth century. *Two Choctaw Indians* is from a set of paintings from the 1850s and 1860s. (National Gallery of Art)

Figure 3.5. For Daniel Parker, "the environs of Natchez on the bluff were beautiful," but the landing under the hill was "a sink of debauchery." There he witnessed a slave being murdered. This picture, based on the artist Henry Lewis's travels in the late 1840s, includes steamboats, which Parker would not have seen in 1810. (Lewis, *Das Illustrirte Mississippithal* [Dusseldorf, Germany: Arnz, 1857], plate 72 [Library of Congress])

oak, bay tree, China tree, and magnolia decorated the former; and the latter was covered with clover six inches high. The environs of Natchez on the bluff were beautiful, but such a sink of debauchery as existed under the hill at the landing could scarcely be found anywhere else. While we stayed there a boatload of slaves was landed and I saw a savage looking white man strike one of them on the head with a club and knock him off the side of the boat. About three days after, a black man was seen floating about in a small basin near the boat with his skull broken and much swelled. He was drawn out and Mr. Denny and I went into town to find a coroner, but the people laughed at us, so we returned and buried him in the sand.[21]

Here we sold two machines for twenty-five dollars apiece, the price up the river being twenty. But this did not satisfy us, for the people told us that in Orleans we could get thirty. The remainder on hand, about twenty, we took thither and after making great exertions we could not sell one. We had been coasting along so slowly that we did not arrive at Orleans until the eighteenth of May. [We] staid until the sixth of June. The sickly season was coming on.[22] Fearing to stay any longer, and having disposed of our other loading, we were obliged to leave all our machines, the cooking utensils, and the boat in care of a man with whom Mr. Bingham had been somewhat acquainted, who promised to do with them the best he could and remit to us the proceeds, but that was the last we heard of him or the property.

We then regretted not having stayed longer at Natchez, but now we were at the end of the market. This was a sad disappointment, and to make it still worse, I was taken sick, from which, however, by taking medicine I partially recovered in a few days. There being at that time no steam boats on the western waters, barges were the only mode of transportation up by water. And it requiring about three months to come up in that manner, with very hard work beside, we had no alternative but to come by land through the wilderness. I was about 1500 miles from home, among strangers, with small means, no one feeling any sympathy (except my good friend Mr. Bingham, who was always very attentive and kind). My past experience on the subject of religion: all these considerations crowded upon me with such force that for a time, I almost wished myself dead.[23] This gloom subsiding in a measure as my bodily strength returned, I determined to put on resolution and make the best of it.

On the sixth day of June we left the city, crossed Lake Pontchartrain in a small schooner, and traveled on foot to Natchez. There I took sick again, and being unable to walk more than a few miles, I bought a small Chickasaw horse, which proved to be a very easy traveler.[24] This was at Washington, six miles back from Natchez. There I got bled and fainted away;[25] was obliged to be helped on my horse, and in this condition I traveled two weeks, passing through the Choctaw and Chickasaw nations on dry provision, at a speed of from thirty to thirty-five miles per day without resting one day, often sleeping in the woods, and having to be assisted both on and off my horse the whole way.[26]

My readers may wonder why I did not stop and rest occasionally. It was because the company, which consisted of some five or six, were not willing to be detained. On that route in those days, travelers had to go in armed bands for fear of robbers, as all who came through from Orleans were suspected of having money. I thought therefore that I had rather die in the company of friends than be left to die among savages, for I had faint hopes of ever getting into the states, much less to my father's house.[27] But it pleased God, who had brought me through so many trials, to spare my life.

I remember well my feeling on seeing the first white woman after passing through the Chickasaw nation. This was a Mrs. Grinder. The house was located exactly on the [southern] line of Tennessee. It was here that Mr. Lewis, who first crossed the Rocky Mountains with Captain Clark, shot himself.[28] Mrs. Grinder was very kind and gave me the best nourishment she could command. This was the last day of June.[29]

I WILL here transcribe a portion of my journal, which was written after I recovered sufficiently to do it:

> July 1st
>
> Rode about twenty miles to Columbia, a new town on the Duck River, a branch of [the] Tennessee, seat of justice for Murry County.[30] Here we stopped and fed at a tavern. I lay down on a palate, being very sick. Took a short rest and rode fourteen miles toward Nashville. At

night put up at Mr. Giddins's.[31] I was so far gone with sickness and fatigue that I could scarcely get into the house, which was no sooner entered than, lying on the bed, I fell into a kind of convulsion in which I expected to expire. But being somewhat delirious, I imagined my case more dangerous than it really was. Mr. Bingham, who had treated me as a brother through the wilderness (being very unwell himself), now paid the greatest attention, holding me up in the bed that I might enjoy the fresh air. Toward ten o'clock I fell asleep, and a violent sweat ensuing, I felt considerably revived in the morning, yet very weak. At this house we continued four days, during which time I had many severe turns. The landlady was very kind, but being ignorant of my situation, supposed it to be hypochondria, and observed that if I would "eat hearty and stir about lively," I should do well enough; while in truth I was hardly able to stand or eat.

JULY 6th:[32] Traveled four and one half miles farther and stopped at the house [of] a Baptist preacher by the name of Lester. He held slaves but treated them pretty well. Here we stayed nearly a month, by which time I was so far recovered as to work moderately. We had by this time spent nearly all the money we had, having paid Mr. Denny, who had left us some time before. We lost also at this place by some means a gold doubloon worth sixteen dollars.[33] Our clothing too was nearly worn out. We each had a horse, but these only increased our expenses. A heavy debt, incurred by purchasing the patent, hung over us, while as yet we had made nothing clear. Could we have reached home, we did not like to go in such a condition. Having no earthly reliance but the business of washing machines and patent rights, we hired a workman to assist me, and in the town of Franklin, by the tenth of August, we had a machine completed, which was sold to a gentleman living some distance in the country and was highly approved. Thus we commenced once more our business, which had been some time suspended.

Shortly after this, Mr. Bingham disposed of several county rights for some store goods, two good horses, and a quantity of manufactured tobacco. We also exchanged the horses we rode through the wilderness for the same article, and having procured about 400 dollars' worth, well put up in kegs delivered at Nashville, sent it by a respectable young man to Orleans. The young man was taken sick and died there. The tobacco was sold with other property, and after his expenses were paid there were remaining due to us ninety-five dollars, which we never got. We had, however, good clothes and each of us a good riding horse. My health improved gradually, but I did not recover my full strength under a year from the time I was taken sick.

The following winter was spent in Tennessee, principally in the counties of Williamson, Davidson, and Sumner. Near Gallatin, seat of justice of the latter, Mr. Bingham got married.[34] This event changed the complexion of affairs and not many months afterward rendered necessary a different arrangement in our business. In the mean time, my partner made other sales by which we acquired considerable property, but not much money except what was procured by selling machines, the making of which devolved entirely upon me. It suited him to take the property which fell to my share, for which he finally gave me obligations to the amount of several hundred dollars. Having exchanged a life of celibacy for that of matrimony, his attention was, of course, more concentrated at home, and consequently drawn off in some measure from our common interest. Finding that the burden rested principally upon me, I proposed a dissolution of partnership, offering to take myself the right of Kentucky and give him all the balance. This arrangement was finally made. Soon after he moved to Ohio and I commenced on my own footing in Kentucky.

During all the time since my departure from home, the subject of religion was never wholly banished from my mind, and I embraced every opportunity to attend meetings, especially in Tennessee, where I frequently met with devoted Christians, in whose company I enjoyed much satisfaction. The following extract from my diary, dated September 9th, 1810, will shew some of my thoughts at that time on the subject of party spirit:

> On Sunday I accompanied the family to meeting one mile, where a pathetic discourse was delivered by Mr. Hodge from John 1:29. This was a Presbyterian congregation of the old order. Though there is a variety of other sects in this part of the country, who, like sectarians in every other place, esteem their own way of thinking the most unexceptionable, looking on their dissenting neighbors as having, either willfully or

ignorantly, departed from the true faith. In discoursing with different professors, I could discern a degree of the spirit which actuated the Pharisee in the Temple,[35] of which the Lord complains, by one of the prophets, when speaking of those who say unto others, "Stand thou there. Come not near to me. I am holier than thou."[36] Although none are willing to acknowledge this as applicable to themselves, yet it evidently applies where the spirit of charity is wanting. One lays a particular stress on this and another on that point of doctrine, while all too much neglect to cultivate in themselves, and inculcate to others, that mutual forbearance and brotherly love which are the proper fruits of true religion.[37]

THE FOLLOWING of Oct. 30, 1810, exhibits some of the mental conflicts I experienced:

Today I am out of employment. Having no business to do in the line of my present occupation, I am waiting with anxiety for Mr. Bingham's arrival. My mind is dejected and disposed to give way to disconsolate thoughts. My reflections lead me to realize the instability of human nature, the uncertainty of all earthly enjoyments, and their insufficiency to satisfy the unhappy mind.

Although I at present am blessed with a good degree of health, am surrounded with all the comforts which nature requires, and have reason to believe possess the good will of the family with whom I reside, and that of my acquaintances around; yet all these are not sufficient while my *mind* is depressed to afford any happiness.

My present experience proves to me the existence of a state where minds can be filled with more substantial joy than what is to be found in this fluctuating scene of transitory pleasures. Why should I be endowed with this thinking part, if the only design of its creator was to qualify me for temporal pursuits—when that very part is least satisfied with the greatest worldly acquisitions? Or why should I be unhappy on the ground of remorse, if I pursue the very end for which I was designed? And yet there appears at times a fatality in my actions, which seems to baffle volition.

Such a complicated mixture of rational and animal propensities do I find in myself that I appear to be an inexplicable riddle. Sometimes the rational gets the upper hand, and then again the animal assumes the seat of judgment, deciding all in its own favour.

> At other times a severe conflict ensues between the two, and like the north and south wind, alternately prevail; or in the severity of the contest both for a moment sink exhausted through loss of power and leave the controversy undetermined. Well might the poet say,
>
> "He hangs between; in doubt to act; or rest;
> In doubt to deem himself a god or beast;
> In doubt his mind or body to prefer,
> Born but to die, and reasoning but to err."[38]

OFTEN TIMES would my past experience come up with vivid recollection, accompanied with a strong impression that my labours in the ministry would yet be resumed. The case of Jonah fleeing to Tarshish would sometimes present itself,[39] and I would reproach myself for giving way to the desire of acquiring earthly possessions at all; and yet the fact that my best days were passing by, and that it was prudent for one to provide something for old age, operated as a salvo against self-reproach. Many times I have retired from all company into the woods and spent hours in deep meditation and secret devotion, giving vent to my feelings in trying to compose hymns occasionally.[40]

I will here insert a few more extracts before proceeding with my narrative. The following on the subject of slavery will show that I was not an indifferent spectator to the cruel system and its deleterious influence on both races:

> Wednesday, 16 May 1810, on the Mississippi coast:
>
> Arose before day and floated on past the Red Church[41] one league below on the left, four leagues below which we were obliged to land again on the right, where the wind kept us until evening. During our stay I took a walk through the fields, planted with corn and cotton (in alternating rows). Here I saw the poor Africans drudging in the hot sun with scarcely a rag of clothes to cover their nakedness. One in particular I discovered who had not a stitch except one small rag which modesty demanded. Next to him was a poor old negro, half bent with age, and apparently past the power to labour, with a dejected countenance and very scanty covering, hoeing along with his fellow sufferers.
>
> I stood some time (with tears in my eyes) looking at the unhappy creatures, contrasting their situation with that of their cruel masters,

who live in idleness and luxury at their expense. I thought to myself, "Will not the God of justice at some period avenge the cause of these innocent beings, who are dragged from their native country by the arbitrary power of usurpers, and made to toil and sweat in the fields of foreigners to support their sumptuous banquets, while they themselves are scarcely allowed the means of subsistence."[42]

Sumner Co., Tenn., Sept. 30th, 1810

Here it is easy to discover the baneful fluence which slavery has on the rising generation. Those parents who possess large estates and have a great number of slaves suffer their children to be raised in idleness, with a domineering disposition over the servants and a haughty, ostentatious carriage toward their white equals in more moderate circumstances. While on the other hand, such as are opposed to slavery bring up their children in the practice of industry, plain and familiar manners, thus making them useful and honest citizens. Nor are the effects confined to manners, but may be discovered in the arrangements of their farms. Those who attend to and take care of their dwellings and fields have everything in much better order and enjoy much more satisfaction in the bounties of providence.[43]

ONE MORE extract on the subject:

Davidson Co., Tenn., Nov. 11th, 1810

I sat down this morning to add a little to my diary, but hardly know what to write, as nothing extraordinary has lately occurred. It may not be amiss just to mention a few principal traits in the character of our landlady. In the first place, she is a woman of uncommon size, weighing 244 [pounds]. Yet notwithstanding her corpulency, she finds means to trip over the floor with astonishing quickness, especially when matters in the kitchen go contrary to her mind. The strength and activity of her arm is fully realized by the servants, who, under the severity of cowhide-discipline, receive from her liberal hand their full share of daily chastisement. With nice precision she notices the most trivial faults in those under her power; and for small offenses, pinches or pulls on the ear. Her voice, which for strength corresponds to her size, may be heard across the plantation, and what her expressions want in elegance is sufficiently made up in verbosity. As industry is one of her principle virtues, no idleness is suffered about the house, which is kept in the neatest manner. Her table is furnished with a copious supply of good provision and carefully attended during meals by a servant, who anxiously watches the eye of her mistress and runs at the word of command to obey her sovereign mandates. The abrupt plainness of her speech, both in the family and to strangers, bids defiance to dissimulation. If we may look for analogies in the works of nature and suppose her mental qualities to be in proportion to her person, their description would engross too much of my little book. I therefore dismiss the subject with my good wishes and hearty thanks for the kind treatment I received at her house.[44]

DESCRIPTION OF a court day scene in Gallatin, Sumner Co., Tenn., Sept. 13th, 1810:

The town, which was small, was crowded with people from the country, especially the taverns and grog shops. Numbers were reeling to and fro with their bacchanalian cups, while one, not so far gone, was swearing through the streets, leading by the head a favourite horse, on whose dexterity he threw out high, swelling banters. At some more retired spot, perhaps in a mechanic's shop or private house, might be seen little companies of the more civil and sober farmers conversing on the various subjects of husbandry, complaining of dull times, scarcity of money, etc.; while the courthouse was occupied with clients anxious to gain their cases, and lawyers equally anxious to obtain their fees. Waiting evidences,[45] tired by the court's prolixity and desirous to be released, kissed the book and told their story. Listening jurors, balancing testimony, retired a short time and returned with the decisive verdict. Judges aiming to dispense justice and regulate the bar, received the lawful decision and pronounced sentence. Depression and cheerfulness in opposing litigants was the sure result.[46]

Amidst this scene of excitements, one may discover human ambition in various forms. One is emulous of literary and oratorical fame, a second eager for the shining booty. A third craves the inebriating stimulus. A fourth indirectly solicits the suffrage of his neighbors in aiding him to procure an office. All are striving to accomplish some favourite end. Thus man, the most restless of all creatures, endeavours by various means to satisfy his anxious mind and fill that aching void, which after all his toil and bustle remains a vacuum still.

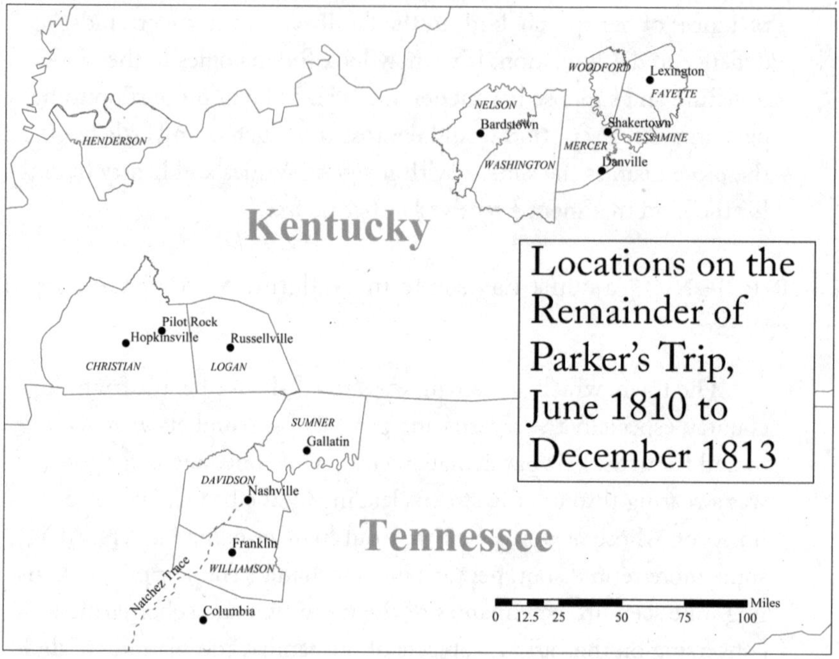

Map 4.1. Map by Matthew Young

CHAPTER 4

"A Kind of Agreeable Dread"

ON LEAVING Tennessee I procured a gig, and tying on behind a box of tools, commenced traveling in a new mode.[1] Entered the state of Kentucky on the south the first day of March, 1811. The next morning, having set out very early with my tools on behind and a wild young creature in the shafts, the road being good and the weather pleasant, I passed westward out of Logan into Christian County, highly gratified with my new plan of traveling.

Here follows straight from my journal of that day:

March 2nd

Set off early, rode briskly through the open barrens six miles, when on a sudden, descending a moderate hill, not suspecting the least danger, but singing to myself, the carriage upset, threw me on the ground and strained one arm. The creature, being young, took the alarm, sprang forward, and wresting the reins from my hand, broke the singletree,[2] disengaged herself from the gig, and fled with full speed through the barrens, and was soon out of sight.

I reflected a few moments on my situation, and on the kindness of God in preserving my life. Then, summoning resolution, pursued the creature and found her about a mile and a half on the road taken up at the house of Esqr. Loflane on the Elk Fork of Red River. The gentleman kindly assisted in filling up my carriage, his lady having bathed and wrapped up my arm. After breakfast I again proceeded,

> but with great caution and no small difficulty arising from lameness and the affrighted beast.
>
> In the afternoon I arrived at Colonel Ewing's in Christian County,[3] nine miles from Loflane's. Mrs. Ewing bound up my arm with comfrey and shewed me much kindness.[4] The Colonel bled me, and the servants were very attentive. One of them by the name of Dick voluntarily went several miles in the night for vinegar to bathe my arm.[5] For several nights I suffered extremely with little sleep. The injury was much worse than at first anticipated.

By this calamity I was prevented several weeks from pursuing my business and detained in the same place, making Colonel Ewing's my principal home, in whose neighborhood I formed some agreeable acquaintances. Among them was a niece of the Colonel, to whom I afterward became much attracted.[6] Her parents had once been in affluent circumstances, but were then quite poor. Her mother was a woman of extraordinary mind and amiable manners; was soon after left a widow.[7] Her husband, Baker Ewing, died down the river while I remained in that section.[8]

Christian County being at that time thinly settled, the prospect of doing much in my business was small. In about two weeks I left these kind friends and traveled eastward into Logan County again. Recovering soon after the use of my arm, [I] commenced work near Russellville,[9] the county seat, at Esqr. Stephen's, where I remained some weeks and found much kindness; meeting also with some success in business.[10]

A large portion of this part of Kentucky consists of open barrens, some of which are very rich and well watered. Many of the smaller streams sink suddenly into the openings through the limestone rock and, running some distance underground, reappear again. The surface is, for the most part, gently undulating. There are many large sink holes in the shape of an inverted cone. At the bottom of some may be seen from the surface limpid streams of pure water flowing past. I saw in one of the largest an overshot grist mill,[11] the whole bulk of which was below the surface. A winding road led down to the stream below, which came from a cave, and after passing over a large wheel sunk still lower into the earth.

I take pleasure in bearing testimony to the generous hospitality of the farmers in this region at that day, the most of whom have no doubt e'er now "gone the way of all the earth."[12] They appeared to think themselves favoured to have a well-behaved stranger take lodgings with them, and would seem hurt if they were offered compensation. I have often been urged to stay with my horse for several days together without the smallest expense except what I chose to give the servants.

The greatest drawback to my satisfaction so far as temporal matters were concerned was the system of slavery. Although I seldom witnessed extreme cruelty, yet to behold human beings created in the image of God reduced to the condition of mere property, kept in profound ignorance and made to labour a lifetime without wages for the comfort of others, would often make my heart ache. In those days very little was said on the subject, and when I would sometimes speak of its injustice among intimate friends, they would stare at me as though they had never once called it in question. Yet after conversing freely, they would often confess that it did appear to be wrong. Some would even go so far as to say they would prefer living in a free state if they could. Especially females have made this confession, but *they* had no control in the matter.[13]

After a residence of some weeks in Logan, I returned again to Christian County; thence visited nearly all the Green River country; thence on westward as far as the red banks in Henderson County; thence up the Ohio, exploring nearly all the river counties from that to Licking River, returning once more to Russellville; passed through the town the seventh of August, 1811; found it crowded with people holding an election, for some remarks on which I once more refer to my journal:

> August 7th
>
> It being the last day of the election, the streets were crowded and the electioneering spirit sparkling in every eye: the several candidates flourishing in the throng, endeavouring to attract attention and acquire votes. In this country, if a man desiring an office does not put himself forward, attend public assemblies for several months previous to the election, get upon stumps and "speechify," as it is called, let his

talents be ever so great or merit ever so conspicuous, he stands but a dull chance of going to the "Big House." But if a brisk stripling of common, or even inferior, education, with a sufficient show of self-importance can set forth his own good qualities if he has any (or if he have none, borrow a few for the present exigency), and be hail-fellow in all companies, the ignorant and profane will shower their votes and encomiums upon him, with a volley of oaths declaring that he shall go because he is a clever fellow. Detraction and scurrility are substituted for argument, and the columns of newspapers crowded with frivolous stuff. Every foible of an opponent is exaggerated and thrown at him in public print with all the spite that party spirit can inspire. Such is the effect of perverted freedom. Liberty and equality is the cry, but libertinism and defamation the practice.[14]

MY BUSINESS calling me once more to Christian County, I revisited again the kind friends of whom mention had been made. Absence had not obliterated the impression which had been made by the attractions of Miss Eliza Ewing.[15] I foresaw, and anticipated with a kind of agreeable dread, the approach of a new trial. I had hitherto not been assailed in that way beyond the power of resistance, and (except [in] my father's house), felt equally at home wherever my lot was cast. But now my thoughts, though fluctuating at times, like the magnetic needle would finally settle in one direction. Reminiscences of the past crowded upon me.[16] Desire prompted forward and caution held me back. I was tired of wandering, and my age indicated the propriety of settling in life, unless I chose one of celibacy. These and a thousand other reflections occupied my mind, while in the mean time many pleasant interviews tended to strengthen an attachment already too strong for my peace.

During the visit I took an excursion to see a natural curiosity called the Pilot Rock,[17] situated in Christian County on the waters of Pond River (two miles from the county seat).

The following is a description given at the time:

On Saturday, 7th of September, 1811, Miss Ewing, her brother, sister, brother-in-law, and myself set out about eleven o'clock on horseback to visit the above curiosity. After riding four and a half

Figure 4.1. Daniel Parker's gentle satirical reflections on democracy on the old western frontier anticipated George Caleb Bingham's painting, *The County Election* (1851), set in Missouri, by several decades. (Saint Louis Art Museum)

miles over very poor land, we arrived at its base. The ground for seventy or eighty rods[18] each way descends very considerably from the Rock, whose summit is perhaps four or five hundred feet above the surrounding country, but is of itself probably not more than 80 or 100 feet. It is not one solid rock, but a huge mass of rocks, separated in many places by narrow passages running in different directions, by which one may pass through near its centre. These internal passages are closed at the top, so that a person may pass over its summit, the area of which is about one acre, covered with scrubby timber of various kinds: grape vines, wortle berries,[19] haw bushes, and moss. An extensive horizon, the sight of numerous farms, a rising column of smoke from distant prairies on fire, flitting clouds, and singing birds with the sound of distant voices conspired to render still more delightful the sublime prospect. There are seven springs issuing from its base, and in many of the internal cavities water stands a great part of the year. The passage by which

> we ascended was about four feet wide. After spending about three hours in conversation and music, closed by an agreeable repast, we descended by another opening two feet in width, mounted our horses and returned.

THIS PLEASING visit, though fascinating for a time, only made me feel more sensibly the contrast on mingling again in the turmoil of business, which necessarily engrossed a large portion of my time. Having embarked in it, and involved myself in debt, I had no alternative but to persevere. I had to combat prejudice arising from the failure of former machines, so that nothing but actual experiment would satisfy the people. This made it very disagreeable on entering new neighborhoods. The improvement was called a "Yankee trick" and a torrent of abuse would often be the first salutation.[20] I was obliged for the most part to board at taverns, and of course could not avoid coming in contact with much disagreeable company. Many times my spirits would sink so low that nothing but the fact of being bound both by law and honor to pay the debt I had incurred would have prevented me from retiring in disgust, but vain regrets availed nothing.

The following reflection was written on Sunday, Sept. 15, 1811:

> Retiring to the woods, pensive and alone, I sat down under an oak to write. I experienced a degree of tranquility in mind, an indifference to the world and its cares; reflected on the goodness and immutability of God, and through his works was led to adore that providence which supported and blessed so changeable a creature as I. Just by where I sat hung a few bunches of grapes.[21] I arose and pulled a cluster with this reflection: the nourishment this sweet fruit affords on this dry and barren ridge is a striking emblem of those moments of consolation granted to mortals while passing through the dreary scenes of this life. I sat musing in my silent retreat till the sun had sunk in the west, and the chirping of evening insects saluted my ear with incessant and increasing noise. My peculiar frame of mind forbade a wish for company and welcomed the sweets of solitude. With reluctance I returned to the house, where domestic tumult interrupted the pleasing train of thought and with my late serene contemplations formed a grating contrast.

IN NOVEMBER of 1811 I left the Green River country, having done but little in my business; bent my course toward the more populous parts of the state eastward. Made a stand for a short time in Washington County, where the Catholics were pretty thickly settled; became acquainted with several families—found them very friendly in matters pertaining to this world, but extremely tenacious of their own religious sentiments. Had an interview with their priest Mr. Baddon, with whom I conversed freely on the principle points of difference between them and the Protestants, particularly those of infallibility, oracular confession, and transubstantiation. He was very learned and polite, but failed to convince me that his system was true. They lent me books, which I read with care, and found in them much to approve and more which seemed to me destitute of scriptural authority.[22]

While in this country, two shakes of an earthquake were felt about the middle of December. My next stand was in Beardstown, seat of Nelson County, where I stayed from the seventh of January 1812 to

Figure 4.2. The New Madrid, Missouri, earthquake of December 1811 and its aftershocks, continuing into 1812, were felt across the eastern half of the United States, including by Daniel Parker in Kentucky, almost three hundred miles away. This *Scene of the Great Earthquake in the West* was published in R. M. Devins's *Our First Century* (Springfield, MA: C. A. Nichols, 1877), 220. (Special Collections, Legacy Library, Marietta College)

the second of February. Here I had better success in business. Experienced another earthquake on the 23rd [of] January,[23] on which occasion I was shocked with the profane and blasphemous remarks of some in reference to the earthquake; was disgusted also with the vulgar language and conduct of young men who would even boast of their extreme wickedness. On one occasion, in my presence, they went to such lengths that I broke out upon them and delivered a pointed lecture on the evil of such conduct and the obligations of morality as connected with respectability in this world. They were a class of young lawyers. At first they attempted to defend themselves, but at the close of my address acknowledged the right, and treated me with great respect. Virtue commands respect, even from the vicious.

From Beardstown I passed on still eastward and arrived in Danville, seat of Mercer County, the fourth of February. Three miles from this town, in the adjoining county of Lincoln, resided old Capt. Warren,[24] the father of Mrs. Ewing, Eliza's mother, who was made a widow and keeping house for her father, who had recently lost his wife. Having no acquaintance in this part of the country, I rode out the same evening to the grandfather of Miss Ewing, who still lived with her mother. The meeting of my friends once more was of course very agreeable, and I received from the old gentleman and his only single son Samuel the most cordial reception.[25] Through them I soon became acquainted with a numerous connection[26] of the Warren family in different sections of the state: all respectable and some of them wealthy. This acquaintance proved a great benefit to me in my business, which began to be more profitable as soon as the people became satisfied of its utility. I pursued my work with assiduity and could dispose of it readily; occasionally sold county rights, but relied for money mostly on making machines, the demand for which continued to increase. In the county of Mercer and those adjoining I remained until the month of June. On the 19th of that month I went to Lexington; made my home at Doctor McCalla's three weeks. His son William was then studying for the ministry; became afterward an eminent Presbyterian preacher and settled in Philadelphia.[27]

[I] remained at Lexington in all six weeks, during which time war was declared against England.[28] When the report of this event reached the place, a number of hot-headed citizens set on foot an illumination, which, though disapproved by the more judicious and sober portion, was complied with to save their windows from destruction, for the war spirit was predominant. A Mr. Sanders who refused to illuminate had his windows broken to pieces; and the Hon. John Pope, one of their most worthy statesmen, was burnt in effigy for voting in Congress against the war.[29] I saw the ridiculous procession, consisting mostly of boys, passing with the image through the streets with all the disgusting demonstrations peculiar to mobs. In the night of July 10th another illumination was made on hearing that Commodore Rogers had obtained a victory at sea, but the report was false and the candles burnt for nothing.[30] During this excitement volunteer companies were collected in Lexington and other neighbouring towns. At a barbecue near Nicholasville, one of the toasts was at first proposed, "May the volunteers prove successful"; but the word "*shall*" was substituted for "*may*."

Such presumption, however, was soon to meet with a check. For shortly after that, the melancholy defeat at the River Raisin occurred, in which Captain Hart of Lexington with the greater portion of his company, consisting mostly of young men delicately brought up, was slain by the Indians.[31] This sad event filled the city with sorrow, and the streets, instead of brilliant illuminations, presented the habiliments of mourning. Although sympathizing deeply with bereaved families, I could not but deprecate their premature rejoicing. For whatever may be urged in palliation of war, it surely does not furnish cause for mirth, but is a great calamity under the most favourable aspect.[32]

Leaving Lexington the first of August,[33] spent some time visiting my friends in Mercer and Lincoln, which tended to strengthen the attachment already mentioned. Returned again to the city on the 18th and worked three more weeks, making my principal home at Doc. McCalla's, who was a most amiable old gentleman: quite charitable on the subject of religion. His wife, an excellent woman and remarkably charitable to the poor, was a real bigot in religion, and no doubt thought it wicked to countenance any other than Presbyterian sentiments. She was so interested in behalf of the soldiers who were among the Kentucky troops that she went through the city and begged cloth of the merchants, which was made into garments under her direction and sent to the army.[34]

I here insert another extract from my journal of that period:

> While the young men were marching toward a foreign enemy, a large company of old men organized under the title of "Silver Greys" as a domestic safeguard against the insurrection of slaves, which seemed to threaten the country. Several combinations and plots had been detected in adjoining counties, and no small alarm among the whites was the consequence. Some, however, apprehended no danger, and esteemed the precaution of others as the effect of ungrounded fear. But I could discover a pretty general uneasiness, particularly in those who saw the injustice of keeping them in bondage.[35]
>
> Amidst the splendor of affluence I could discover a half-disguised misery with now and then a wish that there had never been a slave in America. How often I have viewed the grandeur of envied opulence, acquired through the means of oppression, and felt thankful that my lot was not cast in that state of ill-gotten ease: where I must be a prey to corroding anxiety and continued suspicion; where no confidence could be placed in those on whom I depended for support; to have my rest disturbed by a constant dread that my property or perhaps my life was in danger. These are a few of the innumerable evils that result from the existence of slavery, and from which those are happily free who never knew its baneful influence.
>
> But of all the evils, setting aside the wickedness of the principle, I think the greatest is experienced in bringing up children. It is next to impossible to educate them among the slaves without contamination. The little attention paid by most slaveholders to the minds and morals of their slaves, the natural viciousness in some, and the want of encouragement in all, place them in a deplorable state of corruption, the fruit of which flows out in their conduct before white children, who imbibe their vices, while at the same time they are taught to consider them an inferior race, and exercise towards them the spirit of overbearing haughtiness. It is not uncommon to hear a child of ten years old peremptorily ordering a grey-headed Negro to do some little trifling thing, while the poor slave is worn out with fatigue and the spoiled child pampered in wantonness and luxury. I hardly know which to pity the most, the poor slave or the spoiled child.[36]

> I would not exchange the contentment of the hard-working farmer or mechanic where the spirit of freedom reigns for the richest dainties of the wealthy slaveholder. Oh happy people who are taught from infancy to pursue honest industry, and properly appreciate the value of blessings obtained through diligent attention to the business of life:
>
> Ah! when shall freedom universal reign
> And Adam's race on equal footing stand,
> When each shall strive the rights of man to gain
> And justice reign throughout our favoured land.[37]

THE INSTANCE above cited of an organization to keep down domestic insurrection shews the danger to which society must always be exposed where one portion of the inhabitants are slaves to the other. It is not to be expected that human beings reduced to a state of *chattleism*[38] should feel much interest in the safety and prosperity of those who have thus degraded them. Nor ought we to be surprised at their seeking opportunities for revenge. If, as Solomon says, "Oppression will make a *wise* man mad" (Ecclesiastes 7:7), should we not fear the consequences of an excited ignorant mass? Or will the danger be lessened by procrastinating the work of emancipation? All history shews it will not. The only true policy for individuals and nations is to do righteousness. There can never be a better rule of action than the one given by Christ, "Whatsoever ye would that man should do unto you, do ye even so unto them."[39] But this rule cannot be obeyed where slaveholding is practiced, as no one would choose to be a slave, unless he had beforehand been deprived, by slavery itself, of his manhood.[40]

My business was of such a nature as made me familiar with the domestic economy of slaveholding families. It would have been of little use to make a machine for washing clothes unless I attended closely to its operation. This of necessity brought me in contact with the labour of slaves in the kitchen. I had the best opportunity of observing their management. For the most part, the kitchens were mere hovels with scarcely any conveniences for doing work of any kind as it should be done. Nor did the slaves care how they got through it if they could but escape detection. Having no stimulus but that of fear, the less they did in a given time was to them so much gain, as they were inspired with no higher motive than that of gratifying their present physical wants. It is strange that among republicans, and more especially professors of religion, there should be found a single advocate for the system of unrequited labour. In justice to the citizens of Lexington, I should state that their domestic arrangements and facilities for kitchen work were far superior to what I had seen in other places, and so far as one could judge from appearances, slavery here existed in its mildest form.[41]

In Lexington I became acquainted with Professor Blythe, afterward president of South Hanover College, who lost a son, an amiable young man, at the River Raisin in the defeat which proved so disastrous to the Kentucky troops.[42] Was also intimate with Sawyer Fishback, who was at that time writing a book on theology designed to prove that the idea of a supreme being could never have entered into the mind of man without revelation. He used to read his manuscript and ask me what I thought of it. He afterward became a Baptist preacher.[43] In this city I was treated with much kindness and generous hospitality. Its location is in the heart of a rich and beautiful country, and its suburbs in particular are delightful, being decorated with splendid dwellings generally one story high, built mostly on gently rising hills in view of the city. What a pity that such a country should be cursed with slavery.

My old diary furnishes the following:

> Sept 7th (1812)
>
> Left Lexington and made into Woodford County; stayed at Mr. Taylor's, son in law to old Captain Warren, till next day afternoon.[44] Proceeded thence into Jessamine County and built a machine for Esqr. Hawkins. Left his house the 13th and passed into Mercer. Called on the way to see and hear the worship of the Shakers,[45] which though very singular was yet solemn. A man of considerable talents was preaching with great energy when I entered the meeting house. Parts of his discourse were exceedingly good, but delivered in a manner calculated rather to disgust than convince his hearers, being very dogmatic and accompanied with heavy denunciations against their opposers. During the discourse the members sat down on the floor, each sex its own side of the house. Sermon being ended,

Figure 4.3. Men and women of the congregation, in separate ranks, approach each other in an ecstatic dance at a Shaker meeting, similar to the one Daniel Parker witnessed. This print from the 1830s by an unknown artist is based on a color lithograph of ca. 1826 by Anthony Imbert, titled *Shakers near Lebanon.* (New York Public Library)

> all arose (males and females facing each other) and sang an anthem, with which I was much pleased. The men laid off their coats and prepared to dance. While five or six sang lively tunes, the rest danced excessively half an hour and were then dismissed. The women were dressed in uniform, having dark stiff petticoats, long white loose gowns, and white strap caps, remarkably neat and clean. Their meeting house was also very neat; large, plain and commodious.

A PRINCIPLE object of this memoir being to trace my inward rather than outward travel, and to notice particularly those events in my life which had a special bearing upon my peace of mind or otherwise, and as a crisis in my experience was just before me, the following reflections and candid statement will not be thought inappropriate.

I had from my childhood always been fond of virtuous female society, and believed then as I do now that human happiness is incomplete short of a virtuous union between the sexes. Yet, notwithstanding this predilection, I had—more from a sense of duty than inclination—endeavoured to ward off whatever might interfere with my duty to God (for amidst all my wandering, there still remained a secret conviction that some time or other providence would call me again into the public ministry), and I was for many years under the impression that a life of celibacy would be my lot. With this impression, I had the satisfaction of knowing that in no instance had I ever trifled with the affections of women, or attempted to gain them for dishonorable purposes, such conduct being in my estimation not only dishonorable but very wicked.

In spite of my prudence, however, the attachment for the young lady already mentioned had become so strong that propositions of marriage had been made, and I was on my way to receive a final answer. We had conversed freely on the subject of my past experience, my embarrassments and prospects in business, my family connections, and above all the obligations of religion, not neglecting the subject of slavery. On this last her mind had become so changed that she was willing to live in a free state and give up her slaves, though used to them all her life, acknowledging that she was convinced through my arguments that the practice of slaveholding was wrong.[46]

With this subject bearing with intense weight upon my mind, and with my heart engaged in prayer to God that he would guide me in this important matter and give me resignation to his will, we had on the 14th inst.[47] the decisive interview, in which she with great candour informed me that, although she had given me encouragement and reason to expect an affirmative answer, yet during my absence a young man for whom she had a previous attachment, reciprocated also on his part, but kept in abeyance by some cause not known to her, had stepped in with [a] proposal of marriage; and that although she entertained for me the highest regard as a friend, we could neither of us be happy with the knowledge that her first attachment had been revived. This ingenuous (though to me, painful) announcement disappointed, of course, all my fond anticipations for the present on that subject.[48] Yet I have since seen the hand of providence in this disappointment and been satisfied that the gratification of my wishes then would not have been for my permanent happiness. Eliza was soon after married to the man of her choice (Mr. George Briscoe), and afterward moved to the state of Illinois with my good wishes for their welfare.[49] The revulsion of feeling consequent upon my late trial was in a great measure compensated by being released from a state of suspense.

Having gotten through one more chapter in the book of my experience, another, quite different from any former one, was opening before me, the nature of which is described in the following passage from my old journal:

> The urgent and pressing call for men to repel the enemy encroachments on the Wabash River induced Mr. James Warren and his father in law Major Briscoe to volunteer their services with others.[50] I offered to stay and take care of their families during their absence, especially Mr. Warren's, which proposal they accepted with thankfulness. Accordingly on the 18th of September, 1812. I entered upon a task entirely new, that of managing a set of lazy negroes and superintending the business of a farm (worked by slaves).[51] It made me feel right comical as I approached the house to hear one of the little negroes hallow out, "There comes my young master."
>
> After receiving from Mrs. Warren a memorandum of what her husband wished me to do, I went the same evening to the woods where the boys were chopping and let them know what I should expect from them as standing in the place of their master. They promised very fair, and seemed highly pleased with their new overseer; [and] began to call me Master Parker. This produced feelings as new as my occupation was. I however found it necessary not to appear outwardly what I inwardly felt, but to assume an authority sufficient to command their attention and respect. The first of the following week I took two servants and went with a team eight miles to mill some hemp for spinning. Our next business was to quarry and haul stone for repairing the hearths.
>
> Friday, 25th: went to Danville to procure articles for my landlady. The evening of this day: experienced a dismal, gloomy state of mind, arising principally from contemplating my wandering, peculiar situation of life. Having no particular purpose in view; being disappointed in my

Figure 4.4. The farms that Daniel Parker oversaw in 1812 produced hemp, a major product of Kentucky produced with the use of slave labor, as depicted in *The Hemp Brake* (1850) by Samuel I. M. Major. (Kentucky Historical Society).

late fond expectations; being in doubt with respect to the propriety of resuming again the public station once occupied; seriously impressed with the vanity of all earthly acquisitions; my spirit sunk, and I beheld myself as it were afloat on the broad sea of uncertainty. Thus hurried along the torrent of tumultuous thought and weighed down with a cloud of gloomy reflections, I was forced to retire and give vent to the laborious struggle in secret. My heart felt disposed to seek relief from that source which alone can afford consolation when sublunary joys forsake us. Oh! that I could always feel thus disposed, and place entire confidence in him who will never deceive those that put their trust in him. How often I have pondered over and felt the force of the following expressive lines:

Man, on the dubious waves of error toss'd,
His ship half founder'd, and his compass lost,
Sees, far as human optics may command,
A sleeping fog, and fancies it dry land;

Spreads all his canvas, every sinew plies;
Pants for it, aims at it, enters it, and dies!
Cowper[52]

The perturbation on my mind wore off by degrees, and the following Sabbath I felt quite composed. Looked back on the dark valley I had passed through, and wondered at the sudden transition from darkness to light. The intellectual, like the material world, appeared to have its various seasons of storms and sunshine: gloomy and serene. How grateful to the senses are the exhilarating sunbeams breaking from behind a dark cloud that has long intercepted their influence! But much more so to the benighted soul are those rays of divine light which pierce the mental gloom and enliven the dejected faculties.

Placed as I find myself, in the situation of a master over servants in whose fidelity no confidence can be placed, who substitute promises for performance; and feeling responsibility to my friend in what I have voluntarily undertaken, I find a new kind of experience to which I have hitherto been a stranger. Those with whom I have to do are not only lazy but lying and dishonest. The one I had entrusted to bring home the hemp hid a part of it in a hollow log on the way and then denied it. My landlady, who is one of the neatest housekeepers, is continually tormented with the carelessness of her black woman. She observed to me one day that she would willingly give up all she possessed except a bare living if she could begin the world again without slaves.[53]

I SUPERINTENDED Mr. Warren's business fifty days, and endeavoured to keep up the spirits of his wife and a young woman who lived with her, but sometimes my exertions would fail and we all got "in the dumps together." About the first of November we heard that he was on his way back. One of his neighbours and myself took fresh horses and met him forty miles off and assisted him home.

Relinquishing my charge and receiving the grateful thanks of the family, I left Mercer and, passing once more through Lexington, arrived ten miles north at Mr. Thomas B. Warren's[54] (brother to James), intending to leave in a few days and go home to my father's house. But this intention was frustrated by being thrown from a wild young horse on the 23rd of December, by which accident my right arm was again badly strained. By the time this injury was healed, a variety of other incidents occurred that kept me through the winter.

The spring of 1813 opening with fairer prospects of business, and having lost so much time, being anxious also to acquire all the property I could to liquidate the debt which still remained unpaid, I was induced to spend the following summer and fall in different parts of Fayette and adjoining counties. Working very hard and meeting with good success, was enabled not only to gather considerable property, but to lay up money which was put out on interest to a rich old farmer.

On the 11th of December following, I left for Leading Creek, and once more arrived at home the 21st, having been absent four years, instead of four months as was my intention on leaving. There was of course great joy in the family, but with a great drawback on my part because I saw not my dear mother, who had died during my absence.

How little we know what is to be our lot [in the] future; and how vain often are the calculations we make as to the course we intend to pursue. If anyone had told me before leaving home that in less than five years I should run in debt $700, and that for speculation; that I should go to New Orleans; travel back through the wilderness sick; should be almost engaged to be married;[55] should be an overseer of slaves; should be thrown twice by wild horses and each time have my right arm strained; with all the other changes in body and mind related above, I should perhaps have answered as Hazael did: "Is thy servant a dog that he should do this" (2nd Kings 8:13)? And yet, such was the concatenation of circumstances, and such the gradual influences conspiring to bring about each event, [that] I find it difficult to resist the conviction that the whole was permitted by providence as a school of experience from which to draw lessons of instruction in after life.[56]

I also have the satisfaction to know that through the whole there was on my part no willful departure from moral principle.[57] It was always a rule with me that, let what would happen, or whatever might be the company among whom my lot was cast, I would stand up for truth and right, leaving consequences to God. Yet so far from having anything to boast of, I feel that without the restraining influence of grace, the many strong temptations to which young men are subject might have proved my overthrow. And therefore, "by the grace of God I am what I am."[58] To the influence of an early religious education, as a secondary cause, may also be ascribed much as operating to restrain me from those practices which have proved the ruin of thousands. These remarks are left on record for the benefit of my children or any others who may read this memoir.[59] I spent the remainder of the winter among my relations.

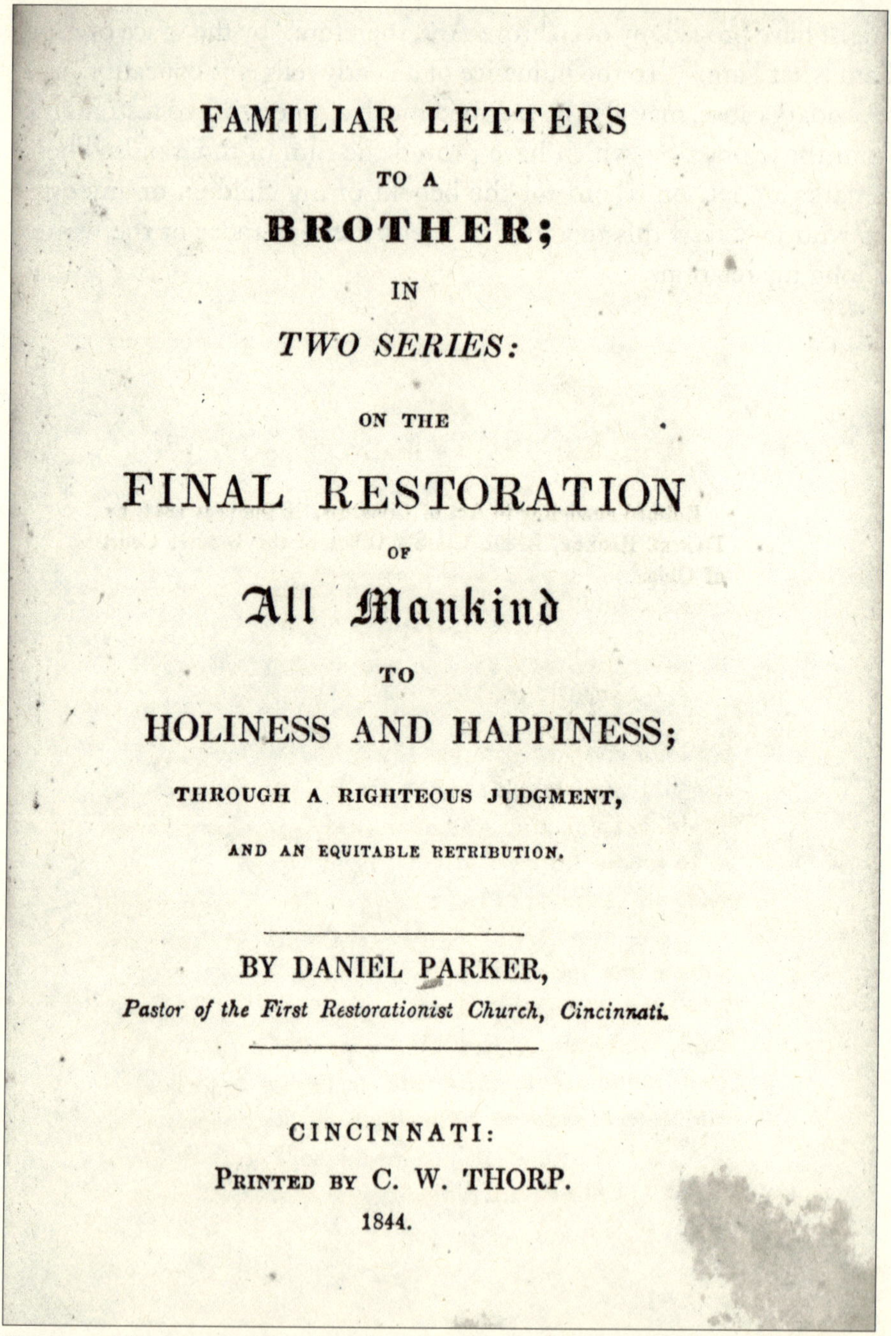

FAMILIAR LETTERS

TO A

BROTHER;

IN

TWO SERIES:

ON THE

FINAL RESTORATION

OF

All Mankind

TO

HOLINESS AND HAPPINESS;

THROUGH A RIGHTEOUS JUDGMENT,

AND AN EQUITABLE RETRIBUTION.

BY DANIEL PARKER,

Pastor of the First Restorationist Church, Cincinnati.

CINCINNATI:

PRINTED BY C. W. THORP.

1844.

Figure 5.1. Title page of Daniel Parker's *Familiar Letters to a Brother*, his only published book, an argument for his "Restorationist" version of universalism. (Special Collections, Legacy Library, Marietta College)

CHAPTER 5

"The Whole Race of Adam Would Be Restored"

APRIL 7TH, 1814: I left home once more to pursue my business again in Kentucky; spent a few days on the way among my old friends in the neighborhood of Mr. Bing, where my first efforts were made in business, and where so much persecution had in former years been suffered by the first members of the Halcyon Church; but instead of persecution, I was received by all the family most cordially. The recollection of past sufferings and joys made our meeting exceedingly interesting.

While watching for a boat in which to get a passage, an old acquaintance by the name of Purdy, from the flats of Grave Creek, came along trading.[1] We soon recognized each other and were glad. I took passage with him and had a pleasant trip. On our way down we stopped all night at the small village of Alexandria below the mouth of the Big Scioto.[2]

Mr. Purdy, knowing that I had once been a preacher, mentioned it to some of the inhabitants, who beset me with earnest entreaty to speak that evening. I replied that although it was true what Mr. Purdy had stated, yet difficulties in my mind had induced me to suspend those labours for a number of years past; that my sentiments on the subject of man's final destiny had changed; that although I was satisfied in my own mind that the whole race of Adam would ultimately be restored, I still had doubts as to the expediency of preaching it, on account of its liability to perversion. Mr. Purdy remarked that perhaps I was putting my "light under a bushel."[3] I felt the force of the observation and after a severe struggle of mind, consented.

The appointment was rapidly circulated and a small number by candlelight was convened. At first I was much embarrassed, not having spoken in public for so long; and being about to commence the propagation of a sentiment which I knew would array against me the larger portion of the religious world, it formed another important crisis in my life. After introducing the subject with the words of Elihu, "I will also shew you mine opinion,"[4] I spoke two hours from Second Timothy 1:10.[5] Embarrassment soon passed away and I enjoyed a degree of light and liberty to which my soul had been a stranger for several years. This was my first sermon on the doctrine of Restorationism; was delivered on Monday evening, the 25th of April, 1814.

From that time till this I have continued bearing witness to the glorious truth that our blessed savior will go on conquering and to conquer until "every knee shall bow and every tongue confess that he is Lord, to the glory of God the Father."[6] With the exception of the one point of final restoration, my sentiments have remained the same as when I was a Halcyonist; and I can now see that the standard we then adopted involved principles which, if carried out, lead necessarily to this conclusion.[7]

I now saw before me a new field of labour. The colt was no longer "tied where two ways met," but he was loosed, because "the Lord had need of him."[8] In the last twelve years I had gone through much remarkable experience both inward and outward; had diligently sought for truth and to know my duty. When in prospect I beheld the opening contest that must ensue from the public announcement of a sentiment so unpopular as that of the restoration, knowing that the great body of learned ministers in most of the churches would be against me, that my doctrine and character would be misrepresented, that honest and pious Christians—not understanding the principle—would shun my fellowship, that wicked men under equally erroneous conceptions would seize the single idea of the final issue without considering the process which must lead to it, would consequently pervert the true meaning, I could not but feel keenly my trying and responsible situation. Yet conscious that my own convictions were the result of a long and faithful search of the scriptures, and that I could not refrain any longer from an open avowal without condemnation—the effect, likewise, which my

Figure 5.2. An illustration of the steamboat *New Orleans* from James T. Lloyd's *Steamboat Directory* (Cincinnati, OH: James T. Lloyd, 1856, 42). It was the "first boat built on the western waters," but probably not the steamboat Daniel Parker saw in 1814. The *New Orleans* had departed for Louisiana for good by then. (Special Collections, Legacy Library, Marietta College)

first public declaration had on my mind, relieving it from anxiety and producing clearness and peace, I determined to go forth once more in the ministry, relying on God, whose aid I had always invoked in every important movement, desiring that if mistaken, the Lord would convince me of the error. The effect produced on the audience at Alexandria was far more satisfactory than could have been anticipated.[9]

The next day about five miles below the Scioto I saw the first steamboat on her way from Pittsburgh. The sight was truly pleasing.[10] On Sunday, first of May, [I] preached again at the mouth of Saltlick Creek (on which is situated the Ohio Salt Works) from Zechariah 3:9.[11] Having left my friend Purdy's boat, spent the two following weeks in the same vicinity, working at my business through the week and preaching on the Sabbath.

Left the place on Monday, 16th of May, in a skift,[12] and arrived at Maysville that night. Next day went out to Washington, where I stayed until the 24th of August, labouring hard on week days and preaching every Sabbath, often to large assemblies: sometimes in the courthouse and often in the woods.

Here my business succeeded well, and I became acquainted with many worthy people, many of whom were religious, and some who had formerly belonged to that branch of the Halcyon Church in Fleming County over which my brother had once presided. These of course were rejoiced to meet one who was still in the same faith, except the point already noticed.

The last week in August was spent in and near Maysville, where I preached to a very large congregation in a ropewalk.[13] In this vicinity and that of Washington there were more skeptical men than I had ever met with before. They would often attack me on the subject of revelation, and for hours together sometimes I had to contend with more than one after preaching a long sermon. Some were Deists, denying revelation, prophecies, and miracles; while others had no faith at all even in the existence of God, ridiculed the idea of man's fall, and considered death an eternal sleep.[14] Such men, possessing as they generally did strong minds, would not be put off with dogmatic assertions, but insisted on reasons addressed to the understanding. Many have confessed to me after hearing my definition of the divine character and benevolent purposes of our heavenly father, that if such views had always been presented to them they should never have denied the Bible; but when I asked them for their particular objections to the book, many of them confessed they had never read it to any extent, by which I discovered that it was possible for a man to have implicit infidelity as well as implicit faith.[15]

To those that acknowledged the existence of God and professed to believe that he was a good being, I used to put the following questions. First: Is God a good and benevolent being? Second: Is it consistent with goodness and benevolence to create intelligent beings subject to such laws as render inevitable to them disorder, pain, and death? Third: Were the laws of nature established by God? Fourth: If man be not a fallen being, whence come disorder, pain, and death? I have often asked these questions, but have never seen a man who denied the fall that did not tie his own hands when he gave a candid answer.[16] However, some honest minds may be embarrassed with abstruse points in theology. I fear that many deny the obligations of religion because of their unwillingness to come under its salutary restraints. Such are the enemies of the cross of Christ.

My old journal says that on the 31st of May I left Limestone and embarked on board a flat boat bound to Cincinnati; that there were two other passengers, one from Virginia, the other from Lexington. The former observed as we pushed off that the river was "damn'd muddy." The young man who had charge of the boat (a citizen of Ohio) replied that he did not know whether it was damn'd or not, but that it was muddy. I took notice of it, and thought there was something good in him. Nor was my impression incorrect, for as we sailed along by pleasant moonlight, we had some agreeable discourse together. He informed me that his mind had been greatly exercised on the subject of man's fall, and that the last Sabbath I had given him much satisfaction. His name was Lanewell.

We landed at 11:00 at night in Augusta, Bracken County, Ky. Saw some slaves burning a lime kiln; enquired the way to Doc. Keeth's, for whom I had brought a box of medicine.[17] He received me kindly and next day introduced me to other citizens. Staid in this town until Sept. 19th, during which time a negro girl was hung for murdering two children. I was requested to preach on the occasion, but declined for special reasons.[18] Near this place I found another old Halcyon member, the widow Tarvin, whose husband was killed on the waterwheel of a grist mill. I find the following notice taken of this location in my diary:

> A vast quantity of human bones are dug up in sinking wells and cellars. Nearly one hundred skeletons were found within the size of one cellar. A citizen informed me that he found five in a hole dug for making mortar. And I saw part of a skeleton raised in digging a post hole. Although no monument appears above ground, yet this place must have been the seat of a numerous population or a common cemetery of some ancient race. The vestiges of a great road up the river-hill on which large trees are now growing prove it to have been a place of great resort.[19]

19th SEPT., 1814. Having settled my temporal business in Augusta, obtained a passage with some gentlemen in a large skift eighteen miles to

Campbell County and arrived about noon at Mr. James Kenedy's, whose wife was a daughter of Cap. Warren.[20] I had heard much of Mr. Kenedy from the Warren family. He being a man of talents, a noted Deist, [I] was anxious to see him, and had once written him a letter containing the four questions above mentioned, a copy of which, without date, I find on the outside leaf of one of my little journal books, and is as follows.

> Dear Sir:
>
> Although a stranger to you, yet being intimately acquainted with your lady's connections and having often heard them speak of you as a person whose natural genius and acquired talents prompted to a deep research into every principle relative to theology, I have, with deference, submitted to your candid investigation the enclosed queries, the impartial solution of which may cast some light on a subject of great importance—one on which we no doubt sincerely differ in opinion. In taking this liberty, my dear sir, I have not been actuated by that spirit of bigotry too prevalent among sectarians,[21] but from a real desire to ascertain the truth, being persuaded that error is not the less erroneous for having the sanction of popular applause, nor truth the less invincible in itself, though the most consummate talents should be arrayed against it.
>
> If Deism be true it will doubtless stand the test of the closest scrutiny, but if on critical inspection any point should be discovered unsupported by rational evidence, it must be acknowledged deficient. On the other hand, if the doctrine of man's fall cannot be maintained on the ground of consistency and rational argument, no hope should be entertained of its ever becoming generally the faith of enlightened men. You will discover that the object of the enclosed questions is confined particularly to that subject, on the authenticity of which depends the truth of subsequent doctrines.
>
> Should you think them worthy of your attention, and will take the trouble to state the several answers to each question in writing, you will oblige me. I may have the pleasure of seeing you at some future period, and of cultivating a personal acquaintance. Till then I remain yours respectfully,
>
> Daniel Parker
>
> James Kenedy, Esqr.

MY EXPECTATIONS of this man were fully realized. He was benevolent, sensible, practical, and the strangest Deist I had ever met with. He believed not only in future existence for man, but also in future rewards and punishments. The former he predicated on the immortality of the soul and the latter on the distinction between virtue and vice. [He] insisted that this might be true without the mediation or resurrection of Christ; that the Deity could do his own work without the aid of a second person. Yet he thought that Jesus Christ was a very good man, and taught excellent precepts. When I asked him how he could be a good man while professing to be the Son of God when (according to his opinion) he was not, he denied that he had ever professed it, but that his biographers put that in the narrative to make out their system.[22] When I required him to prove that man possessed native immortality independent of Christ, he could not do it. Then, said I, if the soul of man be not naturally immortal, how will you prove its conscious existence in a future state without a resurrection? He felt this to be a hard question to answer, inasmuch as philosophy throws no light in the subject, and he denied revelation. Nor could he have found in the volume of revelation, had he admitted its truth, any immortality for man out of Christ, as he is there represented as the only "way, the truth, and the *life*."[23]

I soon discovered that most of Mr. Kenedy's objections to the Christian religion were founded either upon false views of it, or upon the improper conduct of its professors. He was well acquainted with the scriptures, but had read them more for the purpose of detecting apparent contradictions than to ascertain their true meaning. The margin of his Bible abounded with marks of reference, and he had arranged in opposite columns long lists of texts selected from the Old and New Testaments for the purpose of making one contradict the other. Had he taken as much pains to trace out the harmony of the two Testaments, the accordance between prophesies in the Old and their fulfillment in the New, and had he seen that all the evil conduct of professors as individuals or nations was the work of antichrist and not of Christ, he might have enjoyed the benefits of that gospel which confers upon its true disciples a consolation and peace of mind to which the skeptic must be a stranger.

I stayed in this very hospitable family four weeks, made them one of my machines, and devoted much time to the investigation of theological subjects. Mr. Kenedy would often appear to feel as Agrippa did when he exclaimed, "Almost thou persuaded me to be a Christian."[24] He did indeed manifest toward me the spirit of a Christian, as did also his amiable wife and children. Mr. Kenedy was a Scotchman, of a lively turn, and an admirable performer on the violin. He was noted not only for his open defense of Deism, but also for his open-hearted hospitality. His house was the resort of much company; nor did the traveling stranger apply in vain for entertainment, nor his poor neighbours for charity. The latter were often sought out and relieved. I shall have occasion to speak of this kind family more particularly hereafter.

On the 17th of October, 1814, I left Mr. Kenedy's, and passing south through Falmouth, seat of Pendleton County, and Cynthiana, [seat] of Harrison County, arrived once more on the 19th at Mr. T. B. Warren's in Fayette County. Tarried one night, went to Lexington next day on business, passed on to Verseiles,[25] and returned to Mr. Warren's again the 21st. Having met with disappointment in some arrangements by which I intended to have returned home before winter, I assisted my friend to build a small cabin, and in that I worked at my business until the next April, preaching continually on the Sabbath. Was laid up two weeks with another strained wrist. In this neighbourhood I became acquainted with Mr. Thomas Smith, an able preacher of the Christian Connection, who treated me like a Christian.[26] We held several meetings together, although he could not agree with all my sentiments. The restoration doctrine was so new to most people that few had examined it sufficiently to decide, but were induced to read the scriptures anew, and though hoping it was true, feared it was not.

My next location for about two months was near Georgetown, Scott County. Lived very pleasantly at rich farmers' houses, working week days and holding meetings on Sundays, sometimes in the woods, at others in the courthouse. While at work one day in the woods, I saw an old crazy woman coming toward me carrying a budget[27] and muttering to herself. When she came opposite, a lamb ran up to her bleating. She turned short round and, looking the little creature in the face, sang with a sweet voice the following verse:

O the lamb, the loving lamb,
The lamb of Calvary,
The lamb that was slain, but lives again,
To intercede for me.[28]

THIS SINGULAR occurrence excited a train of serious thoughts, as: that the unfortunate maniac might have been made such by intense mental exercise on the subject of religion; the harmless innocence of the little lamb, fit emblem of the "Lamb of God who taketh away the sin of the world"; an impression of thankfulness that I had my reason and was not like this poor woman, wandering about with shattered intellect without a home.[29]

During my stay in this vicinity a report was put in circulation by some ill-disposed person that I was a married man and had run away from my wife. The man with whom I lived came to me quite demurely and developed the secret.[30] I smiled and said that the story gave me no uneasiness. He replied that for himself he did not believe it, but as I was a stranger it might injure my usefulness. The next Sabbath at the close of my sermon (the courthouse being full), I requested the congregation to wait a few moments and then brought the subject forward, desiring that if anyone present had evidence of the fact reported, they would bring it forward that I might meet it; appealing to all who knew how to value character to reflect on the injustice of circulating an injurious report on a stranger. No one said a word, although the man who reported the slander was present, as I was afterward told. The slanderous report being suppressed in the bud, I heard no more of it.

Mr. Samuel Warren from Lincoln, being on a visit to his brother's, urged me to revisit once more my old friends south of the Kentucky River. Complying with his invitation, we rode to Lexington the 19th of June, and next day I found myself among those who had been so long my intimate acquaintances. Reminiscences of the past crowded upon my mind, and mutual congratulations were exchanged. The object of my former attachment had become a wife and a mother, and I spent a night at her house [and] was treated with great kindness by herself and husband. Called on my good friend James Warren, whose business I had overseen. Spent two weeks visiting round, preached twice, and returned again to T. B. Warren's in Fayette, having preached at Lexington on my way back, Sunday the second day of July (1815).

Mr. Warren was not a professor of religion, but his wife was a Baptist and a most excellent woman. Her preacher was a Mr. Vardeman. He was at that time very popular. His preaching produced great excitement through that part of the country. On the evening of the sixth inst. he preached at Mr. Warren's. Mr. Smith, above mentioned, was also present. After sermon a controversy commenced between the two, and they insisted that I should give my opinion, as that differed from both the others. I did so, but my arguments were treated by Mr. Vardeman with contempt instead of being met and refuted. He shewed an overbearing dictatorial spirit, but Mr. Smith treated me like a Christian. The next morning I complained, as did Mr. Warren also, of his course. He regretted having hurt my feelings, and said it was his nature to be blunt. I forgave him and we parted. His popularity, as I was afterward informed, was short lived.[31]

July 11th: Removed into Harrison County. Spent between two and three months in the vicinity of Cynthiana, labouring and preaching. Although I had much more peace of mind than during those years in which my ministerial labours were suspended, yet many times such depression would seize my spirits as was scarcely supportable. The following extract will show the exercise of mind on the eighth of August:

> Reflecting on my lonesome, unsettled situation in this world, I opened my little Testament, as on similar occasions, and the passage that presented itself was First Peter 4:12. "Beloved, think it not strange concerning the fiery trial that is to try you, as though some strange thing happened unto you." Such passages have often afforded comfort, but at this time my mind seemed not susceptible of consolation. One fact that causes me many unhappy hours is that the religious portion of [the] community are so under the influence of sectarianism that they look with suspicion upon every preacher who declares sentiments different from their own, and especially the doctrine of universal restoration, with which is associated in their minds the idea of imposture. I therefore am deprived of that sympathy which all Christians should feel for each other. Consequently, I am

> obliged to associate more than is agreeable with the irreligious, and this brings upon me the reproach that I must be a bad man because of "eating and drinking with publicans and sinners."[32] This I must bear or crowd myself into the company of those who suspect me of having some mischief hid under the cloak of the ministry; and indeed, were I to keep no other company than that of professors, there would be but little enjoyment where there is such want of charity. There exists also a strong prejudice against my temporal occupation, so that I am almost obliged to force my way through in reference to both.[33]

WHILE AT work in the neighbourhood of Cynthiana on the fourth of September, Brother John and Lucy, his companion, came very unexpectedly in sight. We of course were rejoiced to see each other, and had many enquiries to make concerning our friends and the experience through which we had passed. My worldly business was shortly after settled up in this and other parts where I had been, and we three spent some time visiting among my friends in several different counties, my brother and I preaching together on all suitable occasions.

In the course of our travels we came across an old man by the name of Daniel Fink, a very devoted Christian possessing a strong and penetrating mind.[34] It was his opinion that washing of feet should be performed as a religious ceremony, and in the evening desired that he might be permitted to wash ours.[35] Although we did not view it as he did, we consented; and during the service, his exhortations were most solemn and pathetic. He was a strong believer in and advocate of the restoration faith. His arguments in its favour were most cogent and conclusive.

He also believed our views of the Urim, and suggested to us what he thought was intended by the Thummim; and that as the Urim was the seven communicable attributes of God: Love, Wisdom, Power, Holiness, Justice, Goodness, and Truth; the Thummim was the five leading faculties of the human soul.[36] That as there were five senses pertaining to the body, so there were five principle intellectual powers. That these five and those seven, in Christ completely perfect, constituted the true Immanuel ("God with us")[37] or divinity and humanity in one: the only saviour, the antitypical high priest, the judge of [the] quick and [the] dead. That the twelve precious stones in Aaron's breastplate of judgment were types of these twelve, or antitypical, Urim and Thummim.

As no mention of this interview appears in my old journal, I cannot now remember whether he specified the several faculties by name or not; but as this was a subject on which the Halcyon ministers had for many years bestowed much reflection, in order to find what was meant by the Thummim, without having come to any satisfactory conclusion, we were delighted with this beautiful theory brought forward by Brother Fink. It seemed to us like a new revelation. The main idea of the five mental faculties being arrived at, the more we contemplated it, the more reasonable it appeared.

We did not, however, hastily settle down in a positive opinion as to the particular names and arrangement of the faculties. But on our return home the latter part of October, and meeting once more the leading minds of the old Halcyonists scattered in different sections, the suggestion of Brother Fink was presented and received almost as by intuition. There was such a sameness in the travel of all our minds that everyone appeared to be prepared for the discovery. The Bible was still more thoroughly perused, and commentaries consulted. By these last we discovered the meaning of Urim and Thummim to be Lights and Perfections, and we found also that the word "Urim" occurred just *seven* and the word "Thummim" just five times in the Bible, as follows: the two together in Exodus 28:30; Deuteronomy 33:8, Leviticus 8:8, Ezra 2:63, Nehemiah 7:65; the Urim by itself: Numbers 27:21, First Samuel 28:6. That this should be the case, whether it so happened by accident or design, is certainly a very striking correspondence with our view. We consulted metaphysical authors on mental philosophy to ascertain how they arranged the original faculties, and thought that with all their critical acumen the truth was not with them.[38] After a careful analysis of the mind with all the helps we could get, we finally adopted the following names and order of the five radical powers: first, Perception; second, Understanding; third, Affection; fourth, Will; fifth, Memory.[39]

Our reasons for this arrangement were these: that when any subject was presented to the mind for our contemplation, we first perceived its several parts and relations; that by thus perceiving, we were enabled, secondly, to understand, which we could not do without first perceiving, because there was nothing to understand until something had been perceived. Thirdly, when an object or subject had been perceived and understood, if it was desirable, our affection embraced it. This *central* power, both as respects its importance and number in the order laid down—three being the middle number of five—is called in scripture the *heart.* Fourthly, having perceived, understood, and loved an object or subject, the will is brought into exercise to obtain it if possible; but we cannot want what we neither perceive, understand, nor love. Fifthly, the memory comes into operation as the retrospective faculty, retaining all the former exercises, and cannot act prospectively for this simple reason: that we cannot remember what never took place.

With this view of the Urim and Thummim we became more and more enamoured; studied the scriptures with increased anxiety and delight, and thought we could now see why the numbers *seven*, *five*, and *twelve* (the other two combined) occurred so frequently in the sacred oracles. We explained the scriptures by this rule of twelve parts. The seven attributes of divinity and the five rational powers of humanity in Christ, we conceived to be meant by the twelve manner of fruits on the tree of life;[40] the twelve foundations of the New Jerusalem.[41] By this rule also the patriarchs and apostles were chosen. By the number seven the divisions of time were regulated in the weekly and yearly Sabbaths. By twelve: the months of the year, the hours in the day—minutes and seconds by five times twelve (sixty).

Measuring in architecture by twelve inches, seven radical tones in music, seven colours in the rays of light. Also in anatomy: seven avenues in the head—two eyes, two ears, two nostrils, and mouth; seven bones in the upper portion of the spine (cervical vertebrae), twelve in the middle (dorsal vertebrae), and five in the lower (or lumbar vertebrae), forming a column of twenty-four points, or twice twelve. The number five also seems to be special. There are Ten Commandments, the double of five; five members on each hand and foot in the human person. This is but a mere sketch of what may be discovered in the word and works of God, the former especially. The measures of different parts in Solomon's Temple and its appurtenances, which an attentive reader can scarcely fail to observe. The length of the house was sixty cubits (five times twelve). The molten sea, ten cubits diameter, rested on twelve brazen oxen. The inner court was twenty cubits every way (four times five). The two cherubims, each being five cubits, etc.[42]

Whatever others may think of these views, they were exceedingly interesting to us who had received them, associated as they were with so much extraordinary experience. As to the exposition given above of the Urim and Thummim, I must say that nothing has ever been presented to my mind half so reasonable from any other source. Some may say it is not worthwhile to pry into such subjects, that if we follow the plain precepts and examples of Christ, it will be all sufficient for our salvation and that is the one thing needful. If these enquiries tend to make us neglect the service of God, we certainly should not pursue them; but so far have they been from affecting me in that way that I never saw the character of God so attracting, and his service so delightful, as has been the case since these views were made known.[43]

I have seen more beauty in the scriptures since than before. Many parts that used to appear entirely inexplicable have become clear. The character of Christ, [according] to this view, seems to be more easily comprehended. In him we see the substantial Urim and Thummim (the lights and perfections): perfect humanity united with divinity, one Immanuel, the sun of the heavenly world; whose image, formed in the soul, is the "anchor sure and steadfast."[44] According to the above theory, every human soul is a representative of the Thummim. When it becomes united to Christ by a new birth, it then comes into union with the divine Urim, and that is complete salvation.

When Saul the king of Israel forsook the Lord, it is said the Lord answered him no more, "neither by dreams, nor by *Urim*, nor by prophets" (First Samuel 28:6). And in Ezra 2:63, it is said that the people should not eat of the most holy things until a priest should stand up "with *Urim* and *Thummim*." The holiest things of that dispensation were only types of the most holy things of Christ's kingdom. These could not be partaken of in substance before our great High Priest stood up with the antitypical *Urim* and *Thummim*; or in other words, with the glorious attributes of the Father united with the perfections of pure humanity: the only specimen of pure humanity ever existed on earth. In him was presented to God the first fruits of that nature he came to redeem; and it was a perfect offering, made once and for *all* by the grace of God. It was not made for the purpose of reconciling an angry God to man, but angry men to God. In this sublime *atonement*, "God was in Christ reconciling the world unto himself" (Second Corinthians 5:19). "The first fruits being holy, the lump must also become holy" (Romans 11:16).[45] The first ripe sheaf under the law was a type of this first ripe specimen of *human nature*, not that of angels, "for he took not on him the nature of angels, but he took on him the seed of Abraham" (Hebrews 2:16). In this the "head of every man" "was made perfect through suffering" (First Corinthians 11:3 and Hebrews 5:8, 9).[46]

It would be very strange conduct in the husbandman to save only that portion of his harvest that became ripe *first* and burn up all the remainder. Equally strange but much more terrible would it be for the almighty creator to bring back a small portion of wretched fallen man, and either burn up or keep forever burning the remainder.[47]

This great "mystery of godliness" the "angels desired to look into,"[48] not because of any personal interest they had in it, but because they were filled with the love of God, which was the moving cause of the sublime transaction. They had ever taken a lively interest in our welfare from the time "the morning stars sang together and the sons of God shouted for joy"[49] until the "fullness of time" when the multitude of the heavenly hosts exclaimed "Glory to God in the highest, peace on earth, good will toward men."[50] Nor have we any reason to suppose they will remit their solicitude until the last enemy of man shall be destroyed, all things be subdued unto Christ, and God become "all in all."[51] Such a glorious consummation of the divine purpose will reconcile all apparent discrepancies; satisfy the soul of the saviour, who declared while in the flesh that if he should be lifted up from the earth he would "draw all unto him" (John 12:32).[52]

The proper fruit of such a faith is love to God and man, and nothing but gross perversion could ever have produced the belief that its tendency is licentious.[53] It accords with all the holy aspirations of piety in the Christian heart, and fills up the measure of that charity that "believeth all things."[54] If the anticipation of so grand an issue fills the mind with peace and joy now, what must be the rapture produced among men and angels when "faith shall be swallowed up in sight, and hope in real enjoyment."[55] O my soul! Bless thou the Lord for all his benefits, even for those afflictions, which are but for a moment, and if properly improved, work out "a far more exceeding and eternal weight of glory."[56] "For the Lord loveth whom he chasteneth and scourgeth every son whom he receiveth."[57]

> O then exult that God forever reigneth;
> Clouds that obscure him hinder our perception,
> Bind us the stronger to exalt his name
> And shout louder praises.[58]

I HAD been more than eighteen months from home on my last tour. My sister Suky, or Susanna as we sometimes called her,[59] had died in my absence. I find the following notice of the event in my journal:

> October 26th, 1815
>
> The family who still lived were in good health, but Susanna was no more. I visited my sister's grave, which was dug by the side of my mother's, and thought on the ravages of death. She was a faithful seeker after truth, and I doubt not slept with her maternal parent in the arms of her saviour. "O death, where is thy sting? O grave! Where is thy victory?"[60] Thy desolating sway shall be arrested; and he who was once permitted to pass thy gloomy mansions will rob thee of thy power, and by a glorious resurrection deliver his servants and handmaidens from thy voracious jaws.

DURING MY stay among the friends, I spent one night in company with Brother John at Mr. Sarjent's, who had moved into Ohio and had become much more friendly and less disposed to blame us for the division that had taken place in the Halcyon Church.[61] He treated us with Christian kindness and the old attachment was in a measure revived.

I preached in various places, and among the rest at the house of old Mr. Bing on the Ohio. The change in him was somewhat like that in Paul, though not so sudden and miraculous. From a persecutor, he had become an advocate, to some extent, of our views. This was very grateful to my feelings of course, and the revival of our former friendship was the more sensibly felt for having been interrupted.

On the 23rd of November I left Leading Creek once more for the purpose of visiting some of the old Halcyon members who had moved to the Western Reserve.[62] Went by way of Athens and Marietta. Six miles below the latter lived my sister Sally, whose husband Ephraim Cutler, Esqr., was one of the first settlers in Ohio; was a member of the convention that formed the constitution of the state, and generally acquainted with public affairs.[63]

Made my sister a visit, had a very dull meeting in Marietta,[64] and passed northeastwardly on to one of the head eastern branches of the Muskingum, where I found an old sister of the Halcyon Church by the name of Fordice.[65] She was one of those who went through the great fast in Pennsylvania in 1807. She was a person of strong mind naturally, but through intense study on religious subjects had once been partially insane. Her experience had been very remarkable, similar in some respects to that of Amos Parkhurst. She had brought forward, at the time of our strange experience on Ten Mile, the idea that in the true kingdom of Christ male and female character as to the mind would exist, and they would be united in spirit. That there was a radical difference between the sexes intellectually as well as corporally, and that human happiness could not be perfect without the union of the twain. That the two cherubims in Solomon's Temple and a number of other types were emblematical of this truth. That this "double work," as she termed it, was the order of the universe. That the fall of man had disturbed the harmony of this arrangement, and though the distinction of sex obtained, a prolific cause of matrimonial unhappiness was the want of congeniality in the minds of the parties. That this would not be the case in the spiritual world, but each soul would be united to its own proper companion. This sentiment appears to have been entertained by Doctor Watts[66] when he wrote the following poem, inscribed to Mr. Bendish:

Why should our joys transform to pain?
Why gentle Hymen's silken chain
A plague of iron prove?
Bendish, 'tis strange the charm that binds
Millions of hands should leave their minds
At such a loose from love.

In vain I sought the wondrous cause,
Rang'd the wide fields of nature's laws,

And urged the schools in vain;
Till deep in thought, within my breast
My soul retired, and slumber dresst
A bright instructive scene.

O'er the broad land, and cross the tide,
On fancy's airy horse I ride,
Sweet rapture of the mind!
Till on the banks of Ganges' flood,
In a tall, ancient grove I stood,
For sacred use designed.

Hard by, a venerable priest,
Risen with the sun, his god, from rest,
Awoke his morning song.
Thrice he conjured the murmuring stream;
The birth of souls was all his theme
And half divine his tongue.

He sang the eternal rolling flame,
That vital mass, that still the same,
Does all our minds compose
But shaped in twice ten thousand frames;
Thence differing souls of different names,
And jarring tempers 'rose.

The mighty power that formed the mind
One mould for every two designed,
And blessed the new-born pair:
This be a match for this: he said,
Then down he sent the souls he made,
To seek them bodies here.

But parting from their warm abode,
They lost their fellows on the road,
And never joined their hands:
Ah cruel chance, and crossing fate!
Our eastern souls have dropped their mates
On Europe's barbarous lands.

Happy the youth who finds the bride
Whose birth is to his own allied,
The sweetest joy of life:
But O the crowd of wretched souls!
Fettered to minds of different moulds
And chained to eternal strife.

Thus sang the wondrous Indian bard,
My soul with vast attention heard,
While Ganges ceased to flow,
Sure then, I cried, might I but see,
That gentle nymph that twinned with me,
I might be happy too.

Some courteous angel, tell me where,
What distant lands this unknown fair,
Or distant seas detain?
Swift as the wheel of nature rolls,
I'd fly to meet, and mingle souls,
And wear the joyful chain.

A SON of Samuel and Rhoda (as we familiarly called Mr. and Mrs. Fordice)[67] had married my sister Fanny in 1807 and was still living in the neighbourhood where Brother Amos died.[68] With these old friends I tarried one day and two nights, occupying the time in conversing on bygone scenes. Passed on there through Belmont, Harrison, Jefferson, and Columbiana Counties into Trumbull, where lived a number of old friends busily engaged in pursuit of this world's goods, but cold in religion. They appeared highly gratified, however, with my visit and attentive to my public discourses. I enjoyed the company and hospitality of these friends from the 18th of December, 1815, till the first of January, 1816, when, leaving Trumbull, I bent my course toward Pennsylvania to visit Sister Fanny, whom I had not seen for seven years. After a somewhat tedious journey, arrived at her residence in that hilly region, to the no small surprise and joy of her family, consisting of herself, husband, and two children.[69]

Thus after the lapse of many years I found myself, on the fifth of January, 1816, once more near the place where so many wonderful events had transpired. Here follows another extract from the diary:

Sunday, 7th January

Spoke to a small assembly in the Halcyon meeting house from Second Timothy 1:9–10. The Halcyon cause, which nine or ten years ago flourished in this neighbourhood and produced "joy unspeakable" in the minds of its professors, is at this time extremely sunk. Almost every member in this branch, which once consisted of nearly one hundred, has either died or removed to another country, so that I now recognize but four faces in the congregation with whom I was formerly intimate. Every other branch is in nearly the same situation, and the external form of the church reminds me of desolated Jerusalem, left with scarcely "one stone upon the other." It tends also to confirm me in the opinion, which I have entertained since the first exhibition of the Urim by Brother Sarjent, that outward forms would be of little benefit in the latter-day church, but that so far as the spirit of God was felt in the soul, its fruits would be manifested outwardly. For want of this view, many have forsaken the cause altogether, and supposed the whole to be a delusion, because the outward fabric, once supported by human discipline, has been in a singular manner demolished. Others, who were once zealous, are become discouraged in consequence of the extreme trials resulting from the division (and its consequences), which took place in 1807. Others again (their number comparatively small) still preserve the faith that all these trials have been necessary; that the true doctrine of the Millennium has been measurably declared, and that notwithstanding the present darkness, the cause will finally revive and shew itself to be the work of him "who worketh all things after the counsel of his own will." O come quickly! "Hallelujah! Come Lord come!"[70]

IT WILL be difficult for the reader of this narrative to appreciate the sensations I experienced on revisiting the place where so many extraordinary scenes had occurred, and witnessing the general changes which time had wrought, both in outward circumstances and inward feelings. The remembrance of past suffering, once so cheerfully endured by a band of self-denying seekers after truth; the frustration of high hopes in the speedy approach of Messiah's latter-day kingdom; and the general apathy pervading the minds of those few remaining friends, whose faith had been so severely tried.

In the town of Washington and adjacent vicinity I spent the remaining portion of winter, and till the 20th of March working at my business and preaching wherever a door was opened, encountering much prejudice and meeting in many places but a cold reception from old acquaintances.

Leaving Pennsylvania, I returned once more to my father's house, visiting on the way my old friends at Grave Creek, Dilly's Bottom opposite; thence down the Ohio through Newport, Marietta, Warren, Newbury, Shade River Settlement, and Rutland, the residence of my brother William.

The latest date I find in my old journal is April 24th, 1816. I must therefore depend again on memory. Leaving home the same spring, I descended the Ohio in company with Mr. Alexander McGrew, who was moving with his wife from Pennsylvania to Cincinnati.[71] Having been previously acquainted, we were mutually pleased with the opportunity of travelling together. Our progress on the water was slow on account of his stopping to sell clocks. I delivered several discourses during our voyage. My friend would take no compensation for passage on board.

Resuming again my business in Kentucky and pursuing it closely (still continuing to preach on Sundays), I was enabled to deposit—on interest—in the hand of Mr. John Richardson of Lexington $1100.00; having paid off all my old debts, which had accumulated to my creditors about $80.00 interest. It was no small satisfaction to burn the notes, which had stood against me for years; and I take pleasure in stating here that my brother-in-law Ephraim Cutler, Esqr., rendered me great service by taking various kinds of loose property of me and letting my creditors have land to liquidate the claim held by men in New York, the business being transacted through the agency of Lawyer Fearing of Point Hanover, Ohio.[72]

In the fall of 1816 I was located in Newport, Kentucky. Boarded with Mr. Mayo, then postmaster, in whose agreeable family I enjoyed much satisfaction, being treated with the utmost kindness.[73] Was accommodated with shop-room for my business by Mr. David Perry.[74] Here I formed acquaintance with an excellent young man by the name of Reese Gaddis, of whom I shall speak more hereafter.[75]

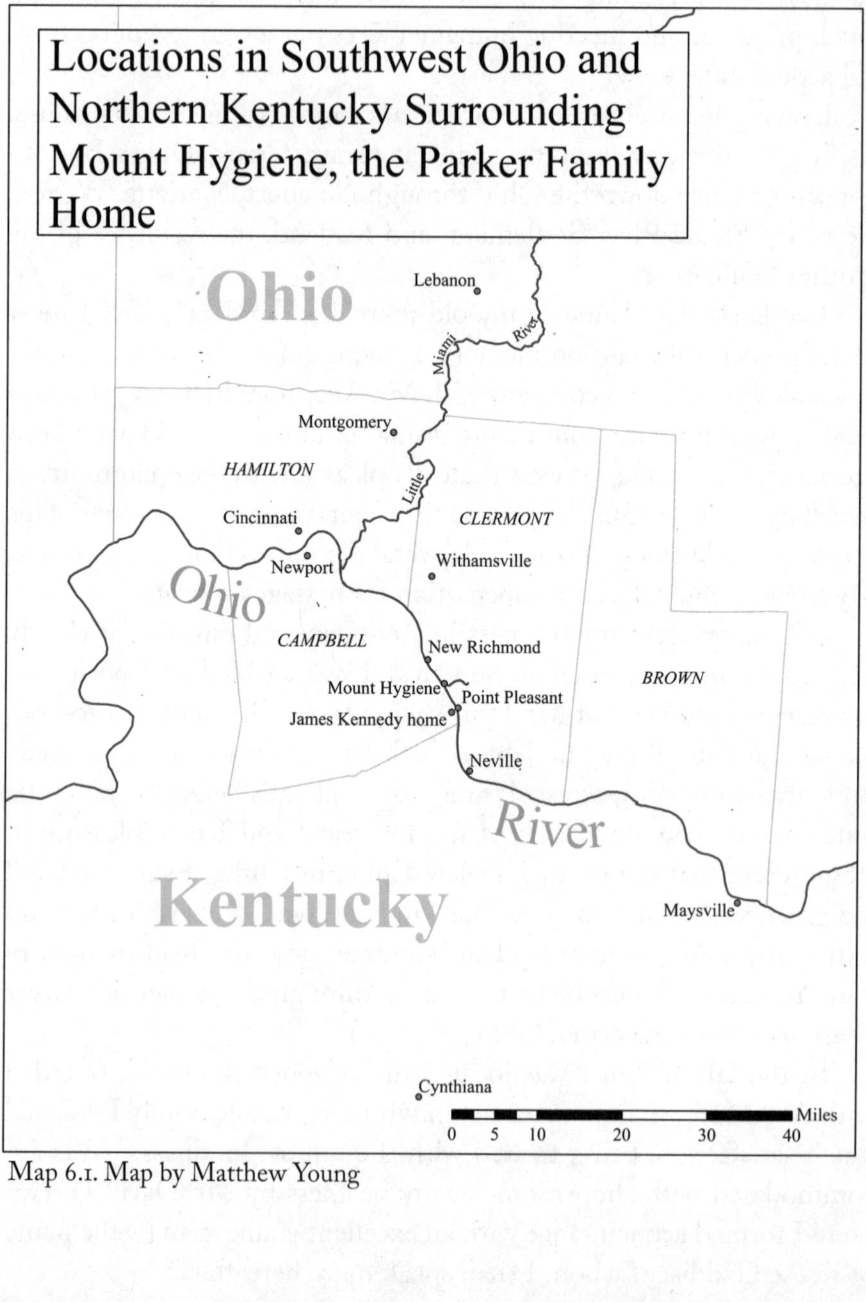

Map 6.1. Map by Matthew Young

CHAPTER 6

"My Best Earthly Friend"

WHILE RESIDING in Newport, I was invited by Col. Francis Carr of Cincinnati to preach in that city.[1] The invitation was accepted, and there being no meeting house accessible, I delivered a sermon on a butcher block in the lower market house on the ninth of October, 1816, from Second Timothy 2:15—"Study to show thyself approved unto God, a workman that needeth not to be ashamed, rightly dividing the word of truth." The congregation was large and attentive, owing somewhat, no doubt, to the novelty of the place, the speaker, and the doctrine. This was my first sermon in the Queen City.

Sometime in the month of June the previous summer, I had preached in Point Pleasant, Clermont County, Ohio, in compliance with an invitation from Mr. James Kenedy. While the congregation was collecting, I looked across the Ohio and saw a company coming down the opposite bank on their way to my meeting. Among them was a female dressed in black. That was Mrs. Ring, whom I saw then for the first time.[2] Before meeting, was introduced to her and accepted afterward an invitation from Mr. Kenedy to spend the night at his house, Mrs. Ring being also prevailed on to accompany us. The evening was spent in social converse, which was always agreeable in the family of my friend, but especially so on that occasion. Why it was the evening seemed shorter than common did not then so clearly appear. Before leaving next morning, however, I began to suspect, and felt a strong desire to spend another such.

Resuming my occupation in Newport, I found it more difficult than usual to keep my thoughts from wandering. They would be straying off up stream. I thought of the meeting at Point Pleasant, of my friend Kenedy, his agreeable household, and "last but not least" of the lady in mourning. A sort of agreeable uneasiness—better felt than told—would steal over me, associated with retrospection and anticipation.[3]

Another appointment was made at Point Pleasant, rather more difficult to fill with singleness of heart. When the time came, which was three weeks from the first, a second interview with the female stranger made the time seem much longer between the last and next appointment. Time passed rather heavily. A third meeting at Point Pleasant was succeeded by a third interview more interesting still.

As our acquaintance became more intimate, my solicitude increased in reference both to her person and history. The former at each succeeding interview became more attractive and drew strongly upon my affections and the latter called forth my warmest sympathy. Although only twenty-three years of age, she had lost a husband and child, the former having been cast away at sea between Bath in Maine and Boston in Massachusetts. The little son died in this country. She had recently come from Holowell,[4] Maine, to Ohio with a relation, and at the time of which I write was engaged in teaching school in Kentucky, near Mr. Kenedy's in Campbell County. I soon became impressed with the belief that at last providence had led me to the person intended for my companion in future life, but as one disappointment in that respect had already occurred in my eventful history, I felt that great circumspection in such an important matter was imperative, and believing that in all important concerns of life we should seek the guidance of wisdom from above, my daily prayer was that I might not be deceived by any impulse inconsistent with my duty to God.

In the school of adversity we had both been taught prudence, and my first proposal of marriage was met on her part with that diffidence becoming a virtuous woman; and which, so great a stranger as I was, ought to expect. Further acquaintance with each other's character and circumstances ultimately removing all objections, we were married the 24th of October, 1816, at the house of our friend, Mr. Kenedy, whose

Figure 6.1. Priscilla Mulloy Parker, portrait by John Frankenstein. (Photograph by Walter Colvin)

daughter Florilla stood up at the same time and was married to Mr. Thomas Gerrard; the ceremony being performed by Mr. Stephens, a Baptist preacher.[5]

So important did this transaction appear to me that on the evening of our union, after the company had assembled, I retired to the woods and prayed that if the approaching connection would prove inimical to my happiness and the glory of God that it might yet be defeated, being well assured that so important a relation as the one in view could not produce happiness without the blessing of heaven. Alas! How many are made wretched for life by disregarding the higher motives of Christian duty and yielding to the imperious influence of passion and avarice.

Not long after our marriage, while on a visit to her relations six miles back of New Richmond, Priscilla, my wife, proposed that we should go a short distance through a grove to see what she called her "cabin": a small log house where she had taught school soon after her arrival in this country. As soon as the cabin appeared in view, it brought forcibly to my mind a dream I had about three years before in Lexington, Kentucky, which I will here relate, although I have but little confidence for the most part in dreams. I have however had some, the impression of which could not be shaken off.

I dreamed in Lexington that being in a wandering and very lonesome condition, not knowing in what direction to turn for relief, I set out and traveled through the woods and came directly to a small log cabin resembling exactly the one we were visiting; and a female, dressed in black with pensive looks, coming out of it, came to me, and seemed to look upon me as one sent to relieve her distress. I thought, in my dream, that we mutually relieved each other.

The recollection of this brought to my remembrance another, which occurred many years before. It appeared to me in my dream that I was standing alone in an open plain in the night, looking at the stars. I looked toward the east, and in the direction of about forty-five degrees from the horizon I saw a star moving westward slowly. It appeared to be labouring among the clouds in distress. The impression came to my mind, while watching its motion, that it signified a woman in trouble. It struggled onward and upward, aiming, as I thought, to get to a star directly over my head. The nearer it approached, the faster it went, until the two uniting formed one, from which the light flashed over the whole hemisphere.

If any who may read this autobiography should be skilled in the science of dreams, they can put their own interpretation upon them. It may be thought very simple in me to record them here. Well, be it so. They were at any rate very pleasant dreams at the close. I know one thing: it is much more agreeable to have pleasant dreams than to have the nightmare or to be tormented with disagreeable waking realities. I wonder if anybody but myself ever dreamed that they fell asleep and had a dream, then waked up and told their dream while they were yet fast asleep dreaming:

> Say, what is sleep?
> And dreams, how passing strange!
> When action ceases and ideas range.
> Phillis Wheatley[6]

A SHORT time previous to my marriage, being on a tour of business through the counties of Clermont and Brown in the state of Ohio, and having heard that an old acquaintance by the name of David Moreton,[7] with whom I had been intimate, and at whose house near Washington, Pennsylvania, I had when a young preacher been often entertained, was settled on the Ohio River between New Richmond and Point Pleasant in Clermont County, I made it my business to call and see him. It was in the dusk of evening when I arrived at his house, situated on a beautiful elevation in sight of the river. Having just emerged from a dark valley and coming suddenly to the opening prospect, it struck me as one of the most delightful locations I had ever seen, and the impression came upon me that if it were in my power to possess such a home, I would seek no farther, but settle down for life, provided success should crown my wishes in reference to a female companion.

My old friend and his family expressed much satisfaction at my having called to see them, and a very pleasant evening was spent in conversation, recalling past scenes and comparing their former comfortable and very independent situation in Pennsylvania with their condition in a new country with but few accommodations. I soon discovered they were not very well contented, notwithstanding the beautiful site on which their house stood; that the farm was mortgaged as security for one half of the purchase money yet remaining unpaid.

Next day Mr. Moreton took me round, and after shewing the whole premises, urged me to buy him out, as he was fearful he should not be able to meet the payment. This, however, I was unable to do without involving myself too much. I had already experienced sufficient anxiety on the subject of debt, although I had not seen in all my travels a place that attracted me so much. When I declined purchasing the whole, consisting of about 160 acres, he proposed selling one half for $1500.00. I told him I would reflect on it, and so we parted. At a subsequent interview we closed the bargain, and I became paymaster to Mr. Newton, of whom he had purchased, agreeing to pay $1000 down, letting the mortgage remain as security for $500. Drawing my money from Lexington and making the first payment, I became owner of the pleasant and salubrious home, Mount Hygiene, my present residence.[8]

Arrangements for business were soon entered into with Mr. Gaddis, with whom I became acquainted in Newport. My patent right to the washing machine being confined to Kentucky, I took an agency of Mr. Abraham Sheppard of Brown County for disposing of the same in Ohio. Mr. Gaddis being a cabinet maker, we united the two branches of business and commenced to work. This was a few weeks before the consummation of my marriage, which as already stated was the 24th of October.

The term of my wife's school in Kentucky continuing several weeks later, we laboured apart during the week and saw each other only from Saturday evening till Monday morning until her school closed. Although we commenced house-keeping with but few conveniences and had a debt of $500 hanging over us, we were happy. For my part, I had become so completely worried out with a wandering life of celibacy, being then thirty-five years of age, and realizing for many years the want of a bosom companion with whom to sympathize in the joys and sorrows of life, that my heart glowed with gratitude to God, who had so ordered events as to prepare for me a home and companion so near together, both as to time and locality. I had prayed for divine

Figure 6.2. Mount Hygiene, the Parker family property near New Richmond, Ohio. This undated photo includes Clermont Academy buildings and the Parker family home. (Clermont Academy Collection, Northern Kentucky University)

direction in this great matter and have reason to believe that our union was brought about in accordance with the will of heaven.

With me, neither wealth nor beauty had been a paramount object in the choice of a wife, well knowing that neither, nor both, without something more durable could confer lasting happiness. The Lord gave me more than I asked for. He sent me one from afar, very comely and neat in person, industrious and frugal in habits, courteous and affectionate in manners, of a clear and intelligent mind;[9] and, what is better than all, pious in heart: a professor of the Christian religion and a member of the Regular Baptist Church.[10]

We were both willing to exercise mutual charity on the subject of difference in our doctrinal views, and agreed to encourage each other in following the saviour's example.[11] She was careful to throw no impediment in the way to hinder my labours in the ministry, whenever or wherever I felt it my duty to go. Those only who have had the experience can appreciate the heart-felt satisfaction enjoyed by one who has been long tossed about the world, having no settled home nor anyone to care especially for him, but at last finds himself pleasantly settled on a spot he can call his own, associated with one from whom no secret need be withheld and who, he knows, takes a deep and lively interest in whatever concerns his happiness. Such were my sensations when the appellation of old bachelor was exchanged for that of husband, and the cold formalities of a selfish world for the endearments of a loving wife.

Mr. Gaddis worked with me about one year, and returning to Newport, married and settled in that vicinity. As I had purchased the undivided half of the farm, it was held in common by Mr. Moreton and myself and rented out for several years. After the birth of our first child, James Kenedy Parker,[12] Sept. 22nd, 1817 (who was named for our friend Mr. Kenedy, from whom we had received many favours), my wife returned to Kentucky and taught school the following winter, while I pursued my mechanical business on the Little Miami; boarded at the house of Mr. Thomas Armstrong;[13] visiting home once a month. The following summer I worked five weeks in Lebanon without seeing home. These and other excursions in pursuit of business, though disagreeable, were necessary for the purpose of making money to pay the balance for my place and procure conveniences for housekeeping, and were continued for several years.

The birth of our daughter, Susanna E. Parker[14] (named for my sister Susanna Everts) tended to strengthen connubial attachment and increase parental solicitude. The following summer her mother taught school at our own residence, receiving into our family several young females from the Armstrong connection, to be boarded and taught. The supervision over these, not only in reference to learning but also their whole deportment, developed and called into exercise a degree of patience and talent in her I had chosen as a help-mate as convinced me still farther that my choice had been judicious. Several young ladies from Kentucky and New Richmond were associated with the school; and one other from Hamilton County—intelligent and amiable—by the name of Ester Haywood, who soon after died of consumption. No event of much consequence occurred that I recollect till the birth of our second son, William Tell Parker, on the 16th of May, 1821. He was named for the great Swiss patriot.[15]

My labours in the ministry were still continued wherever my worldly business might call me, either at home or abroad: pursuing the same course in that respect as before my settlement; working through the week and preaching on the Sabbath. My sentiments being little understood, and consequently much misrepresented in those days, I

Figure 6.3. The Parker family home is today a private residence. This was the second house Daniel and Priscilla lived in at Mount Hygiene. The first was destroyed by fire in 1855. (Editor's photo)

found it necessary to dwell more on doctrinal points then than has of later years been my practice. This of course excited against me nearly all the popular denominations, more especially the Methodists, whose circuit riders were active in circulating injurious reports, some of which were old stories long before worn out in Virginia and Pennsylvania.

Mr. G. C. Light,[16] a very popular preacher at that time in Clermont and adjoining counties, drew me into three public controversies, which, some of his own people said, terminated not much to his credit. He collected a number of the slanderous reproaches that were propagated against Mr. Sarjent; by publishing which on his circuit, probably thought he could make them bear against me, as I had formerly been associated with him [Sarjent] and he had then recently paid me a visit. On a subsequent visit paid me by my old brother, I informed him of Mr. Light's course, and by his request brought about a meeting between them. Mr. Light had written down a long list of charges; and reading them over one at a time, waited for the other to reply; which he did to the satisfaction I believe of all present, there being a goodly number of both his and my friends.

This interview had a salutary effect in suppressing the spirit of persecution near home. I was frequently sent for to preach in distant neighborhoods, and as I had always performed such service without demanding compensation, the larger portion of those who invited me were very willing it should be so. There were, however, a number of honourable exceptions, and occasionally my friends would make me presents sufficient in value to remunerate for the loss of time. Yet in the main such labours were given gratis, and often my temporal business was much neglected.[17]

The report having gone abroad that I did not believe in endless misery, but that all the human family would ultimately be restored, men of no religious profession, and sometimes destitute of even moral principle, would send urgent letters requesting me to come perhaps a day's journey to preach, proposing withal to make suitable returns for my trouble. In many cases I have had the mortification to find they only wanted me to oppose orthodoxy. On all such occasions I took good care to preach plain practical sermons and go home with an empty pocket, often bearing my own expenses.

I have been exceedingly tried by having drunken fellows salute me as one who believed just as they did. They were soon, however, undeceived by being told that no drunkard, as such, could enter the kingdom of God. And that they must not expect me to converse with them on the subject of religion until they were sober. Such persons, having always associated religion with the idea of preaching never-ending torment to the wicked, supposed that a minister who did not preach it must be wicked himself. Little did they think that they themselves would be among the last to practice according to that glorious doctrine which requires us to overcome evil with good.[18]

Another class of persons has often excited my astonishment and pity: professors of Christianity, who thought themselves subjects of the new birth, would say to me, "If I believed as you do, I would take my fill of sin now, for I shall be saved anyhow according to your doctrine." I was *astonished* that they should overlook the important reality of a "judgment to come" followed by a righteous retribution, and *pitied* them for desiring to sin after supposing they were converted.[19]

A third and better class, truly pious but ignorant, were sincerely afraid of me, lest my conversation might lead them into fatal error. Thus I was almost compelled to occupy an isolated position, but I enjoyed an inward consciousness that the sentiments I held were true and that the time would come when the clouds of ignorance and superstition would pass away, and the faith that all things in heaven and earth would be reconciled to God by the blood of the cross become universal.[20]

It is not to be expected that this sublime sentiment should be comprehended by those who have no higher view of salvation than to suppose it consists merely in exemption from endless punishment. Could such persons be sufficiently enlightened as to see that salvation, in its true sense, is deliverance from sin, the cause of misery both here and hereafter;[21] and in connection with this, be made to understand that for every departure from rectitude, there will inevitably follow a just retribution, either in this or the future state; they would be ashamed to bring up such foolish objections, or to betray their want of piety so far as desiring to "sin that grace might abound."[22]

We should not get out of patience, however, with those who are exceedingly zealous for the traditions of their fathers, and who will, when better informed, rejoice in the faith they might have wished to destroy. They who suppose the doctrine of Restorationism is agreeable to the carnal mind are sadly mistaken.[23] Let anyone try to "overcome evil with good" in all his intercourse with mankind, and he will soon discover his want of ability while influenced by his carnal nature, and the necessity of God's grace to help his infirmity. And what is the doctrine in question but the same that Saint Paul taught: that though sin reign unto death, grace will reign through righteousness unto eternal life, and that "where sin abounded grace did much more abound."[24] Does such a faith chime in with the corrupt heart of unregenerate man? Does it gratify the spirit of revenge to love our enemies? Or the spirit of selfishness to turn the other cheek when smitten on one? Or to give a remaining garment when one has been violently taken from you? Or to go two miles when required to go only one? Or to feed an enemy when hungry and give him drink when thirsty? And lastly to pray for them that despitefully treat and persecute you?[25] If not, then the doctrine of the final restoration of mankind from sin to holiness, and consequently from misery to happiness, is not easy to live by unless the carnal mind be changed.

The perversion of this doctrine by wicked men has deterred many honest and pious Christians from giving it that examination its importance demands; and even when subsequent investigation has removed all doubt of its truth, it remains still a question in their minds whether its public promulgation would not be like throwing "pearls before swine."[26] This difficulty I know well how to appreciate, having held it back many years for the same reason, after being convinced of its truth. It is "handling the word of God deceitfully" and not "rightly dividing the word of truth," to preach it unconnected with the importance of repentance and the new birth.[27] It would be to anticipate a final result and overlook the process which is to bring about that result. Every branch of the gospel economy should be insisted on in its proper place. As no mere theory concerning our final destiny, apart from the performance of practical duty, can prepare us for that destiny, whatever it may be, we cannot be too careful in yielding obedience to the precepts and example of Christ, who came into the world to redeem man *from* sin and not *in* it.[28]

We need not fear the consequences of spending our lives in the service of him who has the highest claim upon our hearts, our thoughts, our words and our actions. No one believing in a God will dispute his right to our entire consecration in that service. It is to be regretted that some men have espoused and publicly advocated the doctrine of final restoration who were not sufficiently careful in impressing on their hearers the great importance of practical religion, contenting themselves with establishing by argument the correctness of a theological truth.[29] This, however, should not disparage its worth. Let all seek to be confirmed in a correct faith; then add to that faith "virtue, knowledge, temperance, patience, godliness, brotherly-kindness and charity." We should then be "neither barren nor unfruitful in the knowledge of our Lord and saviour, Jesus Christ."[30]

In the fall of 1822, a severe bilious fever (terminating in my case with typhus) prostrated all the family except the two youngest for seven weeks. I was for some time delirious and my life despaired of by friends, neighbours, and our physician Doctor J. G. Rogers of New Richmond.[31] During the lowest stage of our sickness my wife was kept in a separate room, lest a knowledge of each other's case might aggravate our sufferings and prevent recovery. I was therefore in this affliction deprived of that solace which she above all others would have given, had it been in her power. Near the crisis of my complaint, Doctor Selman of Cincinnati came up to see me, but did nothing except leaving a few drops in a phial and approving Doctor Rogers's course, which was ultimately successful in restoring the family to tolerable health. To this unremitting attention and skillful management, we were, under God, indebted for our recovery.

I take pleasure in mentioning here the obligations we were under to kind neighbours for waiting upon us night and day. Mr. Moreton's family kept the little boy (W. T. P.),[32] then about eighteen months old, until we were able to take care of him. Mr. Charles M. Strader, then a young man having charge of a flouring mill in Neville, sent us by the hand of another kind friend, Mr. Josiah Broadwell, a barrel of flour at a time when our supply of provision was nearly exhausted. Also, Mr. Jacob Broadwell, Sr., living on the Little Miami sixteen miles off, hearing of our distress, went round with his wagon and collected from friends in the country and Cincinnati a large supply of necessaries and brought them to us.[33] We had reason to remember with gratitude also Mr. and Mrs. Cyrus Coffin, who visited us; and interested other friends in the city (among whom was the family of Mr. Richard L. Coleman),[34] who sent us medicines, groceries and other comforts. With these kind friends I had formed a partial acquaintance previously and had preached amongst them both in the city and country, and they had become favourable to my theological views.

On the 12th of September, 1823, our third son, Charles Coleman Parker,[35] was born; and called for a son of Richard Coleman above mentioned. He was so small at birth that a common sized teacup would cover his whole face, and his weight was between five and six pounds. His mother had been subjected to much care and labour in consequence of my still remaining debilitated for a long time after our severe sickness. In the spring of 1824, not being able to work myself, I rented the place to my brother in law Thomas Mulloy,[36] who had some years before come from Maine with his parents and one sister, and to whom we had been under great obligations during our late affliction for his constant and attentive nursing. My nervous system had undergone a great shock, and I was consequently low-spirited. My dear wife did all that a woman could do to comfort me and sustain the family.

Hoping that a change of residence might be beneficial, I accepted an offer made by Mr. William Armstrong, at the Little Miami, of a house and garden rent free; and in the month of March that year, he and his brothers sent up a flatboat and moved us down gratis.[37] In the midst of these generous friends we lived one year, during which time my companion taught school to support the family, still remaining myself unable to work much; but traveled and preached what I could. By this time I had formed acquaintance in the town of Montgomery, fourteen miles back of Cincinnati.[38] It being situated in a very healthy neighbourhood, our friends advised us to move there for the purpose of my recovery. Here again we met with great kindness. The citizens uniting, sent wagons and moved us thither free of cost, and supplied us with firewood during our residence there, which was one year, without charge. In this village our fourth son, Daniel M. Parker,[39] was born the 23rd of November, 1825: the first name for me, the middle one for his maternal grandfather, [Mulloy].[40] The salubrity of this location contributed to the speedy restoration of my strength. At the expiration of one year, the same kind neighbours sent us free of cost to Cincinnati, where we lived six months in the lower part, on Mill Street near a large mound, then standing but now demolished.[41] We rented of, and lived in a part of the same house with, Mr. Edward Powers, whose family was very agreeable.

That summer, my companion was sorely afflicted and brought to all appearance near to death. Her Christian resignation under this affliction rendered her still more dear to me, and the apprehension that she would be taken away, leaving me bereaved of an affectionate wife, in charge of a young and helpless family of children, induced such feelings as I had never before experienced, and now have no adequate words to express. After suffering about two months, it pleased the Lord to restore her once more to an anxious and dependent family. "Bless the Lord! O my soul, for all his benefits."[42]

Shortly after our removal to the city, I made a visit to Leading Creek, to see once more my aged father, then in his eightieth year. Both our meeting and parting were very affecting, as we had reason to think it would be our last interview on earth; as indeed it was, for he died the next November, 1826.[43]

I here mention for the first time in this narrative my worthy and staid friend A. H. Ernst of Cincinnati,[44] although we had been acquainted several years, and I had already experienced many evidences of his kindness, as well as that of his worthy companion. These generous friends were very attentive to my wife in her sickness, furnishing comforts of various kinds, verifying the truth that "a friend in need is a friend indeed."

In the month of September, 1826, we returned again to our own home. On our arrival we found my wife's brother and his wife very sick. They were obliged to send their only child abroad to be nursed. The bilious fever that fall was uncommonly severe throughout the neighborhood and pretty general all along the river. My own family, however, escaped and were enabled to make some little return for their attention to us. That was the most unhealthy season we ever experienced at our residence. The following autumn was somewhat sickly, and my wife, daughter, and son William were prostrated for a time.

A fifth son was born the 17th of March, 1828, whom we named Mason Doan Parker[45] in remembrance of Doctor Mason of Cincinnati and Doctor Doan of Withamsville,[46] both intimate friends who had rendered us gratuitous services in the line of their profession. The latter visited me while sick, both at my own house and while living on the Miami; also my wife in her dangerous sickness at Cincinnati, but would never take pay, saying that as I demanded no pay for preaching he would demand none for doctoring.

Not all who professed to value my ministerial services were this considerate. Many a time have I traveled ten or fifteen miles to preach funerals without receiving even thanks, which was no doubt better for my spiritual interest, inasmuch as rich rewards for preaching tend to make a minister worldly minded and destroy his independence. Had worldly gain been my object in becoming a public speaker, the ministry would have been the last profession for me to adopt, and especially the promulgation of so unpopular a doctrine as that of the final restoration.

No man need expect much favour from the world who has the temerity to oppose popular opinion and fearlessly publish his own honest convictions of truth and duty. He may lay out his accounts for a full share of persecution and a very small amount of pecuniary gain. He may have, however, at the same time, an inward satisfaction, unknown to others, in prospectively contemplating the triumph of true principles over error, ignorance, and prejudice.

> Truths would you teach, or save a sinking land?
> All fear, none aid you, and few will understand.
> Painful preeminence! yourself to view,
> Above life's weakness, and its comforts too.[47]

BEING SETTLED once more at our own pleasant home, restored again to health, and, by strict economy, released from the embarrassment of debt, my time was divided between farming, shop work, and preaching. The latter necessarily called me away from home. This threw a great burden upon my wife, who was not only willing I should go, but always anxious that my labours might be blessed, and therefore took upon herself cheerfully the care of an increasing family; sparing no pains to

Figure 6.4. James K. Parker, the first child of Daniel and Priscilla, at about age thirty. He was the principal teacher at the Parkers' school, Clermont Academy. (Clermont Academy Collection, Northern Kentucky University)

instruct the children in everything appertaining to their physical, intellectual, moral, and religious interest. And it is but justice to her for me to acknowledge that in all these respects her influence has tended more than mine toward fitting them for the duties of life. This concession is most cheerfully made, with the prayer that her faithful labours, if not rewarded in this life, will be in the world to come.[48]

How often has my past experience constrained me to acknowledge an overruling providence in carrying me through such varied scenes as have fallen to my lot, and in providing comforts for so unworthy a pensioner upon the bounty of heaven! I have not always been sufficiently grateful, either to my maker or to her, who has ever been my best earthly friend, as well as the most affectionate and devoted mother to my children, who are therefore under the strongest obligations of filial love and obedience to her. Such a benefactor they will seek in vain to find when released from a mother's care and obliged to buffet the storms of life unaided by maternal protection, although they can never deviate so far from virtue as not to be objects of a mother's love and a mother's prayers. Thoughtless and wayward as children are apt to be while young, the time will come when they will remember with regret past acts of disobedience, and with thankfulness parental restraint and admonition.

This I also know from experience, having had one of the best mothers myself; and am well assured that the early impressions made by her on my mind in childhood have never been entirely erased. Had those impressions been vicious instead of being virtuous, there is no knowing but that I should at this day be more fit for the gallows than the pulpit. I desire that my children, when reading this sketch of their father's life, may reflect on the debt of gratitude they owe to her who has suffered so much for their comfort and happiness. The greatness of this debt they will never realize until they become parents themselves. Could this subject press with the same weight upon their minds now as it will then, they would strive to make suitable returns while in their power, avoiding every act which would lay a foundation of future repentance. That the Lord may help them so to do is my most humble and sincere prayer.

And I also pray that we as parents may duly appreciate the blessing of having children who have not been insensible to the claims of parental authority, nor shewn a disposition, thus far, to pursue a vicious course. Few parents, I imagine, have had more comfort with their children than we, not only in respect of their moral conduct, but also because all their lives are still spared, with an uncommon degree of health: the effect no doubt, in a good degree, of temperate habits with regular exercise and rest. We cannot be too thankful for these mercies:

that we have not been made to lament over the heartbreaking spectacle of a drunken, profane, dissipated child. I would sooner follow them all to the grave than see them in the haunts of debauchery; sooner, indeed, would I see them destitute of intellectual refinement than of moral and religious principle. If they remain ignorant of all these, it will be their own fault. May the Lord prevent such a misfortune to them and their parents.[49]

Thousands of youth have been ruined by early vicious associations, left in a state of orphanage without guardians perhaps; or having them [and], regardless of their advice and example, yielding to the seductions of those who would rob them of virtue and everything that would render them respectable and happy.[50] O! What a heartrending sight! To behold one's own offspring, for whom so much solicitude had been felt, so many prayers ascended, so much care bestowed; or the offspring of others, long since numbered with the dead, walking in the way that leads to misery, turning a deaf ear to wholesome instruction and listening to the deceptive allurements of debasing pleasures, until their physical and intellectual constitutions are destroyed and ending in a premature death. May our Heavenly Father deliver me and mine from such a destiny, and enable us to fulfill the mutual obligations resting upon us now "while it is called today."[51]

Another son was born the 27th of January, 1831, and named Eben Armstrong Parker,[52] for Eben Colson, a nephew of my wife,[53] and our friends the Armstrongs, from whom we had received many favours. Having now six sons and but one daughter, and finding it difficult, often, to procure female help, my being much from home, it became necessary to instruct the boys in those branches of domestic labour usually performed by the other sex. This of course increased the care and responsibilities of their mother and made her task very severe.[54] Her health also, for the most, was not good. She was subject to that distressing complaint, the asthma, which frequently prevented her from sleeping in bed for weeks: sitting up all night in an arm chair, and yet never remitting the performance of daily duties when within her power. No one, I think, ever made more personal sacrifices for the benefit of others, either as a wife or mother, and to withhold this testimony on my part would be unpardonable.

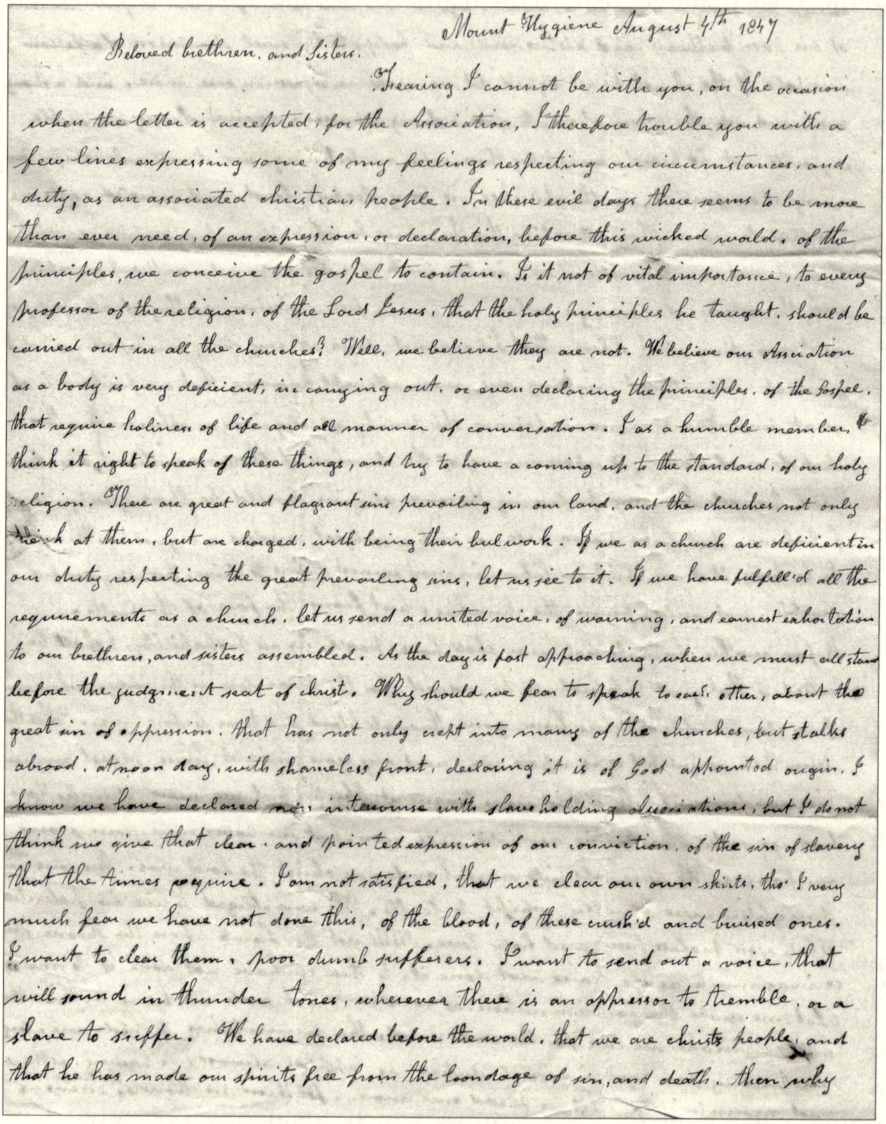

Mount Hygiene August 4th 1847

Beloved brethren. and Sisters.

Fearing I cannot be with you, on the occasion when the letter is accepted, for the Association, I therefore trouble you with a few lines expressing some of my feelings respecting our circumstances. and duty, as an associated christian people. In these evil days there seems to be more than ever need, of an expression, or declaration, before this wicked world, of the principles, we conceive the gospel to contain. Is it not of vital importance, to every professor of the religion, of the Lord Jesus, that the holy principles he taught, should be carried out in all the churches? Well, we believe they are not. We believe our Association as a body is very deficient, in carrying out, or even declaring the principles, of the Gospel, that require holiness of life and all manner of conversation. I as a humble member, think it right to speak of these things, and try to have a coming up to the standard, of our holy religion. There are great and flagrant sins prevailing in our land, and the churches not only wink at them, but are charged, with being their bulwork. If we as a church are deficient in our duty respecting the great prevailing sins, let us see to it. If we have fulfill'd all the requirements as a church, let us send a united voice, of warning, and earnest exhortation to our brethren, and sisters assembled. As the day is fast approaching, when we must all stand before the judgment seat of christ. Why should we fear to speak to each other, about the great sin of oppression. that has not only crept into many of the churches, but stalks abroad, at noon day, with shameless front, declaring it is of God appointed origin. I know we have declared non intercourse with slaveholding associations, but I do not think we give that clear and pointed expression of our conviction, of the sin of slavery that the times require. I am not satisfied, that we clear our own skirts, tho' I very much fear we have not done this, of the blood, of these crush'd and bruised ones. I want to clear them, poor dumb sufferers. I want to send out a voice, that will sound in thunder tones, wherever there is an oppressor to tremble, or a slave to suffer. We have declared before the world, that we are christs people, and that he has made our spirits free from the bondage of sin, and death. then why

Figure 7.1. "I want to send out a voice that will sound in thunder tones, wherever there is an oppressor to tremble or slave to suffer," writes Priscilla Parker in 1847 on the first page of her letter to Ten Mile Baptist Church, where she was a member, calling on them to take a stronger stand against slavery. (Clermont Academy Collection, Northern Kentucky University)

CHAPTER 7

"A Great and Growing Evil"

THE SUBJECT of American slavery as a great and growing evil had occupied my thoughts for many years, and I was anxious that some event in providence might occur which would put it in my power to aid in its removal, believing that if let alone, it would prove the cause of our national overthrow.

I espoused with zeal the colonization enterprise: volunteered my services to the parent society as a lecturer—so far as my domestic duties would admit—without compensation, with the hope that it would lead to emancipation in this country. This was my great aim, and not the getting rid of colored people merely.[1] I was, like many others in the free states, simple enough to believe that all its advocates were actuated with the same motive, but after giving a considerable portion of my time in delivering addresses and collecting money for two years, I was undeceived by conversing with slaveholders in Kentucky who, I found by going among them, were making no move (except in a few instances) to send off their slaves. I asked them for an explanation. They laughed at me and said that I did not understand it as they did, and that when the agent of the Kentucky state society (who was then receiving $600 per annum, while I was lecturing for nothing) came along, he told them that he did not wish to take their servants from them, but the *free blacks* were a nuisance; that they made the slaves uneasy by talking to them of freedom, thereby not only making the slave's condition worse, but that of the master more dangerous.[2]

This open confession from their own mouths satisfied me that, whatever benefits might flow from colonization in Africa, it was espoused and supported by the greater part of slaveholders as a proslavery, and not an antislavery, enterprise. I had also noticed in the *African Repository*, which was sent to me monthly from Washington City, that nearly all the speeches of southern men, whether statesmen or churchmen, were full of the same kind of arguments, urged on and backed up by appeals to self-interest and prejudice against color; together with the supposed impossibility of elevating the colored race here.[3]

Another fact, which tended still farther to open my eyes (and which I might have seen sooner but for want of reflection), was that the first three presidents of the parent society were slaveholders, viz.: Bushrod Washington, James Madison, and Henry Clay; neither of whom, if I was rightly informed, emancipated their slaves even by expatriation (their favorite scheme), much less by giving them freedom in their native country; but either held them still in bondage, sold, or gave them away.[4] It appeared to me that of all colonizationists, their presidents should set the example by placing their unfortunate victims where only, according to their own profession, the blacks could enjoy civil and religious rights.[5]

Upon a careful examination of the whole subject, disgusted with the selfishness of its most preeminent friends, and satisfied that colonization could never be a remedy for slavery in this country, as in twenty years it removed only 5000 to Africa, while the annual increase in the United States was at least 70,000, I gave up the cause, after serving it—as before stated—two years by lecturing among the different denominations and collecting, in small sums, about $80.00, which was sent to Washington and receipted for.

Still, I did not then, nor do I now, oppose colonization as such, provided all parties act perfectly free, in full view of all the consequences, risks, and benefits; and would be glad if the whole western coast of Africa were studded with republican colonies from the Straits of Gibraltar to the Cape of Good Hope.[6] But to make it a condition of freedom to the colored people, in this professedly free country, by saying to them if you do not go home to Africa, "the land of your forefathers," you and your posterity shall be perpetual slaves, I do most heartily abominate. Suppose the same alternative were offered to us, that we

Figure 7.2. Like many other opponents of slavery, Daniel Parker at first supported and later opposed the work of the American Colonization Society. He decided the society was less concerned with ending slavery than with ridding the country of free Blacks. This certificate of membership is signed by former US president James Madison, who was president of the ACS from 1833 to 1836. (McDonough Project, Skillman Library at Lafayette College, https://exhibits.lafayette.edu)

should not be free unless we went to Europe, whence our forefathers came from? Apply the golden rule to it, and the question is answered.[7]

"Ah but the blacks are a degraded race," say they, "and more than that, they are better off in slavery than if they were free, because they have no care, only to do what they are bid, and as to their being educated, it would only make them more unhappy. Nor do they care for wages, so they get plenty to eat with comfortable clothes and shelter; and as to being married, they enjoy much more freedom without;[8] and another thing, it is a greater accommodation to white *gentlemen* (?) the way it is; and also tends to secure white ladies from insult, with many other advantages too 'tedious to mention.' In fine, they are better off than their masters."[9]

Now, if all this be true, and the old adage be also true, that "it is a poor mule that won't work both ways," the masters better change conditions, for everybody likes to be well off.[10] And even if it should set a little hard on the white adults of the present day, the rising generation might be so brought up by beginning with the babies, that they would in time be as well off as slaves! "O! Horrid!"[11]

Meanwhile, the abolition societies began to spring up, first at the east and then at the west. These advocated immediate emancipation, on the soil, as the natural and inalienable right of the slaves; urged the doctrine of human rights contained in our Declaration of Independence and the claims of the gospel upon all mankind, irrespective of color or condition; depicted in glowing language the horrors of slavery with a zeal corresponding to the magnitude and importance of the subject; repudiated worldly expediency, and insisted on the duty of adhering to correct principle, whatever might be the consequences.[12]

The advocates of this radical course were, at first, few in number, but rapidly increased, and great numbers, like myself, forsook the Colonization Society before they were quite ready to join the other.[13] Persecution raged. Rumors of treason, servile insurrection, foreign intrigue, and amalgamation were circulated in every direction. All kinds of misrepresentation were afloat; and mobs raised to break up meetings and printing presses.[14] This last attempt to stop the work put an end to my neutrality, and I became associated with the abolition movement,[15] having some time before espoused and publicly advocated the cause of temperance.[16]

THE LIBERATOR.

VOL. I.] WILLIAM LLOYD GARRISON AND ISAAC KNAPP, PUBLISHERS. [NO. 17.

BOSTON, MASSACHUSETTS.] OUR COUNTRY IS THE WORLD—OUR COUNTRYMEN ARE MANKIND. [SATURDAY, APRIL 23, 1831.

Figure 7.3. The *Liberator*, published by William Lloyd Garrison, was the most recognized publication of the radical abolitionist movement, which Daniel Parker joined after parting with the American Colonization Society. The newspaper adopted this masthead its first year of publication. (The Liberator Files, http://theliberatorfiles.com)

Both of these enterprises, and my so called heretical opinions on theology, made me as unpopular as my worst opposer could wish, and mortified in no small degree the greater part of my professed friends. They remonstrated and said my influence would be ruined and wondered at my imprudence. Satisfied, however, that I was right, and desirous that they might see the importance of these great moral movements, I proposed to hold meetings in the several neighbourhoods where I had been in the habit of preaching, to explain and give reasons for my course; but met with little encouragement, and frequently was threatened with abuse if I attempted to hold a meeting, especially for the defense of abolition; but if I would only preach restoration to them, my congregations would be as large as ever.[17]

I told them that both the antislavery and temperance enterprise, with every other kindred cause, such as those for the encouragement of missions, Sunday schools, circulation of Bibles, and peace societies, were only so many instrumentalities for accomplishing the great work of *restoration*; that they were only nominal Restorationists who stood opposed to the *practical* redemption of all men from every possible wrong condition; that the mere theoretical assent to the best doctrine in the world would only augment the condemnation of those who held "the truth in unrighteousness."[18] Apart from the duty and inward satisfaction of taking such a stand, it had the effect of shaking off a large number of what I denominated "out-side friends," such as "Talkative" in *Pilgrim's Progress*, or those who like religion "when it went in silver slippers," but in heart were "enemies of the cross of Christ."[19]

On the third of March, 1837, we were made to rejoice at the birth of another daughter, whom we named Mary Priscilla—the first for my mother, and the last for her own mother and maternal grandmother. I need not attempt to express how welcome was the little stranger, whose visit was rather unexpected.[20] This event was followed by the marriage of her sister Susanna to Mr. Thomas Donaldson, on the 31st day of August the same year.[21] He had been a merchant in New Richmond, lost a former wife and three children there, and soon after his connection with our family, bought a farm one half a mile below us and was located to the satisfaction of all parties. To the person, character, and circumstances of Mr. Donaldson no objection could be made, and yet it was hard for us to give up our almost only daughter. His settling so near us was, we have reason to think, as much on our account as his own, and this endeared him to us so much the more. His sentiments on the subject of slavery were congenial with our own. He was one of the foremost and most generous supporters of the abolition cause in the neighbourhood at a time when its advocation[22] exposed one to reproach if not to personal danger, the mob spirit being in the ascendant almost everywhere.

When the first antislavery paper (the *Philanthropist*) was started in New Richmond, such was the general feeling among the citizens and surrounding country people that I was quite dubious whether it would be prudent to subscribe for it, but my wife, whose benevolence overcame my caution, going with me to the office, proposed that if I would pay one dollar, she would the other for the paper one year. I could not with a good face decline, although I was afraid it was going to be a terrible paper from what I had heard.[23] When the first number came, it was directed in my wife's name at her request; was full of good sense and couched in very acceptable language; so that in this case as in many others, I found "it is not good for man to be alone." Those who, like me, have really "help meets" would do well not to slight their advice.[24]

Two different presses that issued the *Philanthropist* in Cincinnati were afterward destroyed by mobs,[25] as were also several others of the same character in other places. The name "abolitionist" was associated in the minds of a majority with almost everything odious, while at the same time they were principally the most pious, self-sacrificing men and women[26] in the country; would not retaliate abuse with violence, though assailed often with brickbats and rotten eggs.[27]

Colonization and abolition were soon fairly at issue. The former was very popular, both in the free and slave states. Its tendency was to encourage prejudice against the colored race, and nourish a false hope that slavery would be removed by removing the slaves. The latter was advocated on the ground that slavery, being a violation of natural and divine law, should be done away with by ceasing to violate those laws, and changing the slave's character and condition instead of his location. The former was more selfish; the latter more just.[28]

The Philanthropist.

PUBLISHED BY THE EXECUTIVE COMMITTEE OF THE OHIO STATE ANTI-SLAVERY SOCIETY.

VOLUME I. NO. 48. NEW SERIES. CINCINNATI, TUESDAY, DECEMBER 18, 1838. WHOLE NO. 147.

Figure 7.4. The Parkers were among the first subscribers to Ohio's best-known abolitionist newspaper, the *Philanthropist*, published by James G. Birney. The first issue was published in New Richmond, near the Parkers' home. The newspaper later moved its press to Cincinnati, where it was twice attacked by mobs, but continued to publish. (Ohio History Connection)

My companion had laboured very hard, not only to support the family but to educate the children. The common school in our vicinity being of an inferior grade, the older portion of our sons approaching manhood, and not being able to send them abroad for instruction, we became very anxious on the subject of their education. At length, after long deliberation, we concluded to erect an academy on our own place: let our oldest son go to college and, being prepared to teach the rest, become the principal in our own institution.[29]

This course was accordingly pursued. Our son James went two sessions to South Hanover College, Indiana, and one to Mr. Lang's academy near Cincinnati.[30] In the meantime, by hard work and perseverance, a house was built on our own premises at our own expense, and a high school was put in operation. It soon attracted notice and succeeded better than we anticipated. A prospect was thus opened for the improvement of our own children, those in the neighbourhood, and others from abroad—put under our care to be boarded and taught. Such

Figure 7.5. Clermont Academy buildings. (Clermont Academy Collection, Northern Kentucky University)

is the history, so far, of Clermont Academy: a real independent family concern—without charter, trustees, or support from public funds.

My son, being a professor of religion and a member of the Baptist Church with his mother, introduced his school with prayer, reading the scriptures and sometimes singing. He repudiated corporeal punishment, and governed more by appeals to the understanding and conscience than to the principle of fear. Both sexes were taught in the same apartment.[31] A Lyceum was soon established, holding its meetings once a week for the purpose of improving the members in composition and debate. A yearly course consisted of two sessions, five months each, with an examination and exhibition at the close of each session. Addresses, declamations, and music drew together at such times large crowds. Literary gentlemen were invited to deliver occasional lectures on subjects connected with scientific and moral improvement, and a general invitation extended to preachers of all denominations in good standing to preach in the Academy whenever it suited them. This tended to allay sectarian prejudice and promote Christian charity.

I studiously abstained from inculcating my peculiar sentiments on theology in the minds of young persons entrusted to our guardianship,

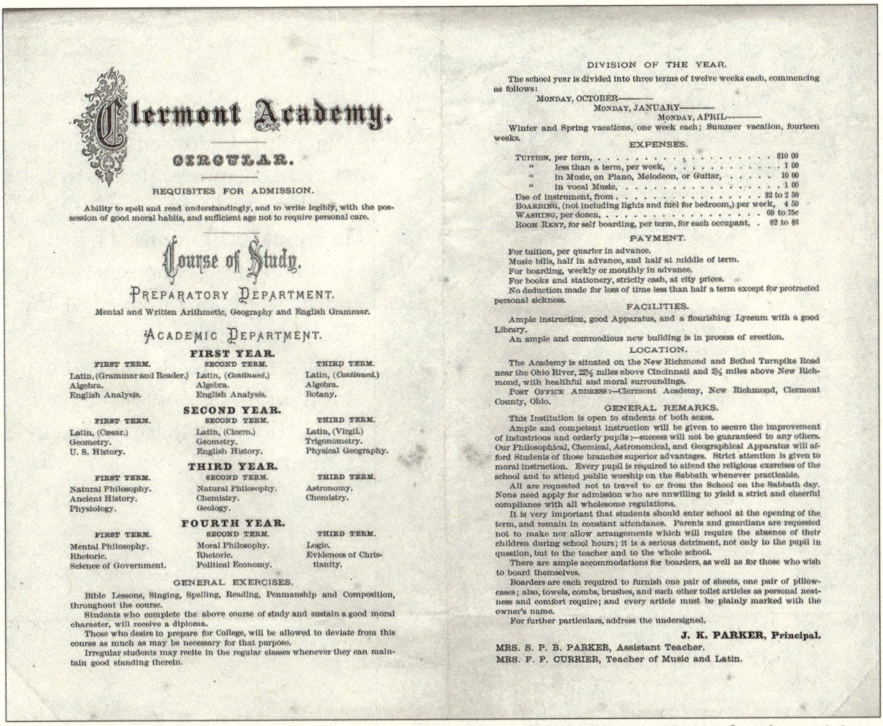

Clermont Academy.

CIRCULAR.

REQUISITES FOR ADMISSION.

Ability to spell and read understandingly, and to write legibly, with the possession of good moral habits, and sufficient age not to require personal care.

Course of Study.

PREPARATORY DEPARTMENT.

Mental and Written Arithmetic, Geography and English Grammar.

ACADEMIC DEPARTMENT.

FIRST YEAR.

FIRST TERM.	SECOND TERM.	THIRD TERM.
Latin, (Grammar and Reader.)	Latin, (*Continued.*)	Latin, (*Continued.*)
Algebra.	Algebra.	Algebra.
English Analysis.	English Analysis.	Botany.

SECOND YEAR.

FIRST TERM.	SECOND TERM.	THIRD TERM.
Latin, (Cæsar.)	Latin, (Cicero.)	Latin, (Virgil.)
Geometry.	Geometry.	Trigonometry.
U. S. History.	English History.	Physical Geography.

THIRD YEAR.

FIRST TERM.	SECOND TERM.	THIRD TERM.
Natural Philosophy.	Natural Philosophy.	Astronomy.
Ancient History.	Chemistry.	Chemistry.
Physiology.	Geology.	

FOURTH YEAR.

FIRST TERM.	SECOND TERM.	THIRD TERM.
Mental Philosophy.	Moral Philosophy.	Logic.
Rhetoric.	Rhetoric.	Evidences of Christianity.
Science of Government.	Political Economy.	

GENERAL EXERCISES.

Bible Lessons, Singing, Spelling, Reading, Penmanship and Composition, throughout the course.

Students who complete the above course of study and sustain a good moral character, will receive a diploma.

Those who desire to prepare for College, will be allowed to deviate from this course as much as may be necessary for that purpose.

Irregular students may recite in the regular classes whenever they can maintain good standing therein.

DIVISION OF THE YEAR.

The school year is divided into three terms of twelve weeks each, commencing as follows:

MONDAY, OCTOBER———
MONDAY, JANUARY———
MONDAY, APRIL———

Winter and Spring vacations, one week each; Summer vacation, fourteen weeks.

EXPENSES.

TUITION, per term,	$10 00
" less than a term, per week,	1 00
" in Music, on Piano, Melodeon, or Guitar,	10 00
" in vocal Music,	1 00
Use of instrument, from	$2 to 2 50
BOARDING, (not including lights and fuel for bedroom,) per week,	4 50
WASHING, per dozen,	60 to 75c
ROOM RENT, for self boarding, per term, for each occupant,	$2 to $3

PAYMENT.

For tuition, per quarter in advance.

Music bills, half in advance, and half at middle of term.

For boarding, weekly or monthly in advance.

For books and stationery, strictly cash, at city prices.

No deduction made for loss of time less than half a term except for protracted personal sickness.

FACILITIES.

Ample instruction, good Apparatus, and a flourishing Lyceum with a good Library.

An ample and commodious new building is in process of erection.

LOCATION.

The Academy is situated on the New Richmond and Bethel Turnpike Road near the Ohio River, 22¾ miles above Cincinnati and 2¾ miles above New Richmond, with healthful and moral surroundings.

POST OFFICE ADDRESS:—Clermont Academy, New Richmond, Clermont County, Ohio.

GENERAL REMARKS.

This Institution is open to students of both sexes.

Ample and competent instruction will be given to secure the improvement of industrious and orderly pupils;—success will not be guaranteed to any others. Our Philosophical, Chemical, Astronomical, and Geographical Apparatus will afford Students of those branches superior advantages. Strict attention is given to moral instruction. Every pupil is required to attend the religious exercises of the school and to attend public worship on the Sabbath whenever practicable.

All are requested not to travel to or from the School on the Sabbath day. None need apply for admission who are unwilling to yield a strict and cheerful compliance with all wholesome regulations.

It is very important that students should enter school at the opening of the term, and remain in constant attendance. Parents and guardians are requested not to make nor allow arrangements which will require the absence of their children during school hours; it is a serious detriment, not only to the pupil in question, but to the teacher and to the whole school.

There are ample accommodations for boarders, as well as for those who wish to board themselves.

Boarders are each required to furnish one pair of sheets, one pair of pillow-cases; also, towels, combs, brushes, and such other toilet articles as personal neatness and comfort require; and every article must be plainly marked with the owner's name.

For further particulars, address the undersigned.

J. K. PARKER, Principal.

MRS. S. P. B. PARKER, Assistant Teacher.

MRS. F. P. CURRIER, Teacher of Music and Latin.

Figure 7.6. Clermont Academy admission requirements, curriculum, faculty, tuition and expenses, and even a packing list were all contained on a two-page, occasionally revised, printed circular. This edition, printed after 1867, hardly differs from those printed decades earlier. (Clermont Academy Collection, Northern Kentucky University)

lest their parents might think I took advantage of my position. Unless particularly requested, I seldom said anything on the subject of Restorationism in my own family. Yet the faith in so great and glorious a result was to me a source of much consolation. Some thought very strange of this reserve, but in my judgment it was the more prudent course, and would be the most likely to satisfy our patrons. We were careful, however, to impress upon the minds of those under our care the importance of moral and religious obligation.[32] My wife spared no pains in this respect, and also in forwarding the studies of those living with us.[33]

I cannot express the feelings of gratitude that sprang up in my heart at the time we commenced our school. From being a wandering old bachelor, with no permanent home and no one to care especially

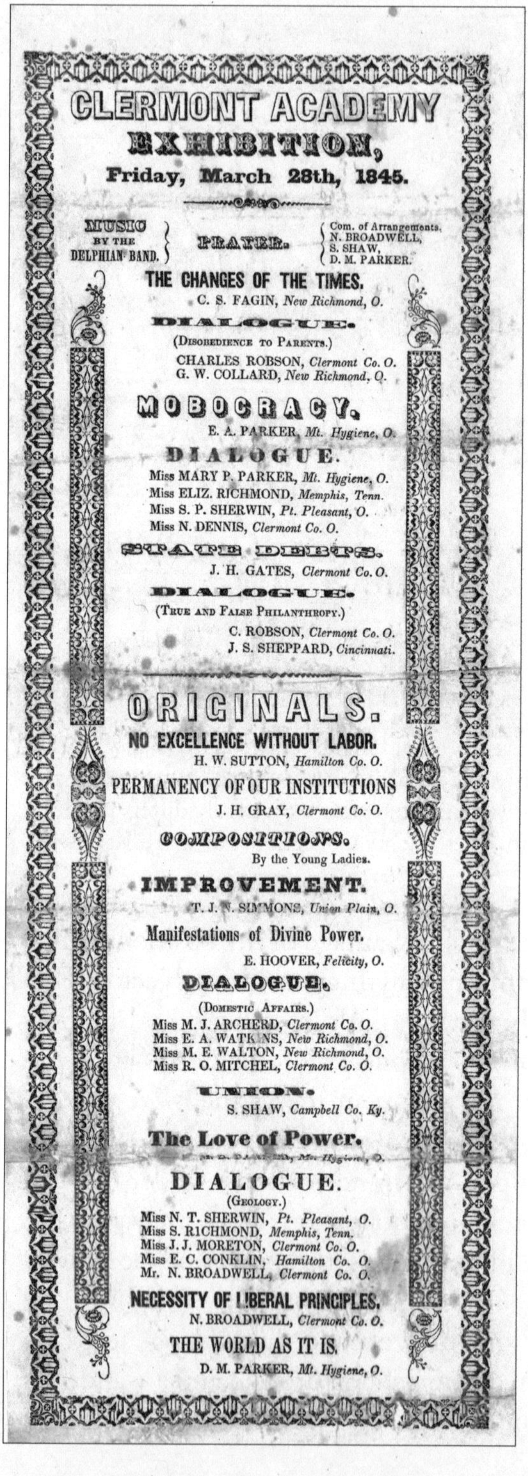

CLERMONT ACADEMY
EXHIBITION,
Friday, March 28th, 1845.

MUSIC BY THE DELPHIAN BAND.
PRAYER.
Com. of Arrangements. N. BROADWELL, S. SHAW, D. M. PARKER.

THE CHANGES OF THE TIMES.
C. S. FAGIN, *New Richmond, O.*

DIALOGUE.
(Disobedience to Parents.)
CHARLES ROBSON, *Clermont Co. O.*
G. W. COLLARD, *New Richmond, O.*

MOBOCRACY.
E. A. PARKER, *Mt. Hygiene, O.*

DIALOGUE.
Miss MARY P. PARKER, *Mt. Hygiene, O.*
Miss ELIZ. RICHMOND, *Memphis, Tenn.*
Miss S. P. SHERWIN, *Pt. Pleasant, O.*
Miss N. DENNIS, *Clermont Co. O.*

STATE DEBTS.
J. H. GATES, *Clermont Co. O.*

DIALOGUE.
(True and False Philanthropy.)
C. ROBSON, *Clermont Co. O.*
J. S. SHEPPARD, *Cincinnati.*

ORIGINALS.

NO EXCELLENCE WITHOUT LABOR.
H. W. SUTTON, *Hamilton Co. O.*

PERMANENCY OF OUR INSTITUTIONS
J. H. GRAY, *Clermont Co. O.*

COMPOSITIONS.
By the Young Ladies.

IMPROVEMENT.
T. J. N. SIMMONS, *Union Plain, O.*

Manifestations of Divine Power.
E. HOOVER, *Felicity, O.*

DIALOGUE.
(Domestic Affairs.)
Miss M. J. ARCHERD, *Clermont Co. O.*
Miss E. A. WATKINS, *New Richmond, O.*
Miss M. E. WALTON, *New Richmond, O.*
Miss R. O. MITCHEL, *Clermont Co. O.*

UNION.
S. SHAW, *Campbell Co. Ky.*

The Love of Power.
[illegible]

DIALOGUE.
(Geology.)
Miss N. T. SHERWIN, *Pt. Pleasant, O.*
Miss S. RICHMOND, *Memphis, Tenn.*
Miss J. J. MORETON, *Clermont Co. O.*
Miss E. C. CONKLIN, *Hamilton Co. O.*
Mr. N. BROADWELL, *Clermont Co. O.*

NECESSITY OF LIBERAL PRINCIPLES.
N. BROADWELL, *Clermont Co. O.*

THE WORLD AS IT IS.
D. M. PARKER, *Mt. Hygiene, O.*

Figure 7.7. Clermont Academy students demonstrated their speaking and writing abilities in annual exhibitions. This program of 1845 announces that music would be provided by the Delphian Band, which included James K. Parker and his brothers. (Clermont Academy Collection, Northern Kentucky University)

Figure 7.8. Clermont Academy classroom with two unidentified students. A banner contains the Latin slogan *nulla dies sine linea* (no day without a line), an exhortation to diligence from Pliny the Elder. (Clermont Academy Collection, Northern Kentucky University)

for me, I had become pleasantly settled with a worthy companion, on a fertile and healthy farm, in view of the beautiful Ohio, surrounded by a pretty large family of children, with the prospect of being able to give them a decent education at home. On one occasion in attempting to give utterance to my sensations before a large audience in the Academy, the tears began to flow, and I could not proceed. It appeared to me that Providence had bestowed upon me far more than sufficient to compensate for all the labours of body and mind through which I had passed and that I did not deserve so happy a lot. May I never be unmindful of his goodness, who has led me safely through many trying scenes, and more than compensated me for all my troubles!

The antislavery agitation became more and more intense. Societies multiplied on every hand. Thorough discussions, both private and public, were of the most exciting character. The poor slaves availed themselves of the interest felt by abolitionists in their behalf, and hundreds fled to Canada through the free states.[34] This enraged their masters, who came over with armed bands to reclaim them, threatening terrible vengeance to those who assisted the fugitives; but they could not be deterred from doing what they conceived the obligations humanity required. A law was passed in Ohio to pacify Kentucky, making it a crime to help runaways, but the people would not regard it, and the next year the legislature repealed it (They might as well have legislated against sunshine).[35] Large rewards were offered in slave states for prominent abolitionists in the free.[36]

I was engaged four years in a book agency, which required me to travel, carrying books with me.[37] Having an extensive acquaintance in Kentucky, I took a horse load of books and went some forty miles into the state; sold books and delivered temperance lectures in several towns where I used to preach. My old friends for the most part treated me the same as formerly, but some looked shy. One old man, after buying a book, asked me where I came from. I told him Ohio.

"Then,"[38] said he, "I suppose you are an abolitionist."

I said yes.

Then said he, "If I had known that I would have cut your throat."

"O! I reckon not without giving me a trial," said I. We then had a long conversation on the subject of slavery and at the close he asked my name. I told him.

"Are you a brother to the preacher?"

"No sir, I am the man himself."

"O! really, Mr. Parker, I have used you rather roughly, but now I know you, and have heard you preach. If everybody would do what you tell them, they would do well enough. Can't you come over and preach for us?"

"Perhaps I will, but suppose I should come out on these great evils of slavery and intemperance, etc.?"

"Well, I suppose we should have to put up with it."

"The people would not permit me to speak in public against slavery, but would against intemperance," said I.

"Well, if you do come, you must stay at my house. My son-in-law told me of your lectures at his house, and that he signed the pledge."[39]

"So he did; and if I come over, you may expect me at your house."

So I got off without having my throat cut. Slaveholders respect antislavery men who will fearlessly stand up for their principles much more than cringing dough-faces; and whether they did or not, we should always do it.[40] He who is afraid to advocate the truth in the presence of its enemies deserves, and will get, the scorn of even the vicious and profligate. My neighbors wondered that I should venture into Kentucky, but I knew there was no danger.

On another occasion, in Augusta, Kentucky, the seat of a Methodist college,[41] where I had been delivering a temperance lecture, a number of young students from the South were standing in the street. One of them observed that John Rankin ought to have his throat cut.[42] "Ah," said I, "what has Mr. Rankin been doing?"

"Why, stealing negroes."

"Is it possible? I did not think he would steal. I have been acquainted with him some years and always thought him an honest man. He is a minister of the gospel. I think there must be some mistake about it. O! now I suppose I know what you mean. It is likely that when he sees a poor slave running away with the legs his maker gave him, he may pity and assist him with food, lodging, or perhaps money to help him escape from bondage. Do you call that stealing? Would you not think such assistance a benevolent act if done to yourself, were you in the slave's place? I perceive, sir, you do not understand the alphabet of abolitionism. I will explain it. You think the abolitionists are your enemies, whereas they are the best friends the South have. They wish you to do away the evil of slavery before it does you away, which will most assuredly be the case unless prevented by emancipation."

"What!" said he, "Free them here, and let them stay amongst us? I would fight to my knees in blood before they should be permitted to enjoy equal rights here, and amalgamate with the whites."

"I suppose sir," said I, "you will not deny that amalgamation is already going on among you, and that in violation of the seventh commandment?"[43]

"O! yes, to be sure, there is some of that; but then, they are not recognized."

"I know they are not recognized as standing on equal footing, yet they might be recognized in a way you would not like any better. Suppose we were to be involved in war with some foreign power, and the enemy were to come onto the southern coast and offer them liberty, feed, clothe, and arm them? What would become of you?"

"O! My father has fifty, and they would fight for him to the last man."

"I do not know your father, nor his slaves, but sometimes appearances are deceptive; and now, I'll tell you a piece of history which you may not have read. At the time of our last war with England, a member of the British parliament proposed that an army be sent with the intention I have stated. The plan was objected to by another member for the reason that England had slaves in the West Indies, and that the Americans might retaliate in the same way, and more effectually, because there was a larger proportion of slaves in the British Islands than in the southern states.[44] But now they have converted 800,000 slaves into free people, have black soldiers trained and training in their armies, and they could probably land 100,000 colored troops on our southern border, who would feel strong sympathy with their brethren in bondage, while the love and prospect of liberty in the latter would induce them to join the invaders.[45] Then sir, you would see on which side your father's slaves would fight. Now we want you to emancipate and make friends of those men while it is in your power, for though you may not realize it now, the slaveholders are sleeping, as it were, over a volcano."

The young man looked astonished and replied, "Well Mr. Parker, I am glad to hear you talk so reasonable."

"We go," said I, "for reason on our side of the river, and not for cutting throats."

Another instance of a somewhat different character I will relate. A very wealthy slaveholder in the town of Cynthiana, Kentucky, about forty miles from my residence, had been very kind and generous to me at a time that I was in the habit of preaching in that vicinity, insisting always that his house should be my home when in the village; and went so far that he built a meeting house on his own ground, partly on my account, and free for other traveling preachers. We had conversed very freely in private on the subject of slavery, and he had acknowledged it to be a great evil, especially in a pecuniary point of view: making careful estimates of profit and loss, deciding in favour of free labour; and when I asked him why he continued it? "O," he said, "it was convenient."[46]

One of this man's male slaves ran off with his so called wife, belonging to another friend two miles in the country, at whose house I had often preached and who had told me that he would willingly give up his two slaves (all he had) if others would do the same, admitting that the system was wrong.[47] This man came to my house in pursuit of the runaways. I saw that his horse was very much worried, and insisted that he should be put up and the friend stay for dinner, but he declined, saying he was in a great hurry, searching for runaway negroes.

I then reminded him of what he told me, and said to him that as they had gone off without his consent, the law could not hold him accountable for their maintenance, and inasmuch as he considered slavery an evil, why should he pursue them? He did not seem to like it, and replied that if he could find the woman, he would "put her in his pocket" (meaning he would sell her). My wife, overhearing the conversation, came into the room and said, "Do go home like a Christian and let the poor things go."[48]

Meanwhile, the other man sent an advertisement promising $50.00 reward, enclosed in a bank envelope directed to me, as much as to say "stick it up." I would not have done it if he had offered a thousand dollars. When the man returned and told the other where he had been and what we said, he, being of a violent temper, was raving mad and immediately sent me a short, crusty letter, ironically thanking us, but especially my wife, for our politeness to Mr. R., saying, "We have got our property, and no thanks to the people your side of the river, which I hope will hereafter separate us" (the slaves were taken up twelve miles distant).

I immediately answered his letter with a very long one, and after thanking him for all his former kindnesses, informed him that I would rise at midnight to serve him in any other way, but to require me to violate my principles was asking too much, leaving him to judge whether I had not done right. I received no reply.

The affair made a great noise in Cynthiana, but he got no sympathy and I no blame, even among his slaveholding neighbours, who commended me for adhering to my principles, and some of them said they would rather hear me preach after than before it happened. I saw the man afterward in one of my tours through the place. He saluted me very friendly but did not invite me to his house. I have no doubt he respected me more than ever in his heart. A time-serving, cringing

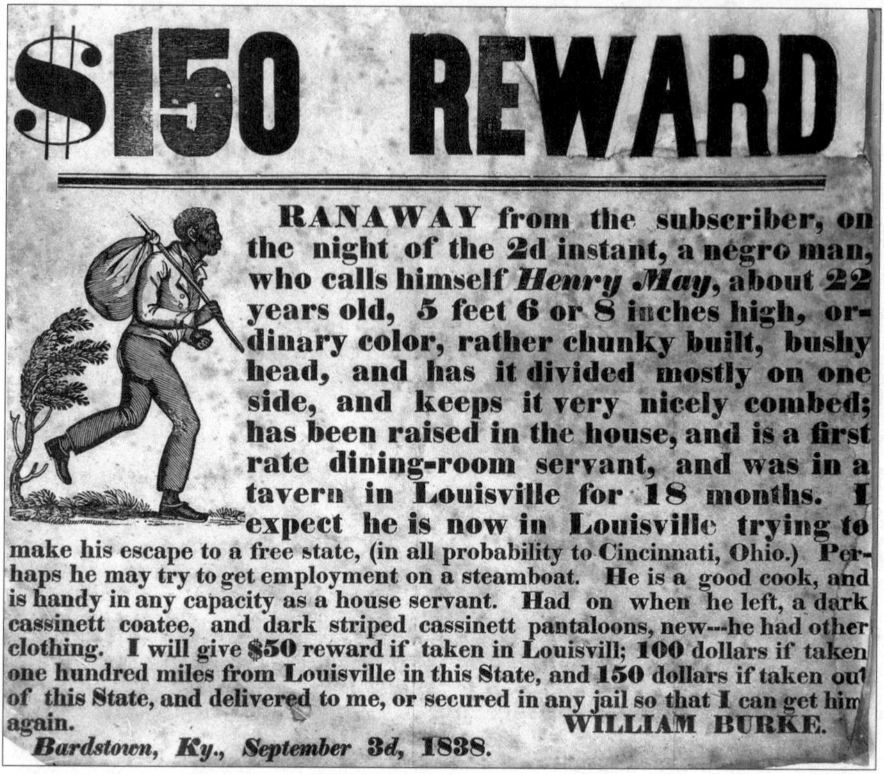

$150 REWARD

RANAWAY from the subscriber, on the night of the 2d instant, a negro man, who calls himself *Henry May*, about 22 years old, 5 feet 6 or 8 inches high, ordinary color, rather chunky built, bushy head, and has it divided mostly on one side, and keeps it very nicely combed; has been raised in the house, and is a first rate dining-room servant, and was in a tavern in Louisville for 18 months. I expect he is now in Louisville trying to make his escape to a free state, (in all probability to Cincinnati, Ohio.) Perhaps he may try to get employment on a steamboat. He is a good cook, and is handy in any capacity as a house servant. Had on when he left, a dark cassinett coatee, and dark striped cassinett pantaloons, new---he had other clothing. I will give $50 reward if taken in Louisvill; 100 dollars if taken one hundred miles from Louisville in this State, and 150 dollars if taken out of this State, and delivered to me, or secured in any jail so that I can get him again.

WILLIAM BURKE.

Bardstown, Ky., September 3d, 1838.

Figure 7.9. A broadside offers a $150 reward for the capture and return of a man who escaped slavery in Kentucky and went "in all probability to Cincinnati, Ohio." (Library of Congress)

policy is despised by everyone whose good opinion is worth having, and no man pursuing it can be satisfied with himself. The portrait of a sycophant ought to be painted without eyes.[49]

Large colonization societies in the county of Clermont were superseded by others advocating immediate emancipation; and I was appointed to lecture through the county, what time I could spare from other avocations, during one winter.[50] It was a hard service. The travelling was uncommonly bad, many parts of the county thinly settled. Ignorance and prejudice, like a thick cloud, hung over the people. They were made to believe that if the slaves were set free, they would murder their former masters, overrun the free states—either as idle, worthless, thieving vagabonds, or else would underwork the whites and thus monopolize all the employment; in fine, that nothing would be so likely to ruin the country, north and south, as the destruction of slavery, the very thing that, if let alone, was most likely to prove its ruin. Abolition lecturers were looked upon as incendiaries, disturbers of the public peace, and enemies of the country, influenced by foreign emissaries, and therefore tories.[51]

It was not an easy task to contend with such opposition, and yet whenever the people could be prevailed upon to hear the subject discussed, the opposition became less, and many who had been bitter enemies became warm friends. The greatest difficulty was to get hearers. Some were afraid to go, lest the house might be assailed by a mob. Many threats were made, and one lecturer had been abused in an obscure place where I had an evening appointment, in a schoolhouse surrounded with woods.

I had traveled a long distance to fill it, and when near the place, a friend suggested that perhaps it would be better to forego the meeting. I told him if anybody was afraid to go with me I would go alone, that I did not think there would be any disturbance, but if there should, it was my duty to fulfill the mission on which I had been sent. O, he said, if there was any fighting to be done, he would not let me be abused. I told [him] I was not afraid to go alone. It turned out to be a very peaceable meeting.

One old woman near the place said she wished I was roasted and she had my fat to grease her shoes. She would have had a hard bargain, for I had about as much fat as she had delicacy, both of us being very lean in these respects.

Numerous petitions were sent to Congress, praying that slavery might be abolished at the seat of government in the District of Columbia, but they were treated with contempt, laid on the table; and finally, a standing rule adopted, forbidding them to be received, read, or acted upon in any way.[52]

We were tauntingly told to go into the slave states and lecture where the evil existed, that there was no slavery at the north and everybody there was opposed to it.[53] The reply was that the south would not permit the subject to be discussed there; that prominent southern senators had threatened in Congress that if abolitionists were caught in the south they would be hung despite of all law. That although there were no slaves in the free states, there were many slaveholders living at the north upon the money wrung from the unrequited labour of slaves, which they owned on southern plantations. That the proslavery spirit infected the whole country. That so far as Congress had jurisdiction over the subject, it was as much the business of northern as of southern men. It was therefore not only very proper but highly important that correct public sentiment and moral action should be promoted everywhere; that the reflex influence of the same through the press must be felt even where the voice of a lecturer could not be heard.[54] And moreover, that slavery in the southern churches exerted a deleterious influence upon those connected with them in the north, and prevented the latter from bearing testimony against it for fear of division.[55] Proslavery clergymen in both sections, using their moral power and talents to prove it a divine institution, attempting to make it identical with Jewish servitude and sanctioned by apostolic precept—all these and many other reasons were assigned by abolitionists to justify agitating the subject in free states.

The sharp collision of mind with mind on this exciting topic could not fail to elicit much truth, and although not always conducted by either party in the spirit of that charity that "thinketh no evil," the substantial interest of the whole nation required it. As the noxious effects of a stagnant pool are more deadly to the physical man than those of the roaring cataract, so is the intellectual man more likely to suffer from mental sloth than even imperfect intellectual activity.[56]

My ministerial labours since the year 1815 had not been confined to any one place.[57] I traveled much in various directions, both in the free and slave states; passed often up and down the Ohio on steamboats, which brought me frequently in contact with slaveholders who well knew my sentiments on the absorbing question. Many a stirring conversation and long argument took place in the cabin, the result of which I leave for others to tell. One thing, however, it is my duty to say: that except in one instance, I was always treated by my opponents on that subject with courtesy while travelling on the packets.[58] Nor did they, in general, attempt to justify their practice on the ground of principle, but on that of expediency only. While many of their apologists in free states, professing to believe slavery to be a great moral evil, yet labored hard to prove from the Bible that it was a divine institution.[59] This concession is freely made because justly due.

The exception above mentioned was as follows. In passing to Cincinnati on the packet one Saturday evening, a citizen of Maysville, who knew me, asked if I was going to preach next day in the city. I said yes. He replied that he had heard me there some ten years before in the courthouse. I asked if he lived in Cincinnati. He said no, he lived in Maysville, and then asked me what I thought of abolition. I replied that I had always thought it was right to abolish whatever was wrong, that I had been taught to believe slavery was wrong, and that if it were possible I must have been born an abolitionist. "But," said he, "I want a direct answer. Do you think it right to aid runaway slaves?"

I replied that if I were a slave I would run away if I could, and that when anybody came to my house hungry, I fed him. If belated, I let him stay all night; that it was a duty to "feed the hungry and take in the stranger."[60]

"Well," says he, "you come to our town and you'll get well whipped. You'll get your back well cut up."

"Ah," said I, "and whose fault would that be?" He then whirled round and left the cabin, full of wrath.

I was not long after invited to deliver a temperance lecture in Maysville by one of its prominent citizens, and went for the purpose; but the meeting failed through the carelessness of those who were requested to circulate the notice. Many expressed regret and apologized to me for the disappointment, but I neither got whipped nor my "back cut up." Nor was there the least danger in a place where I was so well known. It might have been imprudent for a stranger with my antislavery sentiments, but I had many acquaintances that would not have permitted any such violence.

In fact, there was more mobbing done in Ohio than in Kentucky, though in some instances they were instigated by Kentuckians, especially those in Cincinnati, for they were seen in the crowd when the *Philanthropist* office was broken open and the press destroyed.[61] It would have been a dangerous example to set in a slaveholding state, lest the slaves might pursue the same course, and the mobbers in their turn be mobbed themselves.

I happened to be in Cincinnati at the time one of the great mobs occurred; and meeting on the sidewalk an old acquaintance who appeared to be in a great fright, he took hold of my hand with both of his and said, "Do for God's sake stop this abolitionism."[62]

"Why?" says I, "what's the matter?"

"Why, don't you see what it is doing?"

I told him it was not abolitionism but the enemies of it that were doing the mischief; that as to stopping abolitionism, you might as well try to stop the sun from shining; and as to myself, the people knew I was an abolitionist.

"O well, maybe they don't," said he.

"If you see anybody that does not, I wish you would tell them," said I.

That evening I had an appointment for preaching, but very few met, and they proposed that we should give it up, lest the meeting house should be assailed. I remarked that I did not apprehend any danger, as the police was out watching;[63] but should it be, it was no time for Christians to flinch; but if anybody was afraid, they had better go home; that I had come to hold meeting and should do it. I read the last chapter of Ephesians,[64] made a few remarks, sung and prayed, and felt much better for having done my duty, and so did the rest, no doubt.

Epilogue

DANIEL PARKER'S autobiography ends abruptly here, unless one were to consider the note he wrote on the back of the last page the actual ending: "Be careful of me, and return me" (a reminder to anyone who borrowed the manuscript). Perhaps the author intended to add to his life's story at some point. In fact, he was to have several healthy years and more adventures ahead to describe. Fortunately, he did describe them in other documents, which have been preserved and copied.[1]

One of these documents is the journal that Daniel Parker kept of a trip he took in 1845, the same year that he began writing his autobiography. In the spring of that year, Parker traveled from Cincinnati to New Orleans by steamboat, making in a few weeks the journey that as a younger man took him over four years, albeit with a number of diversions. In his journal, Parker noted the developments along the riverfront, and especially in the city of New Orleans, which "had grown enormously since I saw it in 1810." While in that city he visited the United States Mint and took an enthusiastic mechanic's interest in the "melting, bleaching and stamping process." He also availed himself of the opportunity offered by "a liberal minded minister" of the "use of his meeting house to preach" on a Sunday evening.[2]

Parker's overriding concern on his journey south was to inquire into the practice of slavery. With characteristic open-mindedness, the

Figure E.1. Fannie Parker (later Fannie Parker Currier), the daughter of James K. Parker and granddaughter of Daniel Parker. She was an infant at the time Parker began writing his autobiography and was around sixteen years old in this picture, close to her age in 1861, the year Daniel Parker died. She taught Latin and music at the Clermont Academy. (Clermont Academy Collection, Northern Kentucky University)

abolitionist tried to ascertain if there was any truth to the proslavery argument that it was a misunderstood, benign institution. Visiting a sugar mill on the trip downriver, Parker befriended a "mulatto" slave who quickly disabused him of the notion, saying that "who ever said so were fools." The man, who also happened to be a Baptist preacher, explained that slaves worked fourteen-hour days, that while a good master would give them cornmeal, "none would give them meat," and that slaves got whipped for trying to have their own church services. Parker trusted the testimony of his fellow minister of the gospel, saying "the expression of his voice and countenance indicated that he was a truth-telling Christian."[3]

However, Parker was confused by other reports, including some from acquaintances he trusted, that slaves were not always so badly mistreated. He expressed frustration at his limited access to information, exacerbated by the fact that "almost every white person I converse with in this country is either an advocate or an apologist for the system."[4] He concluded that whatever "palliation" more humane slaveholders might offer, it remained "a cruel system which requires hearty and strong laborers to work all their lives for coarse victuals and clothes without the stimulus of wages, the advantages of education, or the right of legal marriage."[5]

The following year, Parker, along with his daughter Susanna and some friends, made a journey east. He described his trip in a letter to his sister Sally and brother-in-law Ephraim Cutler. As tourists in "Washington City," the nation's capital, Parker saw the usual sites: "Congress, the President's house, the National Institute."[6] He also visited the infamous Williams's Slave Jail. Five years before, it had housed the kidnapped Solomon Northup (a fact that would not be generally known until after his rescue and the publication of his memoir, *Twelve Years a Slave*, in 1853).[7] Profoundly affected by the sight of a slave trader's holding pen within eyeshot of the Capitol, Parker left the keeper with a quote from Thomas Jefferson, "I tremble for my country when I remember that God is just."[8]

From there the party traveled to Philadelphia, where he saw the Liberty Bell, and then onward to New York City. Parker was impressed by the "remarkable objects there, from the Battery on the south to the great bridge over the Haarlem River at the north end of Manhattan Island (a stupendous work)." He was disturbed, however, by the "loathsome receptacle of debauches at 'Five Points'" (a neighborhood that would be a main focus of Herbert Asbury's *The Gangs of New York*).[9]

Leaving the city by train, he was amazed to travel the whole length of Long Island, "93 miles in 3 ½ hours." From there he traveled to Boston and "went thence to Newburyport, my native town." Finding his old house still standing, he "examined it from cellar to scuttle," and "saw where I tumbled down the old cellar door when a small child, crying after Mother."[10]

In addition to documents authored by the man himself, these papers also include typescripts of documents written by Daniel Parker's relatives. One of these is a "Note," written by Daniel Parker's grandson Charles M. Parker,[11] appended to the former's autobiography. Apparently, like his grandfather, Charles Parker assumed that the autobiography might one day reach a broad audience and added this epilogue for their benefit, intending to compensate for the abrupt ending by adding information about the last years of Daniel Parker's life. It is quoted in full below as an appropriate conclusion to this volume.[12]

> The foregoing history ends so abruptly that I have thought it might interest the reader to know something of the closing hours of its author and of his condition and employment in later years. His labors in the ministry and for the great causes of temperance, anti-slavery, and everything which bettered the condition of humanity were continued to the last, so far as his failing strength would permit. He always took the deepest interest in the welfare of the school which he had established and which is still successfully progressing, now (1878) completing its 39th year. He often visited the school room and addressed the students but never on his peculiar tenets. As long as he was able he preached the annual Thanksgiving sermon in the Academy and seemed to delight in it; praise and thanksgiving were favorite themes with him.
>
> In the year 1855,[13] he had the misfortune to lose his house by fire together with almost all his household goods, his diary, and a fine cabinet of geological and prehistoric specimens which

Figure E.2. Priscilla Parker after 1861. (Clermont Academy Collection, Northern Kentucky University)

Figure E.3. Daniel Parker in 1850, aged sixty-eight or sixty-nine. (Clermont Academy Collection, Northern Kentucky University)

Grandmother had gathered with great care. The night was bitterly cold and the inmates of the house escaped with barely clothing enough for the scantiest protection. Until a new house was erected by the sons then at home,[14] Daniel and Eben, all the family were housed in the more capacious dwelling of their son James. This was a terrible stroke on these old people. Grandfather used to say, however, that even this calamity had its good features, for he never should have known how kind and numerous his friends were, but for the many offers of assistance, sympathy and the contributions of material comforts which were so freely and voluntarily made to them in this hour of need.

Shortly before his death he called his family together to tell them of his feelings and thoughts. He had all his life dreaded death, but expressed a happy freedom from that feeling as the hour of dissolution approached. He abhorred expensive funerals and costly caskets, with their futile attempt to defeat nature and prevent "dust from returning to dust," and requested to be buried in a tasteful but inexpensive wooden coffin; that his resting place be marked by two granite boulders (such as abound in that neighborhood) one at the head, the other at the foot, on which might be inscribed his name and the dates of his death and birth. These instructions were carried out to the letter. He died March 22, 1861.

Shortly before his death he remarked that he hoped to see the end of the struggle against slavery, but immediately consoled himself with the thought that perhaps his vision of it would only be the clearer in another state of existence. Grandmother died Sept 4th, 1874.

NOTES

Editor's Introduction

1. Daniel Parker's manuscript autobiography (hereafter referred to as MS) consists of sixteen octavo notebooks that were numbered and bound together in one volume. Citations for quotes from the MS will include an octavo number. This quote is from Octavo 13.

2. MS, Octavo 13.

3. Biographical information about Daniel Parker's parents and other significant persons he mentions will be provided in endnotes as they are first mentioned by Parker himself in the body of this autobiography.

4. MS, Octavo 2.

5. MS, Octavo 13.

6. Richard Eddy, *Universalism in America: A History*, vol. 2, *1801–1886* (Boston: Universalist Publishing House, 1886), 169. Parker is also mentioned in other Universalist histories: J. A. Stoner, "Before and after Winchester," in *The Winchester Centennial, 1803–1903: Historical Sketch of the Universalist Profession of Belief* (Boston: Universalist Publishing House, 1903), 121, 122; Elmo Arnold Robinson, *The Universalist Church in Ohio* ([Akron?]: Ohio Universalist Convention, 1923), 26; and Russell E. Miller, *The Larger Hope: The First Century of the Universalist Church in America, 1770–1870* (Boston: Unitarian Universalist Association, 1978), 697.

7. The full title is *Familiar Letters to a Brother in Two Series: On the Final Restoration of All Mankind to Holiness and Happiness; Through a Righteous Judgment, and an Equitable Retribution* (Cincinnati: printed by C. W. Thorp, 1844).

8. MS, Octavo 1.

9. MS, Octavo 1.

10. MS, Octavo 8.

11. MS, Octavo 9.

12. A notable reference is in Mary Walton Ferris's two-volume *Dawes-Gates Ancestral Lines: A Memorial Volume Containing the American Ancestry of Rufus R. Dawes.* References to Daniel Parker's autobiography are in volume 1, *Dawes and Allied Families* (Milwaukee, WI: privately printed, 1943), 473–81. Rufus R. Dawes and Mary Beman Gates were the parents of US vice president and Nobel Peace Prize winner Charles G. Dawes (1865–1951), who commissioned the publication of the volumes. Dawes was descended from Daniel Parker's sister Sally and her husband, Ephraim Cutler.

13. This copy (hereafter referred to as the "Family Copy") was written in a large manuscript book with printed page numbers, which will be included in citations. See "Note on Text" in this volume for further explanation of the manuscript and its copies.

14. For the progress of the Parker Academy Archaeological Project, see its website, https://parkeracademy-nsfreu.weebly.com.

15. Later end notes will give more information and sources for historical events such as the New Madrid earthquakes and the death of Meriwether Lewis as they are mentioned in Parker's autobiography.

16. The complexity of the time period covered by Parker's autobiography is evident in the organization of Eric Foner's widely used college textbook, *Give Me Liberty! An American History*, 4th ed. (New York: W. W. Norton, 2014), 282–465. It breaks off its chronological organization for this period and instead covers it thematically in five separate chapters.

17. Foner, *Give Me Liberty!*, chap. 8, "Securing the Republic," 282–319; Gordon S. Wood, *Empire of Liberty: A History of the Early Republic, 1789–1815* (New York: Oxford University Press, 2009), 133–39, 696–700. As a child, Daniel Parker watched federal troops, led by President George Washington, march past his family home in the woods of western Pennsylvania to quell the Whiskey Rebellion (MS, Octavo 1). As an adult sojourning through Kentucky, he documented the home-front excitement caused by the War of 1812 (Octavo 8).

18. The westward movement of Anglo-American "pioneers" from the eastern states (or British colonies, before they were states) preceded the time period of Parker's memoir and continued decades afterward, with far-reaching consequences for migrant settlers, for Native Americans who already occupied the territories, and for the United States as a whole. The western movement was accelerated in the 1780s by congressional land ordinances, including the Northwest Ordinance of 1787, which the Parkers benefitted from as shareholders in the Ohio Company. See Foner, *Give Me Liberty!*, 252–54; Peter S. Onuf, *Statehood and Union: A History of the Northwest Ordinance* (Bloomington: Indiana University Press, 1987), xiii–xiv; and Andrew R. L. Cayton, "The Significance of Ohio in the Early American Republic," in *The Center of a Great Empire: The Ohio Country in the Early Republic*, ed. Cayton and Stuart D. Hobbs (Athens: Ohio University Press, 2005), 1–9.

19. Foner, *Give Me Liberty!*, chap. 9, "The Market Revolution," 318–54. John Lauritz Larson describes the market revolution as a "dramatic transformation" of the

United States from the end of the American Revolution to the beginning of the Civil War, which expanded manufacturing and industry, increased the country's territory and population, brought financial and technological innovations, and altered cultural values (*The Market Revolution in America: Liberty, Ambition, and the Eclipse of the Common Good* [Cambridge: Cambridge University Press, 2010], 1). See also Charles Sellers, *The Market Revolution: Jacksonian America, 1815–1846* (Oxford: Oxford University Press, 1991), 5.

20. Foner, *Give Me Liberty!*, chap. 10, "Democracy in America, 1815–1840," 355–93. The expansion of American democracy is popularly associated with the presidency of Andrew Jackson (1829–37), especially since the publication of Arthur Schlesinger's *The Age of Jackson* in 1945. The French writer Alexis de Tocqueville famously made the observations that formed the basis of his *Democracy in America* in the 1830s. Historians note, however, that expanded political participation and the accompanying populist political culture, brought about by the elimination of property requirements for voting and other factors, were well underway before the election of Jackson, particularly in the West. The frontier election-day scene that Parker describes occurred in 1811 (MS, Octavo 7). The expansion of American democracy in the early nineteenth century did not include all Americans. Women, African Americans, and Native Americans actually lost political rights during this period. The nature of American democracy during the years covered by Daniel Parker's autobiography continues to be debated by historians, as do other themes and periodizations of the time. See Harry L. Watson, *Liberty and Power: The Politics of Jacksonian America*, rev. ed. (New York: Hill and Wang, 2006), 3–15; Sean Wilentz, *The Rise of American Democracy: Jefferson to Lincoln* (New York: W. W. Norton, 2005), 116–18, 177–78; Alexander Keyssar, *The Right to Vote: The Contested History of Democracy in the United States* (New York: Basic Books, 2000), 26–52, 53–60; and James A. Ramage and Andrea S. Watkins, *Kentucky Rising: Democracy, Slavery, and Culture from the Early Republic to the Civil War* (Lexington: University Press of Kentucky, 2011), 3–4.

21. Foner, *Give Me Liberty!*, 342–47; Nathan O. Hatch, *The Democratization of American Christianity* (New Haven, CT: Yale University Press, 1989), 3–16; and Jon Butler, *Awash in a Sea of Faith: Christianizing the American People* (Cambridge: Harvard University Press, 1992), 177–91, 236–56.

22. Foner, *Give Me Liberty!*, chap. 11, "The Peculiar Institution," 395–429; Ira Berlin, *The Making of African America: The Four Great Migrations* (New York: Viking, 2010), chap. 3, "The Passage to the Interior"; and Peter Kolchin, *American Slavery, 1619–1877*, rev. ed. (New York: Hill and Wang, 2003), 93–99, 169–70.

23. Foner, *Give Me Liberty!*, chap. 12, "An Age of Reform," 432–65; and Robert H. Abzug, *Cosmos Crumbling: American Reform and the Religious Imagination* (New York: Oxford University Press, 1994), 3–8.

24. Sydney E. Ahlstrom, *A Religious History of the American People* (New Haven, CT: Yale University Press, 1972), 429–58. Nathan O. Hatch and Jon Butler, while making different arguments, together attest to the plurality of causes of the religious energy and ferment of the nineteenth-century United States. See Butler, *Awash*, 164–65, 177–91, 236–56; and Hatch, *Democratization*, 3–16, 225–26. For the burned-over district of western New York, see Whitney R. Cross, *The Burned-Over District: The*

Social and Intellectual History of Enthusiastic Religion in Western New York, 1800–1850 (Ithaca, NY: Cornell University Press, 1950), 3–51. Daniel Parker's memoir is evidence of the diversity of American religion in the West. The Cane Ridge–style camp meeting was important, but only one of its many different aspects.

25. Ahlstrom, *Religious History of the American People*, 77–81, 84–98, 124, 455–58.

26. Congregationalists and Presbyterians were both Calvinist in their theology, but differed over matters of polity. For Congregationalists, each congregation was self-governing. For Presbyterians, churches were governed by a college of "elders" ("presbyters" in New Testament Greek) elected from congregations and organized into graduated church courts. From the time of the Pilgrims of 1620, the "Congregational way" was the predominant church polity among the English-descended Puritans of New England. Presbyterians tended to be of Scottish or Scots-Irish ancestry and came to the North American colonies and the United States largely through Pennsylvania. However, a minority of New England Puritans adhered to a Presbyterian system even in the seventeenth century. Their numbers increased through Scots-Irish immigration into New England in 1718. The Parkers belonged to the First Presbyterian Church of Newburyport, commonly known as (and now officially called) the Old South Presbyterian Church of Newburyport, which was organized in 1746 in the wake of a visit from George Whitefield, famous English itinerant of the First Great Awakening. Jonathan Parson was their first minister. Whitefield died on a return visit to Newburyport in 1770 and was buried, according to his wishes, in a crypt underneath the pulpit at Old South. There were tensions between American Presbyterians and Congregationalists, but there were also instances of cooperation. The two denominations agreed to a "Plan of Union" in 1801, which for a time allowed for combined Presbyterian and Congregationalist churches in the western territories. However, though the Parkers lived in the West, their Presbyterian loyalties were prior to and unrelated to the Plan of Union. See Alexander Blaikie, *A History of Presbyterianism in New England* (Boston: Alexander Moore, 1881), 154; Harry S. Stout, *The Divine Dramatist: George Whitefield and the Rise of Modern Evangelicalism* (Grand Rapids, MI: W. B. Eerdmans, 1991), 269–87; the website of Old South Presbyterian Church, http://www.oldsouthnbpt.org/History-Church; Leonard J. Trinterud, *The Forming of an American Tradition: A Re-examination of Colonial Presbyterianism* (1949; reprint, New York: Books for Libraries Press, 1970), 7–37; and John Von Rohr, *The Shaping of American Congregationalism, 1620–1957* (Cleveland: Pilgrim, 1992), 262–65.

27. MS, Octavo 1.

28. Helpful definitions of evangelicalism include the often-cited "Bebbington Quadrilateral," for which see David W. Bebbington, *Evangelicalism in Modern Britain: A History from the 1730s to the 1980s* (London: Unwin Hyman, 1989), 2–17. See also the four emphases of American revivalism in A. Leland Jamison, "Religions on the Christian Perimeter," in *The Shaping of American Religion*, ed. James Ward Smith and A. Leland Jamison (Princeton, NJ: Princeton University Press, 1961), 197–98.

29. William G. McLoughlin, *Revivals, Awakenings, and Reform* (Chicago: University of Chicago Press, 1978), 1–23; and Hatch, *Democratization*, 220–26. For a challenge to the broadly accepted concept of the Great Awakening as a historical movement, see Jon Butler, "Enthusiasm Described and Decried: The Great

Awakening as Interpretive Fiction," *Journal of American History* 69, no. 2 (September 1982): 305–25; and Butler, *Awash*, 164–65.

30. For the Arminian (from the Dutch theologian, Jacobus Arminius) emphasis of nineteenth-century evangelicals, see Jamison, "Religions"; Mark A. Noll, *A History of Christianity in the United States and Canada* (Grand Rapids, MI: W. B. Eerdmans, 1992), 170; and Timothy Smith, *Revivalism and Social Reform: American Protestantism on the Eve of the Civil War* (New York: Harper Torchbooks, 1965), 24–28. This is not to say that there were not also important Calvinist evangelicals in the nineteenth century.

31. MS, Octavo 8.

32. For the generally hostile attitudes of nineteenth-century American Protestants toward Catholics, see Ray Allen Billington, *The Protestant Crusade, 1800–1860: A Study of the Origins of American Nativism* (New York: MacMillan, 1938), 1–25, 32–48; and Jenny Franchot, *Roads to Rome: The Antebellum Protestant Encounter with Catholicism* (Berkeley: University of California Press, 1994), 3–15. Ann Lee Bressler notes that Universalists were notably less hostile to Catholics than other American Protestants in *The Universalist Movement in America, 1770–1880* (New York: Oxford University Press, 2001), 67.

33. Elizabeth A. DeWolfe, *Shaking the Faith: Women, Family, and Mary Marshall Dyer's Anti-Shaker Campaign, 1815–1867* (New York: Palgrave MacMillan, 2004), 7.

34. MS, Octavo 9.

35. MS, Octavo 10. Daniel Parker spells the name "Kenedy," but the correct spelling was probably "Kennedy." In this volume, the body of Parker's biography will use his spelling, "Kenedy," and the Editor's Introduction and notes will use "Kennedy." See note 20 with citations in chap. 5 dealing with the spelling of this name.

36. MS, Octavo 11.

37. Daniel Parker consistently uses the spelling "Fordice," as do some other documents written by members of the Parker family, but other sources use the name "Fordyce." In the available primary sources there seems to be a higher degree of uncertainty as to how Rhoda herself would spell her last name than there is for James Kennedy (see note 35 above). Therefore, in this volume the body of Parker's autobiography will use his spelling, "Fordice," and the Editor's Introduction and notes will use either or both spellings depending on context.

38. The leader of the Halcyon Church preferred the spelling "Sarjent" for his own name. "Sargent" is the spelling most often used by other writers, both his contemporaries and later historians, and he may have occasionally used this spelling himself. Daniel Parker, after using "Sargent" a few times early in his autobiography, uses "Sarjent" for the remainder. This volume will use "Sarjent" except in notes when quoting sources that use other spellings.

39. Some of these qualities are why Nathan O. Hatch offers Sarjent as exemplary of "the democratization of American Christianity" (*Democratization*, 3–16, 75–76).

40. As is evident in the title of Sarjent's pamphlet *The Urim, or Halcyon Cabala.* The lengthy subtitle follows: *Containing the Fundamental Principles of the Halcyon Church of Christ in Columbia; Otherwise Called the Columbian Church, in Defence of the Genuine Christianity and in Opposition to "Lo Here, and Lo There"; Consisting of*

One Supreme Object and Seven Leading Topicks (Cincinnati: Carpenter and Findlay, 1801).

41. Physician and local historian Samuel Hildreth describes the Halcyon tenets as similar to those "of the modern Millerites, combined with a portion of the Mormon faith" in "Biographical Sketches of the Early Physicians of Marietta, Ohio," *New England Historical & Genealogical Register* 3 (1849): 53. *History of Washington County, Ohio, with Illustrations and Biographical Sketches* (Cleveland: H. Z. Williams, 1881; repr., Washington Co. Chapter, Ohio Genealogical Society, 1989) compares the Halcyon Church to "modern Second Adventists," 394, 408.

42. For Mormonism as the quintessential "American religion," see Harold Bloom, *The American Religion: The Emergence of the Post-Christian Nation* (New York: Simon & Schuster, 1992), 111. Hildreth ("Biographical Sketches") and Ray Swick ("Abel Morgan Sarjent," *West Virginia Encyclopedia*, West Virginia Humanities Council, http://www.wvencyclopedia.org/print/Article/178) point out similarities between Sarjent's Halcyon Church and the Mormons. John L. Brooke notes the similar terminology used by the Halcyon Church and Latter-day Saints in *The Refiner's Fire: The Making of Mormon Cosmology, 1644–1844* (Cambridge: Cambridge University Press, 1994), 102, but does not give evidence of the earlier group's direct influence on the later. Fawn Brodie mentions Abel Sarjent as a prophetic leader who preceded Joseph Smith in *No Man Knows My History: The Life of Joseph Smith, the Mormon Prophet*, 2nd ed. (New York: Alfred A. Knopf, 1971), 98, but does not claim any direct influence or even mention the most striking similarities between the two figures.

43. For the origins and beliefs of the Latter-day Saints, see Matthew Bowman, *The Mormon People: The Making of an American Faith* (New York: Random House, 2012), 1–95. For a briefer summary, see Kathleen Flake, "Latter-day Saints," in *Encyclopedia of Religion in America*, ed. Charles H. Lippy and Peter W. Williams (Washington, DC: CQ Press, 2010), 3:1215–21. The name "Zion," referring both to the current community of believers and the future millennial community, is one of several terms used similarly in Halcyon and Mormon theology. See "When Zion from Her Closet Comes," Hymn XIII in *The New Hymn-Book for the Use of the Free Church* (New York: printed for A. M. Sarjent, 1811), which describes "Zion brought from her invisible to her promised visible state" (21).

44. Andrew Jenson, *Latter-Day Saint Biographical Encyclopedia: A Compilation of Biographical Sketches of Prominent Men and Women in the Church of Jesus Christ of Latter-Day Saints* (Salt Lake City: Andrew Jenson History Company, 1914), 3:228.

45. His date of birth and other details of Abel Sarjent's life are recorded in his own hand in his family Bible, which is in the Blennerhassett Island Historical State Park archives in Parkersburg, WV. Some other details are from Dale Broadhurst, "Chronology: Adapted from Nancy Reynolds' *Abel Morgan Sargent, Sr. Timeline* (from Her Studies, Online Data, and Contributions from Various Other Sargent Family Researchers)," Spalding Research Project, http://solomonspalding.com/SRP/saga/saga01b.htm#chrn01.

46. Abel Sarjent, "Circular Epistle from the 9th Concilium of the Halcyon Church" (1810), in *New Hymn-Book*, 220.

47. Andrew R. L. Cayton and Paula R. Riggs, *City into Town: The City of Marietta, Ohio, 1788–1988* (Marietta, OH: Marietta College, Dawes Memorial Library, 1991), 99; Robinson, 16–17.

48. Stoner, 121–22. Russell Miller, 25–27.

49. Robinson, 15.

50. Abel Sarjent, "Introductory Discourse," *Halcyon Itinerary and True Millennium Messenger* 1 (August 1807): 7–11. Sarjent will be considered the author of all articles in this journal that are not otherwise attributed. The given author of this article is "the bearer of the millennium message, by the authority of Emmanuel"—clearly a reference to Sarjent.

51. Sarjent, "Phenomenon of the Heavenly Host in North Carolina," *Halcyon Itinerary* 2 (September 1807): 48–53. This article is a collection of newspaper reports of strange visions around the country, which Sarjent implies are evidence of the approaching millennium.

52. Sarjent, "Introductory Discourse," 9.

53. Sarjent, "Western Messenger; to the Saints throughout the World," in *New Hymn-Book*, 246. Sarjent is the presumed author of uncredited prose entries in this book. The "Western Messenger" is clearly a reference to Sarjent.

54. Sarjent, "Address to America," *Halcyon Itinerary* 3 (October 1807): 100–103; Sarjent, "A Brief Hint of the Universal Dominion of Emmanuel [continued]," *Halcyon Itinerary* 5 (December 1807): 158. The first part of this article breaks off in midsentence on page 144 of issue no. 4 and continues on the first page (numbered 145) of issue no. 5.

55. Sarjent, "A Brief Hint of the Universal Dominion of Emmanuel [part one]," *Halcyon Itinerary* 4 (November 1807): 120; "A Brief Hint . . . [continued]," 162–63.

56. Sarjent, "Address to America," 111–12; "A Brief Hint . . . [continued]," 147–48; "Imperial Rudiments for the Halcyon and Political Church; Introductory to the Age of Science," *Halcyon Itinerary* 6 (January 1808): 186–97.

57. Sarjent, "A Brief Hint . . . [part one]," 126–27, 136–37; "A Brief Hint . . . [continued]," 156–57.

58. Sarjent, "A Brief Hint . . . [continued]," 166–67. See also Sarjent, "Theology vs. Mythology: In Vindication of Genuine Christianity," in *New Hymn-Book*, vii–viii.

59. Norman T. Burns, *Christian Mortalism from Tyndale to Milton* (Cambridge, MA: Harvard University Press, 1972), 1–8, 34.

60. Sarjent, "The Doctrine of Endless Miseries Investigated; or The Sinews of Antichristian Religion Exploded," *Aletheian Critic; or Error Exposed, by an Exhibition of Truth* 1 (April 1804): 5–33. Sarjent is the presumed author of articles in this journal unless others are specifically named. The given author of this article is "the Aletheian Cabinet."

61. Robinson, 11–17. Richard Eddy claims that the leader of the Halcyon Church and the editor of the *Free Universal Magazine* were two different people with similar sounding names, the former being "Abel Sergent" and the latter being "Abel Sarjent." See *Universalism in America: A History*, vol. 1, *1636–1800*, 2nd ed. (Boston: Universalist Publishing House, 1886), 417–18. Russell Miller states, however, "What is known about the chronology indicates that it was probably the same person, although this cannot be stated definitively" (951–52n3).

62. Dell DeChant, "Apocalyptic Communities—Seventh-Day Adventists and Jehovah's Witnesses," in *World Religions in America*, 3rd ed., ed. Jacob Neusner (Louisville, KY: Westminster John Knox, 2003), 192, 197.

63. John J. Collins, "From Prophecy to Apocalypticism: The Expectation of the End," in *The Continuum History of Apocalypticism*, ed. Bernard J. McGinn, John J. Collins, and Stephen J. Stein (New York: Continuum, 2003), 85–86.

64. Sarjent's political rhetoric ranged from affirmations of accepted American democratic principles of natural rights and government by the consent of the governed ("A Brief Hint . . . [continued]," 146–47, 156–57, 158–59) to a more radical, anarchic disavowal of all earthly governments. His rhetoric was most radical when he attacked slavery. See "Imperial Rudiments," 184–95. For more on Sarjent's political rhetoric in context, see Nathan O. Hatch, "The Christian Movement and the Demand for a Theology of the People," *Journal of American History* 67, no. 3 (December 1980): 553–54; and Hatch, *Democratization*, 75–76. See also Cayton and Riggs, 96–99; and Brian Smith, "Abel Sargent and the Halcyon Church" (senior capstone project, Marietta College, 2010), 1–2.

65. Sarjent, "Introductory Discourse," 15. See also "A Declaration of the Constitution and Standard of the Millennium Church," *Aletheian Critic* 1 (April 1804): 57–60.

66. "Urim and Thummim," *HarperCollins Bible Dictionary*, ed. Paul J. Achtemeier (San Francisco: HarperOne, 1996), 1188. Biblical references include Numbers 27:21; 1 Samuel 14:41, 28:6.

67. Sarjent, "Declaration of the Constitution," 43–60.

68. MS, Octavo 11.

69. Sarjent, *Urim, or Halcyon Cabala*; "Declaration of the Constitution," 43–60; "Further Explanations of the Urim and Thummim," *Halcyon Itinerary* 2 (September 1807): 61; and "A Brief Hint . . . [part one]," 134–35. Hymn CCIII of *New Hymn-Book*, "O for an Angel's Tongue to Raise," attributed to "H. C." (presumably Halcyon Church), explains the Urim and Thummim in verse (195–96).

70. Daniel Parker, MS, Octavo 11, Octavo 3. See also Sarjent, *Urim, or Halcyon Cabala*, 9–10; "Declaration of the Constitution," 57–60; and the Halcyon Church hymn, "O for an Angel's Tongue to Raise" for references to Jesus Christ as the exemplar and mediator of Urim and Thummim. Interestingly, though Sarjent rejected the traditional doctrine of the Trinity (Sarjent, "A Protest against Idolatry: Or Tritheism Exploded," *Aletheian Critic* 1 [April 1804]: 39–42), he (and Parker) still alluded to Jesus Christ as, in some sense, the incarnation of God. See the endnote on the Halcyon Christology in chap. 2.

71. "An Address to the Human Family at Large (Circular Letter, Nov. 1804, By order of the 3d Concilium of the Halcyon Church, &c. held in Mason County, Virginia, near Point Pleasant, on the 3rd, 4th, and 5th of November, 1804)," *Aletheian Critic* 1 (April 1804): 64–67. This article is "signed by the order of the Concilium, 6th November, 1804, JOHN PARKER, Moderator," Daniel Parker's brother (69), but clearly had the input of Abel Sarjent.

72. MS, Octavo 11.

73. One of the prominent theologians Sarjent anticipated would be the Universalist Hosea Ballou. Sarjent criticized the idea of vicarious atonement in his *Free*

Universal Magazine (1793–94) before the publication of Ballou's *Treatise on Atonement* in 1805 (Eddy, 1:414–17). Of course, this is not to claim that Sarjent was the first ever to challenge the traditional Western idea. Though he was probably unaware of the similarity, Sarjent's atonement theology was similar to that of Eastern Orthodox Christianity, in which Jesus Christ is primarily understood to be the victor over sin and death (rather than a sacrificial victim) and salvation is mystical union with God. See Timothy Ware, *The Orthodox Church*, new ed. (Baltimore: Penguin Books, 1997), 222–29, 231–38.

74. Peter Cartwright, *Autobiography of Peter Cartwright, the Backwoods Preacher*, ed. W. P. Strickland (New York: Carlton & Porter, 1856), 99–101; James B. Finley, *Autobiography of Rev. James B. Finley*, ed. W. P. Strickland (1853; Cincinnati: Methodist Book Concern, 1872), 257–58; C. E. Dickinson, *A Century of Church Life: A History of the First Congregational Church, of Marietta, Ohio* ([Marietta, OH]: E. R. Alderman and Sons: 1896), 31; and Alfred Creigh, *History of Washington County from Its First Settlement to the Present Time* (Harrisburg, PA: B. Singerly, Printer, 1870), 211–13. The preceding sources are essentially hostile to Sarjent and the Halcyon Church. Other sources aim at a more neutral or balanced approach but lack detail and tend to take the criticism from Sarjent's opponents at face value. See Hildreth, 53–54; and *History of Washington County, Ohio*, 392.

75. William R. Browning to S. P. Hildreth, August 27, 1847, Hildreth Papers, vol. 1, letter 100, Slack Research Collections, Legacy Library, Marietta College, Marietta, OH.

76. John Corrigan, "Religious Prejudice," in *Encyclopedia of Religion in America*, 4:1852–57. See also Philip Jenkins, *Mystics and Messiahs: Cults and New Religions in American History* (Oxford: Oxford University Press, 2000), 3–24. "Mainstream" religions are a society's "most populous and socially well-established" religious organizations (Timothy Miller, "Introduction," in *America's Alternative Religions*, ed. Timothy Miller [Albany: State University of New York Press, 1995], 2). In Parker's context these would be Reformed and, increasingly, evangelical Protestant churches.

77. See, for example, "In Chancery, January 13, 1804: Abraham Faw, versus Abel Sarjent," *National Intelligencer*, February 27, 1804. A creditor placed this advertisement notifying Sarjent he had defaulted on his debt and was required to appear in court or else forfeit his mortgaged property in Allegany County, Maryland.

78. Methodist minister Peter Cartwright, while clearly Sarjent's adversary, admits "his followers were numerous in town and country. The Presbyterian and Congregational ministers were afraid of him" (Cartwright, 99).

79. In addition to Daniel Parker, Universalist minister Alpheus Sweet offers a sympathetic portrait of Sarjent (quoted in Robinson, 15–16). Hannah Adams, a pioneering scholar of comparative religions, sought to describe the Halcyon Church (and other religious groups) with scholarly impartiality, using their own terminology, in the fourth edition of her *Dictionary of All Religions and Religious Denominations: Jewish, Heathen, Mahometan, Christian, Ancient and Modern* (New York: James Eastburn, 1817; facsimile of the 1817 fourth edition, with an introduction by Thomas A. Tweed, Atlanta, GA: Scholars Press, 1992), s.v. "Halcyons" (102).

80. One of the more "respectable" members was Dr. Nathan McIntosh of Marietta, Ohio (Hildreth, 53–54; and *History of Washington County, Ohio*, 392, 408).

81. MS, Octavo 2.

82. MS, Octavo 4.

83. MS, Octavo 5.

84. MS, Octavo 5.

85. Finley, 258; Hildreth, 53–54; Dickinson, 31; and Creigh, 211–13. Endnotes to chap. 2 will analyze these nineteenth-century accounts to demonstrate that they were based on the rumors Parker refers to.

86. Brodie, 98; and David S. Reynolds, *Waking Giant: America in the Age of Jackson* (New York: HarperCollins, 2008), 145. See analysis in the notes to chap. 2 of this volume.

87. Daniel Parker writes that Sarjent "opposed our cause with all his influence and, as we thought sometimes, with a wrong spirit" (MS, Octavo 4). See also endnotes to chap. 2 for Sarjent's denunciations in his own words.

88. "The belief that an all-good and all-powerful God saves all souls may be virtually as old as Christianity; in the view of some biblical scholars, Saint Paul himself preached a definite if often muted doctrine of universal salvation" (Bressler, 6). Two biblical texts that Universalist apologists often cited were Romans 5:18 ("the free gift came upon all men unto justification") and 1 Timothy 2:4 ("[God] will have all men be saved"). The church father Origen of Alexandria espoused universal salvation in the third century. See Mason Olds, "Unitarian Universalism: An Interpretation through Its History," in Miller, *America's Alternative Religions*, 87.

89. Russell Miller, 3–33, 98–110; Bressler, 14–15, 23–29.

90. Ernest Cassara, *Universalism in America: A Documentary History* (Boston: Beacon, 1971), 5; and E. Brooks Holifield, *Theology in America: Christian Thought from the Age of the Puritans to the Civil War* (New Haven, CT: Yale University Press, 2003), 218–20.

91. Russell Miller, 53–75. The name "General Convention" was used informally for an annual meeting of delegates from Universalist churches as early as 1794. The meeting adopted a series of official names: "General Convention of Universalists in the United States" in 1833, "Universalist General Convention" in 1866, and "Universalist Church in America" in 1942, which it remained until its 1961 merger with the Unitarian denomination (65).

92. Russell Miller, 696.

93. On the title page of *Familiar Letters to a Brother*, Parker identifies himself as pastor of the First Restorationist Church in Cincinnati. There follows (on pp. vi–vii) a dedication of the volume to his congregation, in which Parker claims that "this little Church is the only one of the kind, known by the writer, to exist in the Mississippi Valley," by which he probably meant the only church in the region that affirmed Parker's particularly "Restorationist" version of universalism. The church's existence is confirmed by several other sources. Daniel Parker's son, William Tell Parker, in a manuscript ("Memoir of Our Mother," unpublished MS, November 27, 1874, Bertha Currier Hardman Clermont Academy Collection, Department of History and Geography, Northern Kentucky University, Highland Heights, KY, Northern Kentucky

University [hereafter, Clermont Academy Collection]) wrote that the church came into existence around 1840 and provided his father with the first regular salary he had ever received from preaching (23). It is unknown to this editor how long the church existed, but it apparently did not outlive Daniel Parker or have any other minister besides him. Interestingly, Parker makes no reference to this congregation in his autobiography and identifies himself primarily as an itinerant. See also Charles Cist, *Cincinnati in 1841: Its Early Annals and Future Prospects* (Cincinnati: published by the author, 1841), 98; Cist, *The Cincinnati Miscellany*, vol. 1 (Cincinnati: published by the author, 1845), 81; "Charles C. Parker, M.D.," in *The United States Biographical Dictionary and Portrait Gallery of Eminent and Self-Made Men: Iowa Volume* (Chicago: American Biographical, 1878), 357–59; "Charles C. Parker, MD," in *Portrait and Biographical Album of Fayette County, Iowa* (Chicago: Lake City, 1891), 586–88; Robinson, 26; and Russell Miller, 697.

94. MS, Octavo 16.

95. Robinson, 26.

96. Russell Miller, 44–49.

97. Russell Miller, 48, 105–10.

98. Daniel Parker, *Familiar Letters to a Brother*, 137–42.

99. Russell Miller, 111–26; Bressler, 42–48.

100. Bressler, 46; Cassara, 27; Russell Miller, 124–25. This theological conflict may explain why Parker never formally joined the Universalist denomination, and its resolution may partially explain the disappearance of Parker's First Restorationist Church. Its members possibly drifted to the nearby Universalist Society in Cincinnati when the theological disagreements that separated the two communities dissolved.

101. MS, Octavo 9.

102. Interestingly, the few other Universalists of Parker's day who affirmed a version of Christian mortalism combined it with the "ultra" position, rather than Parker's "Restorationist" position, on future retribution (Bressler, 45).

103. MS, Octavo 13. This would place Parker's concept of future retribution closer to that of the first-generation Universalist Elhanan Winchester than to that of the first generation's John Murray (Holifield, 226–27). For Parker's restorative understanding of divine justice, see *Familiar Letters to a Brother*, 89–93.

104. MS, Octavo 15. See also *Familiar Letters to a Brother* (105–9) for the activist dimension of Parker's Restorationism. Other Universalists, as well as many American Christians in general, also saw social reform as a necessary extension of faith, though particular theological considerations led different groups and individuals to approach reform in different ways (Russell Miller, 485–638). See also Timothy Smith, 8.

105. MS, Octavos 5, 6, and 9.

106. MS, Octavo 14. For an outline of the moderate, gradualist "emancipationist" antislavery position, see David Torbett, *Theology and Slavery: Charles Hodge and Horace Bushnell* (Macon, GA: Mercer University Press, 2006), 42–47. For the history of the African colonization project, see P. J. Staudenraus, *The African Colonization Movement, 1816–1865* (New York: Columbia University Press, 1961), 59–68, 29.

107. MS, Octavo 14.

108. MS, Octavo 15.

109. MS, Octavo 15.

110. For an outline of the more radical abolitionist position, see Torbett, 47–50. For a thorough recent history of abolitionism, emphasizing the racial and gender diversity of the movement, see Manisha Sinha, *The Slave's Cause: A History of Abolition* (New Haven, CT: Yale University Press, 2016). See also Louis Filler, *The Crusade against Slavery, 1830–1860* (New York: Harper and Row, 1960), 48–81; and John McKivigan, *The War against Proslavery Religion: Abolitionism and the Northern Churches, 1830–1865* (Ithaca, NY: Cornell University Press, 1984), 93–110.

111. MS, Octavo 15.

112. Merton L. Dillon, *Elijah P. Lovejoy, Abolitionist Editor* (Urbana: University of Illinois Press, 1961), viii–ix, 143–70.

113. MS, Octavo 15.

114. MS, Octavo 2.

115. MS, Octavo 6.

116. MS, Octavo 15.

117. MS, Octavo 14.

118. MS, Octavo 9.

119. At the time, Daniel Parker wrote a letter to his brother William containing similar jarring racial language, along with references to the awkwardness of his situation and his distressed emotional state: "I have the charge of a bad set of Negroes, which you must know is pretty trying to one who becomes more and more opposed to slavery." He mentioned that he was keeping a journal, "but it is a jumbled up mess, just like my feelings" (Daniel Parker to William Parker [II], October 2, 1812, Special Collections, Legacy Library, Marietta College, Marietta, OH).

120. MS, Octavo 8.

121. Foner, *Give Me Liberty!*, 424.

122. Ronald C. White, *A. Lincoln: A Biography* (New York: Random House, 2009), 276.

123. Matthew Salafia, *Slavery's Borderland: Freedom and Bondage along the Ohio River* (Philadelphia: University of Pennsylvania Press, 2013), 80–88.

124. Andrew R. L. Cayton, *Ohio: The History of a People* (Columbus: Ohio State University Press, 2002), 117–18.

125. MS, Octavo 15.

126. Sarah Baker Parker, "History of Clermont Academy," unpublished MS, 1884, Clermont Academy Collection, Northern Kentucky University, 11–13.

127. Sarah Baker Parker, 13. Gary L. Knepp considers the possibility that the Academy might have sheltered fugitives on the Underground Railroad in *Freedom's Struggle: A Response to Slavery from the Ohio Borderlands* (Milford, OH: Little Miami, 2008), 131–37.

128. Kevin F. Kern and Gregory S. Wilson, *Ohio: A History of the Buckeye State* (Chichester, UK: John Wiley and Sons, 2014), 148. Early Ohio law actually forbade African Americans from attending tax-supported public schools with White children (151).

129. Filler, 64–65.

130. "Clermont Academy," in Ohio State Centennial Educational Committee, *Historical Sketches of the Higher Educational Institutions, and also of Benevolent and*

Reformatory Institutions of the State of Ohio ([Columbus, OH]: [State Commissioner of Common Schools], 1876). See also Roy C. Thompson, *The Schools of Clermont: A Study in the Development of Education in Clermont County, Ohio* (Cincinnati: Little Miami Lithopress, 1962), 14–22.

131. MS, Octavo 15.

132. Several printed Clermont Academy circulars are in the Clermont Academy Collection at Northern Kentucky University. Most are two-page pamphlets on a single folded sheet of paper. The 1849 circular is six pages including a front and back cover and a directory of students.

133. Clermont Academy Circular, undated, probably 1867–1876, Clermont Academy Collection, Northern Kentucky University.

134. Sarah Baker Parker, 11. There is also a history of Clermont Academy, including a list of the university degrees, professions, and other prominent achievements of former students, in J. L. Rockey and R. J. Bancroft, *History of Clermont County, Ohio: With Illustrations and Biographical Sketches of Its Prominent Men and Pioneers* (Philadelphia: L. H. Everts, 1880), 171–73.

135. Printed flier for "Clermont Academy Exhibition, Friday, March 28, 1845," Clermont Academy Collection, Northern Kentucky University.

136. Charles N. Sinnett, *Our Thompson Family: In Maine, New Hampshire and the West* (Concord, NH: Rumford Printing Co., 1907), 218–20; Fannie Parker Currier, "A History of the Parker Family," unpublished MS, 1928, and "A Sketch of the Administration of James Kennedy Parker as Principal of Wilberforce Academy," unpublished MS, 1916, both in Clermont Academy Collection, Northern Kentucky University.

137. MS, Octavo 15; Clermont Academy Circular [1867–76?]; Sarah Baker Parker, 1–14; Currier, "A History of the Parker Family."

138. Sarah Baker Parker, 10.

139. MS, Octavo 14.

140. MS, Octavo 7.

141. The following biography of Priscilla is taken from this autobiography by Daniel Parker, the memoir of William Tell Parker, a ten-page "sketch" titled "Mrs. Priscilla M. R. Parker" by her daughter Susan Parker Donaldson (Clermont Academy Collection, Northern Kentucky University), and Sinnett's ten-page biography of her, which cites several sources, including a "sketch" by her grandson Parker Donaldson (208–18).

142. MS, Octavo 16. According to family history, Priscilla was more forward than her husband not only in opposition to slavery but in the temperance movement as well. She and fellow activists "entered every grocery, dramshop and tavern in New Richmond, O., where drinks were sold, and exhorted the proprietors to desist from their traffic" (Parker Donaldson, quoted in Sinnett, 210).

143. William Tell Parker, 31.

144. Priscilla Parker to "Beloved brethren and sisters" of the Ten Mile Baptist Church, c/o Andrew Coombs, August 4, 1837, Clermont Academy Collection, Northern Kentucky University.

145. MS, Octavo 13.

146. MS, Octavo 14.

147. Bressler, 55, 66–67.
148. MS, Octavo 15.
149. Sarjent, "Western Messenger: To the Saints throughout the World," 241.

Note on Text

1. James Donald Parker to David Torbett, email, August 10, 2016.
2. Family Copy, 6.
3. For examples of irregular spelling from the time period, see letters and diaries quoted in Lewis O. Saum, *The Popular Mood of Pre–Civil War America* (Westport, CT: Greenwood, 1980), xvi–xix.
4. Parker's variant spellings are "Cillibacy" (Octavo 6), "Celibacy" (Octavo 7), and "Celibicy" (Octavo 9).
5. For example, Parker's opening sentence is "Autobiography of Daniel Parker, began to be written at the request of his family and friends, mostly from memory in the 64th year of his age, 1845." The Family Copy begins, "Autobiography of Daniel Parker, commenced to be written in the 64th year of his age (1845) at the request of his family and friends." The second sentence is perhaps more elegant, but not any more clear, and it leaves out the charming qualification, "mostly from memory."
6. MS, Octavo 11.
7. Even when republishing printed (as opposed to manuscript) material from the nineteenth century, some historians have found it necessary to revise punctuation when the original "distorts the sense for modern readers." See Mark A. Noll, ed., *The Princeton Theology, 1812–1921: Scripture, Science, and Theological Method from the Age of Archibald Alexander to Benjamin Warfield* (Grand Rapids, MI: Baker Academic, 2001), 48.
8. "Black and White: A Matter of Capitalization," *CMOS Shoptalk* (blog), *The Chicago Manual of Style*, June 22, 2020, https://cmosshoptalk.com/2020/06/22/black-and-white-a-matter-of-capitalization/.
9. Kwame Anthony Appiah, "The Case for Capitalizing the *B* in Black," *Atlantic*, June 18, 2020, https://www.theatlantic.com/ideas/archive/2020/06/time-to-capitalize-blackand-white/613159/.

Chapter 1

1. The MS hyphenates "Newburyport" as "Newbury-Port" and follows a similar pattern for other place names. This edition will usually use more familiar spellings of place names with some exceptions, such as when Parker's spelling indicates a different pronunciation from the modern spelling.
2. William Parker was born in Malden, Massachusetts, on June 5, 1745, according to Ferris, *Dawes-Gates Ancestral Lines*, vol. 1. His biography in that volume agrees with (and was in part derived from the manuscript of) this autobiography by Daniel Parker. Ferris also includes additional details, including that William was successful as a cabinet maker, "even to the extent of employing journey men and exporting furniture to the West Indies where it found a profitable market. Specimens of his

work are still cherished in Illinois and Ohio." His financial success allowed him to purchase his share of land with the Ohio Company (473–74).

3. Mary Warner was on February 5, 1753, in Gloucester, Massachusetts (on Cape Ann), the daughter of Philemon and Elizabeth Woodward Warner, and died in Meigs County, Ohio, on February 17, 1811 (Ferris, 657). Ferris, noting her writing ability, credits her for educating her highly literate (but formally unschooled) children (478). Daniel Parker describes her as a religiously devout and loving mother and records how she was affected by the isolation and privations of frontier life.

4. Ferris (657) records that Ezekiel Warner, born in Gloucester, Massachusetts, in 1762, was "a member of the crew of the privateer 'America' under Captain John Somes of Gloucester" and that he was imprisoned in the Revolutionary War. He was said to have written an account of his escape that is now lost. He died sometime after 1798, probably in western Pennsylvania. William Warner was born in Gloucester in 1766. He was mentally disabled ("non-compos mentis, simple, not violent" [657]), reportedly by a childhood injury. He migrated west with Daniel Parker's family and is the subject of a dramatic episode in this chapter of this autobiography.

5. The MS renders "Charlestown" as "Charleton" (Octavo 1), which may be a slip of the pen. The Family Copy has "in the Charlestown area" (19).

6. Elizabeth Warner Parker was born in Newburyport, Massachusetts, in 1773 and migrated west with the Parker family in 1788. She died in 1850, never having married or had children (Ferris, 481).

7. The younger William Parker, born in Newburyport, Massachusetts, in 1775, married Betsey Wyatt in 1802. According to Ferris, "Theirs was the first wedding performed in Ames Township and probably the second in Athens County [Ohio]" (481). The couple settled and remained in Rutland, Ohio. He died in 1855.

8. Sally (Sarah) Parker, born 1777, became the second wife of Ohio statesman Ephraim Cutler in 1808. Daniel Parker mentions Sally several times in this autobiography. She died in 1846 in Warren Township, Washington County (Ferris, 481). See note 63 in chap. 5 for more of her biography.

9. John Parker was born in 1779. He married Lucy Cotton in 1807. He, like his brother and father, was a carpenter and mechanic. He died in Washington County in 1849 (Ferris, 481). In this autobiography, Daniel Parker describes John as his confidante, especially in spiritual matters, their having served together as ministers in the Halcyon Church.

10. Polly Parker was born in 1783 in Newburyport, Massachusetts. She married Judge Cushing Shaw (Ferris, 481). According to the couple's grave marker in Old Salem Cemetery in Wilkesville, Meigs County, Ohio, she died in 1869. The marker gives her name as Polly W. Shaw, but according to Daniel Parker none of his siblings except Elizabeth Warner Shaw had middle names. See photograph on Find a Grave, https://www.findagrave.com/memorial/71241999/mary-w-shaw.

11. Nancy Parker was born in Newburyport, Massachusetts, in 1785 and married Stephen Strong (Ferris, 481). She died in what was then Salem Township in Meigs County, Ohio, in 1864, according to her grave marker in Old Salem Cemetery. See photograph on Find a Grave, https://www.findagrave.com/memorial/70038541/nancy-strong.

12. Ferris writes that "Susanna Parker" was born in Newburyport, Massachusetts, in 1787, married Sylvanus Everts, and died in 1815 (481). Daniel Parker gives "Suky" as her actual name and "Susanna" as a nickname (what "we sometimes called her"), in contrast to both Ferris and the Family Copy. See note 59 in chap. 5.

13. Fanny Parker was born in 1789 in or near McKeesport, Pennsylvania (Ferris, 481). See further biographical information about Fanny, including her marriage to John Fordice (or Fordyce), in fig. 2.4 and the notes to chap. 5 below.

14. Ebenezer Parker was born near McKeesport, Pennsylvania, in 1792. He married Mary Swett. He died in 1873 near Cincinnati, Ohio (Ferris, 481).

15. Parker consistently spells his sister's name "Clarrissa," as does the Family Copy. Ferris uses the spelling "Clarissa." She was born near McKeesport, Pennsylvania, in 1795. She married Peter Shaw, brother of her sister Polly's husband, Cushing Shaw. She died in 1817 (Ferris 481).

16. "Down cellar": thus in both the MS (Octavo 1) and the Family Copy (20). Parker often omits words (in this case, "the" between "down" and "cellar") that present-day readers might expect to be included.

17. "Mr. Murry" was John Murray (1742–93), installed as the second minister of the Old South Presbyterian Church in Newburyport in 1781. He had previously served a congregation in Boothbay, Maine. He had a reputation as a powerful preacher and as a fierce advocate of American independence, so much so that the British government put a bounty on his head of five hundred pounds sterling (Alexander Blaikie, *A History of Presbyterianism in New England* [Boston: Alexander Moore, 1881], 175–82; and E. [Euphemia] Vale Smith, *History of Newburyport: From the Earliest Settlement of the Country to the Present Time; With a Biographical Appendix* [Newburyport, MA: n.p., 1854], 375–76). Ironically, considering Daniel Parker's later beliefs, Murray was a vehement opponent of the idea of universal salvation, particularly as it was promoted by one of its earliest advocates in the United States, an English immigrant who (to double the irony) shared the name John Murray (1741–1815). Their contemporaries quickly distinguished the Universalist as "Salvation Murray" and the Presbyterian as "Damnation Murray" (Kathryn Gin Lum, *Damned Nation: Hell in America from the Revolution to Reconstruction* [Oxford: Oxford University Press, 2014], 19–26).

18. To be "religious" in the sense that Parker describes his parents and yet not be church members was common in pre–Civil War America. Many people affirmed beliefs, prayed, studied and practiced other religious disciplines, identified with Protestant denominations, and attended and participated in Protestant churches without formally joining them. This was partly due to the more demanding criteria for full church membership employed by such churches before the twentieth century. See George C. Rable, *God's Almost Chosen Peoples: A Religious History of the American Civil War* (Chapel Hill: University of North Carolina Press, 2010), 11–12. On the other hand, Ferris (474) and Stillman Carter Larkin (*The Pioneer History of Meigs County* [Columbus, OH: Berlin Printing Company, 1908], 41) state simply that the couple were both "members" of the Presbyterian Church. These later authors may be working with a more informal definition of church membership than Parker. The Parkers were unusual in that they identified as Presbyterians as opposed to

Congregationalists, in contrast to most other New England Calvinists of English ancestry. See "Parker and American Religion" in the Editor's Introduction with accompanying endnotes for an explanation.

19. The modern spelling of this river is Youghiogheny. This volume retains Parker's original spelling, "Youghogena," as it indicates Parker might have pronounced the word differently.

20. The history of the Ohio Company and the "first settlement" on the confluence of the Muskingum and Ohio Rivers can be found in Cayton and Riggs, 13–93; Cayton, *Ohio: The History of a People*, 40–43; and Kern and Wilson, 100–17. The settlement was first named Adelphia (Greek for "brotherhood") and later changed to Marietta in honor of Queen Marie Antoinette of France in gratitude for French support of American independence. Marietta was "first" only in that it was the first officially recognized European-American settlement in the Northwest Territory. Thousands of Native Americans already lived in the territory that would become the five states of Ohio, Indiana, Illinois, Michigan, and Wisconsin, as well as part of Minnesota, as did thousands of Whites who settled there without the approval of or purchasing land from the United States government as directed by the Northwest Ordinance of 1787.

21. The genealogy that introduces the Family Copy includes a "biographical note" about William Parker that gives the very precise number of 1,173 acres for his share in the Ohio Company (5), but keeps Daniel Parker's original number of 1,500 acres in the actual copy of this part of his autobiography (21). Ferris writes that William's share amounted to "1200 or 1500 acres" (474).

22. The Treaty of Greenville of 1795 followed the Battle of Fallen Timbers of 1794, in which the forces of General "Mad" Anthony Wayne defeated the pan-tribal Western Confederacy and, in the following months, burned villages and crops of Native Americans, reducing them to starvation. The treaty effectively ended unified Indian resistance to American settlement of the old Northwest, until it was revived again a decade later by Tecumseh and his brother, who would be known as the Prophet Tenskwatawa. The Parkers, though they would delay a few years before moving from western Pennsylvania, would be one of many families that poured into Ohio in the aftermath of the Treaty of Greenville. See Gregory Evans Dowd, *A Spirited Resistance: The North American Indian Struggle for Unity, 1745–1815* (Baltimore: Johns Hopkins University Press, 1992), 110–16; James H. O'Donnell III, *Ohio's First Peoples* (Athens: Ohio University Press, 2004), 73–100; and Kern and Wilson, 87–99.

23. Using paper soaked in oil or grease, making it waterproof and translucent, such windows would be a frontier practice for decades to come. Laura Ingalls Wilder, author of the popular *Little House* books, describes her family's dugout home in Minnesota in the early 1870s as having "a small greased paper window by the door" (*On the Banks of Plum Creek*, rev. illus. ed. [New York: HarperCollins, 1953], 10). Daniel Parker's wife Priscilla would make and sell similar craftwork, waterproof oilcloth "for covering tables and other furniture" to help support their family (William Tell Parker, 25).

24. "Linsey" is short for "linsey-woolsy," linen and wool, *Oxford English Dictionary*, 2nd ed., s.v. "linsey."

25. Apparently, "sick wheat" was and remained mysterious to many others. Writing about agriculture in early nineteenth-century Champaign County, Ohio, J. W. Ogden relates, "Occasionally, a field would be grown producing what was called 'sick wheat,' so named from its tendency to cause vomiting. . . . We have been unable to ascertain whether the 'sick-wheat' was the product of a particular variety of wheat, or from certain localities, from the condition of the undrained soil, or made its appearance generally the same year. It has been described as differing little or none from the wheat now grown, except in the appearance of a red spot on the grain or an indication of sprouting. Some have claimed that it was simply malted wheat" (J. W. Ogden, *The History of Champaign County, Ohio* [Chicago: W. H. Beers, 1881], 221).

26. For comparable experiences of migrant women under the stress of isolation and deprivation on the frontier, see Cayton, *Ohio: The History of a People*, 31–34.

27. The "Sheppard" and Porter families Parker refers to may be related to a number of families with New England roots bearing variations of the name Shepard (Shephard, Shepherd) and Porter who settled in Marietta and the surrounding towns in Washington County, Ohio (*History of Washington County* [1881], 58, 92–93, 368, 407, 444, 544, 590–91, 687). Parker mentioned the settlement of the Ohio company "at the mouth of the Muskingum" previously, but this is the first time in his memoir he mentions Marietta by name.

28. Parker refers to land speculator and entrepreneur Ebenezer Zane, which he misspells as "Zanes." Zane procured federal funding to turn a trail he began blazing in 1796 into Ohio's first long-distance road, Zane's Trace (Kern and Wilson, 163). As Parker indicates, Zanesville, Ohio, built on land he originally owned, is named after him.

29. John McKee was born in Ireland in 1746 and immigrated with his family to Pennsylvania around 1750. His father, David McKee, acquired land at the confluence of the Monongahela and Youghiogheny rivers in 1755, where he operated a ferry service across the two rivers. The location became known as McKee's Ferry. In 1795, John McKee divided the land deeded to him by his father into lots and advertised in the *Pittsburgh Gazette* for investors in "a new town," which would eventually become McKeesport. He died in 1807. Walter S. Abbot and William E. Harrison, *The First One Hundred Years of McKeesport: An Historical and Statistical Description of the City from Its Inception until Its Centennial in 1894* (McKeesport, PA: Press of McKeesport Times, 1894), 8–16.

30. Ezekiel 16:49. Parker addresses his children with moral instruction several times in his autobiography. He quotes and paraphrases the Bible often, sometimes but not always giving a citation. Parker's own chapter-and-verse citations appear either in parentheses or as direct textual reference (e.g., "the injunction in First Corinthians 16:20," below). Citations not given by the author are provided in the notes.

31. Though the excise tax applied to the whole nation, resistance to it centered in western Pennsylvania and spread to other frontier communities. The Whiskey Rebellion of 1794 was "the single largest example of armed resistance to a law of the United States between the ratification of the Constitution and the Civil War" (Thomas P. Slaughter, *The Whiskey Rebellion: Frontier Epilogue to the American Revolution* [New York: Oxford University Press, 1986], 5). It consisted less of shooting battles than of

diffuse protests, assaults on persons and property, dramatic standoffs, and, as Parker indicated, extraordinary mobilizations of personnel. In July, seven thousand rebels advanced on Pittsburgh. To quash the revolt, President George Washington personally led an army of almost thirteen thousand militiamen, approximating the size of his Revolutionary Continental Army. As indicated in the Editor's Introduction, historians describe the rebellion as a key moment in the "early republic" period of American history, laying bare political, regional, and economic differences in the new nation, between the "friends of order" who favored a strong federal government and "friends of liberty" who opposed the excise tax as federal overreach (221); between the settled east and the unsettled west; and between the economic elite and the poorer classes who saw the tax as disproportionately affecting them (Patrick Griffin, *American Leviathan: Empire, Nation, and Revolutionary Frontier* [New York: Hill and Wang, 2007], 222–39).

32. Parker mistakenly conflates John Neville (1731–1803), the actual excise agent, with his son, Presley Neville (b. 1755). John Neville was born in Virginia, the son of wealthy planters, a Revolutionary War general, slaveholder, and the proprietor of Bower Hill, the first large estate in the Pittsburgh region. Slaughter describes him as "an unrelenting symbol and active agent of all the contrasts and conflicts between the cosmopolitan East and the frontier West that the excise represented" (154). In the confrontation with the Mingo Creek Militia at Bower Hill on July 16–17, 1794, John Neville fired the first fatal shot of the Whiskey Rebellion. Several buildings on his property were burned (177–84). Presley Neville was, like his father, born in Virginia, a Revolutionary War veteran, and a large landholder in western Pennsylvania. He was on his way to support his father at Bower Hill when militia captured him along with two others. All three managed to escape. Presley Neville was, as Parker indicated, the proprietor and namesake of the village of Neville in Clermont County, Ohio, where he died in 1818. See Rockey and Bancroft, 370; David P. Barr, *A Colony Sprung from Hell: Pittsburgh and the Struggle for Authority on the Western Pennsylvania Frontier, 1744–1794* (Kent, OH: Kent State University Press, 2014), 263, 265; and Leland D. Baldwin, *Whiskey Rebels: The Story of a Frontier Uprising*, rev. ed. (Pittsburgh: University of Pittsburgh Press, 1968), 45–46, 120–25.

33. David Bradford, born around 1760, immigrated to Washington County in western Pennsylvania around 1782. He was a successful lawyer and deputy attorney general for the county, one of the more "respectable" citizens who stepped up to lead the rebellion after the battle at Bower Hill. In his "incendiary" speeches, he called for secession and an independent state in the west. He did in fact, as Parker indicated, flee south when the rebellion was defeated, resettling in Bayou Sara, Louisiana Territory, where he lived the remainder of his days. President John Adams pardoned Bradford for treason in 1799. It is unclear why Daniel Parker refers to Bradford as "Colonel"; Bradford referred to himself as "major general" during the rebellion (Slaughter, 183, 267; Barr, 266; Griffin, 233–38; Baldwin, 265).

34. With thousands of participants in the rebellion either fleeing before Washington's army arrived or taking advantage of offers of amnesty, "the army was left with about twenty obscure characters in custody to shoulder the blame." In November of 1794, they were brought to Philadelphia, then the seat of the federal government, for

trial. All but two were acquitted and the remainder were convicted of treason but pardoned by President Washington (Slaughter, 219).

35. "Kine pox" is a synonym for cowpox. If Parker's family was in fact vaccinated in the technical sense (exposed to cowpox in order to prevent smallpox), then this would have been one of the earliest such vaccinations in the United States. Parker may be referring to an older, riskier practice of inoculation, which exposed the patient directly to smallpox. See Elaine G. Breslaw, *Lotions, Potions, Pills, and Magic: Health Care in Early America* (New York: New York University Press, 2012), 103–4.

36. When Parker describes his neighbors in western Pennsylvania as being of "Irish descent," he undoubtedly means Scots-Irish descent, from Scottish Protestants who immigrated to the Ulster province in the north of Ireland beginning in the early seventeenth century, and whose descendants migrated from there to North America, largely during the eighteenth century. The three religious groups Parker refers to were different Presbyterian subgroups with primarily ethnically Scottish membership (Ned C. Landsman, *Scotland and Its First American Colony, 1683–1765* [Princeton, NJ: Princeton University Press, 1985], 50–56, 232–36). His neighbors' dialect, which Parker describes below, can be found in part in Michael Montgomery, *From Ulster to America: The Scotch-Irish Heritage of American English* (Belfast, Northern Ireland: Ulster Historical Foundation, 2006), 36, 68, 83, 152, and 159.

37. The "Covenanter" and "Seceder" churches shared historical roots and similar beliefs, tracing their origins to Scotland and the National Covenant of 1638, a rejection of the mainline Scottish Presbyterian Church's accommodations to secular power. The majority of the membership of their American counterparts, the Reformed Presbytery (Covenanters) and the Associate Presbytery (Seceders), united in 1782 to form the Associate Reformed Synod, but a significant minority from each group, citing fine theological distinctions, refused to join the union and continued their separate denominations (William L. Fisk, "The Seceders: The Scottish High Church Tradition in America," *Journal of Presbyterian History* 62, no. 4 [Winter 1984]: 291–97). "Mr. Black" is John Black, born in Ireland in 1768 and educated in Scotland. He immigrated to the United States in 1797. He was the "first Covenanter minister settled west of the Allegheny mountains, and the pioneer missionary in the new West," gathering an "extensive congregation" centered in Pittsburgh and including several smaller "societies" throughout the region (W. Melancthon Glasgow, *History of the Reformed Presbyterian Church in America: With Sketches of All Her Ministry, Congregations, Missions, Institutions, Publications, etc.* [Baltimore: Hill and Harvey, 1888], 440–42). "Mr. Henderson" was Matthew Henderson, who became the pastor of the Bethesda Associate Reformed congregation in Elizabeth Township, Allegheny County, in 1785 (Thomas Cushing, *History of Allegheny County, Pennsylvania* [Chicago: A. Warner, 1889], 308). His father, of the same name, was a better-known Seceder minister in neighboring Washington County, Pennsylvania (Boyd Crumrine, ed. *History of Washington County, Pennsylvania: With Biographical Sketches of Many of Its Pioneers and Prominent Men* [Philadelphia: L. H. Everts, 1882], 708–9). "Dr. Watts," whose name Daniel Parker misspells as "Wats" in the MS (Octavo 1), is the famous English hymnist Isaac Watts (1674–1748). The singing of hymns (that is, composed religious songs) was

a matter of recurrent controversy in Reformed churches. Some believed congregations should sing only metrical settings of the 150 psalms in the Bible. Parker implies that this was the item of contention between the two ministers, but in fact both Covenanters and Seceders rejected hymn-singing (Glasgow, 58; Fisk, 291). See also George M. Marsden, *Jonathan Edwards: A Life* (New Haven, CT: Yale University Press, 2004), 143–44.

38. Parker is referring to the Calvinist doctrine of double predestination: the idea that, as determined from the beginning of time, not only are some people among the "elect," destined for salvation, but others are "reprobate," destined for damnation. Whether this system is a source of comfort, as it has been for many, or a source of anxiety, as it was for John Parker and many others, depends on how confident one is of being among the elect. Often it is a source of both for the same person, a famous example being the English poet William Cowper (1731–1800). He apparently was first rescued from insanity and later driven to despair by the same idea (Deborah Heller, "Cowper's Task and the Writing of a Poet's Salvation," *Studies in English Literature, 1500–1900* 35, no. 3 [Summer 1995]: 575–77). See "Parker and American Religion" in the Editor's Introduction for the influence of Calvinist theology on the Parker family and American religion in general.

39. The MS renders "tracks" as "tracts" (Octavo 2). The Family Copy has "tracks" (29).

40. Parker and the Family Copy use the spelling "Kenhawa," though in this one instance Parker apparently accidentally writes "Kenhwa" (Octavo 2). The modern spelling "Kanawha" is applied to the river, a tributary of the Ohio that winds through present-day West Virginia.

41. During the pre-Columbian era a series of ancient Native American groups lived in the Ohio country, but they had dispersed by around the middle of the fourteenth century. Beginning in the seventeenth century the region was repopulated by Algonquian-speaking Indians, then by Iroquois, then by several Native American groups coming "from all directions," in part because of pressure exerted by European expansion. In the eighteenth century, Shawnee, Miami, and Delaware Indians established multiethnic and multilingual villages north of the hill country (where Parker would live) but preserved the area south of the Ohio River as a hunting ground (Salafia, 18–19). This would fit Parker's description of Leading Creek as a commuting route to hunting grounds to the south. See Stephen Aron, *How the West Was Lost: The Transformation of Kentucky from Daniel Boone to Henry Clay* (Baltimore: Johns Hopkins University Press, 1996), 6–13. I have not found a confirmation of Parker's explanation of the Native American origin of the name "Leading Creek," which is not to say that it is not accurate.

42. Parker's regret for how the US government treated the Ohio Indians was unusual (though not unheard of) for a nineteenth-century White settler on the western frontier, and certainly well placed. The story of the government's relationship to "Ohio's first peoples" is long and complicated, with diverse actors having complex motivations. The simple summary is that, through warfare, legislation, and finally through removal, Indians were forced off their lands so that White people could take them. The Wyandot, the last Native American group living in Ohio, was forced to

migrate to reservations in Oklahoma in 1843, two years before Parker began his autobiography (O'Donnell, 124–26).

43. The Family Copy reads "We often wore moccasins in the summer" (30), which is Parker's essential intended meaning, though the handwriting in the MS is unclear (Octavo 2).

44. Native Americans utilized Ohio's salt water springs (licks) as early as eight thousand years ago. In the late eighteenth and early nineteenth centuries, entrepreneurs like Joseph Conklin in Scioto extracted salt by boiling brine from the licks in large kettles (Kern and Wilson, 14, 80).

45. The Family Copy reads "We made our own sugar" (30), which is Parker's essential intended meaning, though the handwriting in the MS is unclear (Octavo 2).

46. Parker's nostalgia for the simplicity of frontier culture parallels similar memoirs of Ohio written at the time (Cayton, *Ohio: The History of a People*, 102), which is not to say his description of the pioneer life was inaccurate.

Chapter 2

1. This wording is the Family Copy's (34). The MS (Octavo 2) reads "a sea vessel then building by Mr. James Whitney."

2. Beginning in 1800, oceangoing vessels were built in Marietta and sent via the Ohio and Mississippi rivers to the Gulf of Mexico. This industry thrived in the first years of the nineteenth century until it was interrupted by Thomas Jefferson's embargo of 1807 against the United Kingdom and France. It later revived briefly in the 1840s. James Whitney (ca. 1774–1852) was a principal shipbuilder in Marietta in the early period and Colonel Abner Lord (ca. 1760–1821) was one of several Marietta merchants who commissioned ships. The *Brig Marietta,* built by Whitney for Lord, weighing 150 tons, was completed in 1802 and commanded by Captain O. Williams. See Martin R. Andrews, ed. and comp., *History of Marietta and Washington County, Ohio, and Representative Citizens* (Chicago: Biographical Publishing Company, 1902), 306–7; Cayton and Riggs, 51–55; *History of Washington County, Ohio* (1881), 366; A. T. Nye, "Ship Building at Marietta," *Marietta Register*, March 24, 1881.

3. See "Parker and American Religion" in the Editor's Introduction for the growing influence of this "Arminian" concept of free will, in contrast to the Calvinist view of predestination, among American Protestants in the nineteenth century.

4. See "The Halcyon Church" and related topics in the Editor's Introduction for more of Abel Sarjent's biography and the controversy surrounding him.

5. Daniel Parker emphasizes the words "*living death*" in the MS by underlining them (Octavo 2). This is the case for all of Parker's words set in italics in this edition.

6. Sermons vividly depicting the terrors of hell were a standard part of a Protestant preacher's repertoire in Parker's time. The most famous American hellfire sermon of the eighteenth century was Jonathan Edwards's "Sinners in the Hands of an Angry God," anthologized in *A Jonathan Edwards Reader*, ed. John E. Smith, Harry S. Stout, and Kenneth P. Minkema (New Haven, CT: Yale University Press, 2003), 89–105. See also Marsden, 221. John "Damnation" Murray, the Parkers' pastor at the Old South Presbyterian Church in Newburyport, was renowned for his eloquence

"when portraying the terrors of eternal punishment" (E. Vale Smith, 375). A published text of one of these hellfire sermons, "The Last Solemn Scene," was a best seller for Murray, with at least four printings (Lum, 25–26).

7. Parker's memory of never having used profane language or even heard it in his home might surprise twenty-first-century readers, but is plausible in his time and context. His contemporary, Princeton theologian Charles Hodge, remembers cursing only one time in his life, after stubbing his toe when he was thirteen or fourteen years old, and was "thankful no similar experience ever occurred to me" (quoted in Archibald Alexander Hodge, *Life of Charles Hodge* [London: T. Nelson, 1880], 14). Parker's aversion to profanity recurs several times in this autobiography.

8. Parker's affinity for music is a recurrent motif of this autobiography.

9. Here Parker first describes Abel Sarjent's Arminianism (emphasis on free will) and secondly his "annihilationism," a view of the distribution of justice in the afterlife that rejects the traditional concept of eternal punishment for the wicked but stops short of the universal salvation that Daniel Parker would later espouse. See "The Halcyon Church" and related topics in the Editor's Introduction for further explanation of Sarjent's theology and their place in the broader context of religion in nineteenth-century America.

10. Despite the Halcyon Church's unorthodox theology, Parker's experience as described in this chapter has the hallmarks of a typical evangelical conversion experience, with a notable exception being any motivation by threats of hell. In this instance, the first of many similarities to be noted, Parker makes a distinction between his "theoretical conversion" (i.e., intellectual assent to idea) and his later experiential conversion, which engages the heart and the will, implying that both aspects are necessary for an authentic conversion: a long-standing assumption of evangelical revivalism (Marsden, 281–90).

11. This was John R. Bing, who according to family history recorded by Virginia Lee Hubman Kane was born in Chester County, Pennsylvania, 1747. By 1774 he was living in Augusta County, Virginia, where he married Mary Young, and where all their children were born (Kane, John R. Bing Family Group Record, Bing Binder, 1998, Gallia County Historical Society, Gallipolis, OH). See also *History of Gallia County: Containing a Condensed History of the County; Biographical Sketches; General Statistics; Miscellaneous Matters &c* (Gallipolis, OH: St. Peter's Episcopal Church, 1976), facsimile reprint from *Historical Hand Atlas* (Chicago: H. H. Hardesty, 1882), iii, iv, v, xxiv, 3–4, 32–34; and *Cemeteries of Addison Township, Gallia County Ohio* (Gallipolis, OH: Gallia County Historical/Genealogical Society, 2003), 17. The Bing family moved to Gallia County, Ohio, in 1800. From 1802 until around 1804, Gallipolis township meetings were held in Bing's house, "the first frame building erected in the town" (*History of Gallia County*, v). He served in several Gallia County and Gallipolis Township political offices and owned property in various locations in Gallia and Athens Counties. James Weldon, presumably the wheelwright Daniel Parker mentions, was a witness when John Bing deeded one hundred acres to his son, also named John Bing (*Gallia County Deed Book*, vol. 2, 277; copied by Kane).

12. Alcohol consumption ("strong drink") was indeed, as Parker implies, an ordinary aspect of social life for most Americans in the early nineteenth century.

Attitudes toward (and aggregate consumption of) alcohol changed significantly with the formation of the American Temperance Society in 1826 (Abzug, 81–82). Parker, who would become a temperance advocate, here seems less troubled by drinking per se than by what it led to: dancing. Moral distaste for dancing was another value that Parker shared with evangelicals (Marsden, 296–97; Cartwright, 34). A "frolic" or "ballroom" as a moral low point was a trope that Parker's narrative shares with other nineteenth-century conversion stories; see Zilpha Elaw, *Memoirs of the Life, Religious Experience, Ministerial Travels, and Labours of Mrs. Zilpha Elaw, an American Female of Colour* (London: published by the author, 1846), repr. in *Sisters of the Spirit: Three Black Women's Autobiographies of the Nineteenth Century*, ed. William L. Andrews (Bloomington: Indiana University Press, 1986), 63. That Parker was an enthusiastic musician and an opponent of dancing might be ironic, but was not unusual. Catherine Beecher remembers that her father Lyman Beecher, the famous evangelist and Parker's contemporary, also played the violin, "and every day practiced the liveliest airs. But if any of the girls began to take a dancing step, he would make the violin give a doleful screech, and thus always ended every attempt to dance" (quoted in Lyman Beecher, *Autobiography, Correspondence, etc. of Lyman Beecher*, ed. Charles Beecher [New York: Harper, 1865], 145).

13. Parker describes being convicted of sin as a prelude to his receiving grace, yet another similarity to the typical evangelical conversion narrative. See Virginia Lieson Brereton, *From Sin to Salvation: Stories of Women's Conversions, 1800 to the Present* (Bloomington: Indiana University Press, 1991), 3–10.

14. Such was the sentiment of Alfred Creigh, who called Sarjent's denial of hell a "very convenient" doctrine in his history of Washington County, Pennsylvania, in a section on local "superstitions" (211).

15. Mark 11:4. Parker is referring to a verse within an account of Jesus's entry into Jerusalem: "And they went their way and found the colt tied outside by the door at a place where two ways met, and they loosed him" (KJV). He interprets it as an allegory for his own indecision. Parker's unusual metaphorical interpretation of the passage, which he will use more than once, depends on wording that is particular to the King James Version, not other English translations.

16. According to Sarjent, the Halcyon Church "commenced its visible existence, in its present visible form, in Kenhawa county (now Mason county), in the state of Virginia, on the 11th day of July, 1802" ("Circular Epistle from the 9th Concilium of the Halcyon Church," 219). Parker's (often justified) perception of being excluded or even persecuted for holding unpopular opinions will recur even after he leaves the Halcyon Church, when he espouses "restoration" (universal salvation) and later when he becomes an abolitionist.

17. "From darkness to light. . .," Acts 26:18. Parker gives an example of Abel Sarjent's characteristically figurative interpretation of the Bible. Also, while he does not yet use the terms explicitly, Parker here makes his first allusion to the Halcyon symbolic interpretation of the Old Testament terms "Urim and Thummim." As Parker will later explain, the "seven attributes of God" in Sarjent's sermon are symbolically represented by "Urim." See "Urim and Thummim" in the Editor's Introduction and later notes in this chapter for further explanation.

18. Romans 1:16; 1 Peter 1:8.

19. Parker's ecstatic "joy" at the knowledge of his salvation is yet another way that his experience resembles the typical evangelical conversion. In addition to the works already cited on this topic, see Dickson D. Bruce Jr., *And They All Sang Hallelujah: Plain Folk Camp Meeting Religion, 1800–1845* (Knoxville: University of Tennessee Press, 1974), 63–69.

20. Thomas "Waddle" was probably Thomas Waddell, who was born in Augusta County, Virginia, in 1759, served in the American Revolution, and died in 1839, according to his veteran's pension application, made in 1832 in Mason County, [West] Virginia (Revolutionary War Pension and Bounty-Land Warrant Application Files, NARA Publication M804, Roll 2645).

21. A call to preach, following closely after (or coinciding with) a conversion experience, is also a common element of evangelical autobiographies; see Charles G. Finney, *Memoirs of Charles G. Finney, Written by Himself* (New York: Fleming H. Revell, 1876), 24–26. Parker's initial resistance to his call has precedents as well; see Jarena Lee, *The Life and Religious Experience of Jarena Lee* (Philadelphia: published by the author, 1836), repr. in *Sisters of the Spirit*, 35–38.

22. Parker quotes from the King James Version, 1 Corinthians 1:21; Luke 21:15; and Mark 13:11, respectively. The last passage is actually "take no thought beforehand what ye shall *speak*."

23. Mrs. Bing was Martha Young Bing, born ca. 1750 in Augusta County, Virginia, and married to John Bing in 1774 (Kane). She died January 12, 1838, according to her death notice in *Gallipolis Journal*, Feb 1, 1839, transcribed in Henrietta C. Evans and Mary P. Wood, *Death Notices, Obituaries, and Marriage Notices Taken from the Gallia County, Ohio Newspapers from 1825 to 1875* (Gallipolis, OH: Gallia County Historical/Genealogical Society, 1986), 6.

24. Parker's reference to the stones crying out if he remained silent is an allusion to Luke 19:37–40, another episode from Jesus's triumphal entry into Jerusalem. The "depression" that Parker refers to here as subsiding is the storm that kept Parker's party from crossing the river back into Ohio, not any person's mental state.

25. Parker is alluding to 1 Corinthians 14:15. The actual wording of the King James Version is "I will sing with the spirit, and I will sing with the understanding also" (a recurrence of the motif of music in this autobiography). Parker perceives that his call to preach is confirmed when it bears fruit in the form of a listener's conversion experience. This is yet another trope of evangelical conversion narratives (Finney, 24–26; Jarena Lee, 42–48).

26. Parker might mean that he had less than one year of schooling in his life, or that he had one year of schooling in addition to whatever he had at or before the age of seven, when his family lived in Massachusetts. In any case, he had at the most two years of formal schooling.

27. Parker's irenic personality, discussed in "A Human Story" in the Editor's Introduction, is evident throughout his autobiography. At times his aversion to conflict (and his desire for approval) became burdensome as he embraced unpopular opinions.

28. Daniel Parker describes his whole family as disapproving of his and his brother John's involvement in the Halcyon Church, but within a few years of their

joining the attitudes of some of their siblings may have softened. A small collection of hymns published by Abel Sarjent, probably in 1806 (from a bound collection of Halcyon publications, title page is missing), contains three poems purportedly written by "a little girl, named Clarissa Parker, about 10 years old: the daughter of Mr. Wm. And Mrs. Mary Parker in Gallia County, and sister to Elders John Parker and Daniel Parker" (Untitled Hymn Collection, 40–42). The same collection has a poem by "Susanna Parker" (28). However, the poems themselves contain broadly Christian ideas and, except for using the word "millennium" once, do not refer explicitly to specific Halcyon beliefs. There is also the fact of Fanny Parker's marriage to John Fordice (or Fordyce), the son of Halcyon Church member Rhoda Fordice (Fordyce). See fig. 2.4 and notes to chap. 5 below.

29. "Synagogue of Satan" is a reference to Revelation (2:9, 3:9). The term has been (and continues to be) a slur used against any number of religious groups that the speaker might oppose. For example, some American Protestants in Parker's day used it against the Catholic Church, e.g., William Craig Brownlee, *Letters in the Roman Catholic Controversy* (New York: published by the author, 1834), 36.

30. This is probably Esther Bing, a "spinster" daughter, mentioned by John Bing's descendent, Mabel Stannard, in a family history statement included in *Gallia County, Ohio: People in History to 1980* (Gallipolis, OH: Gallia County Historical Society, 1980), 34. There is a grave marker for an Esther Bing in the Bing family cemetery near the grave of John Bing, but the date of death is unreadable (*Cemeteries of Addison Township*, 17). Stannard does not give a birth or death date for Esther Bing. If she died "years before her mother," that would explain why she is not mentioned in John R. Bing's will, written in 1824 (from Gallia County "Will Book B, 401" copied by Kane).

31. This was probably Martha Young Bing, born 1778 in Augusta County, Virginia (Kane), and married to Thomas Sawyers in 1821 (Marriage Records, Gallia County, Ohio, Collection of Gallia County Historical Society, Binder 1, 108; indexed in *Marriage Records: Gallia County, Ohio*, vol. I, *1803–1850* [Gallipolis, OH: Gallia County Historical & Genealogical Society, 2007], 83).

32. Both the MS (Octavo 3) and the Family Copy (47) have "from that to Pittsburgh" (as opposed to "from there to Pittsburgh").

33. According to John Wigger, "Methodism entered Ohio in earnest in the 1790s," rapidly outstripping its significant growth in other regions. Local congregations, called "classes," were served by "circuit-riding" itinerant preachers: "the standard was a four-week circuit . . . about four hundred miles in circumference, with preaching appointments nearly every day of the week (Wigger, "Ohio Gospel: Methodism in Early Ohio," in Cayton and Hobbs, *Center of a Great Empire*, 62–63). "Doing God service" is Parker's paraphrase of John 16:2, a passage predicting the persecution of Christians. The accusation against Abel Sarjent of horse thievery was in line with other assaults on his character by his contemporaries, particularly religious leaders who may have perceived him as competition. See "The Halcyon Church" and "A Mysterious Death" (with notes) in the Editor's Introduction for other examples.

34. The conflict over slavery within the Methodist Episcopal Church had risen to a head in 1844, the year before Parker began writing his autobiography, when

the denomination formally divided over the issue along regional lines. See C. C. Goen, *Broken Churches, Broken Nation: Denominational Schisms and the Coming of the American Civil War* (Macon, GA: Mercer University Press, 1985), 78–90. Parker's epithet for slavery, "*Agag* of America," probably refers to the biblical king of the Amalekites. Parker implies that the Methodist ministers "spare" slavery from just condemnation, just as Saul, the king of Israel, spared Agag from death, disobeying God's command. Both the Methodist ministers and Saul try to rationalize and justify their bad faith (1 Samuel 15).

35. Parker paraphrases Revelation 3:17, a judgment against the materialism of the church in Laodicea. For early persecution of Methodists in southeast Ohio, see Thomas Jefferson Summers, *History of Marietta* (Marietta, OH: Leader Publishing, 1903), 213. Complaints about Methodists declining spiritually as they gained in worldly comforts were common among Methodists themselves in Parker's day (Wigger, 73–74).

36. Peter Cartwright claimed to have been present when this or a similar event occurred and to have personally challenged Sarjent (Cartwright, 100–101).

37. See "A Mysterious Death" (with notes) in the Editor's Introduction for a reference to the fish-stealing accusation. The letter cited, written by William R. Browning, dated August 2, 1847, in response to an inquiry by physician and local historian Samuel Hildreth, confirms that Sarjent was accused of stealing fish but also contains complicating factors. The theft was supposed to have happened in Belpre, Ohio, where Abel "Sargent" supposedly lived only "one summer" in 1801, preaching for a local "Congregational Society," before he had organized the Halcyon Church. Sarjent was supposedly charged *and convicted* for stealing fish off the line of Charles Dana, not a "Dr. Bennet." In the same letter, Browning writes that "Dr. Bennetts residence in Belpre must have been a number of years susequnt to Sargents removal [*sic*]," implying that Hildreth had enquired about Bennett as well. Perhaps Hildreth had heard the same rumor Parker heard and was trying to confirm it. Unfortunately, Hildreth's original letter of inquiry is lost. The "Dr. Bennett" whom Browning refers to (who could not possibly have had such an encounter with Sarjent) was probably physician and colorful character John Cook Bennett (1804–67), who, despite significant accomplishments in medicine, nutrition, and animal husbandry, became most famous for his imbroglio with Mormon prophet Joseph Smith and a related sex scandal (Andrew F. Smith, *The Saintly Scoundrel: The Life and Times of Dr. John Cook Bennett* [Urbana: University of Illinois Press, 1997], ix–xii, 1–3, 187–92). The discrepancies in the two stories might be the result of failing memories (Parker's and/or Browning's), or the result of the confusing rumor mill that spread the story years before, or perhaps Sarjent was accused of stealing fish in more than one place by more than one person.

38. This is probably the family of Samuel Parkhurst, who was a trustee of the North Ten-Mile Baptist Church and donated the land on which its first meeting house was built in 1786 (Crumrine, 669). The United States Census of 1790 (Washington County, Pennsylvania, NARA Publication M637, Roll 9, 168; accessed through Ancestry.com) and of 1800 (Washington County, Pennsylvania, NARA Publication M32, Roll 44, 820–21; accessed through Ancestry.com) confirm that he lived in Washington County with his family.

39. The Halcyon Church used various methods of baptism (pouring, immersion, etc.) based on the preference of the initiate, but only baptized believers of the age of discretion, not infants, according to the introductory statement of *A Circular Epistle, Wrote by Order of the Fourth Concilium of the Halcyon Church, &c., Otherwise Called the Columbian Church* (Marietta, OH: Samuel Fairlamb, 1806), 3. The statement is "signed by order of the Concilium, John Parker," Daniel's brother, representing the church as a whole, but undoubtedly with significant input from Abel Sarjent (8). Amos Parkhurst will figure prominently in this chapter and his biography will be addressed in a later note.

40. Titus 1:13.

41. In this and the following paragraphs, Parker returns to the subject he already alluded to, Sarjent's symbolic interpretation of the Old Testament term "Urim." As Parker states, in Halcyon theology Urim is a "type" or symbol of seven "communicable attributes" of God: love, wisdom, power, holiness, justice, goodness, and truth. "Type" and "antitype," here meaning "symbol" and "referent," are common terms in apocalyptic interpretations of the Old Testament. See R. J. Coggins and J. L. Houlden, eds., *The SCM Dictionary of Biblical Interpretation* (London: SCM Press, 1990), 713–14. Parker refers to the seven attributes collectively as "the Standard" around which the Halcyon community rallies. It is their criteria of truth: their basis for understanding the nature of God, scripture, Jesus Christ, faith, and salvation. In God these characteristics are perfect, constant, unchanging, and consistent with each other. In no true representation of God could these characteristics be imperfect, malleable, or contradictory. If the Bible presents "the Deity as being a passionate, revengeful, malicious, and changeable God," then these passages must be interpreted figuratively and not literally (Sarjent, "Declaration of the Constitution and Standard of the Halcyon Church," 42–60; See also Sarjent, *Urim, or Halcyon Cabbala*, 4–7, and "The Fundamental Principles of the Aletheian Cabinet," *Aletheian Critic* 1 [April 1804]: 34–36). As "communicable" characteristics of God, they can also be shared by human beings. Jesus Christ is the ideal exemplar and conduit of the "influence" of these characteristics to believers. Faith is voluntary submission to the "influence" of these qualities. To the extent that these qualities are perfected in the human soul, the believer is "redeemed." It is essentially a concept of salvation by means of the infusion of virtues. Parker will later explain the second half of the symbolic system, "Thummim," which represents the human faculties by which these divine virtues are appropriated. Some apparent discrepancies between Parker's account of his discovery of the meaning of "Thummim" and the usage of the term in printed Halcyon literature will be discussed in later notes. See also "Urim and Thummim" in the Editor's Introduction.

42. The number seven is in fact "a sacred number in many traditions" and recurs frequently in the Old and New Testaments (Annemarie Schimmel, "Numbers: An Overview," in *Encyclopedia of Religion*, 2nd ed., ed. Lindsay Jones [Detroit: Macmillan Reference USA, 2005], 10:6748). For printed examples of Abel Sarjent's interpretation of this recurrence, see "The Fundamental Principles of the Aletheian Cabinet," 35; "Declaration of the Constitution and Standard of the Millennium Church," 44; and "An Address to the Human Family at Large," 64–67. The second article, while

officially a corporate statement of the church signed by John Parker as moderator, undoubtedly had significant input from Abel Sarjent.

43. A messenger, divinely authorized to uncover lost or concealed divine revelation, is a motif of apocalyptic religion (Christian E. Hauer and William A. Young, *An Introduction to the Bible: A Journey into Three Worlds*, 8th ed. [Upper Saddle River, NJ: Pearson, 2012], 189–90). Mormon prophet Joseph Smith would also assume this role when he appeared on the scene years later. For further discussion of similarities between Sarjent and Smith, see "The Halcyon Church" in the Editor's Introduction.

44. For further explanation of Sarjent's millennial expectations, see "The Halcyon Church" in the Editor's Introduction.

45. Parker is referring to New Salem in Fayette County, Pennsylvania, organized in 1799. See Franklin Ellis, *History of Fayette County, Pennsylvania: With Biographical Sketches of Many of Its Pioneers and Prominent Men* (Philadelphia: L. H. Everts, 1882), 658.

46. Roundtree may have been, or been related to, Daniel Roundtree, who was a teacher in several schoolhouses near New Salem in the 1790s (Ellis, 655).

47. Parker's circuit through southwestern Pennsylvania and the northwest region of what is now West Virginia was roughly 130 miles. Alexander McGrew might have been, or might have been a family member of, an Alexander McGrew who lived in a household with nine members in Nottingham, according to the US Census of 1810 (Nottingham, Washington County, Pennsylvania, NARA Publication M252, Roll 57, 75; accessed through Ancestry.com). Nottingham Township is roughly eight miles from what was in Parker's day Williamsport and is now the city of Monongahela, Pennsylvania (Crumrine, 382).

48. Baltzel may be (or may be related to) Daniel Baltzel, who married Margaret Ware in Monongalia County, (West) Virginia, in 1802 (West Virginia Marriages Index, 1785–1971, online database maintained by FamilySearch, accessed through Ancestry.com). Germans had been immigrating to what would become the United States in large numbers since the eighteenth century, being particularly drawn to the back country and western frontier. See Foner, *Give Me Liberty!*, 112–14, 164, 335; and R. Douglas Hurt, *The Ohio Frontier: Crucible of the Northwest, 1720–1830* (Bloomington: Indiana University Press, 1996), 209–10.

49. Deism is "a belief in a God disclosed in nature and by reason rather than in sacred scripture and by supernatural revelation." This rationalistic belief system was not an organized church and had no set creed. Typically, Deists rejected "scriptural inerrancy, miracles, providence, and ecclesial institutions," but accepted "the existence of a First Cause, the importance of virtuous behavior, and, less unanimously, an afterlife." Deism had its origin in England. Its chief American exponent was Elihu Palmer (1764–1806). Many American founding fathers, including Thomas Jefferson and Benjamin Franklin, had Deist sympathies, while orthodox clergymen like Ezra Stiles attacked Deism as infidelity (Kerry Walters, "Deism," in *Encyclopedia of Religion in America*, 1:527–31). See also Walters, *The American Deists: Voices of Reason and Dissent in the Early Republic* (Lawrence: University Press of Kansas, 1992), 1–50. Parker depicts himself as a respectful opponent of Deists, though he himself held unorthodox beliefs. "Parker and American Religion" in the Editor's Introduction discusses Parker's

encounter with Deists and other representatives of the American Enlightenment. I have not yet found another record of a "noted Deist" named Joseph Reed living near Morgantown, (West) Virginia, during the time to which Parker refers.

50. While Parker's response to the Deist's challenge may have indeed been spontaneous, it was also in keeping with the general tendency of the Halcyon Church to interpret the Bible figuratively rather than literally, especially the Old Testament. See Sarjent, "Introductory Discourse," 15; "A Declaration of the Constitution and Standard of the Millennium Church," 57–60; and "The Doctrine of Endless Miseries Investigated," 18–19. Others, including the bastion of American Reformed Protestant orthodoxy Charles Hodge, offered a similar rational defense of the creation account in Genesis, saying that some biblical language expressed "apparent, and not absolute or scientific truth" (Hodge, *Systematic Theology*, vol. 1 [1871; reprint, Grand Rapids, MI: W. B. Eerdmans, 1997], 569).

51. See Sarjent, *The Urim, or Halcyon Cabala*, 3, on Jesus Christ as the concrete expression of "abstract deity." The question of the Halcyon Church's Christology is one that merits further study. Jesus Christ plays a central role in both Sarjent's and Parker's theological language: as representing God in a unique way, and as giving "form" and intelligibility to the invisible God. He is described as a kind of mediator of salvation, in the sense that he is both the perfect example and also the source of the virtues symbolized by Urim (and Thummim), and he is expected to reign over the earth in the millennium. Both Parker and Sarjent favor the biblical name "Emmanuel" (Matthew 1:23: "God with us") for Christ (Sarjent, "Declaration of the Constitution and Standard of the Millennium Church," 59–60). Despite this incarnational language, Sarjent vehemently rejected the orthodox ("Athanasian") formulation of the Christian Trinity, which describes the Son of God as one of three "persons" sharing a single divine "substance." He did not seem to object so much to the idea of the divinity of Christ, however, as to the idea of there being distinct "persons" in God, affirming instead "that the Messiah, or Son, composes no part of the Godhead: nor yet, that there are three persons, but, three characters composing together one glorious person in the Lord Jesus Christ" (Sarjent, "A Protest against Idolatry: Or Tritheism Exploded," *Aletheian Critic* 1 [April 1804]: 39–40). Those looking to compare Sarjent's view to a third-century Christian heresy might call it Modalism. See J. N. D. Kelly, *Early Christian Doctrines*, rev. ed. (San Francisco: HarperSanFrancisco, 1978), 119–23. Sarjent's language here is very similar to that of the nontrinitarian "Oneness" Pentecostalism that would emerge in the twentieth century. See Robert Mapes Anderson, "Pentecostal and Charismatic Christianity," in *Encyclopedia of Religion*, 10:7029. Daniel Parker, unlike Abel Sarjent, did not clearly reject the traditional Christian trinity, and apparently continued to ponder the question of the nature of Christ in later life. William Tell Parker remembers his father gazing into the fire, possibly thinking about "the nature of Jesus Christ in a pre-existent state," while the more practical Priscilla would "be contriving how to make a pair of new boy's breeches out of two old pairs" (34).

52. See Charles Hartshorne, "Pantheism and Panentheism," in *Encyclopedia of Religion*, 10:6960: "In Greek *pan* means 'all,' *theos* means 'god'. . . . *Pantheism* means that all is God." This concept of divinity is typically associated with religions of Asia. The best known nineteenth-century American thinkers who approached a kind of

pantheism were transcendentalists like Ralph Waldo Emerson, who understood God to be immanent within nature. They became prominent decades after the encounter Parker here recounts. See Daniel Vaca, "Transcendentalism," in *Encyclopedia of Religion in America*, 4:2206–11. See also Catherine L. Albanese, *Nature Religion in America: From the Algonkian Indians to the New Age* (Chicago: University of Chicago Press, 1990), 80–116.

53. MS (Octavo 4) has "prettle" instead of "pretty," probably a slip of the pen.

54. Here Parker introduces his account of the severe fast taken on by a small group within the Halcyon Church. For further discussion of the fast, the death of one of the participants, the controversy, and the consequences of the whole event for Parker personally and for the historical memory of the Halcyon Church, see "A Mysterious Death" in the Editor's Introduction, along with notes. As stated in the Editor's Introduction and as the following notes will demonstrate, Parker's firsthand account offers valuable corrections to and accounts for the origins of inaccurate hearsay reports that found their way into various memoirs and local histories, and were later repeated by historians in the twentieth and twenty-first centuries.

55. Parker and his friends' fast precipitated a division within the Halcyon Church, as is confirmed by Abel Sarjent's writings. Sarjent denounces "John Parker," along with other "deluded disciples and accomplices of Rhoda Fordyce," in "Circular Epistle from the 9th Concilium of the Halcyon Church," 224. He apparently attacks the same group with symbolic language in "The Downfall of the Halcyon Church, Predicted in a Dream," *Halcyon Itinerary* 3 (October 1807): 81–91. Alfred Creigh, in his *History of Washington County* (Pennsylvania) also acknowledges a division, claiming that the events occurred within a splinter "sect" of the Halcyon Church led by "Rhoda Fordyce," called "Rhodianites, after their founder" (213). Other writers appear unaware of the division, saying that, based on either Sarjent's teaching (Dickinson, 31) or on his own initiative (Finley, 258; Cartwright 102), an individual Halcyon member decided that he could live without food entirely. Later writers also differ over where the event took place. Creigh, like Parker, places it near Washington, Pennsylvania. Similarly, Finley, a Methodist minister at the time, says that it happened "in the bounds of my circuit" around Saint Clairesville, Ohio, which could reasonably include the same location. Dickinson, in his centennial history of First Congregational Church in Marietta (1896), relying on the journal of a former pastor, Thomas Robbins, locates the event near Marietta, Ohio, which would be over a hundred miles away.

56. Like several other millenarian groups, the Halcyon Church, based on their understanding of the New Testament book of Revelation, expected the apocalypse to occur in phases (Stanley E. Porter, "Millenarian Thought in the First-Century Church," in *Christian Millenarianism: From the Early Church to Waco*, ed. Stephen Hunt [Bloomington: Indiana University Press, 2001], 64–66). In the Halcyon scenario, "the first resurrection" was a general resurrection of the dead, following which would be a time period in which some people would willfully turn away from God and forfeit the gift of immortality, while others would remain faithful and receive the reward of eternal life with God, a "second resurrection" (Sarjent, "The Doctrine of Endless Miseries Investigated," 24). Parker explains that he and his little band of "pilgrims"

engaging in the fast became convinced they "might never die," meaning they would live to see the imminent dawn of the millennium and be among those living saints who would receive the gift of immortality along with the resurrected dead, a scenario described by the apostle Paul in 1 Corinthians 15, which Parker will refer to. Secondhand accounts by other writers (Dickinson, Cartwright, Finley, Creigh) caricature this Halcyon belief, saying that they (or their "Rhodianite" splinter group) believed they could make themselves immortal by their own holiness aided by a special diet.

57. Parker describes the fast, which consisted of an austere vegetarian diet, as a devotional practice, placing it in the context of Christian scripture and tradition. Secondhand accounts by other writers caricature the fast as a naturally impossible task, either by implying that surviving on a vegetarian diet is in itself impossible (Creigh) or saying that an individual Halcyon member believed that he could go without food entirely for a miraculous forty days (Finley, Cartwright, Dickinson).

58. I have not yet found a second primary source confirming a son of Samuel Parkhurst named Amos (see note 38 on the Parkhurst family, above). A family tree on Ancestry.com does indeed list Amos Parkhurst as a son of Samuel Parkhurst and gives a birthdate of 1794, which would make him close to the age Parker gives him, but unfortunately does not cite a historical document for evidence. However, it is reasonable to assume that Amos Parkhurst was one of the three males under the age of sixteen living with Samuel Parkhurst in 1790 (US Census) and either the one male under sixteen or the one between sixteen and twenty-five in the same household in 1800 (US Census). In Amos Parkhurst, Daniel Parker offers a detailed portrait of a plausible personality with precedented (albeit unusual) religious experience (Ann Taves, *Fits, Trances, and Visions: Experiencing Religion and Explaining Experience from Wesley to James* [Princeton, NJ: Princeton University Press, 1999], 3–6; see also Butler, *Awash*, 225–56) belonging to a historically documented family. Creigh calls the one who died "a man by the name of Parker" (no first name). There were in fact two Parkers (Daniel and John) participating in the fast, but neither of them died. Other secondhand accounts do not give any name: "one of [Sarjent's] followers" (Finley); "one of these Halcyon preachers" (Cartwright); "a son of one of their leading female preachers" (Dickinson).

59. The MS has "trivling" instead of "trifling" (Octavo 5). The Family Copy uses "trivial" (57).

60. "Behold, I shew you a mystery; we shall not all sleep, but we shall all be changed, in a moment, in the twinkling of an eye, at the last trump: for the trumpet shall sound, and the dead shall be raised incorruptible, and we shall be changed" (1 Corinthians 15:51–52, KJV). See note 56 above on Halcyon millennial expectations with reference to this passage.

61. "Magnetic sleep" is a term coined in the eighteenth century by the Marquis de Puységur, a disciple of Franz Anton Mesmer, for what would later be called a hypnotic trance. See Judith Pintar and Steven Jay Lynn, *Hypnosis: A Brief History* (Chichester, UK: Wiley-Blackwell, 2008), 24–30. At the time of Parker's writing, touring "mesmerists" had popularized such language in the United States, and it would be adopted by Spiritualism, the practice of communicating with the dead, which would burst on the American scene a few years later. See Bret E. Carroll,

"Spiritualism," in *Encyclopedia of Religion in America*, 4:2134; and Carroll, *Spiritualism in Antebellum America* (Bloomington: Indiana University Press, 1997), 18, 19, 68, 108–9. Spiritualism would become a preoccupation of Priscilla Parker. See "Priscilla Parker" in the Editor's Introduction.

62. Revelation 19:6.

63. A distance of over one hundred miles.

64. "Skileton" in MS (Octavo 5).

65. By "common man" Parker might be comparing Parkhurst to a working man who would need to be physically strong. Parker uses the phrase "two common days' work" in chap. 1.

66. Creigh writes that Rhoda Fordyce "kept the body concealed in her house for three days and three nights" until the neighbors finally "broke the door open, found the body and buried it." Finley and Dickinson both write that the community predicted a resurrection in three days, but when the prophecy failed they were compelled to bury the decomposing body. While no historical hypothesis is certain, the specificity, detail, and plausibility of Parker's account, in contrast to the vagueness, implausibility, and inconsistency of the secondhand accounts, as well as their acknowledged reliance on hearsay ("It is said. . .," writes Creigh), their acknowledged disdain of the Halcyon "superstition" (Finley and Creigh), and finally, the fact that Parker wrote his unpublished account before these other books were published, leads to the conclusion that Parker's description of the event is accurate, and that the hostile rumors he describes as being spread at the time were repeated over the years until they found their way into these secondhand texts. Even later, these reports would be taken at face value and repeated by historians in the twentieth and twenty-first centuries. Fawn Brodie, in her best-selling biography of Joseph Smith, *No Man Knows My History*, offers Abel Sarjent's Halcyon Church as an example of one of the eccentric sects of the old frontier and says that Sarjent "talked with angels and received revelations, toured the state with his twelve women apostles pretending to raise the dead and preaching the odd doctrine that if one were sufficiently holy one could live without food. The sect suffered eclipse in Marietta, when a convert put the belief to the test, went nine days without eating, and died" (98). Writing in 2008, David S. Reynolds, in *Waking Giant: America in the Age of Jackson*, does not allude to a specific mysterious death but repeats the characterization of Sarjent as a wandering miracle worker who "claimed to raise the dead" and the story that he and his followers "fasted for as long as forty days at a time" before "the cult fell into disrepute" (145).

67. The meaning of this unusual idiom, "made a jumping stick of his measure," may be discerned from the context.

68. The word here rendered as "Amos" is obscured by an inkblot in the MS (Octavo 5).

Chapter 3

1. John Parker married Lucy Cotton in 1807 (Ferris, 481). He apparently continued to find audiences for his preaching despite his falling out with Abel Sarjent,

perhaps among people who had some affiliation with or interest in the beliefs of the Halcyon Church. After the traumatic events of 1807 the Halcyon community might have taken on a more fragmented and informal structure, which could lend itself to John Parker's unauthorized itinerancy. The fact that Sarjent was still denouncing Parker and the "deluded disciples . . . of Rhoda Fordyce" in 1810 ("Circular Epistle from the 9th Concilium of the Halcyon Church," 224–30) indicates factions within the church may have endured for years. In a later chapter of this autobiography, Daniel Parker describes himself and his brother John meeting with a group of current and former Halcyonists in 1815, over a year after Daniel returned from his southern journey.

2. William Parker's family would live on his homestead for at least three generations and over one hundred years. A brief family history with a photograph of the William Parker home is in Larkin's *Pioneer History of Meigs County*, 57–59.

3. The MS has "comfortable provided for" rather than "comfortably" (Octavo 5).

4. In this and the following paragraphs, Parker explains how he moved beyond the annihilationism of the Halcyon Church, which stopped at rejecting the idea of eternal punishment in hell, to embrace true universal salvation. Parker came to believe that ultimately all people would, to use his favored language, be "restored" to "happiness and holiness" and enjoy a blessed eternal life with God. Even as his mind was changing on this topic, Parker continued to retain much of the Halcyon theological framework, including its Christian mortalism and its millennial expectation of a general resurrection of the dead. However, Daniel Parker, like his brother John, would reject the necessity of the "second death," the annihilation of the wicked, which was to occur after the general resurrection (Sarjent, "The Doctrine of Endless Miseries Investigated," 25). See the previous chapter with notes as well as "The Halcyon Church" and "Parker the Universalist" in the Editor's Introduction for further explanation of Parker's developing theology.

5. Parker, in his caution, anticipates a common objection to universalism, that its proponents embraced it only because it was an attractive "conscience-soothing doctrine" (Cartwright, 393). See also Bressler, 33–40.

6. Parker alludes to Acts 17:11. The Bereans "searched the scriptures daily" to see whether the things Paul preached to them were true. Parker's high regard for the Bible compels him to find biblical evidence for universal salvation. Exegetical arguments take up much of the first two thirds of *Familiar Letters to a Brother*, in which Parker makes use of biblical passages with universalizing tendencies, such as 1 Timothy 2:4 (74). The fact that Parker was a Restorationist (as opposed to an "ultra") Universalist, and believed in a postmortem "just retribution" for sin, helped him deal with biblical references to punishment. He did not deny that sin would be punished after death, but only that those punishments would be unending. Therefore, many an objection that "would be good against those who deny future punishment . . . amounts to nothing, against a Restorationist" (46). See also "Parker the Universalist" in the Editor's Introduction. Typically of many on the old frontier, Parker claimed to arrive at his universalist position through his own reflection on scripture, having never read an author or heard a sermon on the topic. By this time, Universalism had existed as an American religious movement for almost forty years but was still concentrated in

New England. The first Universalist society in Marietta, Ohio, would be formed in 1816, some eight years after Parker reached his own conclusions (Russell Miller, 693). Even so, Parker's theological language is similar to earlier Universalist theologians, especially Elhanan Winchester, *The Universal Restoration, Exhibited in Four Dialogues between a Minister and His Friend* (Worcester, MA: Isaiah Thomas, 1803). See also Reiner Smolinski, "Apocalypticism in Colonial North America," in *Continuum History of Apocalypticism*, 460–61.

7. On the brink of another radical change of mind, as he was when he joined the Halcyon Church years before, Parker once again alludes to Mark 11:4 ("the colt tied . . . in a place where two ways met") as a symbol of his uncertainty. However, he resolves to work through his theological dilemma, remembering the deceased "brother Amos" Parkhurst's admonition to "hold on to the standard." The standard, as Parker had "already . . . explained" in the previous chapter, refers to the seven characteristics of God symbolized in Halcyon theology by the Old Testament figure Urim, which include love, justice, and wisdom. Parker will conclude that the necessary consequence of God's love, justice, and wisdom will be universal restoration (salvation), even though Abel Sarjent himself did not reach this conclusion. This is another example of how Parker maintained the Halcyon theological framework even as he embraced a new idea.

8. Matthew 6:7.

9. Alvan Bingham (b. ca. 1781) was the son of Silas Bingham (1758–1840), a prominent early settler to the Athens area, formerly known as the Middletown district, in 1797. Also among those settlers was Silas's brother, the elder Alvan Bingham (1754–1841), and his son, also named Alvan (1788–1843). The Bingham brothers immigrated together with their families, originally from Litchfield County, Connecticut. Silas Bingham served as constable and his brother Alvan as a magistrate of the village of Athens. Silas was also a miller and tavern owner (Charles M. Walker, *History of Athens County, Ohio* [Cincinnati: Robert Clarke, 1867] 115, 119–21, 127–28; Robert L. Daniel, *Athens, Ohio: The Village Years* [Athens: Ohio University Press, 1997], 22, 24, 35, 42, 65, 114; and Donna G. Bingham Munger, email to David Torbett, June 11, 2018). Silas Bingham's two-story log cabin in Athens has been preserved and moved twice. It is currently on the campus of Ohio University and houses its Office of Sustainability (Ohio University Compass, March 4, 2013, https://www.ohio.edu/compass/stories/12-13/3/Office-of-Sustainability-moves-to-Bingham-House.cfm). See also the will of Silas Bingham, probated 1840 (Athens, Ohio, Record of Wills, vol. 3: 1835–1842), 361, accessed through Ancestory.com; and grave markers (photos on Find a Grave) for Silas Bingham (West State Street Cemetery, Athens, Ohio, https://www.findagrave.com/memorial/34105050/silas-bingham); Alvan Bingham [Sr.] (New Plymouth Cemetery, Vinton County, OH, https://www.findagrave.com/memorial/120675801/alvan-bingham); and Alvan Bingham [Jr.] (Higley Family Cemetery, Rutland, Meigs County, OH, https://www.findagrave.com/memorial/33299520/alvan-bingham).

10. Eli F. Hill's "flax and hemp machine" and clothes "washing machine" each received a United States patent in 1809. See *List of Patents for Inventions and Designs Issued by the United States from 1790 to 1847* (Washington, DC: J. & G. S. Gideon, 1847), 73, 314. Unfortunately, the original patent application drawing cannot be

accessed from the United States Patent and Trademark Office database, probably because it was lost in the Patent Office fire of 1836. "Breaking" hemp or flax was the process by which the fiber was separated from the straw in preparation for spinning. Nineteenth-century inventors often sought to profit from their inventions through the sale of patent rights. Those buyers (like Bingham and his associates) in turn attempted to profit from their investment through the sale of the invention as well as through the resale of patent rights, subdivided into smaller geographic units. See Naomi R. Lamoreaux and Kenneth L. Sokoloff, "Intermediaries in the U.S. Market for Technology, 1870–1920," in *Finance, Intermediaries, and Economic Development*, eds. Stanley L. Engerman, Philip T. Hoffman, Jean-Laurent Rosenthal, and Kenneth L. Sokoloff, 209–46 (New York: Cambridge University Press, 2003).

11. Parker is not referring to Henry Lee III ("Light Horse Harry"), governor of Virginia and father of Robert E. Lee, but to his cousin Henry Lee (1757–1845), a Virginia-born Revolutionary War veteran and early Kentucky politician (Lucy C. Lee, "General Henry Lee," *Register of the Kentucky State Historical Society* 1, no. 3 [September 1903]: 82–88). Henry Lee amassed a large fortune by "his great sagacity as a business man" (88), which perhaps included investing in new inventions like Parker's washing machine. I have not found a likely second historic document identifying the New York investors, "Messers Jackson and Crocker."

12. This is one of Parker's first exposures to slavery during his southern trip that would consolidate him in his antislavery position. According to an apocryphal story, Harriet Beecher Stowe, like Parker, also witnessed and was similarly shocked by a slave auction in the same city of Washington, Kentucky, in 1833. Stowe did in fact visit a former student in that location whose family owned slaves, and her memories of their home became the basis of the fictional Shelby Plantation of *Uncle Tom's Cabin* (Nancy Koester, *Harriett Beecher Stowe: A Spiritual Life* [Grand Rapids, MI: W. B. Eerdmans, 2014], 64).

13. Parker's journal, which he evidently kept from 1809 to 1816, is an important source for his autobiography of 1845. The original was lost, probably in a fire of 1855 (see Epilogue). Because of Parker's irregular punctuation, the (at times significant) question of where the quoted journal entries begin and end is at times a matter of interpretation. Possibly controversial editorial choices will be discussed in notes.

14. In chap. 1, Parker states that he never remembered his father or brothers using profanity during his childhood. That the women in his family never did so apparently went without saying, hence his shock when he sees "genteel females" tolerate profane language in their presence.

15. The US Census of 1830 has an Eli F. Hill living in Madison County, New York, which neighbors Onondaga County, the residence listed for Eli F. Hill on the *List of Patents* cited above (1830 US Census, Cazenovia, Madison County, New York, NARA Publication M19, Roll 93, 237; accessed through Ancestry.com).

16. "Esqr. Lemon and his brother" may have been, or more likely were family members of, John and James Lemon, early settlers of Clark County, Indiana. James Lemon was active in the militia, political, and business life of the county. Lewis C. Baird, *History of Clark County, Indiana* [Indianapolis: B. F. Bowen, 1909], 40, 70, 81, 142, 370). "Denny" is possibly John Denny (b. 1789), who according to the US census was living

in Clark County, Indiana, in 1850 and 1860 and was a "cabinet maker" (1850 US Census, Charlestown, Clark County, Indiana, NARA Publication M432, Roll 138, 103A; 1860 US Census, Charlestown, Clark County, Indiana, NARA Publication, M653, Roll 248, 142; accessed through Ancestry.com). In 1802, territorial governor William Henry Harrison had named the seat of Clark County (directly across the Ohio River from Louisville, Kentucky) "Jeffersonville" in honor of President Thomas Jefferson (Andrew R. L. Cayton, *Frontier Indiana* [Bloomington: Indiana University Press, 1996], 234).

17. From December 16, 1811, to late April 1812, New Madrid was the site of a series of earthquakes, among the severest ever to hit the contiguous United States. Conevery Bolton Valencius gives a thorough account of the earthquakes themselves and their far-reaching environmental and cultural consequences (*The Lost History of the New Madrid Earthquakes* [Chicago: University of Chicago Press, 2013], 1–13). See also Jay Feldman, *When the Mississippi Ran Backwards: Empire, Intrigue, Murder, and the New Madrid Earthquakes* (New York: Free Press, 2005), 1–15.

18. Parker is referring to river cane, a North American bamboo that once dominated the Mississippi bottomland ecosystem. Native Americans used cane for roof thatching, basketry, and many other purposes. Canebrakes (to use the standard spelling) also provided habitats for a unique variety of birds, mammals, and reptiles. Already in the early nineteenth century, as Parker witnessed, this wilderness was being cleared for cotton plantations, one of the many consequences of the boom in the cotton export industry (Donald E. Davis et al., *Southern United States: An Environmental History* [Santa Barbara, CA: ABC-CLIO, 2006], 68–70, 127).

19. The Quapaw ("Arkansas") Indians lived primarily in the lower Mississippi valley west of the river. The name "Arkansas" is derived from the pluralized French pronunciation of "Quapaw." The Chickasaws and Choctaws lived to the east of the river. However, members of all three groups at times migrated and traveled through the Mississippi valley, as did Cherokees and migrant Indians from further east (Daniel H. Unser Jr., *American Indians in the Lower Mississippi Valley: Social and Economic Histories* [Lincoln: University of Nebraska Press, 1998], 14 [map], 33–72, 98).

20. Parker passed through during a period of economic disruption and hardship for Native Americans of the Mississippi valley. Their major source of income, the "frontier exchange economy"—trading animal skins, pelts, and food with settlers for goods and cash—was being overwhelmed by the explosion of the cotton export industry. As the market for their goods declined, Native Americans, with encouragement from federal policy, became entangled in "a chronic cycle of trade indebtedness and land cessions, a cycle that would steadily weaken their power and eventually culminate in removal," making room for new settlers to build cotton plantations worked by African American slaves (Unser, 56–72, 79). Both the Choctaw and the Chickasaw made significant land cessions in 1805, and at the time of Parker's journey they were "landless participants in the expanding plantation economy" (Roxanne Dunbar-Ortiz, *An Indigenous Peoples' History of the United States* [Boston: Beacon, 2015], 97). See also Robert V. Haynes, *The Mississippi Territory and the Southwest Frontier, 1795–1817* (Lexington: University Press of Kentucky, 2010), 219–40.

21. See "Parker and Slavery" in the Editor's Introduction for a reference to this event and its effect on him. The enslaved people Parker saw, presumably being

imported for sale, were part of what historian Ira Berlin calls a "second Middle Passage." Between 1800 and 1860 over a million Black people were transported from the eastern states to the southern interior to work on plantations, another effect of the cotton boom. Natchez was an "infamous" terminal of the new domestic slave trade, the consequences of which included an African American population shift, disrupted families, kidnapping (slave traders frequently ignored the distinction between slaves and free people of color), and, as Parker documents, murder (*The Making of African America*, 99–103).

22. Most Americans in the nineteenth century understood season, location, and climate to be primary causes of sickness. See Marli F. Weiner with Mazie Hough, *Sex, Sickness, and Slavery: Defining Illness in the Antebellum South* (Urbana: University of Illinois Press, 2012), 87–92. Possibly the effects of the season and weather on mosquito populations provided evidence for these beliefs.

23. Parker's memory of "past experience . . . of religion" is apparently the last of a list of factors, along with physical sickness, that brought on his desperate state of "gloom." Parker often refers to his mental state and sometimes describes what present-day physicians might diagnose as depression. Parker's pursuit of happiness, and his learning to accept happiness when it finds him, is yet another theme of his narrative. The MS (Octavo 6) punctuates "My past experience on the subject of religion" as a complete sentence by itself, though a verb is lacking. The sentence is here punctuated as in the Family Copy, 68.

24. Legend has it that the Chickasaws stole their first horses from Hernan De Soto's expedition in 1540, but they probably adopted the horse from English traders in the early eighteenth century, quickly becoming "singular horsemen, and are credited with developing a special breed—the Chickasaw horse—famous all along the Mississippi Valley for its long stride, endurance, and striking appearance" (Arrell M. Gibson, *The Chickasaws* [Norman: University of Oklahoma Press, 1981], 42).

25. Bloodletting and other forms of depletion were the common treatments for most diseases in early nineteenth-century America (Breslaw, 46–47).

26. Parker most likely traveled along what would later be known as the Natchez Trace, originally a series of Indian paths and later a federally funded wagon road between Natchez and Nashville, completed in 1809 (William C. Davis, *A Way through the Wilderness: The Natchez Trace and the Civilization of the Southern Frontier* [New York: HarperCollins, 1995], 14–28).

27. Despite his sympathy for Native Americans and the injustices they suffered, Parker still defaults to labeling them (and apparently, to an extent, fearing them) as "savages," a usage so common in Euro-American culture it would be tedious to list examples, one being in the Declaration of Independence. See "Parker and Race" in the Editor's Introduction for a discussion of his views on race in general. However, Parker also called some White people "savage," such as the slave trader he witnessed in the act of homicide. Perhaps he is here referring to White robbers that he and his companions feared, with good reason. Even though the most famous highwayman on the Trace, Samuel Mason (b. 1739), was killed in 1803, travelers still "understood that once they reached Red Bluff Stand at the Choctaw boundary, they were leaving law and order behind" (William C. Davis, 276).

28. The MS has "The house was located exactly on the western line of Tennessee" (Octavo 6). The Family Copy (69) has "probably intended to be southern" in parentheses after "western," which is doubtlessly correct.

29. According to William C. Davis, Robert and Priscilla Griner opened their "stand" (wilderness inn) in 1807 or 1808. People soon mistakenly called it "Grinder's Stand" and the name stuck (32–33). Priscilla Griner is the source of the most detailed account of Lewis's death. She was interviewed three times over a thirty-year period about the event and has been the subject of interest and even suspicion for some. The majority of historians believe Lewis committed suicide. See Clay S. Jenkinson, "Introduction: Meriwether Lewis's Mysterious Death on the Natchez Trace," in *By His Own Hand? The Mysterious Death of Meriwether Lewis*, ed. John D. W. Guice (Norman: University of Oklahoma Press, 2006), 3; Guice, "'It Seems to Be More Probable . . .,'" in the same volume, 101–2; and William C. Davis, 277–78.

30. "Murry County" was actually Maury County, established in 1807 (Marise P. Lightfoot, "Maury County," *Tennessee Encyclopedia*, Tennessee Historical Society, last updated March 1, 2018, http://tennesseeencyclopedia.net/entries/maury-county).

31. This may be the home of James Giddins, who registered sixty acres of land in Williams County, Tennessee, in 1808 (*Early Tennessee/North Carolina Land Records, 1783–1927*, Record Group 50, Warrant 4366, Tennessee State Library and Archives microfilm, accessed through Ancestry.com).

32. Here is a case where it is unclear in the MS where Parker's quoted journal entries from 1810 end and where his 1845 memoir resumes (see note 13 above). Though this section of the manuscript begins with a date, as would a diary entry, the author's perspective in the passage that follows indicates it is a later reflection.

33. In losing their doubloon, Parker and his associates not only lost its value, but their souvenir of the Spanish presence in eastern North America. It might have come into New Orleans through Spanish Florida.

34. A marriage certificate was issued to Alvan Bingham and Jane Baldridge in Sumner County, Tennessee, on December 25, 1810 (*Tennessee State Marriages, 1780–2002*, Tennessee State Library and Archives microfilm, accessed through Ancestry.com). Many years later, perhaps after his wife died, Bingham was recorded as again living in Athens, Ohio (Donna G. Bingham Munger to David Torbett). See also the 1850 US Census, Athens, Athens County, Ohio, NARA Publication M432, Roll 660, 2B; 1860 US Census, Canaan, Athens County, Ohio, NARA Publication M653, Roll 934, 92; accessed through Ancestry.com.

35. Luke 18:9–14.

36. Isaiah 65:5 ("Stand by thyself, come not near to me; for I am holier than thou.")

37. Daniel Parker has a temperamental dislike of religious sectarianism, which he associates with dogmatism and self-righteousness, as does Abel Sarjent, evident in his *Destruction of the Beast in the Downfall of Sectarianism* (Marietta, OH: n.p., 1806), iii–v. The two men differ in that Sarjent advocates separation from the various denominations, while Parker takes a more conciliatory approach. See "A Human Story" in the Editor's Introduction for further discussion of this aspect of Parker's temperament and theology.

38. The tension between the "rational and animal capacities" of human beings is a classic problem of Western philosophy, commonly associated with Plato. Parker quotes Alexander Pope, *An Essay on Man*, epistle II, lines 7–10; published as vol. 3, pt. 1, of *The Poems of Alexander Pope*, ed. Maynard Mack (London: Methuen, 1950), 53–55.

39. The Old Testament book of Jonah is a story of a prophet who flees from but ultimately cannot resist his divine calling.

40. Apparently, Daniel Parker also wrote hymns while he was with the Halcyon Church, which were included in one of its publications. See "The Urim and Thummim" (attributed to "D. P." and dated October 9, 1805) and "Salvation Hymn" (attributed to "D. Parker") in a small collection of hymns published by Abel Sarjent [1806], 25–26, 34–35. This is the same collection that included hymns purportedly written by Clarissa and "Susanna" Parker. See note 28 in chap. 2.

41. It is not clear what "Red Church" Parker is referring to, though his use of capital letters imply it was a specific landmark (MS, Octavo 7).

42. Parker's hope for the ultimate distribution of divine justice for the sins of slavery may be a reason he sided with the Restorationist school of universalism, believing in a limited punishment for sin in the afterlife, rather than siding with the position that all people would experience complete salvation immediately after death. See "Parker the Universalist" in the Editor's Introduction.

43. While Parker's observations of the social consequences of slavery may be accurate, his affirmation of the general moral, social, and economic superiority of a free as opposed to a slave society may be partly shaped by his Ohio regional loyalties. See Cayton, *Ohio: The History of a People*, 120–21.

44. Apparently, Parker, writing his autobiography in 1845, included this passage from his 1810 diary because he saw his landlady's abusive behavior and abrasive personality as symptomatic of slave culture: an example of the "deleterious influence" that slavery had "on both races." His original purpose in writing the passage in 1810 is less clear, however. Because Parker lived in several places in Tennessee, it is not certain to which landlady he is referring. It would not have been Priscilla Griner because he indicates that he stayed at Grinder's Stand only one night, months before the date of this diary entry.

45. By "waiting evidences," Parker means the witnesses who were detained to give evidence. The Family Copy has "waiting witnesses" (77).

46. Towns like Gallatin were on a judicial circuit. The arrival of the lawyers and judges of the traveling court was an opportunity for community celebration that could include horse races, circuses, and other sideshows (Ronald C. White, 85).

Chapter 4

1. A "gig" is a two-wheeled carriage.

2. A singletree is a crossbar for an animal's harness traces, also called a "whiffletree."

3. "Colonel Ewing" was Young Ewing, born in Bedford County, Virginia, ca. 1756. According to a biography in William Henry Perrin's *County of Christian, Kentucky* (Chicago: F. A. Battey, 1884), he was a magistrate of Logan County, Kentucky,

and one of the original surveyors of Christian County when it was formed in 1796. He lived near Hopkinsville, the seat of Christian County, where he served in various offices for twenty-five years, being elected to the county legislature several times. He is described as an unschooled "true pioneer and hunter" and "backwoods politician," popular for his "rude eloquence" and "hail fellow, well met" personality. The rank of colonel came from when he "commanded a regiment against the Indians," but his "campaign was a bloodless one." Even so, when an "election appeared to be doubtful, the Colonel would be seen at public gatherings hobbling about with a cane . . . , complaining loudly of the hardships of a soldier's life. But no sooner was he assured of election than away went his cane." Perrin warns, however, that "the story may be taken with some allowance" (106–8). Young Ewing is on record as leading a regiment of mounted cavalry in the War of 1812 (A. C. Quisenberry, "Kentucky Troops in the War of 1812," *Register of the Kentucky State Historical Society* 10, no. 30 [September 1912]: 58). He was married three times and had one daughter with his first wife. He moved from Kentucky, possibly to western Tennessee, sometime after he lost an election to state senate in 1832, and died a few years later.

4. "Mrs. Ewing" (1769–1825) was Winnifred Warren Ewing, the second wife of Young Ewing (Elizabeth Prather Ellsberry, *The Warrens and You* [Kansas City, MO: Brown-White-Lowell Press, 1958], 260). She provided Daniel Parker with one of the few medical treatments that might have actually helped him, in contrast to the bloodletting Colonel Ewing administered: "Comfrey roots and leaves contain allantoin, a substance that helps new skin cells grow, along with other substances that reduce inflammation and keep skin healthy" (Penn State Hershey Medical Center, Health Information Library, http://pennstatehershey.adam.com/content.aspx?productid=107&pid=33&gid=000234).

5. Presuming the servant "Dick" was a slave, he was the only enslaved person whom Daniel Parker met on his travels that he mentions by name in his autobiography.

6. The "niece" is Eliza Kennedy Ewing. See further notes, below.

7. "Her [Eliza Ewing's] mother" was Letitia Warren Ewing, born ca. 1764, died 1838 (Ellsberry, 260). According to a marriage record from Lincoln County, Kentucky (then Virginia), "Lettice" Warren married Baker Ewing in 1784 (Lucien Beckner, "Lincoln County Records, continued," *Register of the Kentucky State Historical Society* 12, no. 35 [May 1914]: 79). She was the sister of Winnifred Warren Ewing. The two Ewing brothers married the two Warren sisters (Lucien Beckner, "History of the County Court of Lincoln County, Va., Now Kentucky," *Register of the Kentucky State Historical Society* 20, no. 59 [May 1922]: 188n).

8. Baker Ewing, presumably a few years older than his brother Young, was delegate to the Virginia General Assembly from Lincoln County in the Kentucky region and first registrar of the land office of Kentucky in 1788. He served as an officer in the county militia and in various other government positions in Lincoln County, as he did in Franklin County, Kentucky, after it was formed in 1795. See Beckner, "History of the County Court of Lincoln County," 179, 182–85, 187–88, 188n; and L. F. Johnson, *History of Franklin County, Kentucky* (Franklin, KY: Roberts Printing Company, 1912), 6–7, 40. Ewing Street in Frankfort, the capital of Kentucky, is named for him (Jennie C. Morton, "Streets of the Capital of Kentucky," *Register of the Kentucky*

State Historical Society 13, no. 39 [September 1915]: 55). Baker's and Young's youngest brother was Finis Ewing (1773–1841), one of the founders of the revivalist denomination, the Cumberland Presbyterian Church (Franceway Ranna Cossitt, *The Life and Times of Rev. Finis Ewing, One of the Fathers and Founders of the Cumberland Presbyterian Church* [Louisville, KY: L. R. Woods, 1853], 122, 212).

9. The current spelling for this town is Russellville. Parker spells it two different ways in the MS: "Russelsville" and "Russelville" (Octavo 7).

10. Parker appears to have originally spelled the name of his host "Stephenson" and then corrected it as Stephen or Stephens (Octavo 7). The family copy has "Stevenson" (79). The uncertain spelling makes it impossible to identify "Esqr. Stephens" with any precision.

11. An "overshot" mill has a water wheel driven by water flowing into it from above (*Webster's New World Dictionary*, 2nd ed. [1980], s.v. "overshot").

12. Joshua 23:14; 1 Kings 2:2.

13. The lack of "control in the matter" for women, especially southern women, who opposed slavery is why many women began to link antislavery activism with the struggle for women's rights. See Blanche Glassman Hersh, *The Slavery of Sex: Feminist-Abolitionists in America* (Urbana: University of Illinois Press, 1978), 6–35.

14. Parker gives an illustration of frontier populist electioneering at the outset of the "Age of Democracy," as removal of property restrictions in the early nineteenth century allowed more Americans to vote. Compare to Davy Crockett's even more raucous description of his frontier campaign for the Tennessee legislature in 1821 (*A Narrative of the Life of David Crockett of the State of Tennessee* [Philadelphia: E. L. Carey and A. Hart, 1834], 137–42). Of course, expanded American democracy did not include all Americans (African Americans, Native Americans, women). See "Parker's Decades of Change" with notes in the Editor's Introduction. Note also that Parker is describing, disapprovingly, precisely the kind of campaigning that his friend and host Young Ewing was known for (see note 3 above). Parker's distaste for the cruder aspects of politics coheres with his principled honesty and humility. However, it might also be characteristic of the Federalist ethos of the New Englanders who migrated to eastern Ohio, like Parker's politician brother-in-law, Ephraim Cutler (Cayton and Riggs, 20, 62, 82, 88). Federalists believed that the masses of Americans needed to be educated and elevated by strong institutions in order for democracy to succeed (Linda K. Kerber, *Federalists in Dissent: Imagery and Ideology in Jeffersonian America* [Ithaca, NY: Cornell University Press, 1970], vii–xii). Parker's "Federalism," such as it was, took the form of a general ethos rather than party loyalty. Though an active social reformer, Parker showed virtually no interest in party politics, candidates, campaigns, and the like.

15. Eliza Kennedy Ewing was born in 1790 in what was then Lincoln County, Kentucky (Alpheus H. Harlan, *History and Genealogy of the Harlan Family* [Baltimore: Lord Baltimore Press, 1914]: 109, 285–86).

16. The MS has "crowded up me" (Octavo 7). The Family Copy has "crowded upon me" (83).

17. Pilot Rock is mentioned in Christian County local histories (Perrin, 27–28; Charles M. Meacham, *History of Christian County, Kentucky: From Oxcart to Airplane*

[Nashville: Marshall and Bruce, TN: 1930], 9–10]). It is located on what is now the boundary of Christian and Todd Counties along Kentucky Route 507. It is also the location of some prehistoric Native American petroglyphs (Fred E. Coy Jr. et. al., *Rock Art of Kentucky* [Lexington: University Press of Kentucky, 1997], 29–30). Though partially on private land, it was and continues to be a popular hiking and climbing (and more recently, drinking, partying, and graffiti) destination (Damian Phillips, "Pilot Rock – USDA," *Western Kentucky Hiking* [blog], September 1, 2012, https://kyhiker.blogspot.com/2012/09/pilot-rock.html).

18. A rod is equivalent to sixteen and a half feet.

19. The more usual spelling is "whortleberries." Parker is probably referring to huckleberries, or perhaps blueberries (*American Dictionary of Regional English* [2012], s.v. "whortleberry").

20. A "Yankee trick" is "a deception or fraud often associated with Yankees"—that is, people from New England, and, in Parker's time, from Ohio, "where there were many settlers from New England." By the Civil War, "Yankee" would be used by Southerners for all Northerners. Robert Hendrickson, *The Facts on File Dictionary of American Regionalisms* (New York: Facts on File, 2000), 325, 327.

21. Edible wild grapes grow throughout the eastern and central United States. See Lee Allen Peterson, *A Field Guide to Edible Wild Plants of Eastern and Central North America* (Boston: Houghton Mifflin, 1977), 198.

22. "Mr. Baddon" is Stephen Theodore Badin, born in 1768 in Orleans, France. He immigrated to the United States in 1791 in the wake of the French Revolution. In 1793 he became the first Catholic priest to be ordained in the United States, by Bishop John Carroll in Baltimore, who sent him to minister to the growing number of Catholic migrants in Kentucky. There he labored many years, at times as the only priest in the state, gaining the appellation of "the Apostle of Kentucky." In later years he worked with Native Americans in Michigan and Indiana. He acquired land in Indiana that would become the campus of the University of Notre Dame, where he is buried (Benedict Joseph Webb, *The Centenary of Catholicity in Kentucky* [Louisville, KY: Charles A. Rogers, 1884], 159–67; "Badin, Stephen T.," in *The HarperCollins Encyclopedia of Catholicism*, ed. Richard P. McBrien [New York: HarperCollins, 1995], 126). Parker's interaction with Father Badin is quite civil, considering general relations between Protestants and Catholics in the United States at this time. See "Parker and American Religion" in the Editor's Introduction (with notes, including cited sources) for a reference to this discussion.

23. According to the US Geological Survey, the first main shock of the New Madrid earthquakes was at 2:15 a.m. on December 16, 1811, with a significant aftershock a few hours later. Those would be the "two shakes of an earthquake" that Parker "felt about the middle of December." The second major shock was on the precise date Parker gives, January 23, 1812. These shocks were felt across the eastern half of the United States (https://earthquake.usgs.gov/earthquakes/events/1811-1812newmadrid/summary.php). See also Valencius, 14–34.

24. According to a monument in Warrenwood Cemetery, Danville, Kentucky (photograph on Find a Grave, https://www.findagrave.com/memorial/102001823/william-warren), William Warren was born in Spotsylvania County, Virginia, served

with the Eighth Regiment of Virginia, 1776–78, and commanded the fort on the frontier of Jefferson County, Kentucky, in 1779. He settled in what is now Boyle County (and what was then Lincoln County), Kentucky, where he died on September 3, 1819, at age eighty. Boyle County was formed out of Lincoln and Mercer Counties in 1842 with Danville as the county seat. Lucien Beckner's "History of the County Court of Lincoln County, Va., Now Kentucky" mentions William Warren several times as, among other things, surveyor in 1785 of the road that would become the Danville and Hustonville Turnpike and deputy sheriff of the county in 1792 (180–81, 189).

25. Samuel may not have remained single. The US Census of 1830 (Lincoln County, Kentucky, NARA Publication M19, Roll 38, 347; accessed through Ancestry.com) lists Samuel Warren as the head of a household in Lincoln County that included an adult White female and two White children, along with twelve enslaved persons.

26. The phrase "a numerous connection" (as opposed to "numerous connections") is used in both the MS (Octavo 8) and the Family Copy (87).

27. William L. McCalla (1788–1859) served churches in Maysville, Kentucky, and Philadelphia and also made a brief diversion as chaplain to the navy of the Republic of Texas. The temperamental opposite of Daniel Parker, he thrived on controversy and was famous for "his withering sarcasm, his unsparing invective." Even as a candidate for ministry (while Parker was living in Kentucky) he was locked in conflict with a respected senior Presbyterian minister, James Blythe, who objected to his fierce advocacy of the War of 1812. He became an outspoken critic of Roman Catholicism and a vocal combatant on the strictly Calvinist "Old School" side of the Old School/New School Presbyterian conflict of the 1830s (Robert Davidson, *History of the Presbyterian Church in the State of Kentucky* [New York: Robert Carter, 1847], 125, 283n; and Harris Elwood Starr, "McCalla, William Latta," in *Dictionary of American Biography*, ed. Dumas Malone [New York: Charles Scribner's Sons, 1933], 11:564). His father, Parker's host, Andrew McCalla, was a highly regarded physician and philanthropist in Lexington (Davidson, 283n; and Richard H. Collins, *History of Kentucky: By the Late Lewis Collins, Revised, Enlarged Four-Fold, and Brought Down to the Year 1874, by his Son, Richard H. Collins* [Covington, KY: Collins, 1874], 2:195, 2:223).

28. The US Congress declared war on Great Britain on June 18, 1812, the day before Parker, according to his memoir, left for Lexington, not during the six weeks he lived there. As Parker indicates, however, time would have passed before "the report of this event reached the place."

29. John Pope (1770–1845) was one of Kentucky's earliest leaders to achieve national prominence. As a US senator, he voted against the declaration of war on Britain in 1812, which damaged his political career temporarily. It later recovered, however, and he was elected to the House of Representatives three times. See Todd Estes, "Pope, John," in *The Kentucky Encyclopedia*, ed. John E. Kleber (Lexington: University Press of Kentucky, 1992), 728. The intensity of the war enthusiasm, or as Parker puts it, the "war spirit," in Kentucky in 1812 frightened even the "war hawk" Senator Henry Clay (Ramage and Watkins, 97–101). Craig Thompson Friend writes that some Kentuckians were enthusiastic for war as an opportunity to demonstrate White masculinity: "A second war with Britain and a concluding war with the northwestern

Indians would bring glory and recognition to Kentucky's white men, capping off the shift to patriarchy that had been under way for the previous two decades" (*Kentucke's Frontiers* [Bloomington: Indiana University Press, 2010], 248).

30. "Commodore Rogers" was Captain John Rodgers (1772–1838), the senior active naval officer during the War of 1812. Rogers led four cruises during the war, each doing some damage to the enemy, but never won a frigate engagement that caught the public imagination. See Tyrone G. Martin, "Rodgers, John," in *The Encyclopedia of the War of 1812: A Political, Social, and Military History*, ed. Spencer C. Tucker (Santa Barbara, CA: ABC-CLIO, 2012), 452–53; and Donald R. Hickey, *The War of 1812: A Forgotten Conflict* (Urbana: University of Illinois Press, 2012), 92–93.

31. Parker's narrative flashes forward to January of 1813: the "*habitants*" (ethnically French settlers) of Frenchtown on the River Raisin (now Monroe, Michigan) sent emissaries to General James Winchester, whose regiment of Kentuckians was encamped in the Maumee valley of Ohio, requesting protection from British impressment. Winchester's army enthusiastically responded and routed a small British garrison on January 18. But on January 23, British general Henry Procter arrived to defeat them with an army of some twelve hundred British soldiers and Native American warriors. Approximately nine hundred Kentuckians were killed or captured. The next day, some of the Native American force killed at least thirty prisoners. It was a low point for the American military campaign, but the "massacre" became an important propaganda tool and Kentuckians would be inspired by the slogan "Remember the Raisin!" (Hickey, 85; Alan Taylor, *The Civil War of 1812: American Citizens, British Subjects, Irish Rebels, and Indian Allies* [New York: Alfred A. Knopf, 2011], 210–14).

32. Parker's lamentation of the unavoidable evils of war is in keeping with his temperament and principles. Many Universalists, along with some evangelicals and many abolitionists, were also peace activists (Russell Miller, 508–13; Timothy Smith, 198–200). However, Parker's association of the "war spirit" with "disgusting demonstrations peculiar to mobs" (as opposed to the "more judicious and sober portion" of society) could also be an aspect of a Federalist orientation (see note 14 above). Federalists, while not necessarily sharing Parker's general antimilitarism, opposed the American declaration of war against England in 1812. The bitter, at times even violent, conflict between the Federalist and the opposing Democratic-Republican Party was one of many ways the war exacerbated hostilities and divided communities in North America, the theme of Alan Taylor's *The Civil War of 1812*. As an example of its intimate divisiveness, Taylor refers to Captain Nathaniel Hart of Kentucky, whom Parker mentions. Hart had recently hosted British loyalist Captain William Elliott in his home and nursed him through a nearly fatal illness, "But at Frenchtown, Elliott could not save the wounded Hart from the warriors" (133, 175–79, 212).

33. Parker returns to his original chronology: August 1812.

34. Dr. McCalla's wife was Martha (More) McCalla (Starr, 564), of whom Davidson writes, "None who ever saw [her] will soon forget the keen eye and strong character of that ardent mother in Israel. She fell a victim to the cholera in 1833" (283n). Mild-mannered Daniel Parker also acknowledges her charitable works, but uses an uncharacteristically strong term ("bigot") for her religious dogmatism. Her

combative son, William, apparently took after his mother more than his father in this respect (see note 27 above and notes 42 and 43 below).

35. Such anxiety over a servile rebellion "haunted the collective consciousness (and perhaps also the collective conscience) of white Americans" throughout the period of slavery (Torbett, 3). Craig Thompson Friend explains, "as during the Revolutionary War, Kentuckians drew upon the imagery of a dual threat of Indian attacks and slave revolts that had previously been successful in reinforcing the racial constructions of war," though "most Kentuckians had never experienced slave uprisings or Indian attacks" (247–48).

36. Parker's diary entry offers, on the one hand, a valid argument that slavery demoralizes both races of a slaveholding society, especially the children. That the slave system encouraged vice and discouraged virtue among enslaved people was a common antislavery argument, made by Black and White abolitionists. Frederick Douglass wrote that White masters would rather see their slaves "spending the Sabbath in wrestling, boxing, and drinking whisky" than "trying to learn how to read the will of God" (*Narrative of the Life of Frederick Douglass, an American Slave*, ed. John W. Blassingame, John R. McKivigan, and Peter P. Hinks [New Haven, CT: Yale University Press, 2001], 59). On the other hand, for White opponents of slavery, criticism of the moral degradation of slaves often lapsed into paternalistic expressions of racial superiority (Ibram X. Kendi, *Stamped from the Beginning: The Definitive History of Racist Ideas in America* [New York: Nation Books, 2016], 161–76). Parker's reference to "the natural viciousness in some, and the want of encouragement in all" enslaved people should not escape critical analysis. However, Parker's emphasis appears to be on the evil of inculcating a false sense of superiority among the children of White slaveholding families. It is also important to note that for Parker, as a reformer and religious thinker, all people of all races were in need of moral improvement.

37. Parker may have written these verses himself. I have not been able to locate another source for this poem.

38. "Chattleism," in the MS (Octavo 8) and Family Copy (89), was a common nineteenth-century spelling of "chattelism." Chattel slavery legally defines persons as "chattels" (property).

39. Matthew 7:12.

40. Again (see note 36 above), Parker's reference to enslaved people as "an excited ignorant mass" should not escape criticism. Again, however, it is important to place this statement in the context of his general social and religious vision, in which all people are in need of improvement; of his antislavery argument that slavery deprives people of education; and, more importantly, his estimation that the dreaded slave rebellion would be the natural consequence of oppression. See "Parker and Race" in the Editor's Introduction for further discussion.

41. From what Parker was able to observe at the time, he could reasonably conclude that slavery in Kentucky was "mild" compared to the Deep South. There were fewer slaves, smaller slaveholdings, and generally more freedom of movement for enslaved people. On the other hand, "the backbreaking work that slaves performed in the Kentucky hemp industry and the dangerous and unhealthy labor on steamboats were as harsh as that on cotton or rice plantations" (Ramage and Watkins, 6).

The domestic slave trade contributed significantly to Kentucky's economy. African American people lived with the threat of being sold to southern plantations. Slavery in Kentucky, like slavery in every region, was unique and created particular challenges for both enslaved people and free people of color (Salafia, 5, 123–24).

42. This was the same James Blythe who endured a conflict with William McCalla (see note 27 above) over the War of 1812, yet another example of the divisiveness of that war. Blythe (1765–1842) was opposed to the war, though his son enlisted and was killed at the Battle of River Raisin. McCalla, then a candidate for ministry, arraigned Blythe before Presbytery in 1813, charging him with threatening to oppose his licensure because of their political differences. Blythe was ultimately acquitted. In addition to ministering at Presbyterian churches in Kentucky, Blythe was professor of science and mathematics at Transylvania University. He was elected president of Hanover College, then informally known as South Hanover College, in Hanover, Indiana, in 1832 (Davidson, 123–26; William Alfred Millis, *The History of Hanover College from 1827 to 1927* [Hanover, IN: Hanover College, 1927], 57, 292).

43. Parker misremembers the first name of physician James Fishback, who wrote *The Philosophy of the Human Mind in Respect to Religion, or, A Demonstration from the Necessity of Things That Religion Entered the World by Revelation* (Lexington, KY: Thomas T. Skillman, 1813). At the time of publication, Fishback was a Presbyterian layman. William McCalla, true to form, found heresies and brought Fishback before the Presbytery. Fishback later became a Baptist minister, as Parker says, and then became associated with the Restoration movement of Alexander Campbell (not to be confused with Parker's Restorationist universalism). See Leroy Garrett, *The Stone-Campbell Movement: The Story of the American Restoration Movement* (Joplin, MO: College Press, 2002), 87, 238; William L. MacCalla [*sic*], *Remarks on Dr. James Fishback's the Philosophy of the Human Mind in Respect to Religion* (Lexington, KY: printed by M'Call & Downing, for the author, 1814); and Scott Harp, "Dr. James Fishback," History of the Restoration Movement (June 2011), https://www.therestorationmovement.com/_states/kentucky/fishback.htm.

44. Foushee Tebbs Taylor (1785–1842) married Mary (Polly) Warren in Mercer County, 1808 (Marriage Record transcribed in Jordan Dodd, *Kentucky Marriages through 1850*, accessed through Ancestry.com; Ellsberry, 263).

45. Stephen Stein refers to this Shaker community in Kentucky in *The Shaker Experience in America* (New Haven, CT: Yale University Press, 1992), 62–63. See a reference to Shakers in "Parker and American Religion" in the Editor's Introduction.

46. See "Parker and Slavery" in the Editor's Introduction for the significance of this conversation.

47. "Inst." (Latin, *instante mense*): "this month." Parker had the "decisive interview" with Eliza Ewing on September 14, 1812.

48. William Tell Parker wrote about Daniel Parker's life before Priscilla, "I do not think Father ever had an earlier love; at least none of sufficient intensity to disturb his peace. I have heard him admit that he had felt an interest in a lady, in Danville, Ky., a spoiled heiress" (19). This shows how little the son knew (or wanted to know) about his father's romantic life before he met his mother, though this autobiography would have been available to him.

49. George Harlan Briscoe (b. 1788) had served as lieutenant captain in James Barbour's company of the Kentucky Militia from August 1812 to March 1813 (War of 1812 Pension Applications Index, Records of the Department of Veterans Affairs, NARA Microfilm Publication M313, accessed through Ancestry.com). He married Eliza Kennedy Ewing on January 11, 1814. Their six children were born between the years 1815 and 1825. The family moved to Illinois in 1834. George died in 1847 (Harlan, 109, 285–86). According to the Census of 1860, Eliza later lived with the family of her daughter, Phebe (Briscoe) Bacon in Huntsville, Illinois (Huntsville, Schuyler County, Illinois, NARA series M653, Roll 228, 285, accessed through Ancestry.com). She died in 1873 (Harlan, 285). William Tell Parker claims that the "spoiled heiress" from Danville who rejected his father "afterward married a French scamp named Fauntleroy. This lady was reduced to poverty by the vices of her husband, and was drifted to our neighborhood in after years, on the waves of fortune. She visited at our house, when I was a small boy, and I remember her as a pale, skinny, bent lady of forty, dyspeptic, hysterical, querulous, and gloomy. She taught a select school in New Richmond, and sister Susanna was for a while under her instruction. I was always glad she was not my mother." This story is as unlikely as it is interesting. Tell was confusing another lady he met in childhood with the figure in his father's stories. Eben A. Parker writes that Susanna studied with "Miss Fontleroy" in New Richmond (*The Parker Family*, printed booklet prepared for the semicentennial anniversary of Clermont Academy, 1889, Clermont Academy Collection, Northern Kentucky University, 20).

50. James Warren married Phebe Briscoe (b. 1784) in Mercer County in 1803. She was the daughter of Jeremiah Briscoe (1760–1823) and the sister of George Briscoe, who married Eliza Ewing (Harlan, 109; Kentucky County Marriage Records, 1783–1965, online database maintained by Ancestry.com). Jeremiah Briscoe is listed as a major in Lieutenant Colonel Samuel South's regiment of the Kentucky Mounted Militia, organized on September 12, 1812. Warren and Briscoe were possibly recruited for Brigadier General Samuel Hopkins's disappointing expedition into Illinois Territory (Quisenbury, 57; Ramage and Watkins, 103).

51. Parker's brief employment as a slave overseer, and the racial language he uses to describe it, constitute the greatest contradiction to his later career as an abolitionist. See "Parker and Race" in the Editor's Introduction for further discussion and context.

52. Parker is quoting and citing "Truth" by the eighteenth-century English poet William Cowper. See *The Poems of William Cowper*, vol. 1, *1748–1782*, ed. John D. Baird and Charles Ryskamp (Oxford: Oxford University Press, 1980), 280. On Cowper and his own struggles with mental illness, see chap. 1, note 38.

53. This is a case in which the question of where the quoted portion of Parker's travel journal of 1812 ends and where his autobiography of 1845 resumes is consequential, and is also a matter of interpretation (see note 13 in chap. 3). Parker does not mark the transition by closing quotation marks or beginning a new line, so the editor must detect it through a change in style and content. In the following sentence, Parker moves from describing his day-to-day experience in the Warren household, using mostly the present tense, to describing the fifty days as a whole, using only the past tense, indicating that the quoted portion ends here, though it is possible that

the transition occurred earlier or later in the manuscript. That Parker's complaints in the preceding paragraphs, particularly about the behavior of the enslaved people whom he oversaw, are quotes from his younger self of 1812, and not from the mature abolitionist of 1845, is significant for understanding Parker's state of mind and also his changing attitudes toward race. Even so, the mature Parker, introspective and self-critical in so many other ways, does not explicitly criticize his past racial attitudes. See "Parker and Slavery" and "Parker and Race" in the Editor's Introduction for further discussion.

54. The US Census of 1810 lists Thomas B. Warren as living in Fayette County with what appear to be his wife and children and eleven enslaved people (Lexington, Fayette County, Kentucky, NARA Publication 252, roll 6, 42, accessed through Ancestry.com).

55. In the MS, Parker almost forgets the "almost" before "engaged to be married," but later adds it with a caret (Octavo 9).

56. By "after life" in this sentence, Parker means "later life," not life after death (Octavo 9).

57. In the MS, Parker originally made the stronger statement that he made "no departure from moral principle," but then added the qualifying, and humbler, "willful" with a caret (Octavo 9).

58. 1 Corinthians 15:10.

59. Again, Parker addresses his readers, primarily his children but also, he assumes, a broader audience. See the Editor's Introduction for Parker's intent in writing.

Chapter 5

1. "Purdy" may be, or may be related to, Simeon Purdy, one of the founders of the town of Moundsville, (West) Virginia, in the flats of Grave Creek in 1832 (Scott Powell, *History of Marshall County, from Forest to Field* [Moundsville, WV: n.p., 1925], 97–98).

2. Alexandria, once "the undisputed . . . business center" of Scioto County, was already being overshadowed by nearby Portsmouth when Parker gave his first sermon on universal salvation there in 1814 (Nelson W. Evans, *A History of Scioto County, Ohio* [Portsmouth, OH: published by the author, 1903], 412–13). It is now an unincorporated community, not to be confused with the village of Alexandria in Licking County.

3. Matthew 5:15.

4. Job 32:10 ("I also will shew mine opinion").

5. Parker's first sermon on unlimited salvation appropriately uses a text that proclaims "our Saviour Jesus Christ, who hath abolished death, and hath brought life and immortality to light through the gospel" (2 Timothy 2:10).

6. Parker paraphrases Philippians 2:10–11.

7. See "Parker the Universalist" in the Editor's Introduction for an explanation of how he synthesized Halcyon theology with his concept of universal restoration.

8. At last freed of indecision, Parker makes a final metaphorical allusion to the colt who carried Jesus into Jerusalem (Mark 11:1–4), now no longer tied where two

ways met, but ready to be used by the Lord. See his previous references in chaps. 2 and 3.

9. Parker's anxiety that he would be misrepresented, attacked, and shunned by "pious Christians" for preaching his unorthodox universalist doctrine was not unfounded (Bressler, 33–40). Parker is just as worried that "wicked men" would coopt and misuse his ideas, focusing only on the "final issue" (that there is no hell, that all people will go to heaven) and neglecting the more important "process" of personal and social transformation, which Parker understood to be the heart of his theology of universal "restoration." See the Editor's Introduction for further explanation of this emphasis. Parker resolves, nevertheless, to follow his calling, citing among other reasons the peace of mind brought by his first "public declaration" of his beliefs.

10. Parker would not have seen *the* first steamboat that ever departed from Pittsburgh: Robert Fulton's *New Orleans*, which left in 1811 and did not return to that port. Parker might mean he saw *his* first steamboat, perhaps Daniel French's *Comet*, which "made at least two good trips between Louisville and Pittsburgh before departing for New Orleans in 1814." See Michael Gillespie, *Come Hell or High Water: A Lively History of Steamboating on the Mississippi and Ohio Rivers* (Stoddard, WI: Heritage Press, 2002), 10.

11. Parker's text (Zechariah 3:9) refers to "one stone" with "seven eyes," implying that he might have preached on the seven characteristics of God symbolized by Urim in Halcyon theology. See chap. 2.

12. Parker consistently uses the spelling "skift" rather than the more common "skiff" (a flat-bottomed boat).

13. A ropewalk is a long lane or covered pathway used for manufacturing hemp rope, an important industry in antebellum Kentucky. See James F. Hopkins, *A History of the Hemp Industry in Kentucky* (Lexington: University of Kentucky Press, 1951), 112–16, 132–34.

14. For a discussion of various forms of religious skepticism in nineteenth-century America, see James Turner, *Without God, Without Creed: Origins of Unbelief in America* (Baltimore: Johns Hopkins University Press, 1985), 73–113. That Parker would encounter Deists, who questioned different aspects of religious orthodoxy on the basis of reason and experience, is not surprising. However, the true atheists whom Parker met, who denied God's existence entirely, would be quite rare at that time (Turner, 102). Parker apparently sees himself as especially well suited to speak to the concerns of Deists and others informed by the American Enlightenment. Despite holding some unorthodox ideas himself, Parker generally defends traditional Christian supernaturalism in these conversations, but attempts to do so with respect for his audience's intellectual and moral concerns. See "Parker and American Religion" in the Editor's Introduction and Parker's encounter with the "noted Deist" Joseph Reed in chap. 2, along with the explanatory note.

15. Parker found a point of contact with Deists in his understanding of the "divine character" (symbolized by Urim in Halcyon theology): an image of a benevolent, logically consistent God, comparable to the rational supreme being of Deism (Walters, *The American Deists*, 31–33). By "implicit infidelity," Parker meant that some skeptics, just like some believers, did not always think through the ideas they affirmed. Parker

alludes to the Catholic idea of "implicit faith," of which many Protestants had a negative (and not entirely fair) understanding (Franchot, 109).

16. Parker's defense of the traditional Christian doctrine of the fall is a surprising tack for a Universalist, considering that nineteenth-century "liberal religious thought, of both Unitarian and Universalist varieties . . . repudiated the doctrine of original sin" (Olds, 88). Note that Parker considered conviction of sin to be a necessary element of his own conversion to the Halcyon Church. See chap. 2.

17. This is probably Dr. Anderson D. Keith (1784–1869), whom the US Census lists as a physician living in Augusta, Kentucky (1850 US Census, Augusta, Bracken County, Kentucky, NARA Publication M432, Roll 193, 452A; and 1860 US Census, Augusta, Bracken County, Kentucky, NARA Publication M653, Roll 357, 266; accessed through Ancestry.com). See also *Lineage Book*, vol. 91 (Washington, DC: National Society of the Daughters of the American Revolution, 1912), 303; accessed through Ancestry.com. This might also be the same Dr. Keith who thwarted a mob attack on abolitionist J. M. Mallet in nearby Germantown (Caroline R. Miller, "Underground Railroad, Bracken Co.," in *The Encyclopedia of Northern Kentucky*, ed. Paul A. Tenkotte and James C. Claypool [Lexington: University Press of Kentucky, 2009], 903).

18. Parker's "special reasons" for not preaching at an execution could be that Parker was opposed on principle to capital punishment, the abolition of which was a long-standing cause of Universalists (Russell Miller, 499–508).

19. See "Augusta" in *The Kentucky Encyclopedia*, 41: "Because an abundance of prehistoric artifacts have been found there, it is believed that Augusta was once the site of a large permanent Native American Village."

20. James Kennedy married Elizabeth Warren in Lincoln County in 1789 (Beckner, "Lincoln County Records," 87). The US Census lists James Kennedy as living with his family and several slaves in Campbell County in 1810, and specifically in the town of Covington in 1820 (1810 US Census, Campbell County, Kentucky, NARA publication M252, Roll 9, 27; 1820 US Census, Covington, Campbell County, Kentucky, NARA publication M33, Roll 20, 20; both accessed through Ancestry.com). Mary Keturah Jones writes that William Kennedy, "a Scotchman," settled at "Flag Spring" in Campbell County around 1789 with his son James Kennedy, who "played finely on the fiddle" and had been a classmate in Scotland of poet Robert Burns (*History of Campbell County, as Read at the Centennial Celebration of 4th of July, 1876* [Newport, KY: n.p., 1876], 4). Daniel Parker consistently uses the spelling "Kenedy," for his Scottish Deist friend, and even for his oldest son, James "Kenedy" Parker, who was named after him, as does the Family Copy, written by Parker's son Charles (104, 132). Other documents, including those by Parker's other children, are inconsistent, but usually use the spelling "Kennedy." This volume will use Daniel Parker's spelling, "Kenedy," in the body and the more likely spelling, "Kennedy," in the notes.

21. Kerry Walters writes that Deism attacked traditional Christianity on two fronts: it criticized its "supernaturalistic worldview" as illogical, and it condemned "its historical record of intolerance and persecution" (*The American Deists*, 29). Parker seems to be joining the condemnation of intolerance and persecution ("that spirit of bigotry") in order to defend the supernaturalistic worldview.

22. Kennedy's beliefs—rejecting miracles and supernatural revelation, but affirming the existence of God, life after death with rewards and punishments, and Jesus as an excellent teacher and example, but not the son of God—are common Deist beliefs, similar to those of Thomas Jefferson. That Jesus never claimed to be the son of God, but those claims were added to the gospels by later interpolators, is an exegetical principle of Thomas Jefferson's famous abridgement of the New Testament, *The Jefferson Bible: The Life and Morals of Jesus of Nazareth*, ed. Douglas E. Lurton (New York: Henry Holt, 1995). See also Kerry Walters, *Revolutionary Deists: Early America's Rational Infidels* (Amherst, NY: Prometheus Books, 2010), 155–62. It is not exactly clear what made Kennedy "the strangest Deist [Parker] had ever met with," since most of his ideas are typical of Deism. Maybe the other Deists that Parker had met with did not have such affable personalities.

23. Parker quotes John 14:6. Parker's anti-Deist argument takes an unusual turn, based on his belief in contingent as opposed to natural human immortality. The majority of both traditional and liberal Christians of Parker's day would reject this "Christian mortalism," which he retained from his days in the Halcyon Church. Those few Universalists who would agree with Parker on the nature of immortality would disagree with his belief in a limited postmortem punishment for sin (Bressler, 45–46).

24. Acts 26:28.

25. The Family Copy also uses Parker's spelling, "Verseiles" (107). The current spelling of this town in Kentucky is Versailles.

26. The Christian Connection was one of a number of groups in the United States that rejected traditional creeds and denominational structures. They referred to themselves simply as "Christians" or "Disciples." Seeking to restore what they understood to be the simple, "primitive" practices of the New Testament church, these groups came to be known as "Restorationist" churches (not to be confused with the "Restorationist" faction of universalism that Parker belonged to). Important leaders were Elias Smith, Abner Jones, Barton Stone, and Alexander Campbell. Abel Sarjent sympathized especially with the anticlericalism of this movement and reprinted a foundational document coauthored by Stone, "The Last Will and Testament of the Springfield Presbytery," in a Halcyon publication, *The Destruction of the Beast in the Downfall of Sectarianism* (1806), 1–6. Ironically, this anti-denominational movement produced at least two existent denominations: the Disciples of Christ and the Churches of Christ. See Hatch, *The Democratization of American Christianity*, 68–81; and Keith Huey, "Stone-Campbell Movement," in *Encyclopedia of Religion in America*, 4:2162–66. Thomas Smith may possibly be Thomas Stovall Smith (b. 1780) of nearby Jessamine County, who married Mary Michael Locket in 1801 (US and International Marriage Records, 1560–1900, online database maintained by Ancestry.com).

27. The word "budget" originally referred to a purse or similar small bag.

28. Both African American and White congregations at outdoor revival meetings appended this anonymous chorus to Isaac Watts's "Alas and Did My Savior Bleed." It eventually found its way into printed songbooks. See Candy Gunther Brown, *The Word in the World: Evangelical Writing, Publishing, and Reading in America, 1789–1880* (Chapel Hill: University of North Carolina Press, 2004), 205–6.

29. Parker remembered this momentary encounter decades later, revealing he indeed worried about his own sanity, particularly the effects of "intense mental exercise on the subject of religion." While Parker is not devoid of sympathy for the mentally ill homeless woman, his "there but for the grace of God" reaction contrasts with his generally compassionate character.

30. "Developed" in this case means "revealed." See *Webster's New World Dictionary*, 2nd ed. (1980), s.v. "develop."

31. Actually, Jeremiah Vardeman (1775–1842) was "the most successful preacher that ever lived in Kentucky," whose popularity endured for decades after his meeting with Parker, according to J. H. Spencer in *A History of Kentucky Baptists* (Cincinnati: J. R. Baumes, 1885), 1:232. At the time of meeting Parker, Vardeman was pastor of David's Fork Baptist Church in present-day Lexington. In addition to his pastoral duties, he traveled as an evangelist in Tennessee and Ohio. He finished his career in Missouri.

32. Matthew 9:11; Mark 2:16; Luke 5:30. Parker is referring to Jesus, regarded with suspicion by religious authorities because he associated with moral failures.

33. In addition to holding what were at the time unpopular theological ideas, traveling Universalist preachers like Parker were the targets of popular prejudices against itinerants of all kinds. Critics dismissed them as showmen who appealed to the lower elements of society: "gamblers, scoffers, infidels, blasphemers and topers" (Bressler, 55–56). As a traveling preacher and a traveling salesman, Parker was hit with it from two sides.

34. This may be the Daniel Fink whom the US Census of 1820 records living in Elksburg in Lewis County, Kentucky (NARA Publication M33, Roll 20, 98; accessed through FamilySearch.org).

35. Some Anabaptist and other Christian groups continue to practice foot washing as an occasional rite, intended to show humility and service in imitation of Jesus, who washed his disciples' feet (John 13:1–17). See James F. White, *A Brief History of Christian Worship* (Nashville, TN: Abingdon, 1993), 25. See also "Parker and American Religion" in the Editor's Introduction for a reference to this conversation.

36. With his familiarity with the Halcyon doctrine of Urim, Daniel Fink indicates that he at one point may have been a member of or a sympathetic fellow traveler with the Halcyon Church. In the following paragraphs, Parker, in conversation with Fink and others, builds on his previous understanding of the sevenfold symbolism of Urim, adding the fivefold significance of Thummim. In his elaboration, he lists what he understands to be significant recurrences of the numbers seven, five, and twelve (seven plus five) in the Bible and in nature. He also connects Urim and Thummim to his understanding of the person and work of Jesus Christ. See "Urim and Thummim" in the Editor's Introduction for further explanation of these ideas. See also note 39 below for a discussion of problems related to his memory of the timing of his discovery of the meaning of Thummim.

37. Matthew 1:21.

38. Unfortunately, Parker does not name these "metaphysical authors" who wrote about "mental philosophy." The most influential theory of human knowledge of the time was Thomas Reid's Common Sense Realism. See Sydney E. Ahlstrom, "The

Scottish Philosophy and American Theology," *Church History* 24, no. 3 (September 1955): 257–72; and Holifield, 173–96.

39. There is an apparent discrepancy between Parker's account of how and when he arrived at the symbolic meaning of Thummim and references to the same concepts in Halcyon Church publications. Parker implies, not only that he first learned of the fivefold symbolism in 1815, but that no one had even fully articulated the idea until that time. However, there are earlier allusions to the significance of Thummim in Halcyon literature, many of which sound similar to Parker's explanation in these paragraphs, going back as far as 1804.

In the 1804 text "The Doctrine of Endless Miseries Investigated" (26), Sarjent says that the human soul is composed of five "faculties": affection, will, memory, reason, and understanding, in that order (cf. Parker's perception, understanding, affection, will, and memory). In another article in the same publication of 1804, "A Declaration of the Constitution and Standard of the Millennium Church," 59, Sarjent writes that Urim and Thummim symbolize, respectively, "the seven communicable attributes of the Deity and five faculties of rational intelligence" that are perfected "in the person of Christ." This formula is essentially restated in "An Address to the Human Family at Large," a "circular letter" authorized by the "3d Concilium of the Halcyon Church" and signed on its behalf by John Parker (64–65). In "A Brief Hint of the Universal Dominion of Emmanuel," written in 1807, during the period of conflict between Sarjent and the Parkers, Sarjent refers to Thummim as "five principle parts of the rational and visible agency of God in his visible church, viz.—the Perception, the Understanding, the Affection, the Will and the Memory" (135). Finally, a hymn written around 1812 and attributed to "H. C." (Halcyon Church) extolls Urim and Thummim in verse ("O for an Angel's Tongue to Raise," Hymn CCIII of *New Hymn-Book*, 195–96).

Failures in Parker's memory could partially explain the discrepancy. Dishonesty on Parker's part should not be ruled out automatically, but is unlikely. While Parker admits to the uncertainty of his memory, his autobiography as a whole does not show a tendency toward misrepresentation, exaggeration, or fudging details. In any case, Parker shows no coherent motive for dishonesty on this issue. He shows no interest in distancing himself from Sarjent or taking personal credit for Sarjent's ideas. A more likely explanation would be this: the Halcyon Church's symbolic understanding of Thummim developed gradually, and not in a vacuum or as the product of a single intellect. Rather it was the product of conversations between Abel Sarjent, other members of the Halcyon Church, and even other freelance religionists like Daniel Fink. The idea found partial expression in Halcyon publications as it developed over the years. Parker, who met with and discussed the idea with current and former Halcyonists, may have contributed indirectly to the full development of the Halcyon doctrine, even after he parted with the Halcyon Church.

40. Revelation 22:2.

41. Revelation 21:14.

42. The references to Solomon's Temple are from 1 Kings 6–7.

43. Parker defends what might seem to his readers an esoteric set of ideas by pointing to its practical results. See reference in "Urim and Thummim" in the Editor's Introduction.

44. Hebrews 6:19.

45. The actual wording of Romans 11:16 in the King James Version is "For if the first fruit be holy, the lump is also holy."

46. The phrase "made perfect through suffering" is actually in Hebrews 2:10. Hebrews 5:8–9, which Parker cites, reads, "Though he were a son, yet he learned obedience by the things he suffered; and being made perfect, he became the author of eternal salvation unto all them that obey him."

47. After extolling the different aspects of Urim and Thummim, Parker states that its natural implication is that all people would experience its benefits. He believes universal salvation is the more likely consequence of this principle than the Halcyon annihilationist doctrine (that some people will experience eternal life and others will simply cease to exist), much less the traditional doctrine of hell (that some people would live eternally in misery). See chap. 2 and the Editor's Introduction for further discussion of these theological positions.

48. 1 Timothy 3:16; 1 Peter 1:12.

49. Job 38:7 ("the morning stars sang together and all the sons of God shouted for joy").

50. Galatians 4:4 ("fullness of the time"); Luke 2:14 ("Glory to God in the highest, and on earth peace, good will toward men").

51. 1 Corinthians 15:28.

52. Parker has closing but not opening quotation marks for this biblical passage (Octavo 11). The full, actual wording of John 12:32 is "And I, if I be lifted up from the earth, will draw all men unto me."

53. Parker again affirms the good practical fruits of his belief system. He also heads off a common charge that belief in universal salvation is a gateway to moral license (Bressler, 33–40).

54. 1 Corinthians 13:7.

55. Parker appears to be quoting Matthew Henry on 1 Corinthians 13 in his popular *Commentary on the Whole Bible* (1708–11; Peabody, MA: Hendrickson, 1991), 2269. The commentary in turn may have been alluding to Augustine, *On Christian Doctrine* 1.38.42.

56. 2 Corinthians 4:17.

57. Hebrews 12:6. In this passage, which actually begins "For whom the Lord loveth he chasteneth," the New Testament author, quoting the Old Testament (Proverbs 3:11–12), describes divine punishment as loving parental chastisement. Parker is making the Restorationist Universalist argument that any future divine punishment would be temporary and for the good of the person being punished, not permanent or an act of revenge.

58. Nathaniel Niles, "The American Hero: A Sapphic Ode, Written in the Time of the American Revolution" (1775), in *Poets and Poetry of Vermont*, rev. ed., ed. Abby Maria Hemenway (Boston: Brown, Taggard & Chase, 1860), 18. Parker slightly misquotes the second line of the stanza, "Clouds, which, around Him, hinder our perception," and formats the lines differently than the printed version.

59. Parker apparently intended to write just what he has written: that his sister's given name was Suky and her nickname was Susanna (MS, Octavo 12). See Parker's

first mention of his sister (and the accompanying note) in chap. 1. The Family Copy reverses the names ("My sister Susanna, or Sukey as we sometimes called her" (118). Flora Haines Loughead considers "Sukey" a derivation of "Susan" in *Dictionary of Given Names with Origins and Meanings*, 2nd ed. (Glendale, CA: Arthur H. Clark, 1981), s.v. "Sukey."

60. 1 Corinthians 15:55.

61. Apparently the division between Sarjent and John Parker had been at one point quite hostile. See note 55 on the fast of 1807 and the death of Amos Parkhurst in chap. 2.

62. The Western Reserve (formerly the Connecticut Western Reserve), is a portion of northeast Ohio, including Cleveland, that was once claimed as a possession of the state of Connecticut. See Cayton, *Ohio: The History of a People*, 29–35.

63. Ephraim Cutler (1767–1853) was probably the most influential political figure with whom Daniel Parker was closely associated. He was born in Edgartown, Massachusetts, the son of Manasseh Cutler, one of the original founders of the Ohio Company of Associates. Ephraim moved permanently to Ohio in 1795 and helped to establish Ames Township (now Amesville) in 1797. Trained as a lawyer, he was elected to the territorial legislature in 1802 and, as Parker states, served as a delegate to the Ohio Constitutional Convention in the same year, taking the lead in securing the constitution's ban on slavery in the new state. As a legislator, Cutler, a Federalist and later a Whig, also advocated for state funding of canals and public education. He was a founder and trustee of Ohio University. Sally Parker became Cutler's second wife in 1808. According to family history (Ferris, 229), Cutler's first wife, Leah Atwood, knowing that she was dying and seeking a mother for their four children, recommended Sally, whom she had met but her husband had not. Together, Ephraim and Sally Cutler had five children. Cutler respected Sally's intellect, writing that she was "well acquainted with history, geography, poetry, and music, and indeed she is no contemptible poet herself." His letters to Sally are full of his concerns about matters of state (Julia Perkins Cutler, *Life and Times of Ephraim Cutler, Prepared from His Journals and Correspondence* [Cincinnati: Robert Clarke, 1890], 117–23). Cutler died in 1853, surviving Sally by seven years. See also Kern and Wilson, 150–51, 202; "Ephraim Cutler," Ohio History Central, http://www.ohiohistorycentral.org/w/Ephraim_Cutler; and other references to Cutler with citations in the notes of this volume. Ephraim Cutler is a major figure in David McCullough's *The Pioneers* (New York: Simon and Schuster, 2019), 121–29, 138–50, 177–83, 241–56.

64. Parker does not explain what kind of meeting he had in Marietta and why it was "dull." Probably, he preached there to an unresponsive congregation. Parker often uses "dull" to mean depressed or unproductive.

65. This is Rhoda "Fordice" (as Daniel Parker, his mother Mary, and the Family Copy spell the name), or "Fordyce" (as others spell it). I have not found a reliable source for Rhoda's maiden name or dates of birth and death, but multiple attestations confirm her existence and the strength of her personality. Neither local historian Alfred Creigh nor Halcyon Church leader Abel Sarjent were among her admirers, but both pay her an unintended compliment in crediting her with leading a splinter group of the Halcyon Church, which Creigh calls the "Rhodianites" (213). Sarjent

also called her, among other things, a "modern Jezebel" ("Circular Epistle from the 9th Concilium of the Halcyon Church," 224–30). In "The Downfall of the Halcyon Church, Predicted in a Dream" (*Halcyon Itinerary* 3 [October 1807]: 88–89), Sarjent (the presumed author), writing in an esoteric, apocalyptic style, apparently attacks her in symbolic language: an unnamed female leader of the Halcyon Church, on whom God "conferred . . . blessings above all others of thy sex," who was entrusted with "the pearl," but who betrayed that trust and forfeited her authority, though she might yet attain divine forgiveness. Daniel Parker writes that her "intense study on religious subjects" once drove Rhoda "partially insane," but it should be noted that he earlier intimates the same about himself. Parker also writes that Rhoda had a naturally strong mind and "remarkable experience." Years later, he is still intrigued by her theories on gender and sexuality. Her story also raises interesting questions about the role women played in the Halcyon Church. Sarjent's critics refer (derisively) to Sarjent's "women preachers" (Cartwright, 99–100; Dickinson, 31). Daniel Parker does not indicate that women were "regularly ordained" as ministers of the Halcyon Church like he and his brother were (chap. 2), but he does not indicate they were not, either. Halcyon Church literature is not as explicitly in favor of gender equality as it is of racial equality. Some language implies that women and men had equal roles in "church government and discipline," but does not spell out what this means (John Parker, *Circular Epistle* [1806], 2).

66. This is Isaac Watts (1674–1748), the famous hymnist mentioned in chap. 1. The poem, "The Indian Philosopher," written in 1701, is printed in *The Works of Rev. Isaac Watts, D.D., in Nine Volumes*, vol. 9 (London: printed by Edward Baines, 1813), 278. The spelling, punctuation, and some words in the MS (Octavo 12) differ from the printed edition of Watts's poem. The Family Copy (120–21) and this edition generally follow the MS.

67. Ferris, as does Parker, writes that Samuel "Fordyce" along with his wife Rhoda were members of the Halcyon Church (481). I have not found a reliable source for dates of his birth and death.

68. In 1807 Fanny Parker married John Fordice (or Fordyce), the son of Samuel and Rhoda Fordice (Fordyce) (Ferris, 481). Mary Parker (Daniel's and Fanny's mother) wrote a letter to Daniel, signing both her and her husband's name to it, expressing their disapproval explicitly of the recent marriage and implicitly of the Halcyon Church (Mary Parker to Daniel Parker, [1807], Special Collections, Legacy Library, Marietta College, Marietta, OH). See fig. 2.4. Ironically, Daniel and John Parker and Rhoda Fordice had their own conflicts with the Halcyon Church at that time, with Abel Sarjent charging them with schism. See the account of the "great fast of 1807" in chap. 2.

69. Fanny Parker and John "Fordyce" later moved to Salem Township in Meigs County, Ohio, where they were farmers and "lived and died." They had several children (Larkin, 41). The US Census of 1850 lists John and Fanny Fordyce living in the same household with "Peace Fordyce" (a schoolteacher, aged 27, born in Ohio), presumably their daughter, in Salem Township, Meigs County, Ohio (NARA Publication M432, Roll 710, 12B; accessed through Ancestry.com). Another likely daughter, Alleluia, married Samuel Vale in Meigs County in 1842 (Meigs County Courthouse

Record, Ohio, County Marriage Records, 1774–1993 [online database maintained by Ancestry.com]; 1850 US Census, Pomeroy, Meigs County, Ohio, NARA Publication M432, Roll 710, 127A; accessed through Ancestry.com). These would not have been the two children that Daniel Parker met in 1816. John and Fanny Fordyce died after 1850.

70. The quotation marks are Parker's (Octavo 12). The first quote is from Ephesians 1:11. The second one might be a paraphrase of Revelation 22:20 ("Amen. Even so, come, Lord Jesus"). Parker, despite disappointments, maintains his millennial hope for personal, social, and cosmic salvation, a hope which he will integrate into his belief in universal restoration and his efforts at social reform.

71. See Parker's reference to Alexander McGrew in chap. 2 (with endnote).

72. This may be Paul Fearing (1762–1822), another of the Ohio Company's "first settlers" and the first lawyer to practice in the Northwest Territory (Samuel Hildreth, *Pioneer History: Being an Account of the First Examinations of the Ohio Valley, and the Early Settlement of the Northwest Territory* [Cincinnati: H. W. Derby, 1848], 232).

73. Daniel Mayo was appointed first postmaster of Newport, Kentucky, in 1795 (Mary Keturah Jones, 7).

74. Colonel David Perry was a new settler to Campbell County in the early nineteenth century. His descendants would become prominent citizens (Jones, 9).

75. Reese Gaddis, born ca. 1795, died after 1880 (Jones, 11; 1870 US Census, Highland, Campbell County, Kentucky, NARA Publication M593, Roll 453, 266A; 1880 US Census, Highland, Campbell County, Kentucky, NARA Publication T9, Roll 407, 356A; accessed through Ancestry.com).

Chapter 6

1. Colonel Francis Carr, born 1771, died 1833, according to a grave marker in Spring Grove Cemetery, Cincinnati (photograph on Find a Grave, https://www.findagrave.com/memorial/18339958).

2. See the biography of Priscilla Mulloy Ring, who will become Daniel Parker's wife, in the Editor's Introduction.

3. Parker, ever attentive to his own feelings, recognizes the sensation of falling in love, "an agreeable uneasiness," which he earlier describes as "a kind of agreeable dread" (chap. 4).

4. "Holowell" is Parker's spelling of Hallowell, Maine, which is just south of Augusta.

5. According to William Tell Parker (20) and Susanna Parker Donaldson (5) in their respective memoirs of their mother, the second groom's name was Thomas Garrett, rather than Gerrard. Both Parker children also recall another family story, that the Baptist minister, John Stephens, who served at least two congregations near Kennedy's residence in Campbell County, Kentucky (Spencer, 281, 422), confused the grooms at the double wedding, and tried to marry Daniel Parker to Florilla Kennedy. Tell Parker writes that the results of the Garrett-Kennedy marriage "were such as were usual among the first families of Kentucky: a gay life for a time, with plenty of slaves, dissipation, idleness, waste, poverty, abuse, separation, vagabondage" (23).

The narrator offers no evidence for this denouement, however, and has a tendency to favor a good story over a likely story.

6. Here Parker quotes and cites Phillis Wheatley's lengthy, meditative "Thoughts on the Works of Providence," lines 85–86, from *Poems on Various Subjects, Religious and Moral* (1773; reprinted in Joseph Lavallée, *The Negro Equalled by Few Europeans, Translated from the French: To Which Are Added, Poems on Various Subjects, Moral and Entertaining* [*sic*], *by Phyllis Wheatley* (Philadelphia: William W. Woodward, 1801), 195. Wheatley (1754–84), a slave in Boston, transported from Africa at seven or eight years old, is widely credited with being the first African American published poet.

7. David Moreton came from Pennsylvania to Clermont County, Ohio, around 1815 and bought the land Parker describes, at the mouth of a stream called Boat Run in Monroe Township. He sold a portion of the land to Daniel Parker and lived on the remaining property the rest of his life. He had three sons (Rockey and Bancroft, 384, 388).

8. The Parkers called their homestead Mount Hygiene because they thought it was a healthy place to be, both for its natural beauty and its moral environment. The Clermont Academy Circular (1849) advertised, "The Academy is situated on the farm of Rev. Daniel Parker, on the Ohio River, twenty-two and a half miles above Cincinnati, and two and a half above New Richmond, Clermont Co., Ohio. It is easy of access, either by the river or public road. The location is remarkable for being a healthy one, and entirely removed from the evil influences of town or city" (4).

9. Parker adds some of this description between the lines in the MS (Octavo 13), as if, on rereading, he decided his wife deserved some more compliments.

10. The "Regular Baptist Church" was comprised of Baptist congregations in fellowship with the Philadelphia Baptist Association, formed in 1707. The other major Baptist group in the United States at the time was the "Separate Baptists." See Robert Torbet, *A History of the Baptists* (Valley Forge, PA: Judson, 1950), 211–14, 223.

11. "Mutual charity" in the face of theological differences is a principle that Parker affirms throughout his memoir, including in his personal relationship with his spouse. See "A Human Story" in the Editor's Introduction.

12. James K. Parker, born 1817 in Clermont, Ohio, was principal teacher of the Clermont Academy from 1839 to 1892, except for March 1857 to June 1858, when he was principal professor at Wilberforce University, one of the first historically Black colleges in the United States. He married Sarah Preston Baker in 1842. They had five children. He died in 1894 (Sinnett, 218–20; Fannie Parker Currier, "A History of the Parker Family" and "A Sketch of the Administration of James Kennedy Parker"). See also "Clermont Academy" in the Editor's Introduction with notes and citations of other published and unpublished sources. Daniel Parker gives only the initials "J. K. Parker" for the name of his son in the MS (Octavo 13), as he does for his other children's names, perhaps because he knew his children would be his first readers and editors and could fill in their names, though he might not have anticipated they would disagree about the spelling of James K. Parker's middle name. See note 20 in chap. 5 on James Kennedy/Kenedy.

13. Thomas Armstrong was born in Virginia in 1775 and migrated with his father, Nathaniel Armstrong, to the Miami country of southwestern Ohio in 1800. The

family owned several water-powered grist mills along the Little Miami. Thomas and his brother Leonard built their own mill in the village of Newtown in Hamilton County, originally only for grounding flour. It was later adapted for carding and fulling wool, and ultimately for manufacturing textiles. Thomas Armstrong married Sarah Broadwell in 1806. They had seven children (Henry A. Ford and Kate B. Ford, *History of Hamilton County, Ohio, with Illustrations and Biographical Sketches* [Cleveland, OH: L. A. Williams, 1881], "Biographical Sketches: The Armstrong Family," insert, 254–55).

14. Susanna Everts Parker (the daughter of Daniel and Priscilla Parker) was born in 1819 at Mount Hygiene. She married Thomas Donaldson in 1837. They had eight children, but only two survived them. She died in New Richmond in 1890 (Sinnett, 220–22).

15. William Tell Parker was born at Mount Hygiene in 1821. He graduated from the Eclectic Medical College in Cincinnati in 1847. Afterward he began a medical practice in Birmingham, Erie County, Ohio. He married Anne Denman, probably in 1849, with whom he had two children. He left for California in 1850 to seek his fortune in gold. After two years he returned to Ohio. Anne Denman died, probably in 1859. In 1860 he married Sarah Kaufman (or Aumond), with whom he had one child. He moved to Tracy City, Tennessee, around 1869 and practiced medicine there. He died in 1875. He was called "Tell" by his family. His brother Eben testifies to his sense of humor (evident in his memoir of their mother) and writes that he would sometimes treat his patients with an "anecdote" rather than an "antidote" (Eben A. Parker, 21–22; Sinnett, 222; there are discrepancies between the two sources, and at least one error in the latter, which is why some dates and a name are uncertain).

16. Rev. George C. Light (b. ca. 1785) was the grandson of the founder of New Richmond. The "eloquent" Methodist minister is mentioned several times in Rockey and Bancroft's *History of Clermont County, Ohio* (144, 174, 400, 415–16), as is Daniel Parker, including his former association with "Abel Sargent" (171). The conflict and the meeting between Light and Sarjent that Parker describes is not mentioned, and the authors do not imply that Sarjent was a controversial figure. Light was an agent for the American Colonization Society. He sided with the southern faction of the Methodist Church after it divided over slavery in 1844 and eventually became a bishop of the Methodist Episcopal Church, South. He died in Vicksburg, Mississippi, in 1860 (Knepp, 39). See chap. 2 for Parker's previous conflicts with circuit-riding Methodist ministers.

17. In short, Parker did not ask for payment for his preaching, but usually accepted it when freely offered, which was rare.

18. Parker alludes to Romans 12:21, "Be not overcome of evil [in modern English, 'Do not be overcome by evil' (NRSV)], but overcome evil with good." This text encapsulates his Restorationist Universalist theology, on which he expounds in the following paragraphs in response to typical objections. As a Restorationist, Parker did not believe that sinners would escape the consequences of their wrong actions in the afterlife, but he denied that these consequences would be unending punishment. More importantly, for Parker the "process" of becoming righteous, holy, and, he would add, happy, was the more important part of his message than the "final

result" of escaping punishments or receiving rewards. See also "Parker the Universalist" in the Editor's Introduction.

19. The preeminent Universalist theologian Hosea Ballou, like Parker, was shocked that professed converted Christians would make the fundamental error of assuming sin is "more happifying than righteousness." See *A Treatise on Atonement*, 4th ed. (Boston: Universalist Publishing House, 1882), 87–88. See also Bressler, 25. Parker's ideas are similar to Ballou's in several ways. The main difference between the two is that Parker, as a Restorationist, believed in a limited postmortem retribution for sin, whereas Ballou rejected any intermediate step between death and salvation.

20. Parker alludes to a universalizing New Testament text, Colossians 1:20: "And having made peace through the blood of his cross, by him to reconcile all things unto himself."

21. Universal salvation as Parker understands it is not just the denial of the existence of hell, but a total victory over sin within every individual and reconciliation of all people to God and to each other. Sin, according to Parker and other Universalists (Ballou, 73, 87–90), is a basic alienation from God, which is ultimately contrary to human happiness.

22. Parker alludes to Romans 6:1. The "just retribution" that Parker speaks of need not be understood as spiteful divine retaliation, but as the pain naturally involved in alienation from God and in the repentance that leads to reconciliation. As a Restorationist Universalist, Parker believed that this often painful process of repentance continues for many even after death, until the whole human family is reconciled to God and each other. See "Parker the Universalist" in the Editor's Introduction for further discussion.

23. Authentic faith in universal salvation, according to Parker, is not simply the acceptance of abstract ideas about divine forgiveness, but a life dedicated to repentance and reconciliation.

24. Parker paraphrases Romans 5:20–21.

25. Parker makes several references to Jesus's Sermon on the Mount (Matthew 5–7), which commands the love of one's enemy. This, according to Parker, is the standard by which a life dedicated to reconciliation is measured. The "carnal" or unconverted person is not able to live according to this standard. It requires a "new birth" or inward transformation that can only occur through divine grace.

26. Matthew 7:6.

27. 2 Corinthians 4:2; 2 Timothy 2:15.

28. In keeping with his emphasis on virtuous action, Parker implicitly defines Christian redemption broadly to include not just forgiveness for sin but changed behavior.

29. According to Bressler, nineteenth-century Universalist itinerants were often theological controversialists who favored a combative rhetorical style (55–58).

30. Parker paraphrases 2 Peter 1:5–8: "add to your faith virtue; and to virtue knowledge; and to knowledge temperance; and to temperance patience; and to patience godliness; and to godliness brotherly kindness; and to brotherly kindness charity. For if these things be in you, and abound, they make you that ye shall neither be barren nor unfruitful in the knowledge of our Lord Jesus Christ" (KJV).

31. John G. Rogers (1797–1892) was "one of the most noted and venerable physicians of Clermont" (Rockey and Bancroft, biography of Dr. John G. Rodgers, insert, 415). He is best remembered for delivering the newborn Ulysses S. Grant in 1822. He was an abolitionist, the first president of Clermont County's Antislavery Society, and a sponsor of James G. Birney's famous abolitionist newspaper, the *Philanthropist*, during the year it was published in New Richmond (1836). He was part of the vigilance committee that protected the printing press from being destroyed by mobs (Knepp, 111–13).

32. "W. T. P." is William Tell Parker. Both the MS (Octavo 14) and the Family Copy (138) have only initials here.

33. Rockey and Bancroft list Charles M. Strader as owning a village lot in Neville, on the Ohio River in Clermont County, in the 1820s (368). Josiah Broadwell was a hatter and one of the first settlers of the village of Chilo when it was founded in 1817, just downriver from Neville and on the way to Parker's home near New Richmond (344). Jacob Broadwell Sr. was one of the early settlers of Hamilton County, and lived on the border of Clermont County near Union Township on the east fork of the Little Muskingum (445). The Broadwells were connected by marriage to Thomas Armstrong, who was a friend of the Parkers. See note 13 above.

34. This was probably Richard L. Coleman, a carpenter in Cincinnati who also served on the city council (Henry A. Ford and Kate B. Ford, *History of Cincinnati, Ohio, with Illustrations and Biographical Sketches* [Cleveland, OH: L. A. Williams, 1881], 289, 379–81).

35. Charles Coleman Parker, born at Mount Hygiene in 1823, was a physician and surgeon. He graduated from Starling's Medical College in Columbus, Ohio, in 1850. In 1853 he married Sarah Maria Lakin, with whom he would have six children. They moved to Fayette, Iowa, in 1855, where Charles practiced medicine, residing there until he died in 1906, except for a period of months in 1860, when he prospected for gold around Pike's Peak, and in 1861 and 1862, when he served with the Twelfth Iowa Regiment of the Union Army as a surgeon, participating in the Battle of Shiloh. He was a trustee of Upper Iowa University. See Eben A. Parker, 22–24; Sinnett, 223–27; "Charles C. Parker, M.D.," in *United States Biographical Dictionary*, 357–59; and "Charles C. Parker, MD," in *Portrait and Biographical Album of Fayette County, Iowa*, 586–88.

36. Thomas Mulloy was born in Litchfield, Maine, in 1798. He moved with his father and two siblings to Clermont County, Ohio, in 1817, following Priscilla, who moved there in 1814. He lived in various places in the region (including, for a time, at Mount Hygiene) before settling in Moscow in Clermont County, where he worked as a farmer, sawmill operator, and furniture manufacturer. He was married in 1824 to Susannah Moreton, with whom he had six children. After her death in 1840, the next year he married Susannah Rogers, with whom he had four children. He died in 1863 (Sinnett, 239–47).

37. William Armstrong was the brother of Thomas Armstrong (see note 13 above). He and his brother John owned and operated a water-powered mill in the village of Plainville, which at the time was part of Columbia Township, for which Armstrong served as treasurer and in other offices (Ford and Ford, *History of Hamilton County*,

"Biographical Sketches: The Armstrong Family" [insert, 254–55] and 271–76). Most of the villages that made up Columbia Township were later absorbed into Cincinnati.

38. In the MS (Octavo 14), "14 mile back." The Family Copy has "14 miles back" (140).

39. Daniel Mulloy Parker was born in Montgomery, Ohio, in 1825. According to Eben A. Parker, he grew to be tall and muscular and his mother called him "the Ajax of the family." He attended Clermont Academy. He was very close to his younger brother, Mason Doan Parker. Around 1850, the brothers, still living at home at Mount Hygiene, rowed across the Ohio River under cover of night to help an enslaved man named William, who lived near Belmont, Kentucky, escape before he could be sold away to a plantation in the Deep South. After rowing fifteen miles to meet a relay at the mouth of the Little Miami, the brothers returned home to slip into their beds just "in time to be called to breakfast by father, unconscious of past events of the night." They later received a letter from William saying that he made it safely to Canada (26–27). In 1856, Daniel married Harriet Cook, with whom he had one child. Daniel was a teacher and farmer and lived close to the family home in Ohio until he died in 1878. Harriet afterward moved to Colorado (Sinnett, 228).

40. The Family Copy (140), but not the MS (Octavo 14), includes "Mulloy" at the end of the sentence. Hugh Mulloy was born in 1751 in Albany, New York. His family moved to Maine when he was a child. He married Priscilla Thompson in 1776, while home on furlough from the Continental Army. He enlisted as a private and rose through the ranks to first lieutenant. He was also, according to several accounts, initiated into Freemasonry in the tent of General George Washington. He was in several battles, including Monmouth, where he was wounded. After being honorably discharged he settled in Maine, eventually in Litchfield, where he was a moderator at town meetings, served on the school board, and occasionally taught school. In 1817, he and his wife and three of his children followed Priscilla to Clermont County, Ohio. He died there in 1845 at the age of ninety-four (William Tell Parker, 1–6; Eben A. Parker, 12–13; Sinnett, 190–92).

41. For Indian mounds within Cincinnati, see Charles Theodore Greve, *Centennial History of Cincinnati and Representative Citizens*, vol. 1 (Chicago: Biographical Publishing Company, 1904), 24–34.

42. Parker paraphrases Psalm 103:2, "Bless the Lord, O my soul, and forget not all his benefits."

43. The year 1826 was added later to the MS, above the word "November" (Octavo 15). Other sources give November 26, 1825, as the date of William Parker Sr.'s death, which is probably accurate (Ferris, 473; Eben A. Parker, 8; Larkin, 41).

44. Andrew H. Ernst was born in Germany in 1796. He came to Cincinnati with his brother Jacob and father Zachariah in 1803. Andrew, like his friend Daniel Parker, was a mechanic (Ford and Ford, *History of Cincinnati*, 80, 100), but he became wealthy through land speculation. A horticulturist and landscape architect, his homestead and nursery, Spring Garden, was in the western part of Cincinnati. His first wife was Elizabeth Heffly, with whom he had six children. After her death in 1840, the next year he married Sarah Otis, to whom he was likely introduced by Adin Ballou, a Restorationist Universalist minister and social reformer in Massachusetts.

Sarah Otis Ernst (1809–82) turned out to be "one of the most effective radical abolitionists in the West." She "organized the Cincinnati Anti-Slavery Sewing Circle, whose fairs were a major source of support for the Western Anti-Slavery Society (WASS). When her Garrisonian brand of abolitionism lost favor in the WASS, she organized, financed, and managed the yearly Cincinnati Anti-Slavery Conventions, 1851–1855. These conventions featured nationally known anti-slavery speakers and were nationally publicized" (Walter Herz, "Sarah Otis Ernst," *Dictionary of Unitarian and Universalist Biography*, July 20, 2006, http://uudb.org/articles/sarahotisernst.html). One the speakers at the first convention was Daniel Parker. Andrew and Sarah Ernst were members of Parker's First Restorationist Church in Cincinnati. They had five children. Andrew Ernst died in 1860. See William A. Otis, *A Genealogical and Historical Memoir of the Otis Family in America* (Chicago: [Schulkins], 1924), 288; Julie Roy Jeffrey, *The Great Silent Army of Abolitionism: Ordinary Women in the Antislavery Movement* (Chapel Hill: University of North Carolina Press, 1998), 10–11, 134–35, 139, 159, 185–86; Adin Ballou, *Autobiography of Adin Ballou, 1803–1890*, completed and ed. William S. Heywood (Lowell, MA: Vox Populi, 1896), 355, 394–95, 415.

45. Mason Doan Parker was born in 1828 in Clermont County. He attended Clermont Academy. He was very close to his brother Daniel, with whom he helped a man to escape slavery in Kentucky in 1850 (see note 39 above). Afterward he moved to Cincinnati and became a public school teacher and principal. He married Lucy Herron in 1856. They had two children, one of whom died in infancy. In 1864, at the age of thirty-six, he enlisted in the 138th Regiment, Ohio Volunteer Infantry, and served in Virginia. Eben A. Parker wrote cryptically, "His return from service was soon found to carry the lurking cause of his final dissolution." He died in 1865 (24–30). See also Sinnett, 228–29; and Ford and Ford, *History of Cincinnati*, 527. Daniel Parker spells his name "Doan," but Eben A. Parker and Sinnett spell it "Doane." "Doan" is the generally accepted spelling of his namesake William Doan (see note 46 below).

46. "Dr. Mason" is probably Dr. James M. Mason (1798–1837), who jointly published one of the first medical journals in Cincinnati, the *Ohio Medical Repository*, in 1826 (Ford and Ford, *History of Cincinnati*, 309). He died in 1837 (Greve, 742–43). "Dr. Doan" is William Doan, an eminent physician in Withamsville and member of the US Congress from 1839 to 1843. He was born in Maine in 1792. According to William Tell Parker, his mother Priscilla migrated from Maine to Ohio with the family of William Doan in 1814 (19). The Biographical Directory of the United States Congress has him coming two years before in 1812 ("Doan, William," http://bioguide.congress.gov/scripts/biodisplay.pl?index=D000380). After leaving Congress, he returned to Withamsville to resume his medical practice. He died in 1847.

47. Parker again quotes Alexander Pope, *Essay on Man* (epistle 4, lines 265–69).

48. Daniel Parker's praise for Priscilla in the following paragraphs includes a paean to motherhood that could be read as an example of the nineteenth-century "cult of domesticity," which emphasized the home and the family as the woman's sphere of action and the transmission of virtue to children as her main responsibility (Barbara Welter, "The Cult of True Womanhood: 1820–1860," *American Quarterly* 18, no. 2 [Summer 1966]: 151–74). At the same time, however, Parker frankly and gratefully

acknowledges that Priscilla sometimes financially supported the family, and elsewhere acknowledges the initiative she took in public activity: antislavery advocacy and the founding of Clermont Academy. With these contrasts, Parker's account of his relationship with Priscilla provides rich data to be explored by gender historians of the nineteenth century. See "Priscilla Parker" in the Editor's Introduction.

49. Daniel Parker was survived by all of his eight children, with none of them landing in "the haunts of debauchery." This was rare good fortune for parents in the nineteenth century. Compare to Harriet Beecher Stowe, whose family was touched by death, drug addiction, and alcoholism (Koester, 211, 264–66, 282, 319).

50. Parker's handwriting here (MS, Octavo 14) is unclear, but he possibly intended to clarify his original sentence by adding the "and" that is in brackets in this edition. Parker's intended meaning is that some children are "ruined" because they have no parents to guide them, and others who do have good parents can go to ruin because they disregard their "advice and example."

51. Hebrews 3:13.

52. Eben Armstrong Parker was born at Mount Hygiene in 1831. He studied law and was admitted to the bar in Cincinnati in 1860. Later that year he married Elizabeth Rebecca Barkley, with whom he would have three children. He enlisted as a private in the 153d Ohio Volunteer Infantry in 1864 and rose to the rank of first lieutenant. After the war, in 1866 he moved with his family to Indianapolis, where he continued to practice law. He died in 1898 (Sinnett, 229; Eben A. Parker, 32–35).

53. Sinnett has Priscilla Mulloy Parker's sister Abigail Mulloy as marrying David Colson and then residing in Bath, Maine, but only lists one child, James, not Eben (Sinnett, 193). However, there is a marker in Maple Grove Cemetery in Bath for Eben Colson, who died in 1882 and would have been born in 1809 (photograph on Find a Grave, https://www.findagrave.com/memorial/75327265/ebenezar-colson#view-photo=47321482).

54. Presumably, Parker means to say that Priscilla's *teaching* the boys "domestic labor" is what increased Priscilla's workload, not that their help was in itself a burden that "made her task very severe."

Chapter 7

1. The "colonization enterprise" was a scheme to settle freed American slaves in a colony in Africa established especially for them. The American Colonization Society was founded in 1816 and sent its first settlers to the colony of Liberia in 1822. Many supporters of African colonization, especially in its earliest conception, saw it as a means of gradually ending American slavery by encouraging manumission. However, as Parker indicates, the scheme carried with it an inherent racial assumption that Blacks and Whites could not flourish together as free people in the United States, making racial separation and expatriation virtually a prerequisite for ending slavery. For this reason, African American opponents of slavery generally rejected the colonization solution. However, among White people in the Ohio valley, "colonization gained popularity on both sides of the border throughout the 1820s" (Salafia, 134).

See also "Parker and Slavery" with endnotes in the Editor's Introduction for further explanation of and sources for colonization.

2. As did Parker, many of those who supported colonization did so as an antislavery endeavor. However, as Parker demonstrates, some saw it simply as a means of ridding the country of free Blacks and gave pointedly proslavery arguments for it. Even in Kentucky, colonizationists had a range of attitudes: "There were three major groupings of colonizationists in Kentucky. . . . One group saw colonization as a means of strengthening slavery; the second group saw it as a way to facilitate emancipation; the third group saw it as one mechanism among many to bring about the simple removal of the hated black race from the state" (Harold D. Tallant, *Evil Necessity: Slavery and Political Culture in Antebellum Kentucky* [Lexington: University Press of Kentucky, 2003], 30). The Colonization Society in Kentucky had several "agents" at any given time throughout the antebellum period. The agent Parker quotes reflected the opinion of Robert Wickliffe, the controversial first president of the Kentucky Colonization Society (Salafia, 162; Tallant, 43–44).

3. While White supporters of colonization held different views on slavery and the possibility of emancipation, they almost universally assumed African American inferiority. Whether they considered it a natural condition or the result of the "degradation" of slavery and discrimination, it was a first principle among colonizationists that Blacks could not overcome this disadvantage ("improve") in the United States, which made their removal to Africa a necessity (Salafia, 134; Tallant, 32–33; Torbett, 46–47; Staudenraus, 1–3, 15, 19–22, 28–29). The *African Repository* was the monthly journal of the American Colonization Society. "Washington City" was the common name for Washington, DC, in the nineteenth century (Staudenraus, 23, 100).

4. Bushrod Washington (1762–1829), an attorney and politician from Virginia, served as associate justice of the Supreme Court of the United States from 1798 to 1829, and was the nephew and principal heir of George Washington. He was one of the founders and first president of the American Colonization Society. James Madison (1751–1836), also of Virginia, was one of the principal architects of the US Constitution and the fourth president of the United States. He was elected president of the American Colonization Society in 1833 at the age of eighty-two. Henry Clay (1777–1852) was a congressman, senator, cabinet secretary, presidential candidate, and favorite political son of Kentucky. He was elected president of the ACS in 1836. Bushrod Washington sold fifty-four slaves from Mount Vernon in 1821, bringing criticism from antislavery quarters on him and the Colonization Society. James Madison left his slaves in his will to his wife Dolley, with the stipulation that it was his "desire" that they not be sold against their will. Henry Clay, who was still living at the time of Parker's writing, provided for the gradual emancipation of some of his slaves and their transport to Liberia in his will (Staudenraus, 169–87; Drew R. McCoy, *The Last of the Fathers: James Madison and the Republican Legacy* [New York: Cambridge University Press, 1989], 318; Clement Eaton, *Henry Clay and the Art of American Politics* [Boston: Little, Brown, 1957], 136).

5. Parker's intended meaning in this sentence might be more clear if "where only" were replaced with "the only place where."

6. Parker rejects (and "abominates") involuntary colonization of former slaves, but is not opposed to voluntary emigration, provided it is truly free from coercion. He even holds onto the colonizationist ideal of former slaves spreading American ("republican") ideals to Africa (Sinha, 166). While African Americans generally rejected the colonization scheme of the ACS, some did see voluntary emigration as the best means of achieving independence and freedom from American racism. The preferred destination for such emigrants in the earlier decades of the nineteenth century was not Liberia, however, but Haiti, with its history of a successful slave revolt and Black self-government (Sinha, 168–71, 335–38).

7. Parker unmasks the American Colonization Society's claim to be returning Black people to their ancestral home as coerced exile. This is in keeping with the arguments made by Richard Allen and other prominent African American leaders who criticized the society's program from its earliest days (Staudenraus, 32–33).

8. In this paragraph, Parker has moved from refuting the colonization scheme to attacking various proslavery arguments. The idea that Blacks are racially suited for and "better off" as slaves belongs to the newer "positive good" proslavery position that came to the forefront of southern thought from 1829 to 1831, partly as a reaction against the more forceful abolitionist arguments that emerged at that time. Before 1829, most Americans, North and South, would at least formally describe slavery as "a necessary evil" that should gradually be phased out of society. Generally, Kentucky slaveholders continued to hold to the "necessary evil" position after the Deep South had embraced the "positive good" argument (Salafia, 162–63; Tallant, 1–25). Parker's counterarguments give some insights into the diversity of proslavery arguments he encountered in the Ohio valley in the antebellum period. See also Torbett, 50–53; and William Sumner Jenkins, *Proslavery Thought in the Old South* (Chapel Hill: University of North Carolina Press, 1935), 65–89.

9. Parker attacks a proslavery argument that sexual relationships between male masters and female slaves provided an outlet for White male sexuality and thus protected the virtue of White women. It was common knowledge that such (necessarily unequal and coercive) relationships between masters and slaves existed. It was rare that they were defended morally, at least not formally and in print. See Eugene D. Genovese, *Roll Jordan Roll: The World the Slaves Made* (New York: Random House, 1974), 413–31. Parker's counterargument implies, however, that some were willing to make the argument verbally. See also Kolchin, 123–24.

10. The adage "It's a poor mule that won't work in both ways" was common enough to be repeated by Jacob Biggle in *The Biggle Horse Book: A Concise and Practical Treatise on the Horse* (Philadelphia: Wilmer Atkinson, 1904), 25. It was paraphrased by science fiction writer Isaac Asimov ("It's a poor nuclear blaster that won't work both ways") in *Foundation* (1951; New York: Alfred A. Knopf, 2010), 198. Parker means that if a principle is true it ought to apply to Whites as well as Blacks.

11. The MS (Octavo 15) and Family Copy (148) lack quotation marks for "O! Horrid!" They are added with the presumption that Parker is ironically expressing the slaveholder's reaction to his proposal.

12. As Parker explains, abolitionists, who came to the forefront around 1830, advocated immediate emancipation, unlike more moderate "gradualist" antislavery

advocates. They rejected colonization as a cruel scheme to deport free Blacks, and believed slaves had a right to freedom "on the soil" (i.e., in the United States), not on the condition of emigration. The most famous abolitionist was the White publisher William Lloyd Garrison, who helped to found the American Anti-Slavery Society, which had many regional branches across the country (Torbett, 47–50; Filler, 55–67), but Sinha demonstrates that abolitionism was in its roots a diverse and interracial movement (195–227). Abolitionists appealed to egalitarian passages in the Bible, especially the reciprocity of the golden rule, though their antislavery interpretation of the Bible was not without controversy (Torbett, 28–31). They also upheld the egalitarianism of the Declaration of Independence. The US Constitution, on the other hand, which regulated and implicitly permitted slavery, was problematic. See Ronald C. White, 197; and Mason Lowance, *Against Slavery: An Abolitionist Reader* (New York: Penguin Books, 2000), xxxi.

13. In addition to Parker himself, another example of this gradual radicalization on the issue of slavery was James G. Birney, who went from being a slaveholder to a moderate opponent of slavery (and advocate of colonization), to an advocate of immediate abolition. He moved across the border from Kentucky to Ohio to found the antislavery newspaper the *Philanthropist* in 1836. It was first published near Parker's home in New Richmond, but within a few months moved its headquarters to Cincinnati. See Betty Fladeland, *James Gillespie Birney: Slaveholder to Abolitionist* (Ithaca, NY: Cornell University Press, 1955), 75–124. Daniel Parker will refer to the *Philanthropist* in this chapter.

14. Because of such persecutions, abolitionists considered the 1830s "the Martyr Age" (Filler, 66). Anti-abolitionist activity occurred in every section of the country at this time, North and South, but it was particularly strong in Cincinnati and surrounding southeast Ohio where Parker lived (Daniel Aaron, *Cincinnati, Queen City of the West: 1819–1838* [Columbus: Ohio State University Press, 1992], 294). White businessmen, professionals, and most of the working population were not explicit proponents of slavery, and often supported gradualist plans for emancipation (like the Colonization Society), but rejected the immediatism of abolitionists as disruptive, subversive, and—the most far-fetched accusation—the product of foreign conspiracies. Historians explain anti-abolitionism in southern Ohio in part as a means of maintaining commercial, cultural, and social relationships between White societies across the Ohio River. Ohio rejected the radical abolitionist version of the antislavery argument and Kentucky rejected the radical "positive good" version of the proslavery argument as an implicit compromise with the sensibilities of their partners on the other side of the border. Race was another factor. White Ohioans on the southern border felt threatened by the real or potential influx of free Blacks, which kindled their anxiety about abolitionist excitement and the specter of immediate emancipation. Ohio enacted notoriously discriminatory Black Codes in 1804, and Cincinnati was the site of a disproportionate number of mob attacks on the African American community, which usually accompanied anti-abolitionist riots (Aaron, 294–97; Salafia, 1–8; Nikki M. Taylor, *Frontiers of Freedom: Cincinnati's Black Community, 1802–1868* [Athens: Ohio University Press, 2005], 1–2).

15. The "last attempt to stop the work" that Parker refers to is probably the riot and destruction of the first printing press of the *Philanthropist* in Cincinnati in July of 1836. See further explanation in the following notes.

16. Temperance was another cause of reform-minded Christians in the nineteenth century. As the name implies, temperance proponents originally advocated only moderation of the use of alcohol, but eventually moved toward advocating total abstinence. Alcohol abuse was seen not only as a personal sin but as the source of a variety of social ills, especially for the poor. See Abzug, 81–104; Martin E. Marty, *Righteous Empire: The Protestant Experience in America* (New York: Dial Press, 1970), 96; Richard J. Carwardine, *Evangelicals and Politics in Antebellum America* (Knoxville: University of Tennessee Press, 1997), 101–2; Timothy Smith, 167–68; and Cayton, *Ohio: The History of a People*, 68–72.

17. Opponents of abolitionism often objected that such movements violated "the spirituality of the church" by bringing politics into the pulpit. See Mitchell Snay, *Gospel of Disunion: Religion and Separatism in the Antebellum South* (Cambridge: Cambridge University Press, 1993), 41.

18. Parker cites Romans 1:18. Building on his earlier argument (from chap. 6), Parker adds a social dimension to his understanding of a genuine commitment to universal salvation. One must not only work for reconciliation in personal relationships, but also in society. The "instrumentalities" Parker mentions formed the "benevolent empire" of social reform in the nineteenth century (Marty, 93–96; Timothy Smith, 35–44; McLoughlin, 112–14). These loosely connected voluntary associations were largely run by evangelical Protestants, but Universalists cooperated with them, being particularly active in the "peace societies" (Russell Miller, 485–533, 574–638; Bressler, 81–88). See "Parker the Universalist" in the Editor's Introduction for further discussion of the social aspect of Parker's theology.

19. John Bunyan's allegorical narrative *The Pilgrim's Progress* had been extraordinarily popular with English-speaking Protestants from its first publication in 1678. The character who was "most zealous when Religion goes in his Silver Slippers" was actually named "By-ends," not "Talkative," though a character by the latter name also appears. See Bunyan, *The Pilgrim's Progress*, Oxford World Classics Edition, ed. with an introduction by W. R. Owens (Oxford: Oxford University Press, 2003), xiii, 98. Parker also quotes Philippians 3:18. Parker criticizes those who would be comforted by his Restorationist theology without accepting the cost of discipleship.

20. Mary Priscilla Parker's "rather unexpected" birth at Mount Hygiene occurred in 1837, when her mother was almost forty-four and her father was fifty-five years old. Mary attended Clermont Academy and was a teacher. In 1860, she married George Nichols, with whom she had one child. According to Eben A. Parker the family's happy life was interrupted when Mary was "afflicted" with an unspecified illness "that weakened the physical and darkened her mental powers" (31). She died in Cincinnati in 1880.

21. Thomas Donaldson was a respected citizen of Clermont County and a well-known abolitionist. He was born in London, England, in 1805. His family moved to Wales while he was a child and later migrated to Clermont County in 1821. In 1833, he married Emily Hough, with whom he had three children who died in infancy.

After Emily died in 1836, Donaldson married Susanna Everts Parker in 1837. They had eight children, with two, Ella and Parker, surviving them (see note 14 on Susanna in chap. 6). Thomas Donaldson operated a general store in New Richmond with his brothers. He, like Daniel Parker, was a social reformer: a temperance advocate and abolitionist. As a leader of the American Anti-Slavery Society, he helped to persuade James Birney to publish the first issues of the *Philanthropist* from New Richmond. He gave up his interest in the general store when it would not sustain his practice of stocking strictly free-labor goods, and subsequently made his living as a farmer on land he purchased near Mount Hygiene. Susanna shared his moral commitments. Eben Parker wrote that the Donaldson home was "always a place for the fugitive and the weary to rest." He died in New Richmond in 1894 (Bancroft and Rockey, 423–24; Sinnett, 220; Bethany Marie Pollitt, "The Antislavery Movement in Clermont County" [master's thesis, Wright State University, 2012], 36–37; Eben A. Parker, 21).

22. "Advocation" is a synonym for advocacy, now fallen out of use (*Oxford English Dictionary*, 2nd ed. [1989], s.v. "advocation").

23. This conversation at the *Philanthropist*'s office would have occurred in late 1835, since the "first number" was published from New Richmond on January 1, 1836 (Ann Hagedorn, *Beyond the River: The Untold Story of the Heroes of the Underground Railroad* [New York: Simon and Schuster, 2002], 101; Aaron, 300–301). The newspaper received criticism (and threats) from both sides of the Ohio River even before its first issue was published, as the reputation of its abolitionist editor, James G. Birney, preceded him (Nikki M. Taylor, 109–10). Daniel Parker's anxiety about subscribing to the paper might have been because he would not identify himself fully as an abolitionist until the attack on the *Philanthropist* office in July of 1836. See note 25 below.

24. The "really" in this sentence might be better understood as "true" or "genuine." Parker alludes to Genesis 2:18, "And the Lord God said, it is not good that the man should be alone; I will make him an help meet for him." For a nineteenth-century man, Parker has an unusually (though not uniquely) egalitarian interpretation of the role of "help meet" as partner, advisor, and even an example, rather than as a servant (Hersh, 26), anticipating later feminist interpretations of Genesis. See Phyllis Trible, *God and the Rhetoric of Sexuality* (Philadelphia: Fortress Press, 1978), 88–105.

25. The first attack on the *Philanthropist* in Cincinnati was in July of 1836, at the end of four months that were "as exciting and dramatic as any period in Cincinnati's history" (Aaron, 301). In January, after James Birney published scathing attacks on Kentucky slaveholders in the first issues of the paper, an ad hoc committee of Cincinnati's "men of property and standing" held an anti-abolitionist meeting with over five hundred people attending, warning Birney to stay out of Cincinnati. Birney defied their threats by moving the office of the *Philanthropist* to Cincinnati in April, the same month that a group of rioters in that city burned down an African American tenement while a crowd stood by and watched. On July 12, forty men (representing "an alliance among all classes of white society" [Nikki M. Taylor, 110, 111]) broke into the office of Achilles Pugh where the *Philanthropist* was printed and damaged equipment. Cincinnati's anti-abolitionists, in print, at a public meeting, and through an appointed committee of emissaries, warned Birney to cease publication.

When he did not, a mob attacked the office on July 30, threw the press in the Ohio River, sought to tar and feather Pugh and Birney (but could not find them), and destroyed some African American homes. Mayor Samuel Davies, sympathetic with the rioters, finally dispersed them with what sounded like congratulations, saying they "convinced" the abolitionists "what the public sentiment is" (quoted in Aaron, 309). Birney fished the press out of the river and the *Philanthropist* continued to publish.

26. Parker, significantly, identifies abolitionists as both men and women. A notable aspect of the abolition movement was its outspoken women, who challenged the gender norms of the time by speaking to mixed audiences in public and becoming involved in politics. From their ranks came the first wave of American feminists (Hersh, 6–35; Sinha, 266–98).

27. Many abolitionists were strict pacifists who refused to condone violence under any circumstance (McKivigan, 57–58). A minority of militant abolitionists existed from the earliest days in the movement, and became more prominent as the sectional conflict over slavery heated, John Brown being the most famous (Filler, 239–45, 270–75).

28. While Parker and other abolitionists affirmed racial equality and criticized the implicit racism of the colonization scheme, they also believed in uplifting the slave's "character" in order to prepare the slave for freedom. While such an assumption could seem and often was patronizing toward enslaved people (Kendi, 161–76), it was also based on a commonsense belief in the importance of education for the improvement of all people—a belief that motivated both Black and White philanthropists to found educational institutions for former slaves after the Civil War. See Albert J. Raboteau, *Canaan Land: A Religious History of African Americans* (New York: Oxford University Press, 2001), 63–66.

29. See "Clermont Academy" in the Editor's Introduction for a detailed explanation of the school the Parkers would found.

30. South Hanover College was an informal name for Hanover College, still active in Indiana. See note 42 in chap. 4. The name here rendered as "Mr. Lang" is not clear in the MS (Octavo 15). The Family Copy refers to the second school as "Pleasant Hill Academy" and does not give the name of a person associated with it (152). Pleasant Hill Academy was founded by Freeman Cary in 1832 and was later absorbed into Farmers' College in what is now the College Hill neighborhood of Cincinnati. See Betty Ann Smiddy, ed., *A Little Piece of Paradise: College Hill, Ohio*, 2nd ed. (Cincinnati: College Hill Historical Society, [1999]), 70–71. Sarah Baker Parker's "History of Clermont Academy" says that James K. Parker studied with Freeman Cary at Pleasant Hill Academy (11).

31. Parker does not mention here that Clermont Academy was also racially integrated as well as mixed gender. Parker did publicly affirm this policy in speeches, however. "On 3 February 1841 Parker lectured at Withamsville to a large and attentive crowd and ended by saying that one of James Birney's emancipated slaves, Edwin Mathews [*sic*], was a student at his Clermont Academy" (Pollitt, 36).

32. See "Priscilla Parker" and "A Human Story" in the Editor's Introduction for discussion of Parker's attitude toward theological differences within his own family and at Clermont Academy.

33. Parker apparently added this sentence to the manuscript as a revision—fitting it in with tiny writing at the bottom of one page and the top of the next (Octavo 15). I rely on the Family Copy, which corrects Parker's "forward" with "forwarding" (153).

34. According to estimates at the time, "By the early 1840s, there were approximately fifteen thousand former runaways living in Canada" (Hagedorn, 214).

35. Parker is referring to the Ohio Fugitive Slave Act of 1839, which was repealed in 1843, not one year after it passed, as Parker says. The law was in fact enforced, but amid protest and controversy. See Stephen Middleton, *The Black Laws: Race and the Legal Process in Early Ohio* (Athens: Ohio University Press, 2005), 175–76. While most Ohioans were not abolitionists and did not harbor fugitive slaves, they also were wary of accommodating what they saw as slave power imposing on their state sovereignty, hence the law's unpopularity (Salafia, 205–6).

36. For example, in 1839 "notices were posted in the villages and towns of northern Kentucky . . . announcing the offer of rewards up to $2,500 for the abduction or assassination of Alexander Campbell, John Rankin, Dr. Isaac Beck, and John B. Mahan" (Hagedorn, 143).

37. Daniel Parker's work for the book exchange involved buying and selling used books, a business to which, according to William Tell Parker, "his large acquaintance in Ohio and Northern Kentucky adapted him." He adds that his father's new occupation, along with revenue brought in by Clermont Academy, brought the family "a measure of material prosperity" for the first time (36).

38. The MS (Octavo 15) does not have the given quotation marks for this conversation (or for other dialogues that follow). Quotation marks have been added to this and later conversations in this chapter for the sake of clarity, though determining who is speaking and whether the text is intended as direct quote or paraphrase is a matter of editorial interpretation.

39. "The pledge" was one of total abstinence from alcohol (Russell Miller, 521).

40. The Family Copy clarifies Parker's statement with a paraphrase: "Slave holders respect antislavery men who will fearlessly stand up for their principles, much more than cringing doughfaces, and we should always do so whether they respect us or not" (155).

41. The Methodist-affiliated Augusta College opened in 1825 and closed in 1849. See "Augusta College," in *The Kentucky Encyclopedia*, 42.

42. Presbyterian minister John Rankin (1793–1818) was one of the most famous Ohio conductors of the Underground Railroad. He was born in Tennessee and moved first to Kentucky and then to Ripley, Ohio. In addition to personally protecting several fugitive slaves, he also was one of the founders of the Ohio Antislavery Society. He spoke and published extensively on abolition. He was the founder and president of Ripley College and also organized the abolitionist "come outer" denomination, the Free Presbyterian Church of America. The lamp he placed in the window to alert fugitives of the location of his house on a high hill over Ripley would become an almost mythic symbol of the Underground Railroad. His accounts of fugitive escapes may have inspired portions of *Uncle Tom's Cabin* by Harriet Beecher Stowe, who knew Rankin when she lived in Ohio. See Hagedorn, 57, 99, 61–62, 66–67, 139; and Ellen Eslinger, "The Evolution of Racial Politics in Early Ohio," in Cayton and Hobbs, *Center of a Great Empire*, 85.

43. The seventh commandment is against adultery. Anxiety and ambivalence about "amalgamation" (sexual contact and reproduction between races) pervaded nineteenth-century discussions of slavery and race in America. See Genovese; and Winthrop D. Jordan, *White over Black: American Attitudes toward the Negro, 1550–1812* (Chapel Hill: University of North Carolina Press, 1968), 542–47. As Parker's conversation indicates, slaveholding society (and, to a large extent, White society in the North as well) officially disapproved of miscegenation, but it was widely acknowledged that it occurred.

44. Unfortunately, Parker does not give a source for his account of this episode in the British parliament. Vice Admiral Alexander Cochrane did issue a decree on April 2, 1814, offering all interested Americans the opportunity of either enlisting in the British military or becoming free settlers in British possessions in North America or the West Indies. "Many slaves responded to this call. Some 3,600 found refuge with the British during the war, and of these 550 enlisted in a special Corps of the Colonial Marines" (Hickey, 213).

45. In 1833, Parliament passed an act ending slavery in the British West Indies through a process of gradual emancipation that was complete in 1838 (Sinha, 213).

46. The current consensus among historians is that African American slavery was, on the whole, monetarily profitable in the antebellum years, though, for a variety of reasons, it was often perceived as unprofitable by both northerners and southerners. See Gavin Wright, "Economics of Slavery," in *Dictionary of Afro-American Slavery*, ed. Randall M. Miller and John David Smith (New York: Greenwood: 1988), 201–9.

47. The Family Copy paraphrases this long sentence in a way that clarifies Parker's intended meaning: "One of the man's slaves, together with his so called wife, belonging to another master, ran away. The owner of this escaped woman was also a friend of mine, living two miles in the country, and at whose house I had often preached, and who had often told me, that he would willingly give up his two slaves (all he had) if others would do the same; admitting that the system was wrong" (158).

48. See "Priscilla Parker" in the Editor's Introduction for a reference to this episode.

49. Apparently, this maxim is intended to express disapproval of sycophancy. Other than that, its meaning is obscure.

50. This was the winter of 1840–41, according to a letter and notice published in the *Ripley Bee* (Pollitt, 35–36).

51. "Tory," a term applied derisively to British partisans during the American Revolution, gained traction during the War of 1812 for Americans who were suspected of sympathy with the British (Alan Taylor, 178–79). By the time of Parker's writing, it was a label for anyone suspected of disloyalty to the United States (*Dictionary of American English on Historical Principles*, vol. 4, *Recorder–Zu-Zu* [1944], s.v. "Tory"). That abolitionists were partners in a foreign conspiracy was a common canard (Aaron, 297).

52. An abolitionist petition campaign, beginning in December 1835, called on Congress to abolish the interstate slave trade and slavery in the District of Columbia, where the federal government had jurisdiction. The "Gag Rule" of 1836 required that

the petitions automatically be tabled. This was a compromise with proslavery congressmen who had demanded the petitions be rejected outright (Sinha, 251).

53. See Filler, 64. Most of the remainder of this paragraph is grammatically one sentence, but it is punctuated as several sentences for the sake of clarity.

54. Parker believed that the influence of antislavery lectures in the North would reach the South through print media, which was rapidly expanding in the nineteenth century. This occurred to an extent, though southern efforts to censor antislavery literature and repress dissent were effective. See Clement Eaton, *The Freedom-of-Thought Struggle in the Old South*, 2nd ed. (New York: Harper and Rowe, 1964), 162–215; Genovese, 50; Filler, 97–98.

55. Especially after 1830, larger religious denominations were wracked with sectional tensions over slavery. Sometimes the desire for peace did mute moral argument on the subject. Even the Universalist denomination was affected by such reticence, though it had very few southern members (Russell Miller, 574–609). Eventually, the major evangelical denominations—Methodists, Baptists, and Presbyterians—divided into northern and southern factions, primarily over the issue of slavery. See Goen, 65–107.

56. The irenic Parker is troubled by what he saw as the uncharitable tone on both sides of the slavery debate, but he concludes that the moral benefit of direct debate outweighs the cost of occasional incivility. "Thinketh no evil" is an allusion to 1 Corinthians 13:5.

57. Parker continues to think of himself as an itinerant, though at the time of writing he had his own First Restorationist Church in Cincinnati. See "Parker the Universalist" in the Editor's Introduction.

58. "Packets" were small boats that carried passengers on a regular schedule. Parker is referring to steamboats on the Ohio River, but most "packets" on the Ohio water system were mule-drawn boats that carried passengers on canals (Ronald E. Shaw, *Canals for a Nation: The Canal Era in the United States, 1790–1860* [Lexington: University Press of Kentucky, 1990], 48, 153–54).

59. Parker's observations might add weight to Larry Tise's argument that the South initially lacked a coherent proslavery ideology, and that after 1835 it adopted proslavery ideas from a northern conservative tradition. See *Proslavery: A History of the Defense of Slavery in America, 1701–1840* (Athens: University of Georgia Press, 1987), 308–24. On the other hand, Molly Oshatz suggests that Tise (and abolitionists like Parker) may have been too willing to place moderate opponents of slavery in the proslavery camp if they did not endorse immediate abolition, and especially if they expressed qualms over problematic biblical texts. See *Slavery and Sin: The Fight against Slavery and the Rise of Liberal Protestantism* (Oxford: Oxford University Press, 2012), 56–60; and Torbett, 172–85.

60. Parker is paraphrasing Matthew 25:35.

61. There were "at least three Kentuckians" in the group of forty that broke into the *Philanthropist* office on July 12, 1836 (Nikki M. Taylor, 111).

62. Parker may be referring to the last day of the Cincinnati riot of 1841, really an armed race war, which an African American witness, John Mercer Langston, called "the most detestable moment in Cincinnati's history" (quoted in Nikki M. Taylor,

124). Tensions rose over a fistfight between Irish and African American workers on Tuesday, August 31. "By Thursday, bands of whites were roaming the city attacking innocent African Americans" (Nikki M. Taylor, 120). Anticipating a mob attack like those that had happened in the past, Cincinnati's African American community organized an armed resistance. When a mob of eight hundred, which included White Kentuckians and other "strangers" along with Cincinnati residents, descended on the African American neighborhood in the First Ward, they were met with gunfire. The mob returned fire with a cannon they managed to procure. The city militia and municipal government regarded the African American community as aggressors rather than defenders, and on Friday "swarms of improvised police officers" (some of whom had been part of the rioting White mob), rounded up and jailed three hundred Black men (Langston, quoted in Nikki M. Taylor, 121, 123). On Saturday night the mob "redirected its violence toward abolitionists." The press of the *Philanthropist* was again thrown in the Ohio River and an abolitionist bookstore was destroyed. The mob then "destroyed and looted several homes throughout the city" (Nikki M. Taylor, 123).

63. In MS this reads, "the police was out watching" (Octavo 16). The Family Copy has "the police were out watching" (164).

64. It would be interesting to know what "remarks" Parker made regarding Ephesians 6, a long chapter with several themes. The meaning of Ephesians 6:5–6, which deals with the duties of servants and masters, was a matter of contention in antebellum arguments over slavery.

Epilogue

1. The documents cited in this epilogue were kept by Bertha Currier Hardman, daughter of Fannie Parker Currier, daughter of James K. Parker, the son of Daniel Parker. She typed them in the 1940s and donated her typescripts to the Ohio Historical Society, now the Ohio History Connection. Most of the originals are in Margaret McDiarmid's donation to Northern Kentucky University, and are still being catalogued.

2. Daniel Parker, Diary of a River Trip to New Orleans, 1845, typed copy by Bertha C. Hardman, ca. 1947, Daniel Parker Papers, Manuscript Collections, Ohio History Connection, Columbus, part 2, 5–6.

3. Parker, Diary of a River Trip, part 2, 1–2.

4. Parker, Diary of a River Trip, part 2, 5.

5. Parker, Diary of a River Trip, part 2, 3.

6. Daniel Parker to Ephraim Cutler and Wife, June 27, 1846, typed copy by Bertha C. Hardman, ca. 1947, Daniel Parker Papers, Manuscript Collections, Ohio History Connection, Columbus. Hardman writes that the letter she copied was "in the handwriting of his son, James K. Parker." The typescript is apparently a copy of a copy.

7. Solomon Northup, *Twelve Years a Slave: Narrative of Solomon Northup, a Citizen of New York, Kidnapped in Washington City in 1841, and Rescued in 1853, from a Cotton Plantation near the Red River, in Louisiana* (Auburn, NY: Derby and Miller, 1853), 42–43.

8. Daniel Parker to Ephraim Cutler and Wife.

9. Herbert Asbury, *The Gangs of New York: An Informal History of the Underworld* (Garden City, NY: Garden City Publishing Company, 1928), 21–46.

10. Daniel Parker to Ephraim Cutler and Wife.

11. Charles Mason Parker, the son of James K. Parker and grandson of Daniel Parker, was born at Mount Hygiene in 1847 and was educated at Clermont Academy and Denison University. He was an attorney. He died in 1878 (Sinnett, 219).

12. Note by Charles M. Parker, Grandson of the Writer (ca. 1874), appended to Daniel Parker, Autobiography, ca. 1845; typed copy by Bertha C. Hardman, ca. 1947, Daniel Parker Papers, Manuscript Collections, Ohio History Connection, Columbus, 58–59.

13. The typescript actually reads "In the year 18— (I think the date was March 1855)." Apparently the date on the original manuscript is illegible, and Hardman includes her best recollection of family history.

14. The Parkers' second house is still standing, located on US Route 52 in Monroe Township, and is a private residence.

SELECTED BIBLIOGRAPHY

The purpose of this bibliography is to help readers identify authors in the notes. Most sources in the endnotes are included in this bibliography. I have not included some genealogical evidence (such as census records, wills, marriage records, photographs of grave markers, direct emails to the editor) that are in the endnotes, as the publication or location information I have for these sources is typically in each note. These sources are almost always only cited once.

Primary Sources

Published Writing of Daniel Parker

Familiar Letters to a Brother in Two Series: On the Final Restoration of All Mankind to Holiness and Happiness; Through a Righteous Judgment, and an Equitable Retribution. Cincinnati: printed by C. W. Thorp, 1844.

Unpublished Writings of Daniel Parker

Diary of a River Trip to New Orleans, 1845. Typed copy by Bertha C. Hardman, ca. 1947. Daniel Parker Papers, Manuscript Collections, Ohio History Connection, Columbus.

Letter to Ephraim Cutler and Wife, June 27, 1846. Typed copy by Bertha C. Hardman, ca. 1947. Daniel Parker Papers, Manuscript Collections, Ohio History Connection, Columbus.

Letter to William Parker (II), October 2, 1812. Special Collections, Legacy Library, Marietta College, Marietta, OH.

Published Documents of the Halcyon Church by Abel Sarjent

Sarjent is the attributed author of most of these publications. He is the presumed author of unattributed (or vaguely attributed) prose articles in Halcyon Church publications unless another author is specifically named. The complete titles of Halcyon Church periodicals are:

The Aletheian Critic; or Error Exposed, by an Exhibition of Truth

The Halcyon Itinerary; and True Millennium Messenger

"Address to America." *Halcyon Itinerary* 3 (October 1807): 100–108.

"Address to America [continued]." *Halcyon Itinerary* 4 (November 1807): 109–18.

"A Brief Hint of the Universal Dominion of Emmanuel." *Halcyon Itinerary* 4 (November 1807): 119–44.

"A Brief Hint of the Universal Dominion of Emmanuel [continued]." *Halcyon Itinerary* 5 (December 1807): 145–67.

"Circular Epistle from the 9th Concilium of the Halcyon Church." 1810. In *The New Hymn-Book for the Use of the Free Church*, 217–33. New York: printed for A. M. Sarjent, 1811.

"A Declaration of the Constitution and Standard of the Millennium Church." *Aletheian Critic* 1 (April 1804): 43–60.

The Destruction of the Beast in the Downfall of Sectarianism. Marietta, OH: n.p., 1806. This pamphlet, originally published separately, is included in a bound collection of Halcyon publications, which apparently was donated at some point to the Harvard Divinity School library and has been digitized by Google Books and made available online. The given title of the electronic document is the *Aletheian Critic*, but the first (and only) issue of *Aletheian Critic* from 1804 is only the first of several documents in this bound collection. It also includes an untitled hymn collection, probably from 1806.

"The Doctrine of Endless Miseries Investigated; or The Sinews of Antichristian Religion Exploded." *Aletheian Critic* 1 (April 1804): 5–33.

"The Downfall of the Halcyon Church, Predicted in a Dream." *Halcyon Itinerary* 3 (October 1807): 81–91.

"The Fundamental Principles of the Aletheian Cabinet." *Aletheian Critic* 1 (April 1804): 34–36.

"Further Explanations of the Urim and Thummim." *Halcyon Itinerary* 2 (September 1807): 61.

"Imperial Rudiments for the Halcyon and Political Church; Introductory to the Age of Science." *Halcyon Itinerary* 6 (January 1808): 186–97.

"Introductory Discourse." *Halcyon Itinerary* 1 (August 1807): vii–19.

"Phenomenon of the Heavenly Host in North Carolina." *Halcyon Itinerary* 2 (September 1807): 48–53.

"A Protest against Idolatry: Or Tritheism Exploded." *Aletheian Critic* 1 (April 1804): 39–42.

"A Question Answered." *Halcyon Itinerary* 2 (September 1807): 63–70.

"Theology vs. Mythology: In Vindication of Genuine Christianity." In *The New Hymn-Book for the Use of the Free Church*, iii–ix. New York: printed for A. M. Sarjent, 1811.

The Urim, or Halcyon Cabala: Containing the Fundamental Principles of the Halcyon Church of Christ in Columbia; Otherwise Called the Columbian Church, in Defence of the Genuine Christianity and in Opposition to "Lo Here, and Lo There"; Consisting of One Supreme Object and Seven Leading Topicks. Cincinnati: Carpenter and Findlay, 1801.

"Western Messenger; to the Saints throughout the World." In *The New Hymn-Book for the Use of the Free Church*, 237–56. New York: printed for A. M. Sarjent, 1811.

Published Documents of the Halcyon Church by Authors Other Than or in Addition to Abel Sarjent

These documents either are attributed to specific authors other than Abel Sarjent, or they are anonymous sources of which it is unlikely or doubtful that Sarjent is the primary author, though his influence is evident on all Halcyon Church documents.

"H. C." [Halcyon Church?]. "O for an Angel's Tongue to Raise." Hymn CCIII in *The New Hymn-Book for the Use of the Free Church*, 195–96. New York: printed for A. M. Sarjent, 1811.

Parker, John. "An Address to the Human Family at Large (Circular Letter, Nov. 1804, By order of the 3d Concilium of the Halcyon Church, &c. held in Mason County, Virginia, near Point Pleasant, on the 3d, 4th, and 5th of November, 1804)." *Aletheian Critic* 1 (April 1804): 61–70. This article is "signed by the order of the Concilium, 6th November, 1804, JOHN PARKER, Moderator," Daniel Parker's brother (69), but clearly had the input of Abel Sarjent.

———. *A Circular Epistle, Wrote by Order of the Fourth Concilium, of the Halcyon Church, &c., Otherwise Called the Columbian Church.* Marietta, OH: Samuel Fairlamb, 1806. This is also a corporate statement, signed by John Parker as moderator of the Halcyon Church, probably with input from Abel Sarjent.

Untitled Hymn Collection [1806?], from a bound collection of Halcyon publications, title page missing. This bound collection, which also includes Sarjent's *The Destruction of the Beast in the Downfall of Sectarianism* and the first and only issue of the *Aletheian Critic,* has been digitalized by Google Books and made available online under the title the *Aletheian Critic*. The 1806 hymn collection is different from *The New Hymn-Book for the Use of the Free Church*, published in New York in 1811.

"When Zion from Her Closet Comes." Hymn XIII in *The New Hymn-Book for the Use of the Free Church*, 21–22. New York: printed for A. M. Sarjent, 1811.

Other Published Primary Sources

Adams, Hannah. *Dictionary of All Religions and Religious Denominations: Jewish, Heathen, Mahometan, Christian, Ancient and Modern.* New York: James Eastburn,

1817. Facsimile of the 1817 fourth edition, with an introduction by Thomas A. Tweed. Atlanta, GA: Scholars Press, 1992.

Ballou, Hosea. *A Treatise on Atonement.* 4th ed. Boston: Universalist Publishing House, 1882.

Beecher, Lyman. *Autobiography, Correspondence, etc. of Lyman Beecher.* Edited by Charles Beecher. New York: Harper, 1865.

Brownlee, William Craig. *Letters in the Roman Catholic Controversy.* New York: published by the author, 1834.

Bunyan, John. *The Pilgrim's Progress.* 1678. Oxford World Classics Edition, edited with an introduction by W. R. Owens. Oxford: Oxford University Press, 2003.

Cartwright, Peter. *Autobiography of Peter Cartwright, the Backwoods Preacher.* Edited by W. P. Strickland. New York: Carlton & Porter, 1856.

Cist, Charles. *Cincinnati in 1841: Its Early Annals and Future Prospects.* Cincinnati: published by the author, 1841.

———. *The Cincinnati Miscellany*. Vol. 1. Cincinnati: published by the author, 1845.

Cowper, William. "Truth." In *The Poems of William Cowper*, vol. 1, *1748–1782*, edited by John D. Baird and Charles Ryskamp, 280. Oxford: Oxford University Press, 1980.

Crockett, David. *A Narrative of the Life of David Crockett of the State of Tennessee.* Philadelphia: E. L. Carey and A. Hart, 1834.

Douglass, Frederick. *Narrative of the Life of Frederick Douglass, an American Slave.* 1845. Edited by John W. Blassingame, John R. McKivigan, and Peter P. Hinks. New Haven, CT: Yale University Press, 2001.

Edwards, Jonathan. "Sinners in the Hands of an Angry God." 1741. In *A Jonathan Edwards Reader*, edited by John E. Smith, Harry S. Stout, and Kenneth P. Minkema, 89–105. New Haven, CT: Yale University Press, 2003.

Elaw, Zilpha. *Memoirs of the Life, Religious Experience, Ministerial Travels, and Labours of Mrs. Zilpha Elaw, an American Female of Colour* (London: published by the author, 1846). Reprinted in *Sisters of the Spirit: Three Black Women's Autobiographies of the Nineteenth Century*, edited by William L. Andrews, 49–160. Bloomington: Indiana University Press, 1986.

Finley, James B. *Autobiography of Rev. James B. Finley.* 1853. Edited by W. P. Strickland. Cincinnati: Methodist Book Concern, 1872.

Finney, Charles G. *Memoirs of Charles G. Finney, Written by Himself.* New York: Fleming H. Revell, 1876.

Fishback, James. *The Philosophy of the Human Mind in Respect to Religion, or, A Demonstration from the Necessity of Things That Religion Entered the World by Revelation.* Lexington, KY: Thomas T. Skillman, 1813.

Henry, Matthew. *Commentary on the Whole Bible.* 1708–11. Peabody, MA: Hendrickson, 1991.

Hodge, Archibald Alexander. *Life of Charles Hodge.* London: T. Nelson, 1880.

Hodge, Charles. *Systematic Theology.* Vol. 1. 1871. Reprint, Grand Rapids, MI: W. B. Eerdmans, 1997.

"In Chancery, January 13, 1804: Abraham Faw, versus Abel Sarjent." *National Intelligencer*, February 27, 1804.

Jefferson, Thomas. *The Jefferson Bible: The Life and Morals of Jesus of Nazareth.* 1820. Edited by Douglas E. Lurton. New York: Henry Holt, 1995.

Lee, Jarena. *The Life and Religious Experience of Jarena Lee.* Philadelphia: published by the author, 1836. Reprinted in *Sisters of the Spirit: Three Black Women's Autobiographies of the Nineteenth Century*, edited by William L. Andrews, 25–48. Bloomington: Indiana University Press, 1986.

List of Patents for Inventions and Designs Issued by the United States from 1790 to 1847 with the Patent Laws and Notes of Decisions of the Courts of the United States for the Same Period: Compiled under the Direction of Edmund Burke, Commissioner of Patents. Washington, DC: J. and G. S. Gideon, 1847.

MacCalla [*sic*], William L. *Remarks on Dr. James Fishback's the Philosophy of the Human Mind in Respect to Religion.* Lexington, KY: printed by M'Call & Downing, for the author, 1814.

Niles, Nathaniel. "The American Hero: A Sapphic Ode, Written in the Time of the American Revolution." 1775. In *Poets and Poetry of Vermont*, rev. ed., edited by Abby Maria Hemenway, 17–19. Boston: Brown, Taggard & Chase, 1860.

Northup, Solomon. *Twelve Years a Slave: Narrative of Solomon Northup, a Citizen of New York, Kidnapped in Washington City in 1841, and Rescued in 1853, from a Cotton Plantation near the Red River, in Louisiana.* Auburn, NY: Derby and Miller, 1853.

Nye, A. T. "Ship Building at Marietta." *Marietta Register*, March 24, 1881.

Pope, Alexander. *An Essay on Man.* 1733–34. Published as vol. 3, pt. 1, of *The Poems of Alexander Pope*, edited by Maynard Mack. London: Methuen, 1950.

Watts, Isaac. "The Indian Philosopher." 1701. In *The Works of Rev. Isaac Watts, D.D., in Nine Volumes*, 9:278. London: printed by Edward Baines, 1813.

Wheatley, Phillis. "Thoughts on the Works of Providence." In *Poems on Various Subjects, Religious and Moral.* London: printed for A. Bell, 1773. Reprinted in Joseph Lavallée, *The Negro Equalled by Few Europeans, Translated from the French: To Which Are Added, Poems on Various Subjects, Moral and Entertaining* [*sic*], *by Phyllis Wheatley*, 2:192–96. Philadelphia: William W. Woodward, 1801.

Winchester, Elhanan. *The Universal Restoration, Exhibited in Four Dialogues between a Minister and His Friend.* Worcester, MA: Isaiah Thomas, 1803.

Additional Unpublished Primary Sources

Browning, William R., to S. P. Hildreth. August 27, 1847. Hildreth Papers, vol. 1, letter 100, Slack Research Collections, Legacy Library, Marietta College, Marietta, OH.

Clermont Academy Circular. Printed, 1849. Bertha Currier Hardman Clermont Academy Collection, Department of History and Geography, Northern Kentucky University, Highland Heights, KY.

Clermont Academy Circular. Printed, [1867–76?]. Bertha Currier Hardman Clermont Academy Collection, Department of History and Geography, Northern Kentucky University, Highland Heights, KY.

Currier, Fannie Parker. "A History of the Parker Family." Unpublished MS, 1928. Bertha Currier Hardman Clermont Academy Collection, Department of History and Geography, Northern Kentucky University, Highland Heights, KY.

———. "A Sketch of the Administration of James Kennedy Parker as Principal of Wilberforce Academy." Unpublished MS, 1916. Bertha Currier Hardman Clermont Academy Collection, Department of History and Geography, Northern Kentucky University, Highland Heights, KY.

Donaldson, Susan Parker. "Mrs. Priscilla M. R. Parker," Unpublished, undated MS [1874–1890?]. Bertha Currier Hardman Clermont Academy Collection, Department of History and Geography, Northern Kentucky University, Highland Heights, KY.

Parker, Charles M. Appendix to Daniel Parker's Autobiography. Ca. 1845. Typed copy by Bertha C. Hardman, ca. 1947. Daniel Parker Papers, Manuscript Collections, Ohio History Connection, Columbus, OH.

Parker, Eben A. *The Parker Family*. Printed booklet prepared for the semicentennial anniversary of Clermont Academy, 1889. Bertha Currier Hardman Clermont Academy Collection, Department of History and Geography, Northern Kentucky University, Highland Heights, KY.

Parker, Mary, to Daniel Parker. [1807]. Special Collections, Legacy Library, Marietta College, Marietta, OH. The letter has the names of both of Daniel's parents, Mary and William, but Mary is clearly the author.

Parker, Priscilla, to the Ten Mile Baptist Church, c/o Andrew Coombs. August 4, 1837. Bertha Currier Hardman Clermont Academy Collection, Department of History and Geography, Northern Kentucky University, Highland Heights, KY.

Parker, Sarah Baker. "History of Clermont Academy." Unpublished MS, 1884. Bertha Currier Hardman Clermont Academy Collection, Department of History and Geography, Northern Kentucky University, Highland Heights, KY.

Parker, William Tell. "Memoir of Our Mother." Unpublished MS, November 27, 1874. Bertha Currier Hardman Clermont Academy Collection. Department of History and Geography, Northern Kentucky University, Highland Heights, KY.

Secondary Sources

Aaron, Daniel. *Cincinnati, Queen City of the West: 1819–1838*. Columbus: Ohio State University Press, 1992.

Abbot, Walter S., and William E. Harrison. *The First One Hundred Years of McKeesport: An Historical and Statistical Description of the City from Its Inception until Its Centennial in 1894*. McKeesport, PA: Press of McKeesport Times, 1894.

Abzug, Robert H. *Cosmos Crumbling: American Reform and the Religious Imagination*. New York: Oxford University Press, 1994.

Achtemeier, Paul J., ed. *HarperCollins Bible Dictionary*. San Francisco: HarperOne, 1996.

Ahlstrom, Sydney E. *A Religious History of the American People*. New Haven, CT: Yale University Press, 1972.

———. "The Scottish Philosophy and American Theology." *Church History* 24, no. 3 (September 1955): 257–72.

Albanese, Catherine L. *Nature Religion in America: From the Algonkian Indians to the New Age*. Chicago: University of Chicago Press, 1990.

Anderson, Robert Mapes. "Pentecostal and Charismatic Christianity." In *Encyclopedia of Religion*, 2nd ed., edited by Lindsay Jones, 10:7028–34. Detroit: Macmillan Reference USA, 2005.

Andrews, Martin R., ed. and comp. *History of Marietta and Washington County, Ohio, and Representative Citizens.* Chicago: Biographical Publishing Company, 1902.

Appiah, Kwame Anthony. "The Case for Capitalizing the *B* in Black." *Atlantic*, June 18, 2020. https://www.theatlantic.com/ideas/archive/2020/06/time-to-capitalize-blackand-white/613159/.

Aron, Stephen. *How the West Was Lost: The Transformation of Kentucky from Daniel Boone to Henry Clay.* Baltimore: Johns Hopkins University Press, 1996.

Asbury, Herbert. *The Gangs of New York: An Informal History of the Underworld.* Garden City, NY: Garden City Publishing Company, 1928.

Asimov, Isaac. *Foundation.* 1951; New York, Alfred A. Knopf, 2010.

"Augusta." In *The Kentucky Encyclopedia*, edited by John E. Kleber, 41–42. Lexington: University Press of Kentucky, 1992.

"Augusta College." In *The Kentucky Encyclopedia*, edited by John E. Kleber, 42. Lexington: University Press of Kentucky, 1992.

"Badin, Stephen T." In *The HarperCollins Encyclopedia of Catholicism*, edited by Richard P. McBrien, 126. New York: HarperCollins, 1995.

Baird. Lewis C. *History of Clark County, Indiana.* Indianapolis: B. F. Bowen, 1909.

Baldwin, Leland D. *Whiskey Rebels: The Story of a Frontier Uprising.* Rev. ed. Pittsburgh: University of Pittsburgh Press, 1968.

Ballou, Adin. *Autobiography of Adin Ballou, 1803–1890.* Completed and edited by William S. Heywood. Lowell, MA: Vox Populi, 1896.

Barr, David P. *A Colony Sprung from Hell: Pittsburgh and the Struggle for Authority on the Western Pennsylvania Frontier, 1744–1794.* Kent, OH: Kent State University Press, 2014.

Bebbington, David W. *Evangelicalism in Modern Britain: A History from the 1730s to the 1980s.* London: Unwin Hyman, 1989.

Beckner, Lucien. "History of the County Court of Lincoln County, Va., Now Kentucky." *Register of the Kentucky State Historical Society* 20, no. 59 (May 1922): 170–90.

———. "Lincoln County Records, continued." *Register of the Kentucky State Historical Society* 12, no. 35 (May 1914): 77–88.

Berlin, Ira. *The Making of African America: The Four Great Migrations.* New York: Viking, 2010.

Biggle, Jacob. *The Biggle Horse Book: A Concise and Practical Treatise on the Horse.* Philadelphia: Wilmer Atkinson, 1904.

Billington, Ray Allen. *The Protestant Crusade, 1800–1860: A Study of the Origins of American Nativism.* New York: MacMillan, 1938.

"Black and White: A Matter of Capitalization." *CMOS Shoptalk* (blog), *The Chicago Manual of Style*, June 22, 2020. https://cmosshoptalk.com/2020/06/22/black-and-white-a-matter-of-capitalization/.

Blaikie, Alexander. *A History of Presbyterianism in New England.* Boston: Alexander Moore, 1881.

Bloom, Harold. *The American Religion: The Emergence of the Post-Christian Nation.* New York: Simon & Schuster, 1992.

Bowman, Matthew. *The Mormon People: The Making of an American Faith.* New York: Random House, 2012.

Brereton, Virginia Lieson. *From Sin to Salvation: Stories of Women's Conversions, 1800 to the Present.* Bloomington: Indiana University Press, 1991.

Breslaw, Elaine G. *Lotions, Potions, Pills, and Magic: Health Care in Early America.* New York: New York University Press, 2012.

Bressler, Ann Lee. *The Universalist Movement in America, 1770–1880.* New York: Oxford University Press, 2001.

Britt-Mills, Robert. "Apocalypticism." In *Encyclopedia of Religion in America*, edited by Charles H. Lippy and Peter W. Williams, 1:128–35. Washington, DC: CQ Press, 2010.

Broadhurst, Dale. "Chronology: Adapted from Nancy Reynolds' *Abel Morgan Sargent, Sr. Timeline* (from Her Studies, Online Data, and Contributions from Various Other Sargent Family Researchers)." Spalding Research Project. http://solomonspalding.com/SRP/saga/saga01b.htm#chrn01.

Brodie, Fawn. *No Man Knows My History: The Life of Joseph Smith, the Mormon Prophet.* 2nd ed. New York: Alfred A. Knopf, 1971.

Brooke, John L. *The Refiner's Fire: The Making of Mormon Cosmology, 1644–1844.* Cambridge: Cambridge University Press, 1994.

Brown, Candy Gunther. *The Word in the World: Evangelical Writing, Publishing, and Reading in America, 1789–1880.* Chapel Hill: University of North Carolina Press, 2004.

Bruce, Dickson D., Jr. *And They All Sang Hallelujah: Plain Folk Camp Meeting Religion, 1800–1845.* Knoxville: University of Tennessee Press, 1974.

Burns, Norman T. *Christian Mortalism from Tyndale to Milton.* Cambridge, MA: Harvard University Press, 1972.

Butler, Jon. *Awash in a Sea of Faith: Christianizing the American People.* Cambridge, MA: Harvard University Press, 1990.

———. "Enthusiasm Described and Decried: The Great Awakening as Interpretive Fiction." *Journal of American History* 69, no. 2 (September 1982): 305–25.

Carroll, Bret E. "Spiritualism." In *Encyclopedia of Religion in America*, edited by Charles H. Lippy and Peter W. Williams, 4:2134–39. Washington, DC: CQ Press, 2010.

———. *Spiritualism in Antebellum America.* Bloomington: Indiana University Press, 1997.

Carwardine, Richard J. *Evangelicals and Politics in Antebellum America.* Knoxville: University of Tennessee Press, 1997.

Cassara, Ernest. *Universalism in America: A Documentary History.* Boston: Beacon, 1971.

Cayton, Andrew R. L. *Frontier Indiana.* Bloomington: Indiana University Press, 1996.

———. *Ohio: The History of a People.* Columbus: Ohio State University Press, 2002.

———. "The Significance of Ohio in the Early American Republic." In *The Center of a Great Empire: The Ohio Country in the Early Republic*, edited by Andrew R. L. Cayton and Stuart D. Hobbs, 1–10. Athens: Ohio University Press, 2005.

Cayton, Andrew R. L., and Paula R. Riggs. *City into Town: The City of Marietta, Ohio, 1788–1988*. Marietta, OH: Marietta College, Dawes Memorial Library, 1991.

Cemeteries of Addison Township, Gallia County Ohio. Gallipolis, OH: Gallia County Historical/Genealogical Society, 2003.

"Charles C. Parker, MD." In *Portrait and Biographical Album of Fayette County, Iowa*, 586–88. Chicago: Lake City, 1891.

"Charles C. Parker, M.D." In *The United States Biographical Dictionary and Portrait Gallery of Eminent and Self-Made Men: Iowa Volume*, 357–59. Chicago: American Biographical, 1878.

"Clermont Academy." In Ohio State Centennial Educational Committee, *Historical Sketches of the Higher Educational Institutions, and also of Benevolent and Reformatory Institutions of the State of Ohio.* [Columbus, OH]: [State Commissioner of Common Schools], 1876.

Coggins, R. J., and J. L. Houlden, eds. *The SCM Dictionary of Biblical Interpretation.* London: SCM Press, 1990.

Collins, John J. "From Prophecy to Apocalypticism: The Expectation of the End." In *The Continuum History of Apocalypticism*, edited by Bernard J. McGinn, John J. Collins, and Stephen J. Stein, 64–88. New York: Continuum, 2003.

Collins, Richard H. *History of Kentucky: By the Late Lewis Collins, Revised, Enlarged Four-Fold, and Brought Down to the Year 1874, by his Son, Richard H. Collins.* Vol. 2. Covington, KY: Collins, 1874.

Corrigan, John. "Religious Prejudice." In *Encyclopedia of Religion in America*, edited by Charles H. Lippy and Peter W. Williams, 4:1852–57. Washington, DC: CQ Press, 2010.

Coy, Fred E., Jr., Thomas C. Fuller, Larry G. Meadows, and James F. Swauger. *Rock Art of Kentucky*. Lexington: University Press of Kentucky, 1997.

Cossitt, Franceway Ranna. *The Life and Times of Rev. Finis Ewing, One of the Fathers and Founders of the Cumberland Presbyterian Church.* Louisville, KY: L. R. Woods, 1853.

Creigh, Alfred. *History of Washington County from Its First Settlement to the Present Time.* Harrisburg, PA: B. Singerly, Printer, 1870.

Cross, Whitney R. *The Burned-Over District: The Social and Intellectual History of Enthusiastic Religion in Western New York, 1800–1850*. Ithaca, NY: Cornell University Press, 1950.

Crumrine, Boyd, ed. *History of Washington County, Pennsylvania: With Biographical Sketches of Many of Its Pioneers and Prominent Men.* Philadelphia: L. H. Everts, 1882.

Cushing, Thomas. *History of Allegheny County, Pennsylvania*. Chicago: A. Warner, 1889.

Cutler, Julia Perkins. *Life and Times of Ephraim Cutler, Prepared from His Journals and Correspondence.* Cincinnati: Robert Clarke, 1890.

Daniel, Robert L. *Athens, Ohio: The Village Years*. Athens: Ohio University Press, 1997.

Davidson, Robert. *History of the Presbyterian Church in the State of Kentucky.* New York: Robert Carter, 1847.

Davis, Donald E., with Craig E. Colten, Megan Kate Nelson, Barbara L. Allen, and Mikko Saikku. *Southern United States: An Environmental History*. Santa Barbara, CA: ABC-CLIO, 2006.

Davis, William C. *A Way through the Wilderness: The Natchez Trace and the Civilization of the Southern Frontier.* New York: HarperCollins, 1995.

DeChant, Dell. "Apocalyptic Communities—Seventh Day Adventists and Jehovah's Witnesses." In *World Religions in America*, 3rd ed., edited by Jacob Neusner, 187–99. Louisville, KY: Westminster John Knox, 2003.

DeWolfe, Elizabeth A. *Shaking the Faith: Women, Family, and Mary Marshall Dyer's Anti-Shaker Campaign, 1815–1867*. New York: Palgrave MacMillan, 2004.

Dickinson, C. E. *A Century of Church Life: A History of the First Congregational Church, of Marietta, Ohio.* [Marietta, OH]: E. R. Alderman and Sons, 1896.

Dillon, Merton L. *Elijah P. Lovejoy, Abolitionist Editor.* Urbana: University of Illinois Press, 1961.

"Doan, William." Biographical Directory of the United States Congress, http://bioguide.congress.gov/scripts/biodisplay.pl?index=D000380.

Dowd, Gregory Evans. *A Spirited Resistance: The North American Indian Struggle for Unity, 1745–1815*. Baltimore: Johns Hopkins University Press, 1992.

Dunbar-Ortiz, Roxanne. *An Indigenous Peoples' History of the United States*. Boston: Beacon, 2015.

Eaton, Clement. *The Freedom-of-Thought Struggle in the Old South*. 2nd ed. New York: Harper and Rowe, 1964.

———. *Henry Clay and the Art of American Politics*. Boston: Little, Brown, 1957.

Eddy, Richard. *Universalism in America: A History*. Vol. 1, *1636–1800*. 2nd ed. Boston: Universalist Publishing House, 1886.

———. *Universalism in America: A History*. Vol. 2, *1801–1886*. Boston: Universalist Publishing House, 1886.

Ellis, Franklin. *History of Fayette County, Pennsylvania: With Biographical Sketches of Many of Its Pioneers and Prominent Men*. Philadelphia: L. H. Everts, 1882.

Ellsberry, Elizabeth Prather. *The Warrens and You*. Kansas City, MO: Brown-White-Lowell Press, 1958.

Eslinger, Ellen. "The Evolution of Racial Politics in Early Ohio." In *The Center of a Great Empire: The Ohio Country in the Early Republic*, edited by Andrew R. L. Cayton and Stuart D. Hobbs, 81–104. Athens: Ohio University Press, 2005.

Estes, Todd. "Pope, John." In *The Kentucky Encyclopedia*, edited by John Kleber, 728. Lexington: University Press of Kentucky, 1992.

Evans, Henrietta C., and Mary P. Wood. *Death Notices, Obituaries, and Marriage Notices Taken from the Gallia County, Ohio Newspapers from 1825 to 1875*. Gallipolis, OH: Gallia County Historical/Genealogical Society, 1986.

Evans, Nelson W. *A History of Scioto County, Ohio*. Portsmouth, OH: published by the author, 1903.

Feldman, Jay. *When the Mississippi Ran Backwards: Empire, Intrigue, Murder, and the New Madrid Earthquakes*. New York: Free Press, 2005.

Ferris, Mary Walton. *Dawes-Gates Ancestral Lines: A Memorial Volume Containing the American Ancestry of Rufus R. Dawes*. Vol. 1, *Dawes and Allied Families* [Milwaukee, WI: privately printed, 1943.

Filler, Louis. *The Crusade against Slavery, 1830–1860*. New York: Harper and Row, 1960.

Fisk, William L. "The Seceders: The Scottish High Church Tradition in America." *Journal of Presbyterian History* 62, no. 4 (Winter 1984): 291–305.

Fladeland, Betty. *James Gillespie Birney: Slaveholder to Abolitionist*. Ithaca, NY: Cornell University Press, 1955.

Flake, Kathleen. "Latter-day Saints." In *Encyclopedia of Religion in America*, edited by Charles H. Lippy and Peter W. Williams, 3:1215–21. Washington, DC: CQ Press, 2010.

Foner, Eric. *Give Me Liberty! An American History*. 4th ed. New York: W. W. Norton, 2014.

Ford, Henry A., and Kate B. Ford. *History of Cincinnati, Ohio, with Illustrations and Biographical Sketches*. Cleveland, OH: L. A. Williams, 1881.

———. *History of Hamilton County, Ohio, with Illustrations and Biographical Sketches*. Cleveland, OH: L. A. Williams, 1881.

Franchot, Jenny. *Roads to Rome: The Antebellum Protestant Encounter with Catholicism*. Berkeley: University of California Press, 1994.

Friend, Craig Thompson. *Kentucke's Frontiers*. Bloomington: Indiana University Press, 2010.

Garrett, Leroy. *The Stone-Campbell Movement: The Story of the American Restoration Movement*. Joplin, MO: College Press, 2002.

Genovese, Eugene D. *Roll Jordan Roll: The World the Slaves Made*. New York: Random House, 1974.

Gibson, Arrell M. *The Chickasaws*. Norman: University of Oklahoma Press, 1981.

Gillespie, Michael. *Come Hell or High Water: A Lively History of Steamboating on the Mississippi and Ohio Rivers*. Stoddard, WI: Heritage Press, 2002.

Glasgow, W. Melancthon. *History of the Reformed Presbyterian Church in America: With Sketches of All Her Ministry, Congregations, Missions, Institutions, Publications, etc*. Baltimore: Hill and Harvey, 1888.

Goen, C. C. *Broken Churches, Broken Nation: Denominational Schisms and the Coming of the American Civil War*. Macon, GA: Mercer University Press, 1985.

Greve, Charles Theodore. *Centennial History of Cincinnati and Representative Citizens*. Vol. 1. Chicago: Biographical Publishing Company, 1904.

Griffin, Patrick. *American Leviathan: Empire, Nation, and Revolutionary Frontier*. New York: Hill and Wang, 2007.

Guice, John D. W. "'It Seems to Be More Probable . . .': Why Not Homicide?" In *By His Own Hand? The Mysterious Death of Meriwether Lewis*, edited by John D. W. Guice, 73–105. Norman: University of Oklahoma Press, 2006.

Hagedorn, Ann. *Beyond the River: The Untold Story of the Heroes of the Underground Railroad*. New York: Simon and Schuster, 2002.

Harlan, Alpheus H. *History and Genealogy of the Harlan Family*. Baltimore: Lord Baltimore Press, 1914.

Hartshorne, Charles. "Pantheism and Panentheism." In *Encyclopedia of Religion*, 2nd ed., edited by Lindsay Jones, 10:6960–65. Detroit: Macmillan Reference USA, 2005.

Hatch, Nathan O. "The Christian Movement and the Demand for a Theology of the People." *Journal of American History* 67, no. 3 (December 1980): 545–67.

———. *The Democratization of American Christianity.* New Haven, CT: Yale University Press, 1989.

Hauer, Christian E., and William A. Young. *An Introduction to the Bible: A Journey into Three Worlds.* 8th ed. Upper Saddle River, NJ: Pearson, 2012.

Haynes, Robert V. *The Mississippi Territory and the Southwest Frontier, 1795–1817.* Lexington: University Press of Kentucky, 2010.

Heller, Deborah. "Cowper's Task and the Writing of a Poet's Salvation." *Studies in English Literature, 1500–1900* 35, no. 3 (Summer 1995): 575–98.

Hendrickson, Robert. *The Facts on File Dictionary of American Regionalisms.* New York: Facts on File, 2000.

Hersh, Blanche Glassman. *The Slavery of Sex: Feminist-Abolitionists in America.* Urbana: University of Illinois Press, 1978.

Herz, Walter. "Sarah Otis Ernst." *Dictionary of Unitarian and Universalist Biography.* July 20, 2006. http://uudb.org/articles/sarahotisernst.html.

Hickey, Donald R. *The War of 1812: A Forgotten Conflict.* Urbana: University of Illinois Press, 2012.

Hildreth, Samuel. "Biographical Sketches of the Early Physicians of Marietta, Ohio." *New England Historical & Genealogical Register* 3 (1849): 47–55.

———. *Pioneer History: Being an Account of the First Examinations of the Ohio Valley, and the Early Settlement of the Northwest Territory.* Cincinnati: H. W. Derby, 1848.

History of Gallia County: Containing a Condensed History of the County; Biographical Sketches; General Statistics; Miscellaneous Matters &c. Gallipolis, OH: St. Peter's Episcopal Church, 1976. Facsimile reprint from *Historical Hand Atlas.* Chicago: H. H. Hardesty, 1882.

History of Washington County, Ohio, with Illustrations and Biographical Sketches. Cleveland: H. Z. Williams, 1881. Reprint, [Marietta, OH]: Washington Co. Chapter, Ohio Genealogical Society, 1989.

Holifield, E. Brooks. *Theology in America: Christian Thought from the Age of the Puritans to the Civil War.* New Haven, CT: Yale University Press, 2003.

Hopkins, James F. *A History of the Hemp Industry in Kentucky.* Lexington: University of Kentucky Press, 1951.

Hurt, R. Douglas. *The Ohio Frontier: Crucible of the Northwest, 1720–1830.* Bloomington: Indiana University Press, 1996.

Huey, Keith. "Stone-Campbell Movement." In *Encyclopedia of Religion in America*, edited by Charles H. Lippy and Peter W. Williams, 4:2162–64. Washington, DC: CQ Press, 2010.

Jamison, A. Leland. "Religions on the Christian Perimeter." In *The Shaping of American Religion*, edited by James Ward Smith and A. Leland Jamison, 162–231. Princeton, NJ: Princeton University Press, 1961.

Jeffrey, Julie Roy. *The Great Silent Army of Abolitionism: Ordinary Women in the Antislavery Movement.* Chapel Hill: University of North Carolina Press, 1998.

Jenkins, Philip. *Mystics and Messiahs: Cults and New Religions in American History.* Oxford: Oxford University Press, 2000.

Jenkins, William Sumner. *Proslavery Thought in the Old South.* Chapel Hill: University of North Carolina Press, 1935.

Jenkinson, Clay S. "Introduction: Meriwether Lewis's Mysterious Death on the Natchez Trace." In *By His Own Hand? The Mysterious Death of Meriwether Lewis*, edited by John D. W. Guice, 3–16. Norman: University of Oklahoma Press, 2006.

Jenson, Andrew. *Latter-Day Saint Biographical Encyclopedia: A Compilation of Biographical Sketches of Prominent Men and Women in the Church of Jesus Christ of Latter-Day Saints.* Vol. 3. Salt Lake City: Andrew Jenson History Company, 1914.

Johnson, L. F. *History of Franklin County, Kentucky.* Franklin, KY: Roberts Printing Company, 1912.

Jones, Mary Keturah. *History of Campbell County, as Read at the Centennial Celebration of 4th of July, 1876.* Newport, KY: n.p., 1876.

Jordan, Winthrop D. *White over Black: American Attitudes toward the Negro, 1550–1812.* Chapel Hill: University of North Carolina Press, 1968.

Kane, Virginia Lee Hubman. John R. Bing Family Group Record. Bing Binder, 1998, Gallia County Historical Society, Gallipolis, OH.

Kelly, J. N. D. *Early Christian Doctrines.* Rev. ed. San Francisco: HarperSanFrancisco, 1978.

Kendi, Ibram X. *Stamped from the Beginning: The Definitive History of Racist Ideas in America.* New York: Nation Books, 2016.

Kerber, Linda K. *Federalists in Dissent: Imagery and Ideology in Jeffersonian America.* Ithaca, NY: Cornell University Press, 1970.

Kern, Kevin F., and Gregory S. Wilson. *Ohio: A History of the Buckeye State.* Chichester, UK: John Wiley and Sons, 2014.

Keyssar, Alexander. *The Right to Vote: The Contested History of Democracy in the United States.* New York: Basic Books, 2000.

Knepp, Gary L. *Freedom's Struggle: A Response to Slavery from the Ohio Borderlands.* Milford, OH: Little Miami, 2008.

Koester, Nancy. *Harriett Beecher Stowe: A Spiritual Life.* Grand Rapids, MI: W. B. Eerdmans, 2014.

Kolchin, Peter. *American Slavery, 1619–1877.* Rev. ed. New York: Hill and Wang, 2003.

Lamoreaux, Naomi R., and Kenneth L. Sokoloff. "Intermediaries in the U.S. Market for Technology, 1870–1920." In *Finance, Intermediaries, and Economic Development*, edited by Stanley L. Engerman, Philip T. Hoffman, Jean-Laurent Rosenthal, and Kenneth L. Sokoloff, 209–46. New York: Cambridge University Press, 2003.

Landsman, Ned C. *Scotland and Its First American Colony, 1683–1765.* Princeton, NJ: Princeton University Press, 1985.

Larkin, Stillman Carter. *The Pioneer History of Meigs County.* Columbus, OH: Berlin Printing Company, 1908.

Larson, John Lauritz. *The Market Revolution in America: Liberty, Ambition, and the Eclipse of the Common Good.* Cambridge: Cambridge University Press, 2010.

Lee, Lucy C. "General Henry Lee." *Register of the Kentucky State Historical Society* 1, no. 3 (September 1903): 82–88.

Lightfoot, Marise P. "Maury County." *Tennessee Encyclopedia.* Tennessee Historical Society. Last updated March 1, 2018. http://tennesseeencyclopedia.net/entries/maury-county.

Loughead, Flora Haines. *Dictionary of Given Names with Origins and Meanings.* 2nd ed. Glendale, CA: Arthur H. Clark, 1981.

Lowance, Mason. *Against Slavery: An Abolitionist Reader.* New York: Penguin Books, 2000.

Lum, Kathryn Gin. *Damned Nation: Hell in America from the Revolution to Reconstruction.* Oxford: Oxford University Press, 2014.

Marsden. George M. *Jonathan Edwards: A Life.* New Haven, CT: Yale University Press, 2004.

Martin, Tyrone G. "Rodgers, John." In *The Encyclopedia of the War of 1812: A Political, Social, and Military History*, edited by Spencer C. Tucker, 452–53. Santa Barbara, CA: ABC-CLIO, 2012.

Marty, Martin E. *Righteous Empire: The Protestant Experience in America.* New York: Dial Press, 1970.

McCoy, Drew R. *The Last of the Fathers: James Madison and the Republican Legacy.* New York: Cambridge University Press, 1989.

McCullough, David. *The Pioneers: The Heroic Story of the Settlers Who Brought the American Ideal West.* New York: Simon and Schuster, 2019.

McKivigan, John. *The War against Proslavery Religion: Abolitionism and the Northern Churches, 1830–1865.* Ithaca, NY: Cornell University Press, 1984.

McLoughlin, William G. *Revivals, Awakenings, and Reform.* Chicago: University of Chicago Press, 1978.

Meacham, Charles M. *History of Christian County, Kentucky: From Oxcart to Airplane.* Nashville, TN: Marshall and Bruce, 1930.

Middleton, Stephen. *The Black Laws: Race and the Legal Process in Early Ohio.* Athens: Ohio University Press, 2005.

Miller, Caroline R. "Underground Railroad, Bracken Co." In *The Encyclopedia of Northern Kentucky*, edited by Paul A. Tenkotte and James C. Claypool, 902–3. Lexington: University Press of Kentucky, 2009.

Miller, Russell E. *The Larger Hope: The First Century of the Universalist Church in America, 1770–1870.* Boston: Unitarian Universalist Association, 1978.

Miller, Timothy. "Introduction." In *America's Alternative Religions*, edited by Timothy Miller, 1–10. Albany: State University of New York Press, 1995.

Millis, William Alfred. *The History of Hanover College from 1827 to 1927.* Hanover, IN: Hanover College, 1927.

Montgomery, Michael. *From Ulster to America: The Scotch-Irish Heritage of American English.* Belfast, Northern Ireland: Ulster Historical Foundation, 2006.

Morton, Jennie C. "Streets of the Capital of Kentucky." *Register of the Kentucky State Historical Society* 13, no. 39 (September 1915): 53–56.

Noll, Mark A. *A History of Christianity in the United States and Canada.* Grand Rapids, MI: W. B. Eerdmans, 1992.

———, ed. *The Princeton Theology, 1812–1921: Scripture, Science, and Theological Method from the Age of Archibald Alexander to Benjamin Warfield.* Grand Rapids, MI: Baker Academic, 2001.

O'Donnell, James H., III. *Ohio's First Peoples.* Athens: Ohio University Press, 2004.

Ogden, J. W. *The History of Champaign County, Ohio.* Chicago: W. H. Beers, 1881.

Olds, Mason. "Unitarian Universalism: An Interpretation through Its History." In *America's Alternative Religions*, 87–98, edited by Timothy Miller. Albany: State University of New York Press, 1995.

Onuf, Peter S. *Statehood and Union: A History of the Northwest Ordinance.* Bloomington: Indiana University Press, 1987.

Oshatz, Molly. *Slavery and Sin: The Fight against Slavery and the Rise of Liberal Protestantism.* Oxford: Oxford University Press, 2012.

Otis, William A. *A Genealogical and Historical Memoir of the Otis Family in America.* Chicago: [Schulkins], 1924.

Perrin, William Henry. *County of Christian, Kentucky.* Chicago: F. A. Battey, 1884.

Peterson, Lee Allen. *A Field Guide to Edible Wild Plants of Eastern and Central North America.* Boston: Houghton Mifflin, 1977.

Pintar, Judith, and Steven Jay Lynn. *Hypnosis: A Brief History.* Chichester, UK: Wiley-Blackwell, 2008.

Pollitt, Bethany Marie. "The Antislavery Movement in Clermont County." Master's thesis, Wright State University, 2012.

Porter, Stanley E. "Millenarian Thought in the First-Century Church." In *Christian Millenarianism: From the Early Church to Waco*, edited by Stephen Hunt, 62–76. Bloomington: Indiana University Press, 2001.

Powell, Scott. *History of Marshall County, from Forest to Field.* Moundsville, WV: n.p., 1925.

Quisenberry, A. C. "Kentucky Troops in the War of 1812." *Register of the Kentucky State Historical Society* 10, no. 30 (September 1912): 47–66.

Rable, George C. *God's Almost Chosen Peoples: A Religious History of the American Civil War.* Chapel Hill: University of North Carolina Press, 2010.

Raboteau, Albert J. *Canaan Land: A Religious History of African Americans.* New York: Oxford University Press, 2001.

Ramage, James A., and Andrea S. Watkins. *Kentucky Rising: Democracy, Slavery, and Culture from the Early Republic to the Civil War.* Lexington: University Press of Kentucky, 2011.

Reynolds, David S. *Waking Giant: America in the Age of Jackson.* New York: HarperCollins, 2008.

Robinson, Elmo Arnold. *The Universalist Church in Ohio.* [Akron?]: Ohio Universalist Convention, 1923.

Rockey, J. L., and R. J. Bancroft. *History of Clermont County, Ohio: With Illustrations and Biographical Sketches of Its Prominent Men and Pioneers.* Philadelphia: L. H. Everts, 1880.

Salafia, Matthew. *Slavery's Borderland: Freedom and Bondage along the Ohio River.* Philadelphia: University of Pennsylvania Press, 2013.

Saum, Lewis O. *The Popular Mood of Pre–Civil War America.* Westport, CT: Greenwood, 1980.

Schimmel, Annemarie. "Numbers: An Overview." In *Encyclopedia of Religion*, 2nd ed., edited by Lindsay Jones, 10:6745–51. Detroit: Macmillan Reference USA, 2005.

Sellers, Charles. *The Market Revolution: Jacksonian America, 1815–1846*. Oxford: Oxford University Press, 1991.

Shaw, Ronald E. *Canals for a Nation: The Canal Era in the United States, 1790–1860*. Lexington: University Press of Kentucky, 1990.

Sinha, Manisha. *The Slave's Cause: A History of Abolition*. New Haven, CT: Yale University Press, 2016.

Sinnett, Charles N. *Our Thompson Family: In Maine, New Hampshire and the West*. Concord, NH: Rumford Printing Co., 1907.

Slaughter, Thomas P. *The Whiskey Rebellion: Frontier Epilogue to the American Revolution*. New York: Oxford University Press, 1986.

Smolinski, Reiner. "Apocalypticism in Colonial North America." In *The Continuum History of Apocalypticism*, edited by Bernard J McGinn, John J. Collins, and Stephen J. Stein, 441–61. New York: Continuum, 2003.

Smiddy, Betty Ann, ed., *A Little Piece of Paradise: College Hill, Ohio*. 2nd ed. Cincinnati: College Hill Historical Society, [1999].

Smith, Andrew F. *The Saintly Scoundrel: The Life and Times of Dr. John Cook Bennett*. Urbana: University of Illinois Press, 1997.

Smith, Brian. "Abel Sargent and the Halcyon Church." Senior capstone project, Marietta College, 2010.

Smith, E. [Euphemia] Vale. *History of Newburyport: From the Earliest Settlement of the Country to the Present Time; With a Biographical Appendix*. Newburyport, MA: n.p., 1854.

Smith, Timothy. *Revivalism and Social Reform: American Protestantism on the Eve of the Civil War*. New York: Harper Torchbooks, 1965.

Snay, Mitchell. *Gospel of Disunion: Religion and Separatism in the Antebellum South*. Cambridge: Cambridge University Press, 1993.

Spencer, J. H. *A History of Kentucky Baptists*. Vol. 1. Cincinnati: J. R. Baumes, 1885.

Stannard, Mabel. "Bing Family History Statement." In *Gallia County, Ohio: People in History to 1980*, 34. Gallipolis, OH: Gallia County Historical Society, 1980.

Starr, Harris Elwood. "McCalla, William Latta." In *Dictionary of American Biography*. Vol. 11, edited by Dumas Malone, 564–65. New York: Charles Scribner's Sons, 1933.

Staudenraus, P. J. *The African Colonization Movement, 1816–1865*. New York: Columbia University Press, 1961.

Stein, Stephen J. *The Shaker Experience in America*. New Haven, CT: Yale University Press, 1992.

Stoner, J. A. "Before and after Winchester." In *The Winchester Centennial, 1803–1903: Historical Sketch of the Universalist Profession of Belief*, 113–28. Boston: Universalist Publishing House, 1903.

Stout, Harry S. *The Divine Dramatist: George Whitefield and the Rise of Modern Evangelicalism*. Grand Rapids, MI: W. B. Eerdmans, 1991.

Summers, Thomas Jefferson. *History of Marietta*. Marietta, OH: Leader Publishing, 1903.

Swick, Ray. "Abel Morgan Sarjent." *West Virginia Encyclopedia*. West Virginia Humanities Council. http://www.wvencyclopedia.org/print/Article/178.

Tallant, Harold D. *Evil Necessity: Slavery and Political Culture in Antebellum Kentucky.* Lexington: University Press of Kentucky, 2003.

Taves, Ann. *Fits, Trances, and Visions: Experiencing Religion and Explaining Experience from Wesley to James.* Princeton, NJ: Princeton University Press, 1999.

Taylor, Alan. *The Civil War of 1812: American Citizens, British Subjects, Irish Rebels, and Indian Allies.* New York: Alfred A. Knopf, 2011.

Taylor, Nikki M. *Frontiers of Freedom: Cincinnati's Black Community, 1802–1868.* Athens: Ohio University Press, 2005.

Thompson, Roy C. *The Schools of Clermont: A Study in the Development of Education in Clermont County, Ohio.* Cincinnati: Little Miami Lithopress, 1962.

Tise, Larry. *Proslavery: A History of the Defense of Slavery in America, 1701–1840.* Athens: University of Georgia Press, 1987.

Torbet, Robert. *A History of the Baptists.* Valley Forge, PA: Judson, 1950.

Torbett, David. *Theology and Slavery: Charles Hodge and Horace Bushnell.* Macon, GA: Mercer University Press, 2006.

Trible, Phyllis. *God and the Rhetoric of Sexuality.* Philadelphia: Fortress Press, 1978.

Trinterud, Leonard J. *The Forming of an American Tradition: A Re-examination of Colonial Presbyterianism.* 1949; reprint, New York: Books for Libraries, 1970.

Turner, James. *Without God, Without Creed: Origins of Unbelief in America.* Baltimore: Johns Hopkins University Press, 1985.

Unser, Daniel H., Jr. *American Indians in the Lower Mississippi Valley: Social and Economic Histories.* Lincoln: University of Nebraska Press, 1998.

Vaca, Daniel. "Transcendentalism." In *Encyclopedia of Religion in America*, edited by Charles H. Lippy and Peter W. Williams, 4:2206–11. Washington, DC: CQ Press, 2010.

Valencius, Conevery Bolton. *The Lost History of the New Madrid Earthquakes.* Chicago: University of Chicago Press, 2013.

Von Rohr, John. *The Shaping of American Congregationalism, 1620–1957.* Cleveland: Pilgrim, 1992.

Walker, Charles M. *History of Athens County, Ohio.* Cincinnati: Robert Clarke, 1867.

Walters, Kerry. *The American Deists: Voices of Reason and Dissent in the Early Republic.* Lawrence: University Press of Kansas, 1992.

———. "Deism." In *Encyclopedia of Religion in America*, edited by Charles H. Lippy and Peter W. Williams, 1:527–31. Washington, DC: CQ Press, 2010.

———. *Revolutionary Deists: Early America's Rational Infidels.* Amherst, NY: Prometheus Books, 2010.

Ware, Timothy. *The Orthodox Church.* New ed. Baltimore: Penguin Books, 1997.

Watson, Harry L. *Liberty and Power: The Politics of Jacksonian America.* Rev. ed. New York: Hill and Wang, 2006.

Webb, Benedict Joseph. *The Centenary of Catholicity in Kentucky.* Louisville, KY: Charles A. Rogers, 1884.

Welter, Barbara. "The Cult of True Womanhood: 1820–1860." *American Quarterly* 18, no. 2 (Summer 1966): 151–74.

Weiner, Marli F., with Mazie Hough. *Sex, Sickness, and Slavery: Defining Illness in the Antebellum South.* Urbana: University of Illinois Press, 2012.

White, James F. *A Brief History of Christian Worship.* Nashville, TN: Abingdon, 1993.

White, Ronald C. *A. Lincoln: A Biography*. New York: Random House, 2009.

Wigger, John. "Ohio Gospel: Methodism in Early Ohio." In *The Center of a Great Empire: The Ohio Country in the Early Republic*, edited by Andrew R. L. Cayton and Stuart D. Hobbs, 62–80. Athens: Ohio University Press, 2005.

Wilder, Laura Ingalls. *On the Banks of Plum Creek.* Rev. illus. ed. New York: HarperCollins, 1953.

Wilentz, Sean. *The Rise of American Democracy: Jefferson to Lincoln.* New York: W. W. Norton, 2005.

Wood, Gordon S. *Empire of Liberty: A History of the Early Republic, 1789–1815.* New York: Oxford University Press, 2009.

Wright, Gavin. "Economics of Slavery." In *Dictionary of Afro-American Slavery,* edited by Randall M. Miller and John David Smith, 201–9. New York: Greenwood, 1988.

INDEX

Page numbers in *italics* refer to figures.